W9-AAJ-074

CANADA
365

HISTORICA CANADA
With an introduction by Anthony Wilson-Smith

Collins

To our Historica Canada Board of Directors and all others who similarly give of their time to celebrate Canada in their everyday lives, as well as those who strive to share Canadian stories and are never finished learning.

And to the Bob and Doug McKenzies, the log-driving waltzers, the lovers of CanCon, young hockey players, and their moms and dads; to consumers of donuts and poutine, to wearers of toques and plaid, to sayers of "sorry," to ingesters of maple syrup, and to all who celebrate Canada from sea to sea to sea.

Please enjoy, eh?

Canada 365

Published by Collins, an imprint of HarperCollins Publishers Ltd

First Edition

HarperCollins Publishers Ltd
2 Bloor Street East, 20th Floor
Toronto, Ontario
M4W 1A8

www.harpercollins.ca

Library and Archives Canada Cataloguing in Publication

ISBN: 978-1-44341-835-5

Printed and bound in the United States
QD 9 8 7 6 5 4 3 2 1

Introduction

The problem with Canada, Prime Minister William Lyon Mackenzie King famously observed, is that our country has too much geography and not enough history. Proof of that quote's enduring popularity is that it has been attributed to everyone from Sir John A. Macdonald to Stephen Leacock to John Diefenbaker. (In fact, King made the remark in a 1936 speech to the House of Commons.) But is it true? Our pre-Confederation history dates back thousands of years, to the arrival of the first indigenous peoples. Even our formal founding as a country—Canadian Confederation in 1867—predates that of a surprising number of other nations.

Our history should be seen in context. That means considering items large and small, good and bad, planned and happenstance that play a role in determining the sort of country we are today. At Historica Canada—creators of *Canada 365* in collaboration with HarperCollins Canada—we see our country's history and the values of modern-day Canadian citizenship as inextricably linked.

This book should also be seen in context—for what it is and what it isn't. It is not a definitive recitation of important events in Canada, or even a list of the most momentous occurrences for each day of the year. Much like the *Heritage Minutes* vignettes we also produce, the selections featured here are alternately important, interesting, unusual, and amusing. They may exemplify exceptional, daring, extraordinary achievements or dark moments. We hope to reflect the elements and emotions that make up life. The same is true of the illustrations chosen. They not only represent selected events but also—through the setting, tone, and subject portrayed—demonstrate the different attitudes and atmospheres that prevailed during those moments in time.

Sometimes, it is clear from the outset that an event is of historic importance. The January 1, 1947, enactment of the Canadian Citizenship Act marked the first nationality statute in Canada to define its people as Canadians. It is also clear that we have had a complex relationship with newcomers to this country, as well as members of ethnic, religious, and visible minorities. With that in mind, this book marks events, good and bad, that affected members of these communities. For example, we include events that were discriminatory toward Canada's Black community—which has existed in this country for many centuries—and we also celebrate achievements by its members. Sometimes, we recall people who lived what seemed to be satisfying but unremarkable lives, such as the wife of a nineteenth-century merchant in Victoria, British Columbia. Mrs. Kwong Lee (first name unknown), who reached Victoria on February 29, 1860, is worthy of note because she was the first Chinese woman in Canada. Her arrival marked the beginning of the thriving Chinese Canadian community that today stretches from one end of the country to the other.

There are also the many and varied contributions of Canada's indigenous peoples, along with the challenges they have faced. Some are noted in this book—like the story of painter Alex

Janvier, who helped found the Indian Group of Seven—but again, that list is not definitive. Our *Canada 365* also provides ample reason to feel good about past achievements on many fronts. Some acts of bravery are well known, but others are not, including the story of sealing captain William Jackman, who single-handedly rescued twenty-seven people stranded on a foundering ship. And sometimes events are noteworthy because of the renown of the people involved—even though the occasion cited is not especially dramatic. That's the case with the April 26, 1959, visit to Montréal by Cuban prime minister Fidel Castro shortly after his organization of exiled revolutionaries overthrew the regime of General Fulgencio Batista. Castro held a news conference, and one of the people who interviewed him was journalist René Lévesque, who would later become premier of Québec.

For every event we chose, others were close contenders. We hope the images and descriptions collected here prompt readers to dig further into our past—and that, collectively, these snapshots demonstrate that Canada's history is entertaining as well as important.

A list of this nature is also, by definition, subjective. In coming years, as Canada's achievements and challenges grow and our perception of our country continues to evolve, any subsequent lists will almost certainly include many different choices. But history is a never-ending arc, in which our past provides clues to our future. And it will always be true that the events that came before us help to determine whatever lies ahead.

Anthony Wilson-Smith
President and CEO, Historica Canada

JANUARY

Library and Archives Canada/National Film Board of Canada/Chris Lund/PA-129262.

The first official Canadian citizenship ceremony in Ottawa, Ontario, in January 1947. Armenian-born Yousuf Karsh is in the back row, second from the right.

1947. The Canadian Citizenship Act comes into effect under Prime Minister William Lyon Mackenzie King's government. It was the first nationality statute in Canada to define its people as Canadian rather than as British subjects. Among other things, the Act guaranteed all Canadian citizens right of entry into Canada, regardless of their country of origin, and gave married women full authority over their nationality status, independent of their husbands. Subsequent legislation would standardize and modernize the processes and rules for gaining citizenship.

Did You Know?

With the passing of the Act . . .

Children born abroad to Canadian fathers (or unwed mothers) were given Canadian citizenship.

Immigrants of "good moral character" who knew some French or English could apply for citizenship after five years in Canada.

Immigrants who had served in the Canadian armed forces in the First or Second World War could apply for citizenship after one year in Canada.

The first citizenship ceremony took place on January 3, and Prime Minister Mackenzie King was among the first twenty-six people to receive their certificates.

BORN ON THIS DAY

1793 — Upper Canada lieutenant-governor Francis Bond Head

1926 — opera singer Richard Verreau

1957 — actress Louise Pitre

Library and Archives Canada/William James Topley/PA-009635.

The furnaces at what is now called the Royal Canadian Mint in Ottawa, Ontario, taken in April 1909.

Also on This Day

1727.
Gen. James Wolfe is born in Westerham, England. The British general was mortally wounded on the Plains of Abraham in 1759, in the battle that won New France for England.

1908. The Ottawa branch of Britain's Royal Mint is officially opened—an event commemorated with the striking of a fifty-cent piece. From 1858 to 1907, most issues of Canadian coins had been struck at the Royal Mint in London, England. During its early years, the Ottawa branch produced not just Canadian coins but also British sovereigns and millions of ounces of refined gold. It even produced gun parts for Britain during the First World War. It was not until 1931 that the mint was placed into Canadian hands and transformed into the Royal Canadian Mint. It became a Crown corporation on April 1, 1969. The mint's headquarters still operates at its founding site on Sussex Drive in Ottawa.

Which new Canadian coin was minted in 1996? See February 19.

BORN ON THIS DAY

1881 Group of Seven artist Frederick Varley

1882 aviator and inventor Casey Baldwin

1886 actress Florence Lawrence

1932 children's author Jean Little

THE NICKEL

The word "nickel" comes from Old Nick, which is another name for the devil. In medieval times, miners often mistook nickel for more valuable copper ore and were disappointed when they realized their mistake. German miners called the deceptive metal *Kupfernickel*, meaning "devil's copper."

A 1921 nickel is one of the most valuable Canadian coins. That year, the coin was redesigned, and most of those that had already been minted were melted down. Fewer than five hundred of the original nickels are thought to exist today.

© Richard Buchan/The Canadian Press Images.

During the Second World War, the five-cent piece was changed from pure nickel to a copper-zinc alloy that gave the coin a brownish tinge. To avoid confusion with pennies, the nickel was minted in a twelve-sided, or dodecagonal, shape.

Although they soon went back to a silver colour, nickels kept their twelve sides until 1963. Between 1982 and 1996, Canadian pennies also got the dodecagonal makeover.

The modern nickel is made mostly of iron—it's a steel coin with a thin nickel plating.

The beaver on the coin also has a connection to metal—the enamel in the animal's teeth contains iron. This makes the beaver's teeth unusually hard and resistant to decay. And instead of being white, they're orangey red!

Figures from the 1960s Montréal Art Scene

- Automatiste painter, sculptor, and fimmaker **Marcel Barbeau**
- Stained-glass artist and painter **Marcelle Ferron**
- Painter, photographer, and filmmaker **Charles Gagnon**
- Surrealist-inspired Automatiste painter **Pierre Gauvreau**
- Automatiste and hard-edge abstractionist **Fernand Leduc**
- Abstract painter **Guido Molinari**
- Automatiste painter and multimedia-maker **Jean-Paul Mousseau**
- Experimental Automatiste and abstract painter **Jean-Paul Riopelle**
- Abstract painter **Claude Tousignant**

What importance did the palette knife play in Jean-Paul Riopelle's style? See March 12.

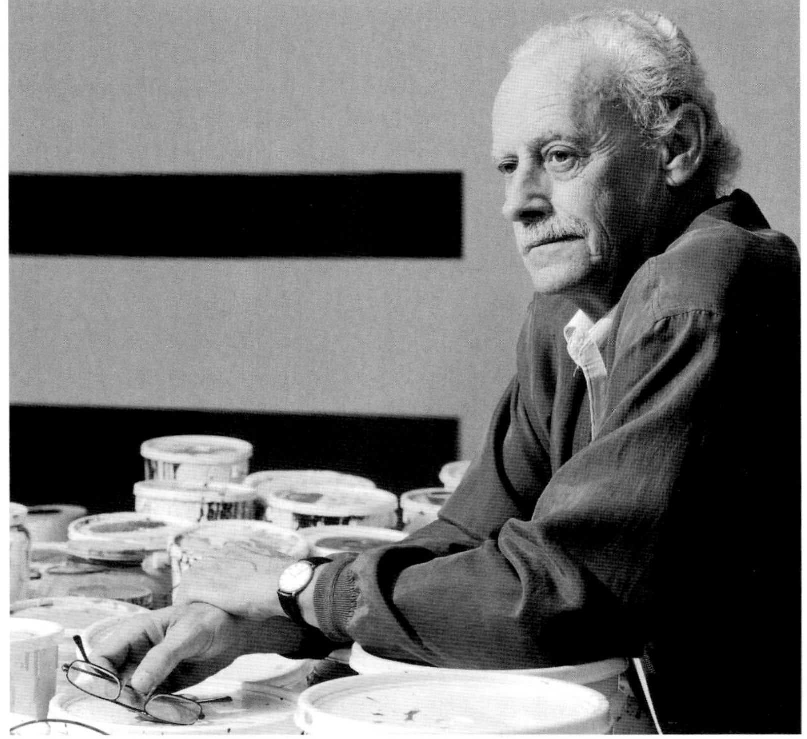

Photograph: Richard Max Tremblay. Courtesy of the Montreal Museum of Fine Art.

Yves Gaucher, 1996.

1947. Painter and printmaker Yves Gaucher is born in Montréal, Québec. Since he began exhibiting in the late 1950s, Gaucher has been one of Montréal's, and Canada's, most important abstract artists. He first made his mark on the art world as a printmaker, pioneering a new embossing technique. Gaucher is best known, however, for his "colour band" paintings, which feature striking horizontal stripes on large-format canvases. These sparse compositions, inspired by colour fields, explore spatial relationships on the canvas while blending Montréal and New York modernist influences.

BORN ON THIS DAY

Temperance advocate Letitia Youmans

1827

1903

Second World War general Charles Foulkes

4 JANUARY

The University of Ottawa/Fonds Association of French Canadians in Ontario/ Ph2-142a.

Schoolchildren protesting against Regulation 17 in Ottawa, Lower Town district, 1916.

1916. The "battle of the hatpins" breaks out when several hatpin- and scissor-brandishing mothers besiege the entrance to the French-language Guigues Elementary School in Ottawa. The women were defending two teachers, Diane Desloges and Béatrice Desloges, who had been banned from school property for their opposition to Regulation 17, issued in 1912 to limit the use of French as the language of instruction in Ontario elementary schools. The "battle" lasted several days, during which police and the school board tried to get the two teachers removed from the school. Parents and students joined forces in the women's defence and in support of their rights as a minority language group. Regulation 17 sparked protests and outrage across French Canada.

Canada's Notable Women Activists

June Callwood, journalist and social activist

Thérèse Casgrain, politician and women's rights activist

Jane Doe, violence against women activist

Mary Two-Axe Earley, Aboriginal feminist who fought for women who lost their status under the Indian Act when they married "non-Natives"

The Famous 5 (Henrietta Muir Edwards, Nellie McClung, Louise Crummy McKinney, Emily Murphy, and Irene Parlby), suffragettes

Marie Lacoste Gérin-Lajoie, pioneering Québec feminist

Madeleine Parent, union organizer

How did the Famous 5 make history? See October 18.

BORN ON THIS DAY

1927 business magnate Paul Desmarais

1963 New Kid in the Hall Dave Foley

1967 actress Marina Orsini

JANUARY 5

Soldiers from Canadian Forces Base Edmonton put up a hydro pylon in St-Césaire, Québec. The soldiers were part of Operation Recuperation, the mission to aid victims of the ice storm.

1998. A severe winter ice storm rages across eastern Canada, causing over $1.8 billion in damage and leaving twenty-eight Canadians dead and over three million without electricity. The total precipitation—which fell as freezing rain, ice pellets, and snow—exceeded 73 mm in Kingston, 85 mm in Ottawa, and 100 mm south of Montréal. It has been called the greatest natural disaster in Canadian history.

BORN ON THIS DAY

1849
North-West Mounted Police superintendent Sam Steele

1915
cartographer Arthur H. Robinson

1950
politician John Manley

MAJOR WINTER STORMS

1942:
Freezing rain drops ice "as thick as a person's wrist" throughout Eastern Ontario

1944:
Twenty-one people die in a Toronto snowstorm in which 57 cm fell over two days

1959:
Strong winds mould 7 m snowdrifts and leave seventy thousand without power in St. John's, NL

1964:
Gusting gales of 160 km/h drub the Maritimes

1976:
Saint John, NB, is hit by 188 km/h winds and 12 m waves on Groundhog Day

1982:
Intense snow, cold, and winds virtually cut off PEI from contact with the mainland

1989:
Temperatures feel like −91°C with the wind chill in Pelly Bay, NT

1996:
A storm drops 80 cm of snow over Victoria, BC, in twenty-four hours

2006:
Winds of up to 119 km/h rip through Vancouver's Stanley Park

Toronto Star archives/getstock.com

Who Was Princess Patricia?

Princess Patricia of Connaught, born on March 17, 1886, was a granddaughter of Queen Victoria. After the creation of the PPCLI, she was named colonel-in-chief. The princess renounced her royal title when she married one of her father's aides, Alexander Ramsay, in 1919. No longer a princess, she still took part in many royal events and was considered an accomplished watercolour artist. She died in 1974 at the age of eighty-seven.

Library and Archives Canada/James Francis Kenney/PA-099796.

The return of Princess Patricia's Canadian Light Infantry, Ottawa, March 1919.

1915. Princess Patricia's Canadian Light Infantry (PPCLI) goes into action, becoming the first Canadian infantry unit to enter the theatre of operations in France during the First World War. The unit was named for Princess Patricia, the youngest daughter of Prince Arthur, the tenth governor general. It was raised at the outbreak of the war, in August 1914, when Canada needed more regular military forces. Montréal entrepreneur Andrew Hamilton Gault offered $100,000 to raise and equip an infantry battalion for overseas service. Within just nine days, the regiment's ranks had been filled with veterans of the South African War and other British imperial conflicts. The PPCLI has since participated in the Second World War, the Korean War, and Afghanistan, as well as in NATO and UN peacekeeping operations.

BORN ON THIS DAY

1859
industrialist Henry Pellatt

1978
actress Tara Spencer-Nairn

1978
opera singer Nikki Einfeld

7 JANUARY

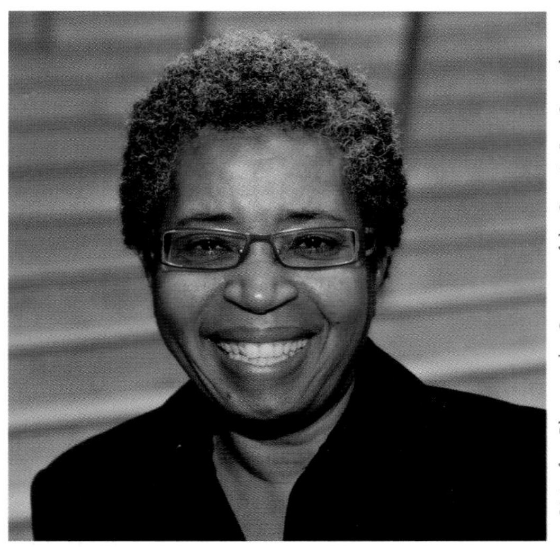

Dionne Brand, 2010.

1953. Poet, writer, and activist Dionne Brand is born in Guayaguayare, Trinidad. Brand came to Toronto in 1970, studying philosophy and English at the University of Toronto before beginning to teach and write. Her innovative work, which pushes the formal and emotional bounds of fiction, dramatizes the lives of Caribbean women in their transplanted homes in Canada. As a triply marginalized storyteller—for her race, gender, and sexuality—Brand is also a committed social activist, critiquing economic and political power structures, speaking against racism and discrimination against women, and working in support of gay and lesbian communities.

Brand is perhaps best known for her poetry and fiction, for which she has won the country's top national prizes. She was appointed poet laureate of Toronto in 2009, and is considered one of Canada's—if not the world's—most eminent poetic voices.

In Her Own Words: Dionne Brand

"She's dreamt riding out to sea, a weeping sea, its eyes translucent, its tears glistening, going to someplace so old there's no memory of it. She wonders what tears that old would taste like. She wonders if they taste like stories she wants to hear."
—from *In Another Place, Not Here*

BORN ON THIS DAY

painter and photographer Roloff Beny
1924

1934
politician Jean Corbeil

JANUARY 8

Also on This Day

1979.
Actress and director Sarah Polley is born in Toronto. She came to notice for her role as Sara Stanley in TV's *Road to Avonlea*, and went on to star in and direct movies. Her feature film directorial debut, *Away from Her*, earned her a number of Genie Awards, including the Claude Jutra Award for best debut feature, as well as those for best motion picture and best adapted screenplay. She also took home the award for best achievement in direction—making her the first woman to receive this honour.

Kenojuak Ashevak, photographed to mark her 2008 Governor General's Award in Visual and Media Art.

2013. Kenojuak Ashevak, an Inuk artist whose work became emblematic of the Canadian Arctic, dies in her home at Cape Dorset, Nunavut, at age eighty-five. Ashevak started drawing in the 1950s; she was the first woman to become involved with the newly established printmaking shop at Cape Dorset. Her father was a revered shaman who had a profound influence on her work, which often features birds, bright colours, and bold lines. She is best known for her famous print *The Enchanted Owl*, which was featured on a Canada Post stamp.

BORN ON THIS DAY

poet Gaston Miron
1928

1955
Loverboy singer Mike Reno

9 JANUARY

The cast of *Little Mosque on the Prairie* with the show's creator, Zarqa Nawaz.

2007. The hit television sitcom *Little Mosque on the Prairie* debuts on CBC. The series sought to bridge cultural divides on screen, showcasing the interaction between Muslim and Christian families living in the tiny fictional Saskatchewan town of Mercy. The plot follows the activities of the local imam, Amaar Rashid, who has left his lucrative law practice in Toronto to take over a congregation in the rented parish hall of the community's Anglican church. The show aired until 2012. It was the first Canadian program to centre on the experiences of an Islamic community.

 Where was the first mosque in Canada built? **See December 12.**

Canadian Comedy Classics

The Beachcombers (1972–90)
King of Kensington (1975–80)
SCTV (1976–84)
Kids in the Hall (1988–95)
The Red Green Show (1991–2006)
Just for Laughs: Gags (2000–)
Trailer Park Boys (2001–)
Slings & Arrows (2003–06)
Corner Gas (2004–09)
Less Than Kind (2008–13)

BORN ON THIS DAY

author Catharine Parr Traill — 1802

women's rights activist Irene Parlby — 1868

broadcaster Lister Sinclair — 1921

wheelchair activist Diane Roy — 1971

Also on This Day

1935.
Singer "Rompin'" Ronnie Hawkins is born in Huntsville, Arkansas. He achieved success in Ontario when he began to play the nightclub scene in 1958, and he contributed greatly to the evolution of rock music in Canada. Hawkins's well-known covers include "Mary Lou," "Who Do You Love?," and "Suzie Q."

Library and Archives Canada/C-009055.

The Canadian delegation at the League of Nations on September 3, 1928.

1902. Canada becomes a founding member of the League of Nations. The international organization, established at the 1919 Paris Peace Conference at the end of the First World War, was founded on the principles of collective security and preservation of peace through arbitration or judicial settlement of international disputes. Sixty-three states became members—though the United States did not—and the League's headquarters was established in Geneva, Switzerland. Canada was a member throughout the League's existence, and served from 1927 to 1930 on the executive council. The League was succeeded by the United Nations in 1945.

BORN ON THIS DAY

1924 — choreographer Ludmilla Chiriaeff

1927 — singer Gisele MacKenzie

1938 — Hockey Hall of Famer Frank Mahovlich

1964 — Crash Test Dummies singer Brad Roberts

11 JANUARY

Library and Archives Canada/Topley Studio/PA-025336.

Sir John A. Macdonald in Ottawa, Ontario, 1868.

1815. John A. Macdonald is born in Glasgow, Scotland. When he was five, his family moved to Kingston, Upper Canada (now Ontario), where he took up law before entering politics as an alderman in 1843. Sir John A. quickly became the dominant player in the Confederation project that united the provinces on July 1, 1867. As Canada's first prime minister, he is best known for linking Canada from sea to sea by railway (despite the Pacific Scandal, which saw him temporarily unseated), as well as for his feisty, charismatic oratory and his bouts of alcoholism. His government dominated politics for a half century and set policy goals for future generations of political leaders.

Scottish Roots in Canada

Alexander Graham Bell, inventor of the telephone

Norman Bethune, surgeon, inventor, political activist

Kim Campbell, first female prime minister

Tommy Douglas, first NDP leader and universal health care pioneer

William Lyon Mackenzie, journalist, rebel, politician

Agnes Macphail, first woman to sit in the House of Commons

Sarah McLachlan, singer-songwriter

Beverley McLachlin, chief justice of the Supreme Court of Canada

Marshall McLuhan, communication and media theorist

Alice Munro, Nobel Prize–winning author

BORN ON THIS DAY

theatre magnate Ambrose Small — 1866

swim coach Gus Ryder — 1899

skier Anne Heggtveit — 1939

JANUARY 12

The Disaster Assistance Response Team (DART)

The Disaster Assistance Response Team (DART) is designed to deploy on short notice anywhere in the world. Its mandate is to conduct emergency relief operations for up to approximately forty days to bridge the gap until national and international aid agencies arrive to provide long-term help. Recent DART missions have assisted people in all corners of the globe:

1998: Honduras, Hurricane Mitch
1999: Turkey, 7.4-magnitude earthquake
2004: Sri Lanka, earthquake/tsunami
2005: Pakistan, 7.6-magnitude earthquake
2010: Haiti, 7.0-magnitude earthquake
2013: Philippines, Typhoon Haiyan

© Neil Brighton.

Canadian relief workers aided in the recovery after the Haitian earthquake.

2010. A devastating earthquake, reaching 7.0 on the Richter scale, rocks Haiti near the capital of Port-au-Prince. Official government counts reported more than 316,000 people dead and thousands more left homeless. Governor General Michaëlle Jean, who came to Canada as a refugee from Port-au-Prince in 1968, lost a close friend—the godmother to her daughter—in the catastrophe. Following an emergency meeting with government heads, Jean made an emotional speech, partly in Haitian, in support of the country's people and Canada's quick aid response. She later met with Haitian prime minister Jean-Max Bellerive at Rideau Hall, the official residence of the governor general, and visited the disaster zone to offer her support.

BORN ON THIS DAY

1899 bush pilot Punch Dickins

1920 sculptor Bill Reid

1930 Hockey Hall of Famer and doughnut shop entrepreneur Tim Horton

1959 synchronized swimmer Helen Vanderburg

1988 hockey player Claude Giroux

13 JANUARY

The Canadian Press/Kevin Frayer.

Members of the Royal Canadian Regiment shovel snow in downtown Toronto.

1999. Just over a week after declaring a "snow emergency" in the city of Toronto, Mayor Mel Lastman calls for military assistance to help clear a record quantity of the white stuff—what would soon amount to about one metre—that immobilized much of the city. As a result, four hundred soldiers and "Bisons-plough-trucks" (armoured vehicles from Canadian Forces Base Petawawa) were sent in to rescue the snow-covered Toronto streets. While the city's dramatic response to the very Canadian winter occurrence remains a source of ridicule, Lastman stood by his decision, stating ten years later that it was the right call for the safety of his citizens.

Major Single-Day Snowfalls

1989: Premier, BC, 146 cm
1999: Tahtsa Lake, BC, 145 cm
1999: Mt. Washington, BC, 135 cm
1989: Brucejack Lake, BC, 130 cm
1985: Pleasant Camp, BC, 127 cm
1885: Cap-de-la-Madeleine, QC, 121.9 cm
1974: Lakelse Lake, BC, 118 cm
1999: Terrace, BC, 113.4 cm
1972: Kitimat, BC, 112.3 cm
1963: Livingston, AB, 111.8 cm
1935: Princeton, BC, 111.8 cm
2002: Whistler, BC, 107 cm
1923: Crofton, BC, 106.7 cm
1976: Stewart, BC, 105.7 cm
1988: Main Brook, NL, 105.0 cm
1968: Kemano, BC, 104.1 cm
2000: Unuk River, BC, 104.0 cm

BORN ON THIS DAY

1919
intelligence officer and Soviet defector Igor Gouzenko

1986
figure skater Joannie Rochette

How did cipher clerk Igor Gouzenko affect Canada's history? **See August 1.**

Also on This Day

1935.
Lucile Wheeler, winner of Canada's first Olympic medal in skiing (a bronze at Cortina d'Ampezzo, Italy, in 1956), is born in Montréal. In 1958, after winning both the downhill and the giant slalom titles at the Alpine World Ski Championships, she was inducted into the Canadian Olympic Hall of Fame and Canada's Sports Hall of Fame.

Vancouver Public Library/Province Newspaper/Gordon F. Sedawie/44666.

Gertrude Guerin on January 6, 1961, days before being elected chief of the Musqueam Indian Band.

1961. Gertrude Guerin becomes the first woman elected chief of the Musqueam Indian Band, on the north shore of British Columbia's Fraser River. Guerin was one of six band members who sued the Crown in 1975 for breach of trust with regard to the lease of sixty-five hectares of Musqueam land for the creation of a golf course. The case went all the way to the Supreme Court, which in 1984 ruled that the government has a fiduciary duty toward the First Nations of Canada. The landmark decision also established Aboriginal title as a distinct right.

BORN ON THIS DAY

1845
Governor General Lord Lansdowne (Henry Charles Keith Petty-Fitzmaurice)

1925
opera singer Louis Quilico

1956
opera singer Ben Heppner

15 JANUARY

Library and Archives Canada/Alexander E. MacDonald Canadiana Collection/NMC51970.

A map of New France, created by Samuel de Champlain in 1632.

1616. Samuel de Champlain—cartographer, explorer, and governor of New France—leaves the Georgian Bay region of Huronia, home to the Wendat (Huron) peoples, to visit the First Nations communities of the Petun (near Craigleith, on Nottawasaga Bay) and the Odawa (Bruce Peninsula, south of Georgian Bay). The visits were part of an effort to promote ties with the French; Champlain extended invitations to the First Nations to come to Québec, which he sought to make the centre of a powerful French colony. At times controversial, Champlain played such a major role in the St. Lawrence River area that he earned the title Father of New France.

Timeline: Samuel de Champlain

1567: Born in Brouage, France

May 26, 1603: Arrives in North America, at the mouth of the St. Lawrence

July 4, 1603: Reaches the future site of Montréal

July 3, 1608: Establishes Québec City

January 9, 1613: Publishes *Les Voyages du Sieur de Champlain*, describing his adventures in New France

March 12, 1618: Establishes a viable colony in New France, as instructed by Louis XIII

May 7, 1620: Becomes governor of New France

May 22, 1633: Reaches Québec after his final voyage

December 25, 1635: Dies in Québec City

BORN ON THIS DAY

1841 — Stanley Cup donor Lord Stanley of Preston (Frederick Arthur Stanley)

1947 — actress Andrea Martin

1975 — tennis player Mary Pierce

In Gord We Trust: Great Canadians Named Gord

Gord Downie, musician, Tragically Hip front man
Sir Gordon Drummond, army officer
Gordon Lightfoot, musician
Gord Martineau, newscaster
Robert Gordon "Bobby" Orr, hockey player
Gordon Pinsent, actor
Gordon Rayner, painter
Gordon Arthur Riley, oceanographer
Gordon Appelbe Smith, painter, printmaker
Gordon Sparling, filmmaker
Gordon G. Thiessen, economist, banker
Gordon V. Thompson, songwriter

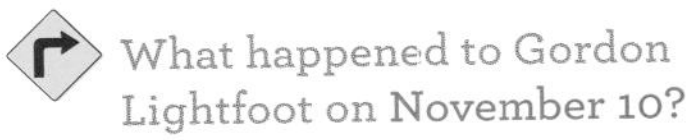
What happened to Gordon Lightfoot on November 10?

Associated Press/The Canadian Press.

Gordie Howe, centre, and his teammate Johnny Wilson offer their congratulations to Maurice Richard after Montréal posted a 4–3 win over Detroit on April 2, 1958.

1960. Gordie Howe of the Detroit Red Wings scores a goal and an assist to surpass Maurice "Rocket" Richard as the leading scorer in National Hockey League (NHL) history. At six feet and two hundred pounds, Howe was legendary for his physical strength. He was recruited to training camp at just fifteen years old, and he played his first NHL game with the Red Wings in 1946, at eighteen. In all, he played thirty-two professional seasons, including twenty-six in the NHL. His career spanned a record-breaking six decades, thanks to a one-game contract he signed with the Detroit Vipers at age sixty-nine. Howe's NHL record for points—1,850 in total—stood until finally surpassed by Wayne Gretzky in 1989. He is still known as Mr. Hockey.

BORN ON THIS DAY

1942
music executive René Angélil

1948
snooker champion Cliff Thorburn

Archives of Ontario.

Pauline McGibbon at her University of Toronto graduation, 1933.

1974. Pauline McGibbon is appointed lieutenant-governor of Ontario, the first woman in Canada to hold the position. She would be sworn in on April 10, 1974, and would retain the position until 1980. A passionate supporter of the arts, McGibbon later served as the first female chair of the Board of Trustees of the National Arts Centre (1980–84) and as a director of Massey Hall and Roy Thomson Hall (1980–90). While she attributed her success to a sense of humour and a love of people, she also acknowledged that her appointment as lieutenant-governor would have been impossible but for the women's movement.

Notable Achievements for Women in Canada

1975: Rosemary Brown, originally from Jamaica, is the first woman to run for the leadership of a federal political party, finishing a close second to eventual NDP leader Ed Broadbent.

1979: Nellie J. Cournoyea is elected to the NT legislature and becomes government leader in 1991. She is the first Aboriginal woman to lead a provincial or territorial government in Canada.

1982: Bertha Wilson is the first woman appointed to the Supreme Court of Canada.

1985: Section 12 of the Indian Act is repealed, meaning Aboriginal women no longer lose their status upon marrying non-Aboriginal men.

1993: Kim Campbell becomes the first female prime minister of Canada.

1993: Dr. Jean Augustine, originally from Grenada, becomes the first Black woman elected to Parliament.

BORN ON THIS DAY

1904 — artist Pegi Nicol MacLeod

1929 — Hockey Hall of Famer Jacques Plante

1946 — musician Domenic Troiano

1962 — actor Jim Carrey

NWT Archives/Department of Public Works and Services/G-1995-001:2928.

The Legislative Assembly in Yellowknife, Northwest Territories.

1967. Yellowknife is named the capital of the Northwest Territories, and the federal government transfers some administrative control to the territory. The commissioner and the territorial government offices were moved north from Ottawa. Three years later, Yellowknife was incorporated as the Northwest Territories' first and only city. It takes its name from the Yellowknives, a Dene people whose traditional territory is around Great Slave Lake, and who travelled as far north as the Arctic coast to obtain copper for knives and other implements. They, in turn, acquired their name from the copper-bladed knives they carried.

BORN ON THIS DAY

1915

Hockey Hall of Famer and pole vaulter Syl Apps

1950

racing driver Gilles Villeneuve

1961

Hockey Hall of Famer Mark Messier

19 JANUARY

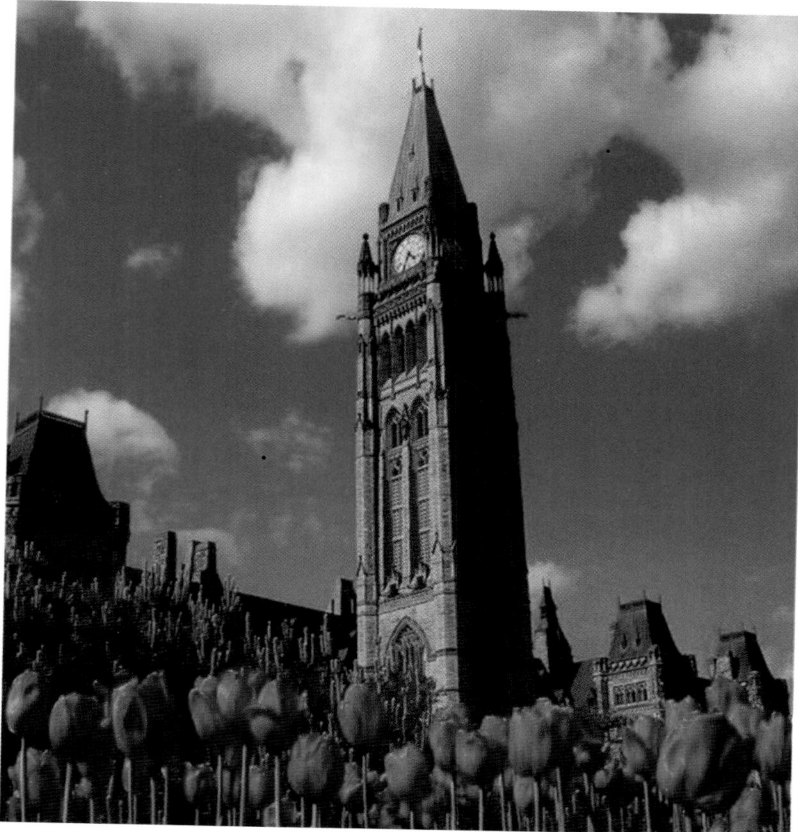

The Canadian Tulip Festival in Ottawa, Ontario.

Also on This Day

1843.
Mount Allison University, in Sackville, New Brunswick, is established. The school's origins go back to a boys' academy founded in 1839. In 1875, it became the first university in the British Empire to award a baccalaureate to a woman, Grace Annie Lockhart, and today it's known for the high number of Rhodes Scholarships awarded to its graduates.

1943. Princess Margriet of the Netherlands is born at the Ottawa Civic Hospital. Her family was living in exile in Ottawa during the Nazi occupation of the Netherlands. To ensure that the infant would have full Dutch citizenship, the Canadian government declared the hospital's maternity ward to be "extraterritorial." As a thank-you, the Dutch royals sent thousands of tulip bulbs to Ottawa. This gift continues as part of the annual Canadian Tulip Festival, during which tulips and tourists come out in equal numbers.

BORN ON THIS DAY

broadcaster Robert MacNeil
1931

1934
broadcaster Lloyd Robertson

politician Frank McKenna
1948

Mass Migrations to Canada

1776: 3,000 Black Loyalists
1783: 35,000 Loyalists from New York State
1815–70: 170,000 Scots
1891–1913: 170,000 Ukrainians
1900–14: 119,770 Italians
1947–52: 250,000 displaced persons from Central and Eastern Europe
1956: 37,000 Hungarians
1968–69: 11,000 Czechs
1972–73: 7,000 Ismaili Muslims from Uganda
1979–80: 60,000 "boat people" from Vietnam

Library and Archives Canada/C-005208.

Doukhobors on board the *Lake Huron*.

1899. Some two thousand Russian Doukhobors land at Lawlor Island in Halifax Harbour, after fleeing persecution for their belief in radical pacifism. They followed the teachings of seventeenth-century renegade preacher Danilo Filipov, who dissented from the Orthodox Church. In 1899 alone, more than seventy-five hundred members of the sect would come to Canada as part of one of the largest mass migrations in Canadian history. The group settled as a community in what is now Saskatchewan, where they continued their activism. Their contemporary descendants number twenty thousand, with approximately one-third remaining active in their culture.

BORN ON THIS DAY

1888 — writer Ethel Wilson

1921 — physician, author, and Rhinoceros Party founder Jacques Ferron

1928 — actor Peter Donat

1815. Lawyer, seigneur, and politician Louis-Joseph Papineau is elected speaker of the House of Assembly of Lower Canada (now Québec). With his self-assurance, skill as an orator, and popular following, he had emerged from a group of young nationalists as leader of the Parti Canadien (later Parti Patriote). His career as a French Canadian nationalist leader was checkered and controversial. Notably, he was part of the Rebellions of 1837—launched to protest against British influence and the power of the anglophone minority—but he was accused of cowardice by other Patriotes after he disappeared just before the Battle of St-Denis was engaged. He opposed the Act of Union, which had united Upper Canada (now Ontario) and Lower Canada, and he advocated joining the United States. He remains known as a strong, if radical, populist leader.

Louis-Joseph Papineau, 1896.

Also on This Day

1901.
A second contingent of Canadian troops sets sail to fight in the South African War. Over the course of the war, four Canadians received the Victoria Cross, nineteen the Distinguished Service Order, and seventeen the Distinguished Conduct Medal. More than one hundred Canadians were also mentioned in dispatches, and Canada's senior nursing sister, Georgina Pope, was awarded the Royal Red Cross.

BORN ON THIS DAY

Hockey Hall of Famer Georges Vézina
1887

1937
cartoonist Jim Unger

wrestler and model Maryse Ouellet
1983

JANUARY  

Library and Archives Canada/James Ashfield/C-003890.

Alexander Mackenzie, 1822–1892.

1874. In the federal election, the Liberals form their first majority government, winning 133 seats. Alexander Mackenzie became the first Liberal prime minister, beating out Sir John A. Macdonald's Conservative government on the heels of the Pacific Scandal (which saw Macdonald take bribes in exchange for the contract to build the Canadian Pacific Railway). Mackenzie served as prime minister until 1878. During his tenure, the Supreme Court and the Auditor General's office were created, and the groundwork for the modern electoral system was laid.

Liberal Prime Ministers

1873–78: Alexander Mackenzie
1896–1911: Sir Wilfrid Laurier
1921–26, 1926–30, 1935–48: William Lyon Mackenzie King
1948–57: Louis St-Laurent
1963–68: Lester B. Pearson
1968–79, 1980–84:
Pierre Elliott Trudeau
1984: John Turner
1993–2003: Jean Chrétien
2003–06: Paul Martin

BORN ON THIS DAY

1799
printer and publisher Ludger Duvernay

1946
Hockey Hall of Famer Serge Savard

1957
Hockey Hall of Famer Mike Bossy

23 JANUARY

1995. Defence Minister David Collenette announces that the Canadian Airborne Regiment, implicated in events that became known as the Somalia Affair, will be disbanded. Canada's participation in Somalia began in 1992 as a humanitarian effort to fight famine and support victims of civil war, but the brutal March 1993 killing of Somali citizens by Canadian soldiers turned it into one of the darkest moments in Canadian military history. The ensuing public inquiry, though controversially cut short, in part revealed that the Canadian Airborne Regiment was a poor choice for the mission, having been trained for combat rather than peacekeeping, and additionally, that the blame lay with the military's top officials for their lack of leadership throughout the mission.

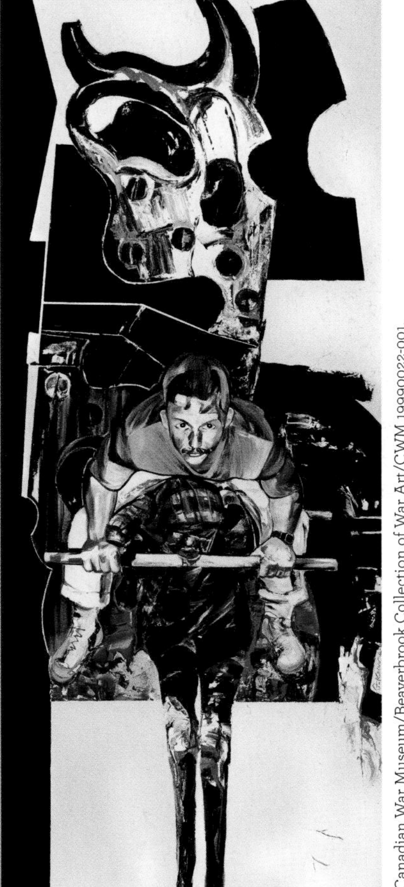

***Somalia 2, Without Conscience,* by Gertrude Kearns, 1996.**

Timeline: The Somalia Affair

December 15, 1992: The Canadian Airborne Regiment arrives in Somalia.
March 4, 1993: Two Somalis infiltrating the Canadian camp are shot, and one dies.
March 16, 1993: Shidane Arone, caught sneaking into the Canadian camp, is tortured and killed.
March 18, 1993: MCpl. Clayton Matchee, arrested in connection with the murder, tries to commit suicide, inflicting brain damage that later keeps him from standing trial.
May 19, 1993: Eight soldiers face court martial, with four convicted.
March 17, 1994: Following his conviction, Pte. Elvin Kyle Brown is sentenced to five years for manslaughter and torture.
January 23, 1995: The Canadian Airborne Regiment is disbanded.
March 21, 1995: A civilian commission of inquiry is established.
March 27, 1996: Information Commissioner John Grace says senior military officers deliberately altered documents related to the Somalia Affair before releasing them to a CBC Radio reporter.
July 2, 1997: The inquiry releases its final report, citing poor leadership and a military cover-up.

BORN ON THIS DAY

1745 — canal engineer William Jessop

1837 — novelist and poet Agnes Machar

1929 — Nobel Prize–winning chemist John Polanyi

1969 — Hockey Hall of Famer Brendan Shanahan

JANUARY 24

Canada Council for the Arts Honour Roll

1959 Senior Arts Fellowships
Irving Layton, poet
Fernand Leduc, painter
Marcel Dubé, author

1959 Arts Scholarships
Leonard Cohen, poet and musician
Mordecai Richler, author
Michael Snow, artist

Library and Archives Canada/e002265645.

Vincent Massey speaking with Oee, an Inuk woman, in Frobisher Bay (now Iqaluit), Northwest Territories, 1956.

1952. Charles Vincent Massey becomes the first Canadian-born governor general. After the Second World War, having recognized Massey as a crusader for Canadian culture, heritage, and identity, Prime Minister Louis St-Laurent had placed him in charge of the Royal Commission on National Development in the Arts, Letters, and Sciences (known informally as the Massey Commission). There, Massey's efforts led to the creation of the National Arts Centre in Ottawa and the formation of what is now the Canada Council for the Arts, the federal government's funding agency for artists and art organizations. Massey has namesake arts and culture institutes across the country.

BORN ON THIS DAY

1927 — architect and philanthropist Phyllis Lambert

1976 — figure skater Shae-Lynn Bourne

25 JANUARY

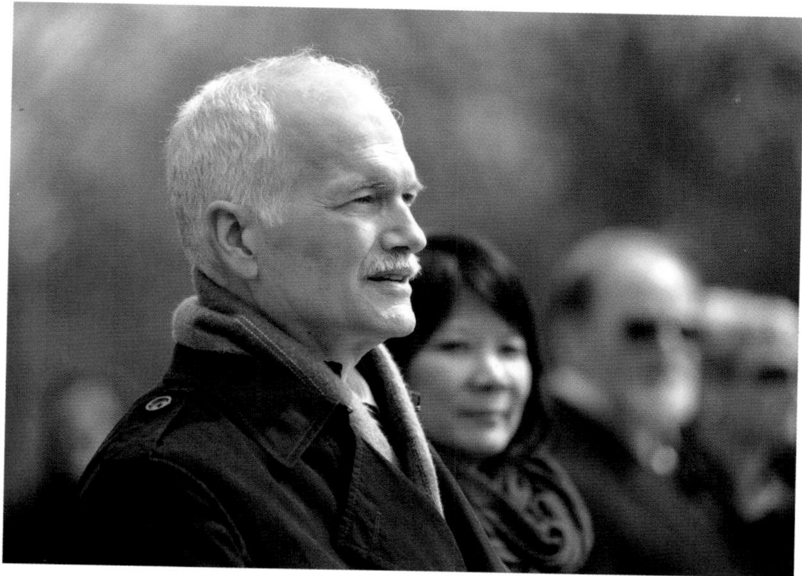

© Henry Chan.

Jack Layton and Olivia Chow at an Easter procession in Toronto, 2011.

2003. Jack Layton is elected leader of the New Democratic Party (NDP). Despite having no seat in Parliament, Layton entered the 2003 NDP leadership race and won a solid first-ballot victory over five rivals, including three sitting MPs. Layton's energetic leadership style garnered attention from the media as well as favourable poll results. He remained party leader until 2011, the year the NDP became Canada's official opposition for the first time. Layton passed away of cancer on August 22, 2011, one month after taking what was meant to be a temporary leave. He is remembered as one of Canada's most inspirational politicians.

You Don't Know Jack: Great Canadians Named Jack

Jack Adams, NHL player and coach
Jack Bush, painter
Jack Chambers, painter
Jack Duffy, comedian, impressionist
Jack Granatstein, historian
Jack Hodgins, author
Jack Humphrey, painter
Jack Jacobs, football player
Jack Kessler, violinist
Jack McClelland, publisher
Jack Nichols, painter
Jack Purcell, badminton player
Jack Warner, producer
Jack Webster, journalist

BORN ON THIS DAY

1867 veterinarian and politician Simon Fraser Tolmie

1960 choreographer John Alleyne

1975 actress Mia Kirshner

JANUARY 26

The Montreal Procedure

Wilder Penfield's epilepsy treatment involved stimulating areas of the brain with electrical probes while the patient, who remained conscious on the operating table, reported any sensations he felt. This technique allowed Dr. Penfield to locate the source of the seizures and surgically remove that section of the brain. It was a successful cure for epilepsy in more than half his cases. The procedure also helped Dr. Penfield draw a map of the human brain, showing how certain regions connected to or influenced the various limbs and organs. "The problem of neurology," he once wrote, "is to understand man himself."

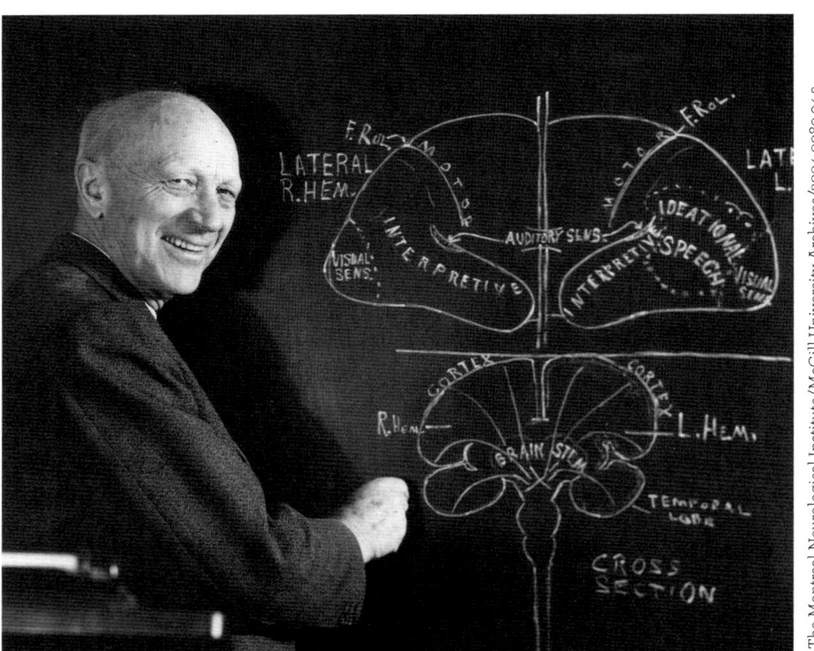

The Montreal Neurological Institute/McGill University Archives/2004-0080.04.2.

Wilder Penfield, 1963.

1891. Famed neurosurgeon Wilder Graves Penfield is born in Spokane, Washington. After arriving in Canada from New York in 1928, Penfield began work at the Royal Victoria Hospital at McGill University. There, he founded the Montreal Neurological Institute and developed the ground-breaking "Montreal procedure" for the surgical treatment of epilepsy. The breakthrough was immortalized in the often-quoted *Heritage Minute* line "Dr. Penfield, I smell burnt toast!"

BORN ON THIS DAY

1925
politician Claude Ryan

1948
musician Corky Laing

1965
actress Allison Hossack

27 JANUARY

Nathan Denette/The Canadian Press.

Susan Aglukark performing at the Canadian Aboriginal Music Awards, 2006.

1967. Inuit singer and songwriter Susan (Uuliniq) Aglukark is born in Churchill, Manitoba. Aglukark's blend of traditional Inuit rhythms and easy-listening pop is distinguished by her gentle voice, upbeat melodies, and inspirational lyrics (sung in both English and Inuktitut). Her lyrics often bring to life personal stories and act as social commentary on issues that have affected many Aboriginal communities, such as child abuse, alcoholism, and suicide. Her album *This Child* (1995) sold more than three hundred thousand copies in Canada, and the lead single, "O Siem," became the first top-ten hit by an Inuk performer. Aglukark has won three Juno Awards over the course of her eight-album career.

BORN ON THIS DAY

dancer Frank Augustyn

1953

1971

hockey player
Patrice Brisebois

JANUARY 28

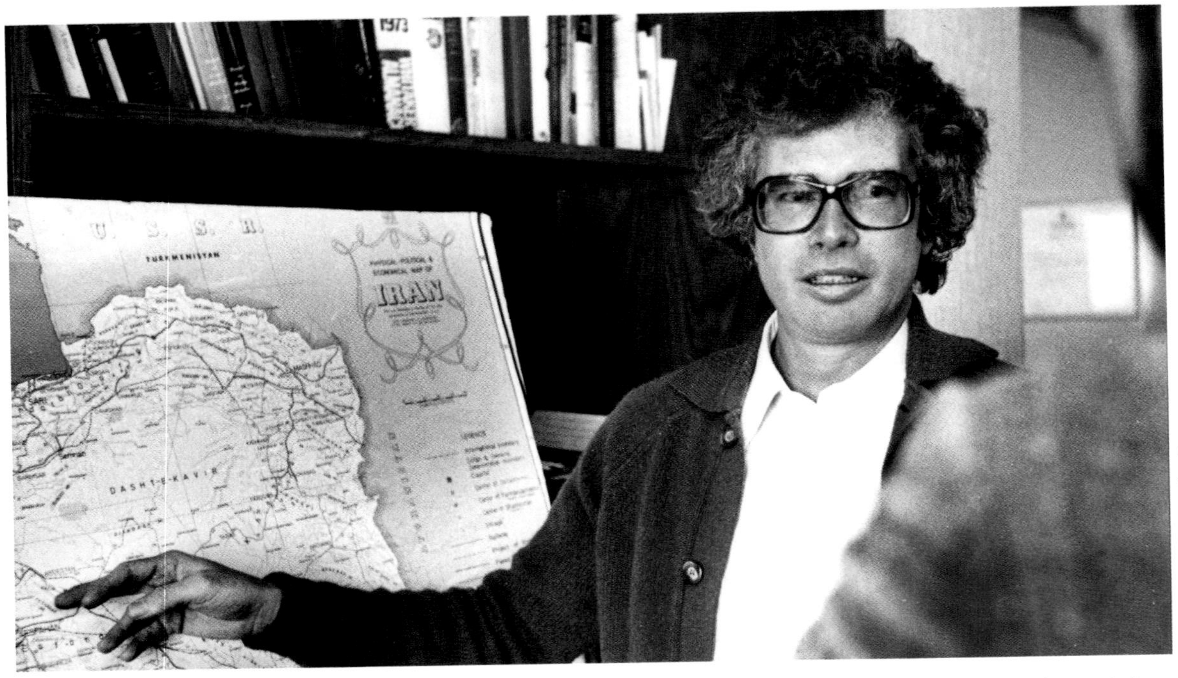

Peter Bregg/The Canadian Press.

Ambassador Ken Taylor briefs Canadian Press reporter Doug Long on the current conditions in Iran, one week before he arranged the escape of six Americans.

1980. Ken Taylor, the Canadian ambassador to Iran, engineers what became known as the Canadian Caper—the escape of six Americans from the revolution-torn country. On November 5, 1979, Iranian revolutionaries captured the US embassy and took sixty-six hostages. In the two months following—at great personal risk—Taylor, immigration officer John Sheardown, and their wives, Pat Taylor and Zena Sheardown, hid the six Americans, who happened not to be at the embassy when it was attacked. No stranger to peril, Taylor had already evacuated 850 Canadian workers from his own embassy. An escape had to be carefully engineered, and Tehran's Mehrabad International Airport was discreetly scouted. Canadian passports and identity documents were arranged for the six Americans, while Canadian embassy staff, in small groups, quietly returned home. On January 28, Canada's American guests navigated their way nervously through the airport and onto an early morning flight to Frankfurt. Later that day, Taylor and the remaining Canadians shut down the embassy and left Iran.

BORN ON THIS DAY

Prime Minister Alexander Mackenzie
1822

1943
hockey player Paul Henderson

rower Marnie McBean
1968

1968
singer-songwriter Sarah McLachlan

FILM VS. REALITY

Bryan Cranston and Ben Affleck in *Argo*.

Ben Affleck's 2012 political thriller, *Argo*, downplays the Canadians' contributions so much that Taylor, who spied for the United States throughout the crisis at the request of President Jimmy Carter, complained, "We're portrayed as innkeepers who are waiting to be saved by the CIA." In reality, Canadians scouted the Tehran airport, travelled in and out of Iran to establish random patterns and obtain copies of visas, purchased three sets of plane tickets, and taught the hostages how to sound Canadian (e.g., by pronouncing Toronto like "piranha"). John Sheardown and his wife, who housed four of the six hostages, are omitted from the film, which gives sole credit to Taylor and his wife. The film's portrayal of a tense outing to a bazaar never happened, and the climactic passage through the airport, depicted on film as fraught with every nail-biting near escape imaginable, was actually completely uneventful.

Painterly Protégés

Many Canadian artists credit the Group of Seven with influencing their craft, among them the following:

Emily Carr, landscape painter
Jock Macdonald, landscape and abstract oil painter
Goodridge Roberts, landscape, portrait, and still-life painter
Harold Town, abstract artist, member of Painters Eleven
Joyce Wieland, mixed-media artist

The Canadian Press/791046.

Lawren Harris, member of the Group of Seven, ca. 1968.

1970. Artist Lawren Harris dies in Vancouver. He was a founding member of the Group of Seven and the first president of the Canadian Group of Painters. Harris's landscapes of Lake Superior, the Rocky Mountains, and the Arctic are at once stark and beautiful, and among the best-loved pieces of Canadian art. He is buried on the grounds of the McMichael Canadian Art Collection, in Kleinburg, Ontario, where many of his paintings are displayed. Harris had a profound influence on the generations of artists who followed.

Who did the artist Harold Town call "the master of absence"? See December 26.

BORN ON THIS DAY

1901 tycoon and horse breeder E.P. Taylor

1924 opera singer Lois Marshall

1986 figure skater Bryce Davison

30 JANUARY

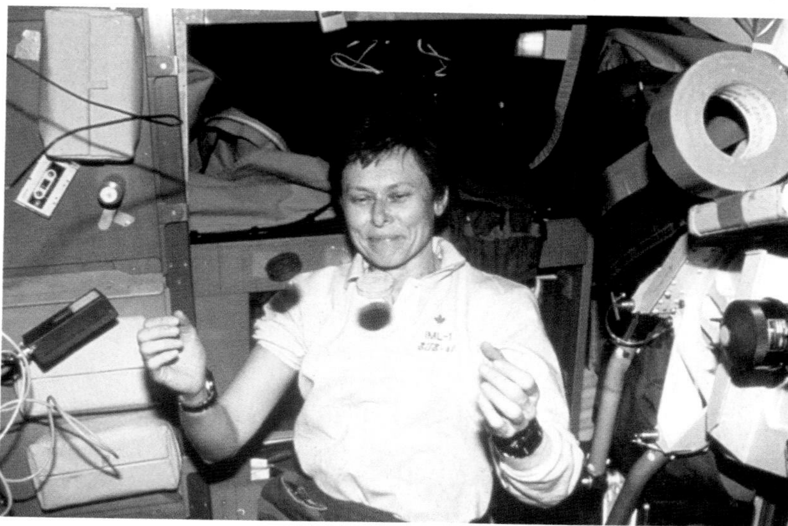

Astronaut Roberta Bondar in space during flight IML-1, 1992.

Blast Off: Canadians Launch into Space

October 5, 1984: Marc Garneau
January 22, 1992: Roberta Bondar
October 22, 1992: Steve MacLean
November 12, 1995: Chris Hadfield
June 20, 1996: Robert Thirsk
August 7, 1997: Bjarni Tryggvason
April 17, 1998: Dafydd Williams
May 27, 1999: Julie Payette
September 30, 2009: Guy Laliberté (first Canadian space tourist)

1992. Physician, educator, and astronaut Roberta Bondar spends her last day aboard the space shuttle *Discovery*. During the eight-day mission, Bondar conducted experiments in the Spacelab and on the mid-deck to discover how to allow future astronauts to undertake longer flights in space. Her McMaster University research on the nervous system and inner ear balancing system made her an ideal candidate for the experimental mission. She was the second Canadian—and the first Canadian woman—in space.

 See what Guy Laliberté was wearing before he blasted off on September 30.

BORN ON THIS DAY

1929
surgeon Lucille Teasdale-Corti

1931
politician John Crosbie

JANUARY 31

Also on This Day

1933.
Aboriginal spokesman, philosopher, statesman, and spiritual leader John Snow (or Intebeja Mani, meaning Walking Seal) is born in Morley, Alberta. Snow was the first member of the Stoney-Nakoda to be ordained in the United Church of Canada. When the Trudeau government tabled the assimilationist 1969 White Paper, Snow presented the Alberta chiefs' response—known as the Red Paper—which asserted Aboriginal and treaty rights.

Fred Chartrand/The Canadian Press.

Gitxsan dancers perform in front of the Supreme Court of Canada in Ottawa, 1997.

1973. The Supreme Court acknowledges the existence of Aboriginal title in modern Canadian law. The decision merely confirmed the existence of the Aboriginal right to hold land. However, the Supreme Court judges remained divided on the nature of such title. Since then, a number of cases have challenged and referred to Aboriginal title, which involves communal, rather than individual, property ownership. Notably, in the 1997 Delgamuukw case, the Supreme Court ruled that claims to title had to show exclusive occupation of a territory by a defined Aboriginal society at the time of the British Crown's assertion of sovereignty. In the same case, the Court ruled that the oral histories of Aboriginal peoples were to be accepted as evidence of historic use and occupation.

BORN ON THIS DAY

1939 singer-songwriter Claude Gauthier

1964 diver Sylvie Bernier

1965 cellist Ofra Harnoy

FEBRUARY

P1000, S4, D83, PH13/Collection Centre d'archives de Québec.

Portrait of Ezekiel Hart, ca. 1910.

1808. Members of the Legislative Assembly of Lower Canada (now Québec) criticize the January 28 swearing-in of Jewish member Ezekiel Hart. Hart had refused to take the Christian oath of office, and instead swore his oath on the Old Testament with his head covered. Because the law of the time required that an oath be sworn "on the true faith of a Christian," assembly members resolved (by a 35–5 vote) that Hart could not sit in the House. Among those who voted for his expulsion was Louis-Joseph Papineau.

In 1815, Papineau became speaker of the Legislative Assembly and no longer held the same ideals as he had when he supported Hart's expulsion. He resolved not to allow prejudice and partisan bickering to interfere with the democratic process. Under Papineau's tenure, the assembly passed a bill in 1832 that guaranteed full rights to people practising the Jewish faith. Twenty-eight years would pass before England and its other colonies granted the same rights.

Also on This Day

1782.
William Johnston, outlaw, is born in Trois-Rivières, Québec. Called the "Pirate of the St. Lawrence," Bill Johnston was a bandit and a smuggler who operated in the Thousand Islands district. During the War of 1812, he deserted to the Americans and served them as a spy and a raider. Later, in 1838, he seized and burned the steamer *Sir Robert Peel*, making off with $175,000 in cash and plunder. The Americans imprisoned him on charges of piracy, but he was granted a full pardon by President William Henry Harrison.

BORN ON THIS DAY

1895
Toronto Maple Leafs founder Conn Smythe

1923
fitness pioneer Ben Weider

1940
sulky jockey Hervé Filion

The Canadian Press.

Roméo LeBlanc, 1977.

1996. Governor General Roméo LeBlanc signs into law an act that gives several provinces (Ontario, British Columbia, and Québec) and some regions (at least two provinces from Atlantic Canada and two from the Prairies, with more than 50 percent of the population in each region) a veto over major constitutional changes. The veto legislation grew out of the 1995 Québec referendum campaign, during which Prime Minister Jean Chrétien said that he would take measures toward recognizing Québec's status as a "distinct society."

Did You Know?

After Conquest in 1760, Québec maintained its civil law, its seigneurial system, and the Catholic Church, preserving the French character of the colony. These "distinct" arrangements were codified in law by the British Parliament in the Quebec Act of 1774 and the Constitutional Act of 1791.

For French Canadians, Confederation is not an agreement to make a country between four provinces but a pact between two peoples, allowing francophones to assert themselves as a distinct society among an anglophone majority.

During the Quiet Revolution of the 1960s, the Québécois began to question their province's role in Confederation, and Premier Jean Lesage wrote: "Our province has particular traits, its own character."

BORN ON THIS DAY

Alberta premier Alexander Rutherford
1857

1867
Marquis wheat inventor Charles Saunders

opera singer Pauline Vaillancourt
1945

What famous trophy survived a fire in 1947? **See February 16.**

Library and Archives Canada/John Boyd/RD-000267.

Firefighters in front of the Parliament Buildings.

1916. Most of the original Centre Block of the Parliament Buildings in Ottawa is destroyed by a fire that kills seven people. The library, along with its irreplaceable collection of books, was saved because an employee closed its iron doors just in time. With the country at war, the event sparked suspicions of foul play. Theories of a terrorist plot led to the questioning of locals with German-sounding names. Ultimately, investigators found that the fire had originated in the House of Commons Reading Room, where members were known to smoke cigars.

BORN ON THIS DAY

1843
railway builder William Van Horne

1863
cartographer James White

1961
Research in Motion co-founder Jim Balsillie

GREAT FIRES IN CANADIAN HISTORY

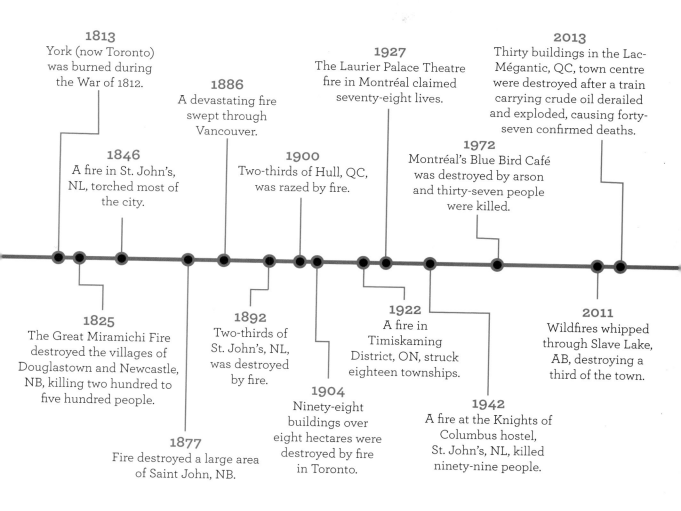

1813
York (now Toronto) was burned during the War of 1812.

1825
The Great Miramichi Fire destroyed the villages of Douglastown and Newcastle, NB, killing two hundred to five hundred people.

1846
A fire in St. John's, NL, torched most of the city.

1877
Fire destroyed a large area of Saint John, NB.

1886
A devastating fire swept through Vancouver.

1892
Two-thirds of St. John's, NL, was destroyed by fire.

1900
Two-thirds of Hull, QC, was razed by fire.

1904
Ninety-eight buildings over eight hectares were destroyed by fire in Toronto.

1922
A fire in Timiskaming District, ON, struck eighteen townships.

1927
The Laurier Palace Theatre fire in Montréal claimed seventy-eight lives.

1942
A fire at the Knights of Columbus hostel, St. John's, NL, killed ninety-nine people.

1972
Montréal's Blue Bird Café was destroyed by arson and thirty-seven people were killed.

2011
Wildfires whipped through Slave Lake, AB, destroying a third of the town.

2013
Thirty buildings in the Lac-Mégantic, QC, town centre were destroyed after a train carrying crude oil derailed and exploded, causing forty-seven confirmed deaths.

Also on This Day

1882.
Poet E.J. Pratt is born in Western Bay, Newfoundland. He studied theology at Toronto's Victoria College and was ordained a minister, but later decided to join the school's faculty of English. He is best known for his epic verses, including *The Titanic*. His great-nephew is Newfoundland artist Christopher Pratt.

Library and Archives Canada/C-008408

Cairine Wilson, undated.

1885. Canada's first female senator, Cairine Wilson, is born in Montréal. A dedicated philanthropist, Wilson championed many social causes, including those supporting women and refugees. From 1938 to 1948, she served as chairman of the Canadian National Committee on Refugees and was an outspoken critic of anti-Semitism in Canada, once stating, "Without a belief in the dignity of man, without indignation against arbitrarily created human suffering, there can be no democratic principles." She was sworn in to the Senate on February 15, 1930, and served in the position until her death in 1962.

Ninety-two women have sat in the Senate since 1930—fifty Liberal senators, thirty-eight Conservatives, three independents, and one NDPer.

BORN ON THIS DAY

War of 1812 scout William "Billy" Green
1794

1873
hammer thrower and Olympic gold medallist Étienne Desmarteau

actor Conrad Bain
1923

1961
Hockey Hall of Famer Denis Savard

5 FEBRUARY

Library and Archives Canada/Frank Prazak/Weekend Magazine Collection/ PA-211916.

Joni Mitchell in Fort Macleod, Alberta, 1969.

1981. Singer-songwriter Joni Mitchell is inducted into the Canadian Music Hall of Fame during the Juno Awards ceremony. She was presented with the award by Prime Minister Pierre Trudeau. Beginning in the 1960s, Mitchell was a forerunner of a style of music with unique, lyric-driven melodies and a breezy vocal approach that has since been adopted by many other performers. Mitchell also became a pioneer for women vocalists by successfully maintaining control of all aspects of her career in the male-dominated music industry. She remains one of the most influential musicians of her generation.

Iconic Joni Mitchell Songs

In 2014, the CBC put together a list of the ten Joni Mitchell songs that everyone should know:

1. **"Both Sides, Now"** from *Clouds* (1969)
2. **"Big Yellow Taxi"** from *Ladies of the Canyon* (1970)
3. **"Woodstock"** from *Ladies of the Canyon* (1970)
4. **"River"** from *Blue* (1971)
5. **"California"** from *Blue* (1971)
6. **"You Turn Me On, I'm a Radio"** from *For the Roses* (1972)
7. **"Help Me"** from *Court and Spark* (1974)
8. **"The Wolf That Lives in Lindsey"** from *Mingus* (1979)
9. **"Lakota"** from *Chalk Mark in a Rain Storm* (1988)
10. **"Sex Kills"** from *Turbulent Indigo* (1994)

BORN ON THIS DAY

stem-cell researcher Charles Leblond

1910

1918

diplomat and thriller writer John Starnes

hockey player, coach, and TV commentator Don Cherry

1934

FEBRUARY 6

Timeline: Queen Elizabeth II in Canada

1926: Born in London, England
1952: Ascends to the throne
1953: Is invested through the coronation ceremony
1957: Delivers Canada's Speech from the Throne, the first reigning monarch to do so
1967: Visits Expo 67
1976: Opens the Montreal Olympic Games
1977: Celebrates her Silver Jubilee for twenty-five years as Queen
1982: Signs Canada's Proclamation of the Constitution Act
1997: Celebrates the five-hundredth anniversary of John Cabot's voyage on the *Matthew* in Newfoundland
2002: Marks her Golden Jubilee for fifty years as Queen
2007: Rededicates the Canadian National Vimy Memorial at Vimy, France
2012: Commemorates her Diamond Jubilee for sixty years as Queen

Library and Archives Canada/National Film Board of Canada/4312140.

King George VI and Queen Elizabeth at the opening of Parliament, 1948.

1952. King George VI dies in his sleep while his eldest daughter, twenty-five-year-old Princess Elizabeth, is visiting Africa. Upon his death, she became Queen Elizabeth II. She was crowned at Westminster Abbey on June 2, 1953, the first monarch to be crowned both head of the Commonwealth and Queen of Canada. Her coronation dress included embroidered maple leaves to represent the former colony. For the first time, television cameras filmed the coronation, and the recording was then flown overseas and aired on the CBC.

 Who did King George VI and Queen Elizabeth pose with for a famous photo during their landmark trip to Canada in 1939? **See May 17.**

BORN ON THIS DAY

1918 poet Louis Dudek

1946 singer-songwriter Kate McGarrigle

Library and Archives Canada/PA-004879.

Richard Jack in 1917, painting *The Second Battle of Ypres, 22 April to 25 May 1915.*

1918. Canadian artists ship off to England to paint scenes of the First World War. Canada's first official war art program—the Canadian War Memorial Fund—had been established in 1916 by Lords Beaverbrook and Rothermere, under the direction of the Canadian War Records Office. The war artists included Group of Seven members F.H. Varley, Arthur Lismer, Frank Johnston, and A.Y. Jackson, as well as Richard Jack and Maurice Cullen. From 1916 to 1921, the Canadian War Memorial Fund hired more than a hundred artists. Since then, war artists have been assigned to numerous conflicts, including the Second World War, Somalia, and Afghanistan.

BORN ON THIS DAY

folk singer Oscar Brand
1920

1968
swimmer Mark Tewksbury

basketball player Steve Nash
1974

Also on This Day

1876.
Although pucks were in use for some time before this date, the NHL marks this day as the puck's birthday based on the word's first appearance in the *Montreal Gazette*. Some sources say the word derives from the Irish "poc"—meaning to punch or poke.

Also on this Day

1924. The Toronto Granite Hockey Club wins Canada's second consecutive Olympic gold medal in ice hockey in Chamonix, France, beating the American team 6–1. The ferocity of play was evidenced by injuries sustained by players like Canada's Harry Watson, who was knocked out cold in the first twenty seconds but went on to score two goals later in the game. The very first Olympic gold in ice hockey was won in Antwerp, Belgium, in 1920 by the Winnipeg Falcons.

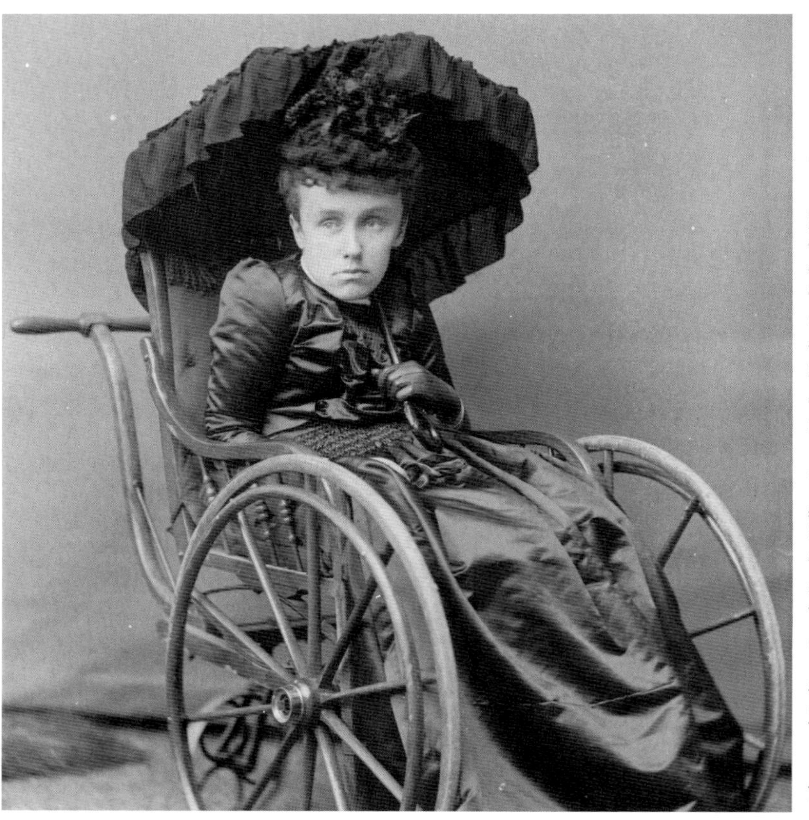

Library and Archives Canada/Credit: William James Topley/Topley Studio fonds/PA-025746.

Mary Macdonald, 1893.

1869. Sir John A. Macdonald and his wife, Agnes, welcome their daughter, Mary Macdonald. Born with serious physical disabilities, Mary was confined to a wheelchair her entire life. She was never able to write, as she couldn't hold a pen, but she could tap out her own letters on the 1922 Corona typewriter her attendant, Sarah Crawford, purchased for her.

BORN ON THIS DAY

1929 senator and Métis activist Thelma Chalifoux

1934 schizophrenia researcher Philip Seeman

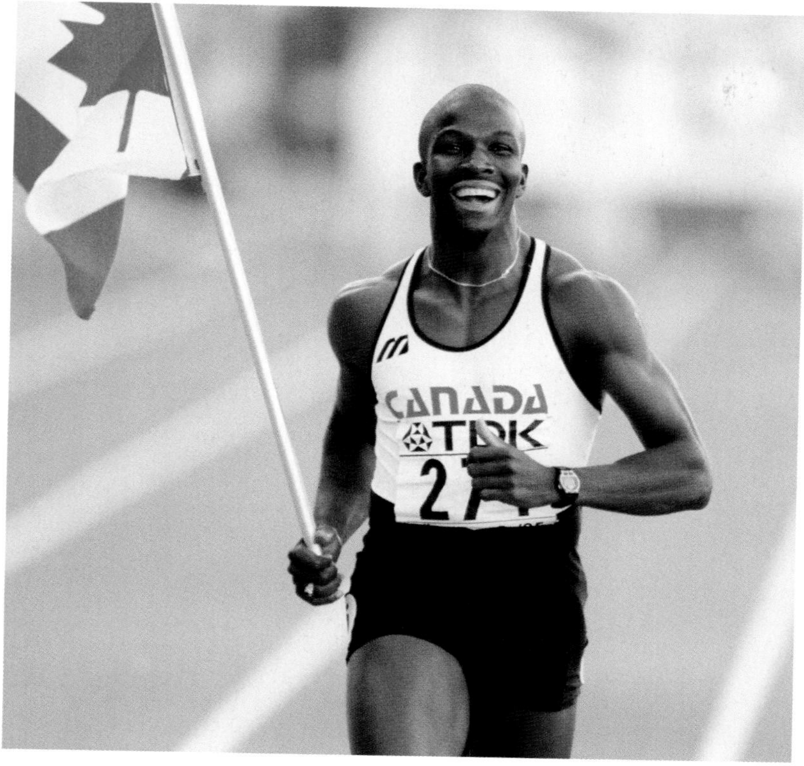

© Claus Andersen.

Prior to his win in Nevada and his two Olympic gold medals, Donovan Bailey won gold at the 1995 World Track and Field Championships in Gottenburg, Sweden.

1996. Canadian sprinter Donovan Bailey sets the indoor 50-metre dash record in Reno, Nevada, at 5.56 seconds. Bailey went on to win gold in the 100 metres at the 1996 Olympic Games in Atlanta, setting a world and Olympic record of 9.84 seconds. At the same Olympics, Bailey also anchored the 4 x 100 metre relay team, which beat out the Americans to win the gold.

Also on This Day

1936.
Country and folk singer-songwriter Stompin' Tom Connors is born in Saint John, New Brunswick. One of the most iconic figures in Canadian music, Stompin' Tom was a working-class, salt-of-the-earth troubadour who travelled across the country for years before launching his musical career in Timmins, Ontario. He developed his signature style of stomping on a board as a way of keeping the beat over the noise at the tavern where he first performed, accepting beer in place of payment. His Canadiana anthems, such as "Bud the Spud" and "The Hockey Song," made Stompin' Tom one of the most overtly nationalist songwriters the country has ever produced.

BORN ON THIS DAY

airman William "Billy" Bishop

1894

1863

Vancouver Historical Society's Citizen of the Century Joseph Seraphim Fortes

In Her Own Words: War Bride Isabella MacDougall

"I met my husband one night at the skating rink, Dundee Ice Rink. There was a bunch of Canadian boys, of course, and we were just young girls, and he fell at my feet, I think! I didn't think he was a very good skater for a Canadian. I thought Canadians were all good skaters, but I guess they just rented these old skates. That was how we met. That's where I met my fate … We were married in November 1945. I was eighteen, but I was almost nineteen in February. Then my husband was sent back home. So he went home in March, but I didn't get over until the last of July the same year, a few months later. He met me in Halifax in a three-ton gravel truck. I think he thought he had a Cadillac! … I had one sister. She married a Canadian too, but she was up in Ontario, in Kitchener. I don't know why we didn't pick men that lived a little closer together!"

—From the *Memory Project*

Isabella MacDougall/The Memory Project Archive.

Isabella and Roland MacDougall in Dundee, Scotland, 1945.

1946. War brides arrive in Halifax from England. The term "war brides" refers to women who married Canadian servicemen overseas during the Second World War. After the war, the Canadian government provided these women with free sea and rail passage from their original homes to their destinations in Canada, and by 1948, over forty-three thousand wives and more than twenty thousand children had immigrated.

Which event caused looting and vandalizing in downtown Halifax? **See May 7.**

BORN ON THIS DAY

1939 broadcaster and Governor General Adrienne Clarkson

1964 swimmer Victor Davis

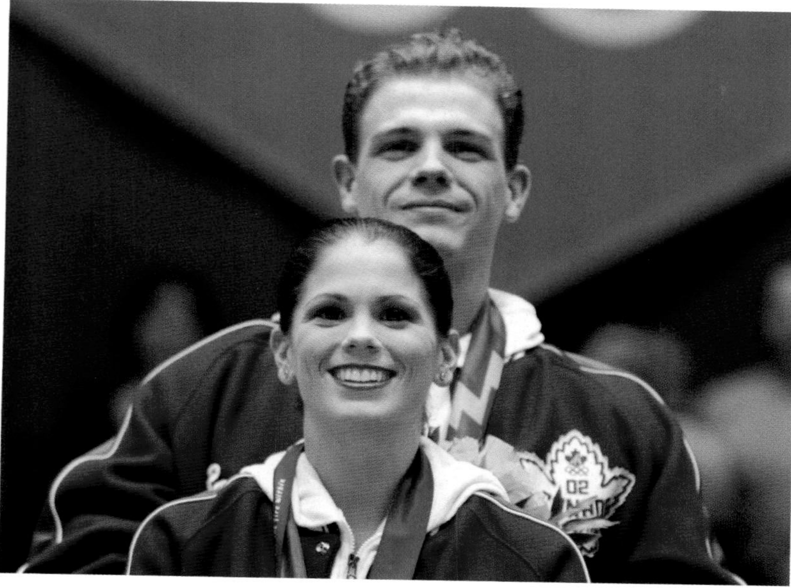

Paul Chiasson/The Canadian Press.

Jamie Salé and David Pelletier during the medals ceremony at the Olympic Winter Games in Salt Lake City, Utah.

2002. Pairs figure skaters Jamie Salé and David Pelletier deliver the performance that would ultimately win them a gold medal at the Salt Lake City Winter Olympics. But despite a clean long program that was expected to clinch the gold, the pair received a second-place ranking, behind the Russian skaters Berezhnaya and Sikharulidze, who had made an error during their routine. The ranking sparked international controversy and suspicions of foul play among the judges, five out of nine of whom had awarded gold to the Russians. The following day, the French judge admitted to being pressured to vote for the Russians (a claim she later recanted). The ensuing scandal, which came to be known as Skategate, saw the French judge and a French official suspended, and gold medals eventually awarded to both the Canadian and the Russian skaters.

Also on This Day

1926.
Actor Leslie Nielsen is born in Regina, Saskatchewan. He grew up in the Northwest Territories and Alberta, and trained as an aerial gunner with the Royal Canadian Air Force during the Second World War, though he was not sent overseas. His television career began in 1950, and he worked as a dramatic actor in movies and on TV before moving on to comedic roles. He most famously played Dr. Rumack in the cult classic *Airplane!* (1980), and is remembered for his deadpan delivery of lines such as "The life of everyone on board depends upon just one thing: finding someone back there who can not only fly this plane, but who didn't have fish for dinner."

Which Canadians became the youngest Olympic winners in ice dancing? **See February 22.**

BORN ON THIS DAY

1944
dancer
Annette av Paul

1947
runner
Abby Hoffman

THE MILK BAG

Visitors to eastern Canada are often surprised to see that milk is sold in plastic bags. The bags must be stored in a special pitcher and snipped open at one corner.

The milk bag was introduced to Canada by the DuPont chemical company in 1967.

While bagged milk is prevalent in eastern Canada, milk is usually sold in jugs or cartons in Manitoba and farther west. Around half of all Canadian milk-drinkers buy their milk in bags.

The Snippit was invented in Toronto in 1979 as a quick and easy way to open milk bags. This simple plastic tool has a stainless steel blade that makes a clean cut, as well as a magnet on the back for storing on the fridge door.

A giant version of the Snippit was developed as an emergency seatbelt cutter.

A YouTube video of a Canadian woman demonstrating how to use a milk bag went viral, generating astonished responses from many American viewers.

12 FEBRUARY

Fred Lum/The Globe and Mail Digital Image.

The opening ceremonies of the 2010 Vancouver Winter Olympic Games.

Also on This Day

1949.
During the first round of the Ice Hockey World Championships in Stockholm, Sweden, Canada beats Denmark in the most lopsided international hockey game ever. The final score was 47–0.

2010. The opening ceremony of the Vancouver Winter Olympic Games is held at BC Place Stadium. It was the first indoor ceremony in Olympic history. The Vancouver games would result in Canada's first Olympic gold medal on home soil, when Alexandre Bilodeau won the moguls event on the second day of the games. This would turn out to be the first of many, with Canadian athletes breaking the record for most gold medals won by a host nation. Canadian pride was on display from coast to coast, with at least one survey showing that more than half of Canadians believed the Vancouver games were a defining national moment more significant than the 1972 Summit Series, Expo 67, or the Montréal and Calgary Olympics.

BORN ON THIS DAY

actor Lorne Greene
1915

1929
marketing guru and K-tel founder Philip Kives

poet and dramatist George Elliott Clarke
1960

Canadian Women Who Flew Past Barriers

1928: Eileen Vollick, first to earn a private pilot's certificate
1950: Marion Orr, first to own and operate a flying club
1959: Molly Reilly, first to pilot corporate aircraft
1973: Rosella Bjornson, first hired by a commercial airline in Canada
1974: Wendy Clay, first female pilot in the air force
1978: Judy Cameron, first female pilot for Air Canada
1989: Deanna Brasseur and Jane Foster, first certified to fly the CF-18 jet fighter

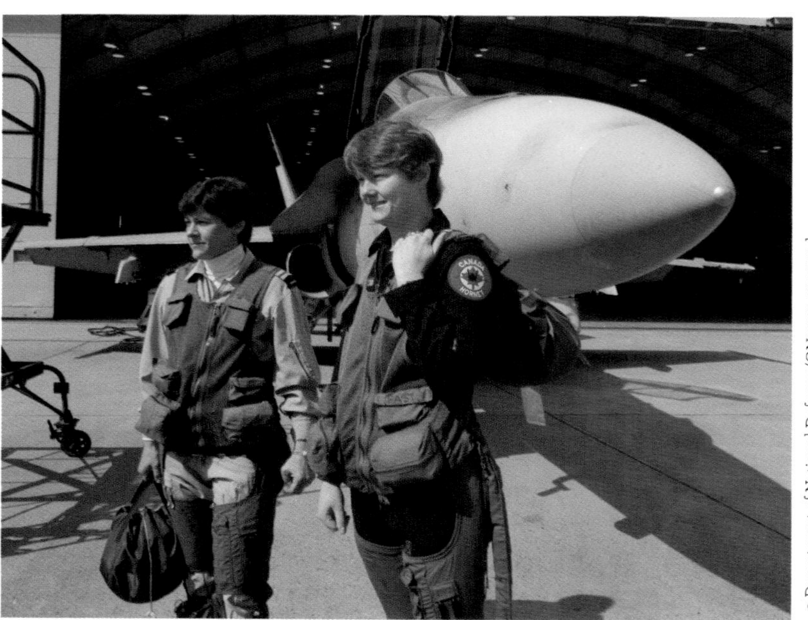

Capt. Dee Brasseur and Capt. Jane Foster, shown here in Cold Lake, Alberta, in 1989, were the first two women in the world to qualify to fly a CF-18 fighter aircraft.

1981. Captains Leah Mosher, Nora Bottomley, and Deanna (Dee) Brasseur become the first Canadian female military pilots to receive their wings, changing the face of the Royal Canadian Air Force (RCAF) pilot community forever. While women had served as pilots during the Second World War, they were classified as commercial (that is, non-combat) pilots. Most, like Ontario's Marion Orr, flew with the Air Transport Auxiliary, shuttling aircraft from factories to bases. In 1988, the RCAF finally started licensing women as fighter pilots—the first Western country in the world to do so.

BORN ON THIS DAY

1819
Father of Confederation James Cockburn

1932
journalist Robert Fulford

1971
Hockey Hall of Famer Mats Sundin

14 FEBRUARY

CBC Still Images Library/Fred Phipps.

Mr. Dressup (Ernie Coombs) with Casey and Finnegan, ca. 1980.

1996. Beloved children's entertainer Ernie Coombs, most famous for the show *Mr. Dressup*, retires from television. Coombs, who originally came to Canada in 1963 as a puppeteer working with Fred Rogers (later of *Mr. Rogers' Neighborhood*), created the character of Mr. Dressup in 1964. The TV show debuted in 1967, delighting generations of children; the name itself has since become part of the Canadian lexicon. Coombs passed away on September 18, 2001, five years after retiring.

Also on This Day

1949.
Some five thousand miners go on strike, paralyzing major asbestos mines in Québec for four months. The brutality of the police response to the strike generated a wave of solidarity, even among powers in the Catholic Church, that showed the labour movement could confront Premier Maurice Duplessis.

BORN ON THIS DAY

1909 poet A.M. Klein

1927 actress and Miss Moneypenny portrayer Lois Maxwell

1960 actress Meg Tilly

Library and Archives Canada/1979-75-120.

Library and Archives Canada/1979-75-129.

Library and Archives Canada/1979-75-118.

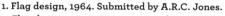

1. Flag design, 1964. Submitted by A.R.C. Jones.
2. Flag design, 1964. Anonymous submission.
3. Flag design, 1964. Submitted by John Ensor.

What colours are used in the Franco-Ontarian flag? **See September 25.**

Also on This Day

1982.
A violent storm sinks the oil-drilling rig *Ocean Ranger* on the Grand Banks, east of Newfoundland. All eighty-four men on board drown in Canada's worst maritime disaster since the Second World War, when ships like the *Nerissa* and the *Empress of Canada* fell prey to German U-boats.

1965. Canada's new flag is officially inaugurated in a ceremony on Parliament Hill. Its adoption was the culmination of many years of discussions, hundreds of designs, and the heated Great Flag Debate in Parliament. Before 1965, Canada did not have an official flag and instead used Britain's Union Jack or the Canadian Red Ensign. The idea of creating a flag unique to Canada was brought before Parliament several times between 1925 and 1960. The debates that followed were never about whether the country should have its own flag, but about what that flag should look like.

BORN ON THIS DAY

financier Joseph Flavelle
1858

1967
musician Jane Child

Boris Spremo/GetStock.com.

Ottawa Rough Riders celebrating with the Grey Cup, 1969.

1970. The Grey Cup trophy, stolen in December 1969 from the offices of the champion Ottawa Rough Riders, is returned to the Canadian Football League (CFL) headquarters. With little fanfare, police had recovered the cup from a locker in Toronto's Royal York Hotel after receiving an anonymous tip. Unwilling to pay the thieves the ransom they were demanding, the CFL was planning to make a replica trophy if the cup was not recovered.

Famous Fumbles

The Grey Cup, intended as a hockey trophy, was donated by Governor General Lord Earl Grey to the amateur rugby football champion of Canada in 1909. It has since endured relentless bumps and blunders. It has been dropped (1978), sat on (1987), head-butted (1993), and decapitated (2006). All these indignities were inflicted by winning teams. It has been stolen three times—as a prank in 1967, for ransom (as described left) in 1969, and briefly in 1997, when Toronto Argonauts' placekicker Mike Vanderjagt lost it in a bar in Oakville, Ontario. It even survived a fire that melted the Toronto Argonaut Rowing Club's trophy collection in 1947.

BORN ON THIS DAY

soldier and colonial administrator John Colborne

1778

1953

Hockey Hall of Famer Lanny McDonald

FEBRUARY 17

Yukon Archives/Thornthwaite/YA 83-22-450.

Peter "Lexee" Alexis, an expert guide from the community of Old Crow, was instrumental in tracking the Mad Trapper.

1932. Albert Johnson, the Mad Trapper of Rat River, is killed in an RCMP shootout on the Eagle River, Yukon. On December 31, 1931, Johnson reportedly shot an RCMP constable who was investigating a trapline complaint. The ensuing chase to apprehend Johnson lasted forty-eight days and covered 240 kilometres in temperatures averaging −40°C. The suspect was so skilled at survival in the isolated landscape that the RCMP had to send out a search party that included flying ace Wilfrid Reid "Wop" May and skilled guide Peter "Lexee" Alexis. By the time of the shootout, a second constable had been wounded and a third was killed. To this day, little is known about Johnson himself and no motive for his crimes has ever been established.

BORN ON THIS DAY

Grand Chief George Manuel
1921

1938
actress Martha Henry

folk singer Loreena McKennitt
1957

1966
Hockey Hall of Famer Luc Robitaille

18 FEBRUARY

Brian J. Gavriloff/The Canadian Press/Edmonton Journal.

First World War veteran John Babcock, 2008.

2010. Canada's last known First World War veteran, John Babcock, dies at the age of 109 at his home in Spokane, Washington. Babcock was raised on a farm near Kingston, Ontario. When he was just fifteen, he lied about his age and enlisted, but authorities caught on to his youth shortly thereafter. He served with the Boys Battalion in the Royal Canadian Regiment and trained in England. He never saw action—the war ended before he reached the front lines in France—and in interviews he said that he felt he had missed what he had "gone over there for." He was the last surviving veteran of more than six hundred thousand Canadians who served in the war.

In His Own Words: John Babcock

"Well, they didn't have conscription then and the Canadian Army was hard up for men at that particular time. And they'd take damn near anybody. So they asked if I wanted to go and I said, sure ... and they signed me up.

"I was physically fit, but my category was A4—I was underage. But for some reason or other, they didn't post my name with those who were turned down. So I put my pack on and got on the train. And when I was getting on the boat at Halifax, the company commander knew my status and he had me step aside ...

"They called for a draft of fifty men to go to the RCR's—that was the Royal Canadian Regiment—peacetime outfit. And so I took my physical, they asked me how old I was and I said eighteen. And I went over on the *California*. And I was seasick damn near all the way ...

"I never did get into battle, but I had a lot of friends that did. And some of them died."

—From the *Memory Project*

BORN ON THIS DAY

1952 politician Bernard Valcourt

1960 hockey player Andy Moog

1970 musician Raine Maida

Coined in Canada

1908: The Royal Mint (now the Royal Canadian Mint) issues the first Canadian-minted coin.
1920: The first Canadian penny is minted.
1922: The nickel is first produced.
1937: The *Bluenose* first appears on the dime.
1987: The "loonie" (one-dollar coin) comes into circulation.
1996: The "toonie" replaces the paper two-dollar bill.
2013: The penny is removed from circulation.

© Njene/Shutterstock.

The Royal Canadian Mint in Ottawa.

1996. The new two-dollar coin, featuring a polar bear on one side and a portrait of Queen Elizabeth II on the other, is introduced by the Royal Canadian Mint to replace the two-dollar banknote. A number of nicknames were suggested for the coin, among them the "bearie" and the "doubloonie." A member of Parliament from Nunavut suggested naming the coin the Nanuq ("polar bear" in Inuktitut) in honour of Canada's Inuit people, but as it had with the "loonie" before it, popular culture won out, and the name "toonie" stuck. In fact, the name became so popular that the mint secured rights to it.

What unusual items did the Royal Canadian Mint produce during the First World War? **See January 2.**

BORN ON THIS DAY

1864 botanist William Francis Ganong

1904 historian Hilda Neatby

20 FEBRUARY

The *Avro Arrow* is unveiled.

1959. The federal government announces the cancellation of the *Avro Arrow*, an advanced, supersonic, twin-engined, all-weather interceptor jet. In addition to cancelling the project, the government also ordered all plans and prototypes destroyed. Many Canadians lamented the critical blow to the country's aircraft industry, and the loss of scientists and engineers who subsequently moved to the United States. The controversial cancellation also renewed Canada's dependence on the American aerospace industry for interceptor aircraft, a field in which Canada might have proved a pioneer if the *Avro Arrow* had been completed.

Black Friday

A product of the Cold War, the *Avro Arrow* was intended to intercept Soviet bomber planes invading northern Canada. Its designers were tasked with creating an aircraft that could fly higher, faster, and farther than any other plane in the world. It would be powered by engines built with space-age materials and strong enough to drive an ocean liner. But cost overruns and a change in government soon doomed the ambitious undertaking, and on what is still called Black Friday by aviation enthusiasts, Prime Minister Diefenbaker killed the project. One crushed *Arrow* supporter predicted, "History will prove this to be one of the most colossal blunders made by a prime minister in the history of Canada."

BORN ON THIS DAY

seaman Joshua Slocum
1844

1850
physician and poet Nérée Beauchemin

war correspondent Kit Coleman
1856

1887
Governor General Vincent Massey

Hockey Hall of Famer Phil Esposito
1942

1945
figure skater Donald McPherson

Timeline: Tim Horton's Legacy

1964: The first store opens in Hamilton, Ontario.
1976: Timbits are launched.
1986: The Roll Up the Rim to Win contest debuts.
2004: The term "double-double" (*noun esp. Cdn.* a cup of coffee with a double serving of both sugar and cream) is added to the *Canadian Oxford Dictionary.*

Also on This Day

2000.
In the remaining seconds of a February 2 game between Boston and Vancouver, the Bruins' Marty McSorley delivers a crushing head blow to Donald Brashear of the Canucks, causing him to fall to the ice and sustain a grade 3 concussion. The widely publicized event resulted in charges for McSorley, who was eventually convicted of assault and suspended for a calendar year. He never played in the NHL again.

Library and Archives Canada/Louis Jaques/Weekend Magazine collection/e002343748.

Tim Horton in his Toronto Maple Leafs uniform, 1962.

1974. Canadian hockey player and doughnut-shop co-founder Tim Horton dies in a motor vehicle accident after losing control of his sports car. Upon Horton's death, Ron Joyce, his partner, bought out the family's share of the business for one million dollars. In 1964, Horton had opened his first doughnut shop in Hamilton, Ontario, featuring (along with the classic doughnuts) his own inventions: the dutchie and the apple fritter. To keep Horton's legacy alive, Joyce started the Tim Horton Children's Foundation, whose mission is to give children from economically disadvantaged communities the opportunity to go to camp.

BORN ON THIS DAY

1808
fur trader Robert Campbell

1935
politician Jean Pelletier

1987
actress Ellen Page

22 FEBRUARY

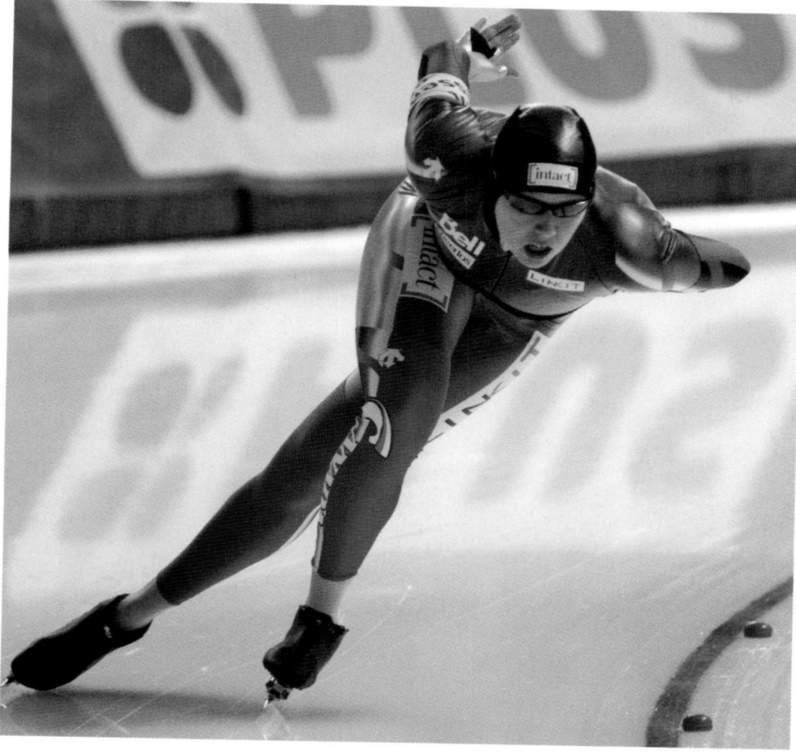

Cindy Klassen at the World Cup Speed Skating Championships.

2006. Winnipeg-born speed skater Cindy Klassen wins Olympic gold in the 1,500 metres, adding it to her already impressive haul of four medals (two silvers and two bronze) at the Turin games. With the win, Klassen became the most decorated Winter Olympian in Canadian history, surpassing short-track speed skater Marc Gagnon's 2002 record. In 2010, speed skater and cyclist Clara Hughes, also of Winnipeg, tied Klassen's Olympic medal count, though hers were earned at both summer and winter games.

Also on This Day

2010.
Skaters Tessa Virtue and Scott Moir win the gold medal in ice dancing at the 2010 Vancouver games, becoming the youngest Olympic winners in the event. It was the first gold medal in ice dancing for Canada and the first-ever gold in the event for an ice-dancing pair from North America.

Which Canadian skaters won hard-earned gold medals in Salt Lake City?
See February 11.

BORN ON THIS DAY

women's education pioneer Grace Lockhart
1855

Hockey Hall of Famer Eddie Gerard
1890

author Morley Callaghan
1903

swimmer Elaine Tanner
1951

FEBRUARY 23

City of Toronto Archives, Fonds 1244, Item 79.

J.A.D. McCurdy sitting in a biplane, 1911.

1909. Aviation pioneer (and later politician) John Alexander Douglas McCurdy flies the *Silver Dart*, an early experimental aircraft, for just under a kilometre in Baddeck, Nova Scotia. McCurdy had taken on the plane's design as a member of the Aerial Experiment Association, a group founded by his mentor, inventor Alexander Graham Bell. Reaching elevations of nine metres during this flight, McCurdy became the first British subject to complete a powered, heavier-than-air flight in the British Empire. The *Silver Dart* would fly more than two hundred times before being irreparably damaged in August 1909.

BORN ON THIS DAY

1955 — fiddler Jerry Holland

1970 — actress Marie-Josée Croze

HIGH-FLYING FIRSTS

1908
Frederick Walker Baldwin is the first Canadian to pilot a heavier-than-air flight.

1909
The *Silver Dart* makes the first powered, heavier-than-air flight in Canada. Several months later, the *Baddeck No. 1*, the first plane made in Canada, also takes flight.

1910
William Wallace Gibson of Victoria builds the first successful Canadian aircraft engine.

1913
In July, Alys McKey Bryant becomes the first woman pilot to fly in Canada. In October, the first commercial cargo flight delivers newspapers from Montréal to Ottawa.

1914
During the First World War, twenty-two thousand Canadians fly with British flight squadrons.

1920
The first commercial passenger flight takes place when two bush pilots fly a fur buyer to The Pas, Manitoba, from Winnipeg.

1939
The first scheduled cross-country passenger service between Montréal and Vancouver departs, makes six stops, and lasts fifteen hours.

1939–45
A quarter of a million men and women serve in the Royal Canadian Air Force during the Second World War.

1949
The *Avro Jetliner*, the first passenger jet in North America, flies outside Toronto.

1958
The *Avro Arrow* becomes the first Canadian jet to break the speed of sound.

1959
The Canadian government scraps the *Arrow* project.

1978
Canadair's *Challenger* business jet takes flight.

Actionstock/getstock.com

Also on This Day

1982.
Edmonton Oiler Wayne Gretzky scores his seventy-seventh goal of the season, breaking the single-season NHL record held by Phil Esposito. By the end of the game he had scored his seventy-ninth, and by the end of the season his ninety-second.

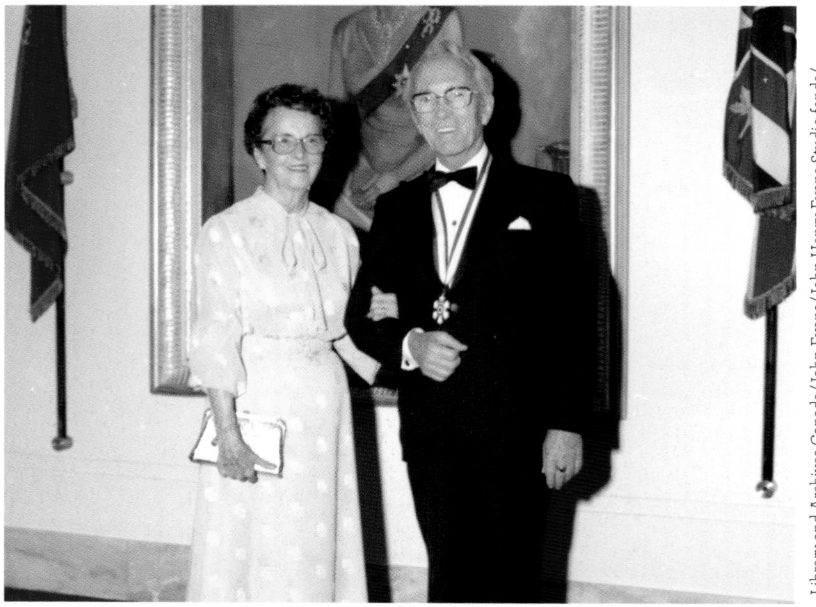

Library and Archives Canada/John Evans/John Henry Evans Studio fonds/ e002505288.

Tommy and Irma Douglas, undated.

1986. Baptist minister turned politician Thomas Clement "Tommy" Douglas passes away. When Douglas moved to Weyburn, Saskatchewan, after being ordained in 1930, he was troubled by the suffering and poverty caused by the Great Depression. He turned to politics to create change, altering the course of Canadian democracy. During his long political career, Douglas served as both premier of Saskatchewan (from 1944 to 1961) and the first leader of the federal New Democratic Party (from 1961 to 1971). He and his party advocated programs such as medicare and a country-wide pension plan. He is remembered today as the leader of the first socialist government elected in Canada and as the father of universal health care.

Which other famous NDP leader made party history in 2003? **See January 25.**

BORN ON THIS DAY

actor John Vernon
1932

1951
actress Helen Shaver

hockey player Manon Rhéaume
1972

1975
fiddler Ashley MacIsaac

25 FEBRUARY

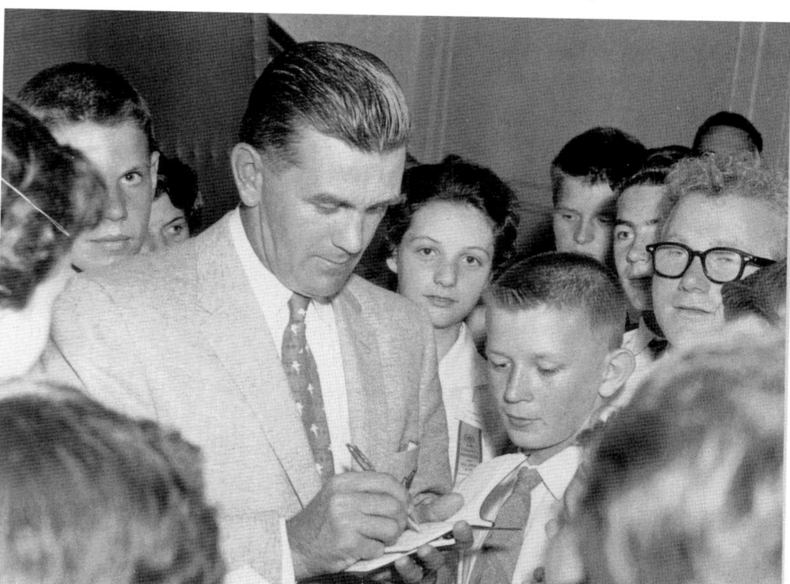

Maurice Richard signing autographs, 1970.

1945. Maurice "Rocket" Richard of the Montreal Canadiens scores his forty-fifth goal of the season to break Joe Malone's NHL single-season record of forty-four goals, set in 1918. The record was one of many that Richard would set at the peak of his outstanding career. In 1944, he scored all five goals in a 5–1 win against Toronto and was named all three of the game's stars—a first in league history. In the 1944–45 season, Richard scored fifty goals in fifty games—a record that would stand until it was matched by Mike Bossy of the New York Islanders in the 1980–81 season and beaten by Wayne Gretzky of the Edmonton Oilers in the 1981–82 season (he scored fifty goals in thirty-nine games). Richard's 544 goals in regular-season play was still an NHL record upon his retirement.

Also on This Day

1752.
John Graves Simcoe, the first lieutenant-governor of Upper Canada, is born in Cotterstock, England. After his arrival in Canada in 1792, Simcoe began granting land to American settlers, confident that they would become loyal colonists and aware that they were the main hope for rapid economic growth. He saw the southwestern peninsula as the future centre not only of the province but of trade with the interior of the continent. He founded York (now Toronto), intending it to be a temporary capital, and laid the foundations of a road system.

BORN ON THIS DAY

1890 — paint roller inventor Norman Breakey

1903 — Hockey Hall of Famer King Clancy

1922 — artist Molly Lamb Bobak

FEBRUARY 26

Memory and Redress

Poet and novelist Joy Kogawa spent her early years in Vancouver. At six years old, Kogawa, along with her parents, was among the thousands of Japanese Canadians forcibly interned during the Second World War. They were relocated first to Slocan, BC, and then to Coaldale, Alberta. Kogawa is best known for her 1981 novel *Obasan*, which is told from the perspective of a middle-aged woman recalling her experience as a child interned during the war. She is celebrated both for her writing and for her work in the Redress Movement to obtain compensation and reparation for her community.

Which Vancouver team was interned before playing its last game in the fall of 1941? See September 18.

Library and Archives Canada/C-057250.

Japanese Canadians being forcibly relocated in British Columbia.

1942. National Defence Minister J.L. Ralston rejects the government's suggestion that the army be enlisted to uproot and relocate Japanese Canadians from British Columbia. Instead, he believes that military personnel should remain focused on home defence. In the aftermath of the December 1941 military strike on Pearl Harbor by the Imperial Japanese Navy, the federal government had announced that all people of Japanese origin living in the coastal regions of British Columbia would be relocated to internment camps in the province's interior or in Prairie farming areas. Under the War Measures Act, approximately twenty-two thousand Japanese Canadians had their property seized, were moved to isolated areas, and had their activities severely restricted. In 1988, Prime Minister Brian Mulroney formally apologized for the devastating events and offered a compensation package of $300 million to the families of individuals who were affected by the relocation.

BORN ON THIS DAY

1886 — Hockey Hall of Famer Moose Johnson

1928 — singer Monique Leyrac

1937 — musician Hagood Hardy

1961 — marathon swimmer Vicki Keith

Thomas Fisher Rare Book Library/University of Toronto/P10103.

Charles Best and Frederick Banting, ca. 1924.

1899. Physiologist Charles Best, co-discoverer of insulin with Sir Frederick Banting, is born in West Pembroke, Maine. Luck played its part in the history-making partnership between the two men—in 1921, Best won a coin toss against one of his classmates to determine who would work with Banting on his quest to find a cure for diabetes. The two men succeeded in isolating a secretion in the pancreas, unlocking a treatment for the debilitating disease. Yet despite his evocative name, Best became the lesser-known partner in the discovery of insulin. He wasn't even recognized by the Nobel Prize committee that honoured Banting for the innovation—although Banting shared his cash award with Best.

The Discovery of Insulin

Banting was working to substantiate his hypothesis that a substance from the pancreas that regulated sugar in the bloodstream could, if isolated, treat diabetes. By the winter of 1920–21, Banting and Best had successfully lowered the blood-sugar level of several diabetic dogs with injections of this pancreatic extract, which would later be called insulin. On January 11, 1922, the first insulin injection was given to a fourteen-year-old boy who was suffering gravely from diabetes. A second injection was given to him on January 23. The boy's recovery proved that insulin could save the lives of people with diabetes.

BORN ON THIS DAY

whisky magnate
Samuel Bronfman

1889

1926

neurophysiologist
David H. Hubel

lawyer
Maureen McTeer

1952

Morning Star, by Alex Janvier, 1993, in the grand hall at the Canadian Museum of Civilization, since renamed the Canadian Museum of History.

1935. First Nations painter Alex Janvier is born on the Le Goff Reserve, near Bonnyville, Alberta. Though he had been painting for years, Janvier's career was launched when he became involved in the organization of the Indians of Canada Pavilion for Expo 67 in Montréal, for which he painted an acclaimed mural. He went on to see his work exhibited at and acquired by the National Gallery of Canada and the McMichael Canadian Art Collection, among other major collections. In 1973, Janvier helped found the Professional Native Indian Artists Incorporation—sometimes called the Indian Group of Seven—a group of Aboriginal artists looking to independently market their work.

Also on This Day

1985.
Holocaust denier Ernst Zündel is convicted of publishing false news (including a pamphlet entitled *Did Six Million Really Die?*) and causing harm to racial tolerance by circulating claims that the mass extermination of Jewish people in Nazi Germany never occurred. The conviction was later overturned on a legal technicality that ultimately resulted in a second trial, in 1988, when Zündel was again found guilty. Zündel lived in Canada from 1958 to 2001, when he left for the United States. He was deported back to Canada in 2003, and ultimately deported to Germany in 2005.

BORN ON THIS DAY

architect Frank Gehry — 1929

actor Don Francks — 1932

director Guy Maddin — 1956

singer René Simard — 1961

actress Rae Dawn Chong — 1961

hockey player Eric Lindros — 1973

29 FEBRUARY

1860. The wife of merchant Kwong Lee arrives in Victoria, British Columbia. While little is known about Mrs. Kwong Lee—not even her first name—she has the distinction of being the first Chinese woman in Canada. She travelled from China via San Francisco to join her husband, who had set up the Kwong Lee Company in 1858. By the time of Mrs. Kwong Lee's landing in 1860, the Chinese population of British Columbia was estimated to be six thousand. The Chinese were first employed as road labourers. Between 1880 and 1885, fifteen thousand Chinese workers completed British Columbia's section of the Canadian Pacific Railway (CPR), with more than six hundred perishing under appalling working conditions during construction. Some sources suggest as many as four thousand Chinese labourers were killed by the time the CPR was completed in 1885. Despite these hardships, these early Chinese settlers laid the groundwork for Canada's Chinese community today.

Library and Archives Canada/William James Topley/PA-011951.

Chinatown in Victoria, British Columbia, ca. 1901.

Timeline: Chinese Immigration to Canada

1788: The first Chinese settlers arrive in Canada.

1858: Chinese immigrants begin to arrive from San Francisco as gold prospectors in the Fraser River Valley, British Columbia.

February 29, 1860: The first female Chinese citizen comes to Canada.

1862: Chinese are first employed in Canada as labourers on the Cariboo Road, a wagon route to the Cariboo goldfields in south-central BC.

1880–85: Some fifteen thousand Chinese labourers complete the British Columbia section of the CPR.

January 1, 1885: Chinese migrants are obligated to pay a fifty-dollar entry (or "head") tax before being admitted into Canada.

March 9, 1885: British Columbia passes the Act to Prevent the Immigration of Chinese. This act and its predecessor, passed in 1884, restrict the entry of Chinese immigrants. Both acts are disallowed by the federal government.

1903: The head tax increases to five hundred dollars.

September 7, 1907: Several hundred people riot through Vancouver's Chinatown to protest Asian immigration to Canada.

July 1, 1923: New legislation virtually suspends Chinese immigration. This discriminatory legislation is not repealed until 1947.

BORN ON THIS DAY

artist
Antoine Plamondon

1804

1936

hockey player
Henri "Pocket Rocket" Richard

MAPLE SYRUP

Maple syrup was discovered by Aboriginal peoples living in what is now eastern Canada and the northeastern United States.

Until the mid-1800s, the maple tree was used mainly to produce sugar. When cheaper cane sugar became more widely available, sugar producers shifted their focus to the delicious syrup.

Most maple syrup comes from Québec. The province produces about three-quarters of the world's maple syrup.

In 2011, scientists discovered an antioxidant compound in maple syrup that had never been seen before in nature. They named it *quebecol*.

Québécois sometimes refer to imitation maple syrup as *sirop de poteau*, or "pole syrup." They say the syrup is produced by tapping wooden telephone poles.

It's sometimes said that the leaf on the Canadian flag is that of the sugar maple. According to the government, however, it's actually a stylized leaf representing a "generic maple species." Canada has ten native maple species, and at least one grows in every province.

MARCH

Also on This Day

1989. The Canadian Space Agency is formed, later establishing its headquarters in St-Hubert, Québec, near Montréal. The agency oversees numerous science and technology programs, develops space robotic technology, and contributes astronauts and equipment to international space missions. Its mandate is to promote the peaceful development of space for the social and economic benefit of Canadians.

City of Vancouver Archives/AM54-S4: Port P509.

Vancouver's mayor-elect J.W. Cornett with the outgoing mayor, J. Lyle Telford, 1940.

1939. Trans-Canada Air Lines, now Air Canada, begins the first transcontinental airmail service. With great fanfare, a Lockheed airliner left Vancouver's Civic Airport on Sea Island at 7:00 p.m., carrying twenty-five bags containing thirty-five thousand letters—315 kilograms of mail in all. The flight landed at Malton Airport, now Toronto Pearson International Airport, at 11:30 a.m. the following day. On board was a letter from the mayor of Vancouver, J. Lyle Telford, to Toronto mayor Ralph Day. In it, Telford wrote, "This attainment has a lesson for Canadians. It shows that despite our geographical distances, in reality, we are close neighbours." Where mail once took four to five days to arrive in Toronto, Ottawa, or Montréal from Vancouver, it would now get there overnight. One month after mail service took off, regular transcontinental passenger service began.

BORN ON THIS DAY

1936 politician Monique Bégin

1947 actor Alan Thicke

1994 singer Justin Bieber

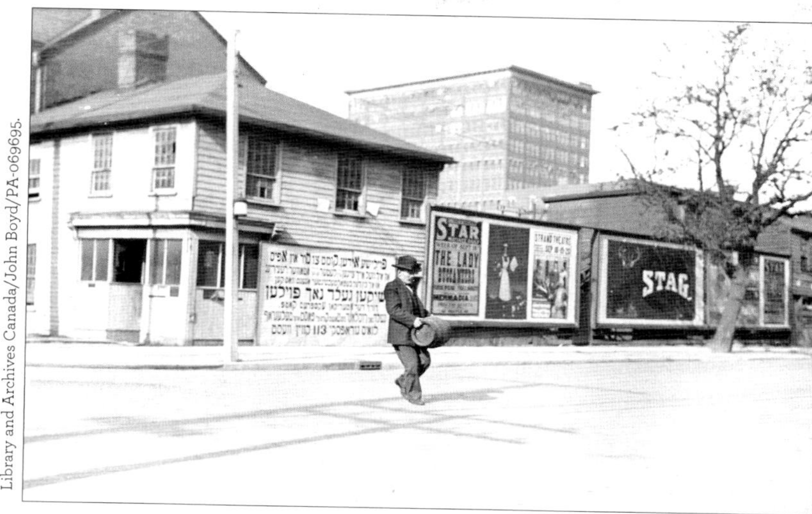

Library and Archives Canada/John Boyd/PA-069695.

A man carrying a keg of beer during Prohibition.

1916. Ontario's Temperance Act passes, making it illegal to possess alcohol (except in a private dwelling) and to sell it in the form of a beverage. The act, which was largely the result of activism by women's groups, including the Women's Christian Temperance Union, sought to curb violence, corruption, and other social ills attributed to alcohol abuse. After its passage, smuggling and bootlegging rose dramatically, as did the number of unlawful drinking places known as "speakeasies" or "blind pigs." One way to drink legally was to be "ill"—doctors could give prescriptions to be filled at drugstores. Scandalous abuse of this system resulted in veritable epidemics and long lineups during the Christmas holiday season.

Timeline: Prohibition in Canada

1864: The Canada Temperance Act is passed, allowing counties and municipalities to prohibit the sale of alcohol.

1877: The Women's Christian Temperance Union forms.

1878: The Canada Temperance Act is extended nationwide.

1898: Sir Wilfrid Laurier's government holds a federal referendum on national prohibition. While 51 percent vote in favour, the government holds off because of regional disparities.

1901: Prince Edward Island goes dry.

1915–17: All provinces except Québec enact Prohibition under the War Measures Act.

1918: The interprovincial trade of liquor is banned.

1919: Québec prohibits the possession and sale of spirits. Beer and wine are not banned.

1921: Québec and British Columbia switch to provincial liquor control systems.

1923: Manitoba follows the lead of BC and Québec.

1924: Alberta and Saskatchewan switch to provincial liquor control systems. Ontario follows suit in 1927.

1948: PEI ends Prohibition.

BORN ON THIS DAY

Canada Dry originator John J. McLaughlin
1865

1935
actor Al Waxman

composer Luc Plamondon
1942

MARCH 3

Also on This Day

1890.
Physician Norman Bethune is born in Gravenhurst, Ontario. His commitment to the Chinese people during the Second Sino-Japanese War, during which he treated sick villagers and wounded soldiers alike, made him a hero in that country and one of the best-known Canadians outside of Canada. He invented or modified over twelve surgical instruments and was the originator of the mobile blood transfusion service.

The godfather of Canadian hip hop, Maestro Fresh Wes, on stage during a celebration of his career at Canada's Walk of Fame Festival in 2013.

1991. Maestro Fresh-Wes wins the first Juno offered in the category of best rap recording for his album *Symphony in Effect*. Maestro put Canada on the international rap map in 1989 with his single "Let Your Backbone Slide," the first top-forty rap hit from north of the border. He became a vocal advocate for Canadian rap on the international scene. His lyrics, in songs like the 1998 singles "Stick to Your Vision" and "416/905 (T.O. Party Anthem)," often include Canadiana references.

BORN ON THIS DAY

1678 — New France heroine Madeleine de Verchères

1847 — inventor Alexander Graham Bell

1920 — actor James Doohan

1927 — artist William Kurelek

1949 — politician Elijah Harper

The Canadian Press/©Warner Brothers/Courtesy: Everett Collection.

Catherine O'Hara as Delia Deetz in *Beetlejuice*, 1988.

1954. Actress and screenwriter Catherine O'Hara is born in Toronto, Ontario. After waitressing at the Toronto Second City Theatre for a year, she got her big start on the television comedy show SCTV, for which she acted and wrote, earning herself an Emmy Award in 1982. O'Hara also played memorable roles in *Dick Tracy* (1990), two *Home Alone* movies (1990 and 1992), and *Beetlejuice* (1988). She reunited with former SCTV castmate Eugene Levy in the mockumentaries *Best in Show* (2000) and *A Mighty Wind* (2003).

Also on This Day

1971.
Prime Minister Pierre Trudeau surprises the country by marrying twenty-two-year-old Margaret Sinclair at a private ceremony in North Vancouver. They went on to have three sons and divorced in 1984.

Which famous Canadian comedy show first aired in 1976? See September 21.

BORN ON THIS DAY

politician Nellie Cournoyea
1940

1949
singer Carroll Baker

politician Svend Robinson
1952

MARCH 5

Timeline: George Brown and the Globe

1844: The *Globe* is founded as a weekly Liberal newspaper with a circulation of three hundred.
1853: The paper begins to publish daily.
1855: George Brown acquires two additional papers, the *Examiner* and the *North American*.
1861–1911: The *Globe* publishes daily morning and evening editions.
1872: T.C. Patterson founds the *Toronto Mail*, a Conservative Party organ.
1887: Sir John A. Macdonald founds the *Empire*.
1895: The *Mail* and the *Empire* merge as the *Mail and Empire*.
1900: The *Globe*'s total circulation approaches seventy thousand; the *Mail and Empire*'s is roughly sixty-two thousand.
1936: George McCullagh purchases both the *Globe* and the *Mail and Empire* within weeks, before merging them as the *Globe and Mail*.

George Brown, undated.

1844. The Toronto *Globe* is founded by politician and Father of Confederation George Brown, with the support of Reform Liberals. In just under ten years, the paper grew from a weekly party journal with a circulation of three hundred to a respected daily newspaper. By 1853, the four-page daily had added a weekly edition for out-of-town subscribers; in 1876, Brown began commissioning early morning trains to take the daily *Globe* to Hamilton and later London. The paper merged with the *Mail and Empire* in 1936 and was renamed the *Globe and Mail*.

BORN ON THIS DAY

1658 — explorer Antoine de Lamothe Cadillac

1813 — engineer Casimir Gzowski

1882 — opera singer Pauline Donalda

1916 — swimmer Phyllis Dewar

6 MARCH

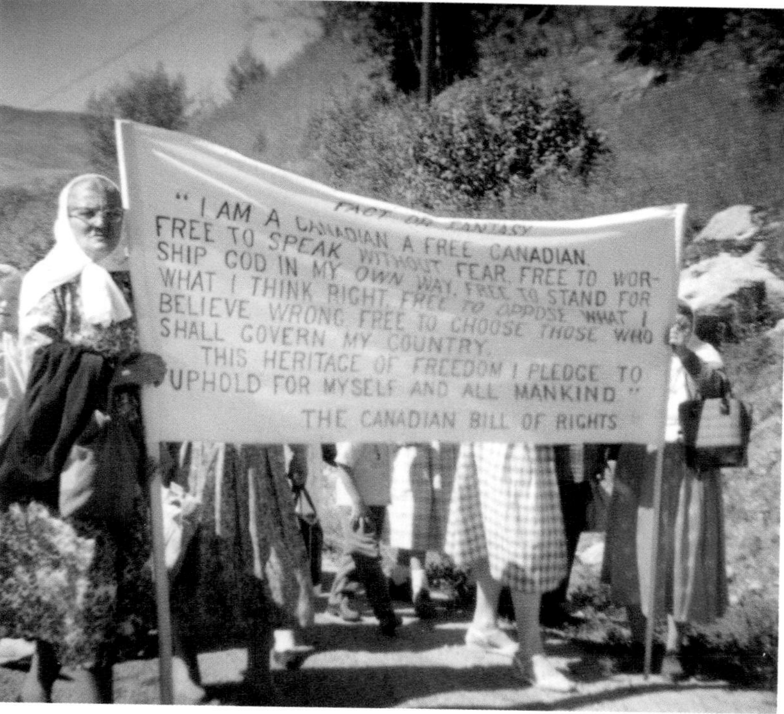

Columbia Basin Institute of Regional History and Kootenay Gallery of Art, History & Science #0131.0280.

Members of the Sons of Freedom sect of Doukhobors, at Crescent Valley, BC, 1962, on their foot trek from Krestova to Agassiz, BC.

1962. A group of radical Doukhobors calling themselves the Sons of Freedom are the prime suspects when a bomb destroys a huge power transmission tower in British Columbia, resulting in a loss of power for thousands. Formed in the 1920s, the Sons of Freedom fought for peace and religious liberty by bombing and burning schools and government buildings. They even destroyed their own property, as well as the property of other Doukhobors, to protest materialism.

Also on This Day

1834.
The city of Toronto (formerly York), Upper Canada, is incorporated with an elected civic government led by the city's first mayor, William Lyon Mackenzie. Born in Scotland in 1795, Mackenzie sailed to Canada in 1820 and settled in Upper Canada. He quickly became a leading voice in the new Reform movement, and in 1828 he was easily elected to the House of Assembly for York County. He served as mayor of Toronto for less than a year before being re-elected to the provincial parliament.

BORN ON THIS DAY

1940 — painter Ken Danby

1955 — actress Alberta Watson

1971 — professional wrestler Val Venis

1979 — baseball player Érik Bédard

The Canadian Press/Ottawa Citizen/Pat McGrath.

Voice of Fire, by Barnett Newman.

1990. The National Gallery of Canada announces its $1.8-million purchase of *Voice of Fire* by American abstract expressionist painter Barnett Newman. The arresting work, which measures 5.4 metres by 2.4 metres and is made up of a red stripe between two blue bands, was painted for Expo 67 in Montréal. Despite Newman's preeminent position in the modernist school of painting, the purchase caused a flood of controversy, with many Canadians irate over the use of taxpayer money to buy what some considered an easily duplicated artwork. The painting has since been estimated to be worth twenty times its original price.

Also on This Day

1934.

Architect Douglas Cardinal is born in Calgary, Alberta. Recognized for his unique artistic vision, Cardinal was instrumental in creating a style of Canadian architecture characterized by organic, curved lines that challenged the most advanced engineering practices. He is perhaps best known for his undulating design for the Canadian Museum of Civilization (now the Canadian Museum of History). He drew inspiration for his curvilinear designs from the Canadian landscape, in particular the rolling plains and badlands of Alberta. This preoccupation with nature is also manifested in Cardinal's emphasis on sustainable building.

BORN ON THIS DAY

1845 — chiropractic medicine founder Daniel David Palmer

1950 — engineer Donald Sadoway

1951 — pentathlete Diane Jones-Konihowski

1965 — politician Alison Redford

THE NATIONAL GALLERY'S PRICIEST PIECES

Virgin and Child with an Angel • Francesco Salviati • $4.5 million

Jupiter and Europa • Guido Reni • $3.45 million

Maman • Louise Bourgeois • $3.2 million

Reclining Male Nude • Jacopo Pontormo • $3 million

No. 16 • Mark Rothko • $1.8 million

Voice of Fire • Barnett Newman • $1.8 million

The Penitent Saint Jerome in His Study
artist unknown • $1.75 million

BY THE QUEEN.

A PROCLAMATION

For Uniting the Provinces of Canada, Nova Scotia, and New Brunswick into One Dominion under the Name of CANADA.

VICTORIA R.

WHEREAS by an Act of Parliament passed on the Twenty-ninth Day of March One thousand eight hundred and sixty-seven, in the Thirtieth Year of Our Reign, intituled "An Act for the Union of Canada, Nova Scotia, and New Brunswick, and the "Government thereof, and for Purposes connected therewith," after divers Recitals, it is enacted, that "It shall be lawful for the Queen, by and with the Advice of Her Majesty's most Honorable "Privy Council, to declare by Proclamation that on and after a Day therein appointed, not being "more than Six Months after the passing of this Act, the Provinces of Canada, Nova Scotia, and "New Brunswick shall form and be One Dominion under the Name of Canada, and on and after "that Day those Three Provinces shall form and be One Dominion under that Name accordingly:" And it is thereby further enacted, that "such Persons shall be first summoned to the Senate as "the Queen, by Warrant under Her Majesty's Royal Sign Manual, thinks fit to approve, and "their Names shall be inserted in the Queen's Proclamation of Union:" We therefore, by and with the Advice of Our Privy Council, have thought fit to issue this Our Royal Proclamation, and We do Ordain, Declare, and Command, that on and after the First Day of July One thousand eight hundred and sixty-seven the Provinces of Canada, Nova Scotia, and New Brunswick shall form and be One Dominion under the Name of Canada. And We do further Ordain and Declare, that the Persons whose Names are herein inserted and set forth are the Persons of whom We have, by Warrant under Our Royal Sign Manual, thought fit to approve as the Persons who shall be first summoned to the Senate of Canada.

FOR THE PROVINCE OF ONTARIO.

JOHN HAMILTON,
RODERICK MATHESON,
JOHN ROSS,
SAMUEL MILLS,
BENJAMIN SEYMOUR,
WALTER HAMILTON DICKSON,
JAMES SHAW,
ADAM JOHNSTON FERGUSON BLAIR,
ALEXANDER CAMPBELL,
DAVID CHRISTIE,
JAMES COX AIKINS,
DAVID REESOR,
ELIJAH LEONARD,
WILLIAM MACMASTER,
ASA ALLWORTH BURNHAM,
JOHN SIMPSON,
JAMES SKEAD,
DAVID LEWIS MACPHERSON,
GEORGE CRAWFORD,
DONALD MACDONALD,
OLIVER BLAKE,
BILLA FLINT,
WALTER MCREA,
GEORGE WILLIAM ALLAN.

FOR THE PROVINCE OF QUEBEC.

JAMES LESLIE,
ASA BELKNAP FOSTER,
JOSEPH NOËL BOSSÉ,
LOUIS A. OLIVIER,
JACQUE OLIVIER BUREAU,
CHARLES MALHIOT,
LOUIS RENAUD,
LUC LETELLIER DE ST. JUST,
ULRIC JOSEPH TESSIER,
JOHN HAMILTON,
CHARLES CORMIER,
ANTOINE JUCHEREAU DUCHESNAY,
DAVID EDWARD PRICE,
ELZEAR H. J. DUCHESNAY,
LEANDRE DUMOUCHEL,
LOUIS LACOSTE,
JOSEPH F. ARMAND,
CHARLES WILSON,
WILLIAM HENRY CHAFFERS,
JEAN BAPTISTE GUÉVREMONT,
JAMES FERRIER,
Sir NARCISSE FORTUNAT BELLEAU, Knight,
THOMAS RYAN,
JOHN SEWELL SANBORN.

FOR THE PROVINCE OF NOVA SCOTIA.

EDWARD KENNY,
JONATHAN MCCULLY,
THOMAS D. ARCHIBALD,
ROBERT B. DICKEY,
JOHN H. ANDERSON,
JOHN HOLMES,
JOHN W. RITCHIE,
BENJAMIN WIER,
JOHN LOCKE,
CALEB R. BILL,
JOHN BOURINOT,
WILLIAM MILLER.

FOR THE PROVINCE OF NEW BRUNSWICK.

AMOS EDWIN BOTSFORD,
EDWARD BARRON CHANDLER,
JOHN ROBERTSON,
ROBERT LEONARD HAZEN,
WILLIAM HUNTER ODELL,
DAVID WARK,
WILLIAM HENRY STEEVES,
WILLIAM TODD,
JOHN FERGUSON,
ROBERT DUNCAN WILMOT,
ABNER REID MCCLELAN,
PETER MITCHELL.

Given at Our Court at Windsor Castle, this Twenty-second Day of May, in the Year of our Lord One thousand eight hundred and sixty-seven, and in the Thirtieth Year of Our Reign.

God save the Queen.

Thomas Fisher Rare Books Library/University of Toronto.

A proclamation for uniting the provinces of Canada, Nova Scotia, and New Brunswick into one dominion under the name of Canada. Published in London by G.E. Eyre & W. Spottiswoode in 1867.

1867. The British North America Act is approved by the British Parliament and given royal assent by Queen Victoria on March 29. It came into effect on July 1, now celebrated as Canada Day. The act, which was the culmination of Sir John A. Macdonald's Confederation project, joined what are now the provinces of Québec, Ontario, Nova Scotia, and New Brunswick into one federal union. In April 1982, the BNA Act was renamed the Constitution Act, 1867, as part of the movement toward patriation of the Constitution.

The Great Coalition

The politics of the Province of Canada in the early 1860s were marked by instability and deadlock. The union of the Canadas had clearly failed, and its leaders were ready to forget old feuds to create a new political order. Reform movement leader George Brown proposed that a multi-party parliamentary committee investigate how the impasse might be broken. Thus the Great Coalition was formed under the leadership of Brown, George-Étienne Cartier, and above all, John A. Macdonald. The broadly based coalition was remarkably successful in meeting its major aims: ending the deadlock and creating a new political entity. It remained largely intact as the government of the Province of Canada until Confederation.

BORN ON THIS DAY

1823 architect Thomas Fuller

1896 Ottawa mayor Charlotte Whitton

1939 dancer Lynn Seymour

1940 actress Susan Clark

The Winnipeg Free Press.

Cpl. Francis Pegahmagabow, undated.

Timeline: Francis Pegahmagabow

1915: Arrives in France with the 1st Canadian Infantry Battalion
1916: Awarded the Military Medal (MM) for bravery
1917: Earns a bar for his MM, for bravery in Passchendaele
1918: Earns a second bar for his MM after the Battle of the Scarpe
1919: Invalided to Canada

1889. Sniper Francis "Peggy" Pegahmagabow is born on what is now the Shawanaga First Nation reserve, near Parry Sound, Ontario. During the First World War, Peggy, a member of the Wasauksing First Nation, killed 378 Germans and captured some 300 more. He was an expert shot and scout, fighting at the Second Battle of Ypres, the Battle of the Somme, and the Second Battle of Passchendaele. At the Battle of the Scarpe, Peggy's company was surrounded with their supply of ammunition almost gone. Under heavy fire from enemy forces, Peggy darted into no man's land to capture ammunition that would help the company beat back the German counterattacks. The act of bravery won him a second bar on his Military Medal, an honour held by only thirty-nine Canadians. Peggy was one of the most highly decorated First Nations soldiers in Canadian military history, and the most effective sniper in the First World War.

BORN ON THIS DAY

Toronto mayor Mel Lastman

1933

1976

TV host Ben Mulroney

Also on This Day

1796.
Julia Catherine Beckwith Hart is born in Fredericton, New Brunswick. She wrote the novel *St. Ursula's Convent*; or, *The Nun of Canada: Containing Scenes from Real Life*. It was the first work of fiction by a native-born Canadian to be published in Canada. Although published in 1824, it was actually written in 1813, when Hart was just seventeen.

The Moorland-Spingarn Research Center/Howard University.

Harriet Tubman, undated.

1913. Underground Railroad pioneer Harriet Tubman dies in Auburn, New York. Tubman grew up in slavery in Maryland and New York. Fearing that she would be sold after the death of her owner in 1849, she fled north on her own, making her way to Philadelphia with the assistance of a number of Quakers active in the Underground Railroad, a secret network of routes and safe houses that helped people escape enslavement. She returned to Maryland in 1850 to guide her daughters and niece out of slavery. Tubman soon earned a reputation as "conductor" on the Underground Railroad, leading rescue missions that would guide enslaved Black people to free northern states. But the Fugitive Slave Act, passed in 1850, made it possible for refugee slaves in free northern states to be returned to enslavement in the South once captured. Tubman changed her escape route to Canada and moved to St. Catharines herself, settling there for ten years. "I wouldn't trust Uncle Sam with my people no longer, but I brought 'em clear off to Canada," she later said. She made at least ten rescue trips and transported at least seventy people, her own family included, to freedom in Canada.

BORN ON THIS DAY

1861
poet Pauline Johnson

1953
screenwriter and director Paul Haggis

1957
model and actress Shannon Tweed

1930. Director Claude Jutra is born in Montréal. One of Canada's most revered filmmakers, Jutra was a central figure in the development of cinema in Québec, and he directed two films of tremendous significance: the autobiographical *À tout prendre* (1964) and *Mon oncle Antoine* (1971), which portrayed a young man approaching adulthood in a small mining town in pre-Quiet Revolution Québec. The latter film won international acclaim, over a dozen international prizes, and eight Canadian Film Awards, including those for best feature film and best direction. In a poll at the Toronto International Film Festival, *Mon oncle Antoine* was voted the greatest Canadian film ever made.

***Claude Jutra*, by Marie-Josée Hudon.**

The Feature Films of Claude Jutra

Les mains nettes (1958)
À tout prendre (1963)
Mon oncle Antoine (1971)
Kamouraska (1973)
Pour le meilleur et pour le pire (1975)
Surfacing (1980)
By Design (1981)
La dame en couleurs (1984)

What Canadian filmmaker was the first woman to win a Genie Award for best achievement in direction? See January 8.

BORN ON THIS DAY

composer John Jacob Weinzweig
1913

1953
musician Bernie LaBarge

swimmer Leslie Cliff
1955

Who Were the Automatistes?

In the 1940s, Paul-Émile Borduas began experimenting with a painting style called automatism, which drew on the unconscious to create spontaneous abstract compositions. His work inspired Jean-Paul Riopelle and several other young artists, who began exhibiting their work around Montréal. "Make way for magic! Make way for objective mysteries! Make way for love! Make way for necessities!" With these words from his manifesto, *Refus global* (Total refusal), Borduas challenged Québec's post-war conservatism and ignited a debate that extended beyond his immediate art-world audience.

Library and Archives Canada/Basil Zarov/Basil Zarov fonds/e010984334.

Jean-Paul Riopelle, undated.

2002. Painter, sculptor, and engraver Jean-Paul Riopelle dies at Isle-aux-Grues, Québec. Early in his career, Riopelle belonged to the Automatistes, a group of artists whose style of painting was spontaneous and free from preconception. He is best known, however, for his work in the 1950s, when he developed his mature style, creating large mosaic paintings by applying a palette knife to paint squeezed directly onto the canvas from the tube. Riopelle has been called the most internationally celebrated Canadian painter of the twentieth century. Over a dozen of his works have gone for more than a million dollars each, including the piece *Composition*, which sold at auction in 2013 for $1.2 million.

BORN ON THIS DAY

1821
Prime Minister John Abbott

1835
astronomer Simon Newcomb

1912
poet Irving Layton

13 MARCH

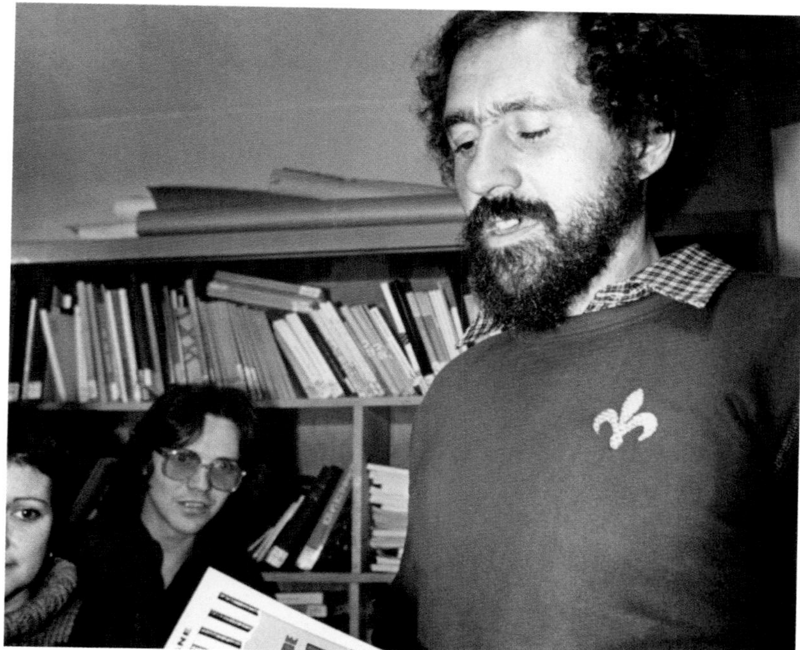

The Canadian Press.

Paul Rose holding a book on prisoners' rights, 1982.

1971. Paul Rose is sentenced to life imprisonment for the murder of Québec cabinet minister Pierre Laporte, whose body had been found in the trunk of a car. A teacher by trade, Rose was the leader of a Front de libération du Québec (FLQ) terrorist cell that kidnapped Laporte in the fall of 1970, during what would become known as the October Crisis. The kidnapping was among a number of militant acts undertaken by the FLQ in an attempt to overthrow the elected government, which they claimed was oppressive to francophone Quebecers. Rose spent just over eleven years in jail before being granted parole.

Timeline: The October Crisis

October 5, 1970: British trade commissioner James Cross is kidnapped by two armed members of the FLQ in Montréal.

October 5–6: The FLQ sends ransom notes to radio stations and newspapers.

October 10: Québec labour minister Pierre Laporte is kidnapped by the FLQ.

October 13: Asked how far he would go in defending elected officials, Prime Minister Pierre Trudeau replies, "Just watch me."

October 15: The Québec government requests assistance from the Canadian Armed Forces.

October 16: Trudeau enacts the War Measures Act, allowing mass raids and arrests. During the crisis, nearly five hundred people are detained; most are eventually released without charges.

October 18: The body of Pierre Laporte is found in the trunk of a car.

November 2: Emergency regulations under the War Measures Act are replaced by similar regulations set to lapse on April 30, 1971.

December 3: James Cross is freed following negotiations with his abductors, who receive safe passage to Cuba.

December 28: Paul Rose and Francis Simard are arrested and subsequently convicted of murder; both receive life sentences and are paroled in 1982.

BORN ON THIS DAY

- 1922 aviator Dick Audet
- 1938 director Peter Pearson
- 1954 comedian Robin Duke
- 1984 actor Noel Fisher
- 1989 racing driver Robert Wickens

MARCH 14

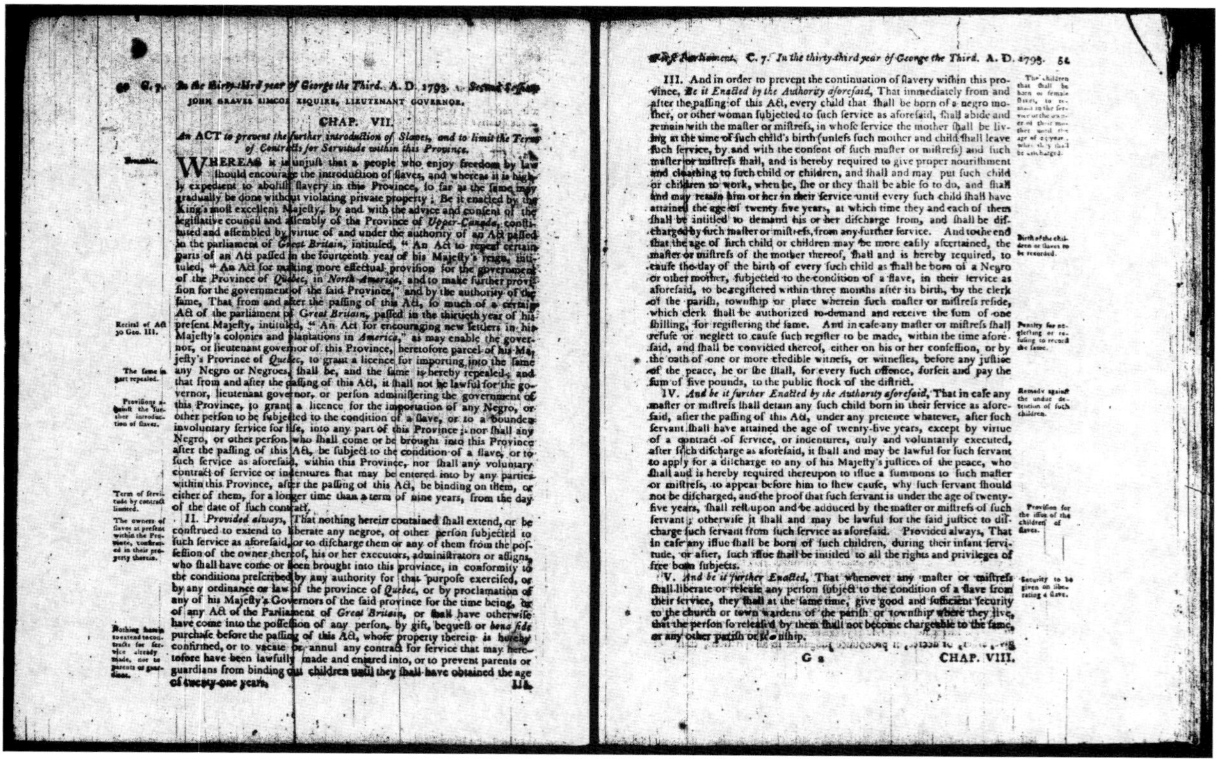

60 C. 7. In the thirty-third year of George the Third. A.D. 1793. Second Seſſion

JOHN GRAVES SIMCOE ESQUIRE, LIEUTENANT GOVERNOR.

CHAP. VII.

An ACT to prevent the further introduction of Slaves, and to limit the Term of Contracts for Servitude within this Province.

Preamble.

WHEREAS it is unjuſt that a people who enjoy freedom by law ſhould encourage the introduction of ſlaves, and whereas it is highly expedient to aboliſh ſlavery in this Province, ſo far as the ſame may gradually be done without violating private property; Be it enacted by the King's moſt excellent Majeſty, by and with the advice and conſent of the legiſlative council and aſſembly of the Province of *Upper-Canada*, conſtituted and aſſembled by virtue of and under the authority of an Act paſſed in the parliament of *Great Britain*, intituled, "An Act to repeal certain parts of an Act paſſed in the fourteenth year of his Majeſty's reign, intituled, "An Act for making more effectual proviſion for the government of the Province of *Quebec*, in *North America*, and to make further proviſion for the government of the ſaid Province," and by the authority of the ſame, That from and after the paſſing of this Act, ſo much of a certain Act of the parliament of *Great Britain*, paſſed in the thirtieth year of his preſent Majeſty, intituled, "An Act for encouraging new ſettlers in his Majeſty's colonies and plantations in *America*," as may enable the governor, or lieutenant governor of this Province, heretofore parcel of his Majeſty's Province of *Quebec*, to grant a licence for importing into the ſame any Negro or Negroes, ſhall be, and the ſame is hereby repealed; and that from and after the paſſing of this Act, it ſhall not be lawful for the governor, lieutenant governor, or perſon adminiſtering the government of this Province, to grant a licence for the importation of any Negro, or other perſon to be ſubjected to the condition of a ſlave, or to a bounden involuntary ſervice for life, into any part of this Province; nor ſhall any Negro, or other perſon who ſhall come or be brought into this Province after the paſſing of this Act, be ſubject to the condition of a ſlave, or to ſuch ſervice as aforeſaid, within this Province, nor ſhall any voluntary contract of ſervice or indentures that may be entered into by any parties within this Province, after the paſſing of this Act, be binding on them, or either of them, for a longer time than a term of nine years, from the day of the date of ſuch contract.

Recital of Act 30 Geo. III.

The ſame in part repealed.

Proviſions againſt the further introduction of ſlaves.

Term of ſervitude by contract limited.

II. *Provided always*, That nothing herein contained ſhall extend, or be conſtrued to extend to liberate any negroe, or other perſon ſubjected to ſuch ſervice as aforeſaid, or to diſcharge them or any of them from the poſſeſſion of the owner thereof, his or her executors, adminiſtrators or aſſigns, who ſhall have come or been brought into this province, in conformity to the conditions preſcribed by any authority for that purpoſe exerciſed, or by any ordinance or law of the province of *Quebec*, or by proclamation of any of his Majeſty's Governors of the ſaid province for the time being, or of any Act of the Parliament of *Great Britain*, or ſhall have otherwiſe have come into the poſſeſſion of any perſon, by gift, bequeſt or *bona fide* purchaſe before the paſſing of this Act, whoſe property therein is hereby confirmed, or to vacate or annul any contract for ſervice that may heretofore have been lawfully made and entered into, or to prevent parents or guardians from binding out children until they ſhall have obtained the age of twenty-one years.

The owners of ſlaves at preſent within the Province, confirmed in their property therein.

Nothing herein to extend to contracts for ſervice already made, nor to parents or guardians.

III.

First Parliament. C. 7. In the thirty-third year of George the Third. A.D. 1793. 61

III. And in order to prevent the continuation of ſlavery within this province, *Be it Enacted by the Authority aforeſaid*, That immediately from and after the paſſing of this Act, every child that ſhall be born of a negro mother, or other woman ſubjected to ſuch ſervice as aforeſaid, ſhall abide and remain with the maſter or miſtreſs, in whoſe ſervice the mother ſhall be living at the time of ſuch child's birth (unleſs ſuch mother and child ſhall leave ſuch ſervice, by and with the conſent of ſuch maſter or miſtreſs) and ſuch maſter or miſtreſs ſhall, and is hereby required to give proper nouriſhment and cloathing to ſuch child or children, and ſhall and may put ſuch child or children to work, when he, ſhe or they ſhall be able ſo to do, and ſhall and may retain him or her in their ſervice until every ſuch child ſhall have attained the age of twenty five years, at which time they and each of them ſhall be intitled to demand his or her diſcharge from, and ſhall be diſcharged by ſuch maſter or miſtreſs, from any further ſervice. And to the end that the age of ſuch child or children may be more eaſily aſcertained, the maſter or miſtreſs of the mother thereof, ſhall and is hereby required, to cauſe the day of the birth of every ſuch child as ſhall be born of a Negro or other mother, ſubjected to the condition of a ſlave, in their ſervice as aforeſaid, to be regiſtered within three months after its birth, by the clerk of the pariſh, townſhip or place wherein ſuch maſter or miſtreſs reſide, which clerk ſhall be authorized to demand and receive the ſum of one ſhilling, for regiſtering the ſame. And in caſe any maſter or miſtreſs ſhall refuſe or neglect to cauſe ſuch regiſter to be made, within the time aforeſaid, and ſhall be convicted thereof, either on his or her confeſſion, or by the oath of one or more credible witneſs, or witneſſes, before any juſtice of the peace, he or ſhe ſhall, for every ſuch offence, forfeit and pay the ſum of five pounds, to the public ſtock of the diſtrict.

The children that ſhall be born of female ſlaves, to remain in the ſervice of the owner of their mother until the age of 25 years, when they ſhall be diſcharged.

Birth of the children of ſlaves to be recorded.

Penalty for neglecting or refuſing to record the ſame.

IV. *And be it further Enacted by the Authority aforeſaid*, That in caſe any maſter or miſtreſs ſhall detain any ſuch child born in their ſervice as aforeſaid, after the paſſing of this Act, under any pretence whatever, after ſuch ſervant ſhall have attained the age of twenty-five years, except by virtue of a contract of ſervice, or indentures, duly and voluntarily executed, after ſuch diſcharge as aforeſaid, it ſhall and may be lawful for ſuch ſervant to apply for a diſcharge to any of his Majeſty's juſtices of the peace, who ſhall and is hereby required thereupon to iſſue a ſummons to ſuch maſter or miſtreſs, to appear before him to ſhew cauſe, why ſuch ſervant ſhould not be diſcharged, and the proof that ſuch ſervant is under the age of twenty-five years, ſhall reſt upon and be adduced by the maſter or miſtreſs of ſuch ſervant; otherwiſe it ſhall and may be lawful for the ſaid juſtice to diſcharge ſuch ſervant from ſuch ſervice as aforeſaid. Provided always, That in caſe any iſſue ſhall be born of ſuch children, during their infant ſervitude, or after, ſuch iſſue ſhall be intitled to all the rights and privileges of free born ſubjects.

Remedy againſt the undue detention of ſuch children.

Proviſion for the iſſue of the children of ſlaves.

V. *And be it further Enacted*, That whenever any maſter or miſtreſs ſhall liberate or releaſe any perſon ſubject to the condition of a ſlave from their ſervice, they ſhall at the ſame time, give good and ſufficient ſecurity to the church or town wardens of the pariſh or townſhip where they live, that the perſon ſo releaſed by them ſhall not become chargeable to the ſame, or any other pariſh or townſhip.

Security to be given on liberating a ſlave.

G 2 CHAP. VIII.

The Archives of Ontario.

An Act to Prevent the further Introduction of Slaves and to limit the Term of Contracts for Servitude.
Statutes of Upper Canada, Chap. 7, 33 George III, 1793.

1793. Chloe Cooley, an enslaved Black woman from Queenston in Upper Canada (now Ontario), is captured and sold across the Niagara River in New York State. The incident, and her struggle to break free, was reported to Lieutenant-Governor John Graves Simcoe. Simcoe, who had been influenced by the growing abolitionist movement in England prior to his arrival in Upper Canada, used the event as the impetus to introduce legislation to abolish slavery in the region. After the passage of his Act to Limit Slavery in Upper Canada on July 9, 1793, Simcoe expressed his hope that those who were enslaved "may henceforth look forward with certainty to the emancipation of their offspring."

BORN ON THIS DAY

1868 women's rights activist Emily Murphy

1888 artist Marc-Aurèle Fortin

1899 entrepreneur K.C. Irving

1932 artist Norval Morrisseau

1961 BlackBerry co-founder Mike Lazaridis

1968 actress Megan Follows

SLAVERY IN CANADA

March 1685
King Louis XIV's *Code noir* permits slavery for economic purposes and establishes strict guidelines for the ownership and treatment of slaves.

1709
Louis XIV formally authorizes slavery.

July 13, 1787
The United States passes the Northwest Ordinance, the first anti-slavery law in North America. The act applies to its Northwest Territory, a region between the Ohio River and the Great Lakes where government authority is not clearly defined.

1790
The Imperial Statute of 1790 allows settlers to bring enslaved persons to Upper Canada duty-free.

July 9, 1793
The Act to Limit Slavery in Upper Canada is passed, the first piece of legislation to limit enslavement in the British Empire.

August 1, 1834
The Slavery Abolition Act formally frees nearly eight hundred thousand slaves; there are fewer than fifty slaves remaining in British North America.

September 18, 1850
The Fugitive Slave Act is passed by the American Congress, giving slave-owners the right to track down and arrest fugitives anywhere in the United States. Thousands seek refuge in Canada.

Which route did many enslaved Blacks use to escape to Ontario? See March 10.

MARCH 15

Also on This Day

1857.
Ishbel Maria Hamilton-Gordon (Lady Aberdeen) is born in London, England. An author, supporter of women's rights, and the wife of Canada's seventh governor general, she is remembered for introducing Prime Minister William Lyon Mackenzie King to automatic writing, a technique of spiritualism used to contact the dead.

© Sandeep Singh Brar. Courtesy of the SikhMuseum.com.

Sgt. Baltej Singh Dhillon at the Remembrance Day ceremony for First World War soldier Pte. Buckam Singh, 2010.

1990. The federal government alters the RCMP's official dress code to allow Sikh officers to wear turbans while on duty. Baltej Singh Dhillon, who had been told that his turban would be unacceptable, was supported in his request to don the headdress by RCMP commissioner Norman Inkster. Following pressure, the government amended the policy and Dhillon became the first officer permitted to wear a turban while on duty. The case ignited controversy, with thousands of Canadians signing petitions to retain the traditional dress code; however, the policy was not overturned.

BORN ON THIS DAY

composer Colin McPhee
1900

1918
hockey coach Punch Imlach

artist Mary Pratt
1935

1943
director David Cronenberg

16 MARCH

The Canadian Press/Jacques Boissinot.

Students protest in front of the Québec National Assembly.

2005. One of the largest protests in Canadian history takes place when some eighty thousand students take to the streets of Montréal to demonstrate against funding cuts. The demonstration supported a strike that ran from February until April in protest of the government's $103-million cut to bursary funds. Almost a quarter of a million college and university students from nearly every region of the province boycotted classes for six weeks. Québec students would quit classes for even longer—more than six months—in opposition to tuition hikes in 2012.

Also on This Day

1949.
Actor Victor Garber is born in London, Ontario. The versatile performer has appeared on stage and in movie and TV roles. His first success was as Jesus in the musical *Godspell*, with a cast that also included Canadians Martin Short and Andrea Martin. He is internationally recognized for his work in the films *Legally Blonde* and *Titanic*, and for playing CIA double agent Jack Bristow alongside Jennifer Garner in the TV show *Alias*.

BORN ON THIS DAY

singer Patricia Rideout-Rosenberg
1931

1934
Governor General Ray Hnatyshyn

actress Kate Nelligan
1951

MARCH 

Library and Archives Canada/1983-33-1115.

A campaign poster from 1891.

1866. The United States ends reciprocity with Canada. The Reciprocity Treaty, which also included free trade on many products, had been signed into law in 1854. The treaty extended free trade to dozens of products, including animals of all kinds; fish of all kinds; hides, furs, skins, or tails; timber; dyestuffs; burr or grindstones; lard, horns, and manures; coal; and unmanufactured tobacco. At first, the treaty was popular in both countries, but owing to a combination of political and economic factors, it fell out of favour. Opposition centred on the fear that it was a stepping stone toward the American absorption of British North America, which caused concern on both sides of the border. Canadian opponents feared their colonies would be swallowed by the Americans. Opponents in the United States, particularly in the South during the Civil War, feared a merger would increase the power of the northern states. Today, trade between both countries is regulated by the World Trade Organization.

Did You Know?

Americans were given the right to navigate the St. Lawrence River and its canals between the Great Lakes and the Atlantic; the British had the right to navigate Lake Michigan.

British (Maritimes) and US fishermen were granted mutual access to each other's northern Atlantic coastal waters.

BORN ON THIS DAY

artist LeMoine FitzGerald
1890

1948
author William Gibson

composer Nick Peros
1963

1972
musician Melissa Auf der Maur

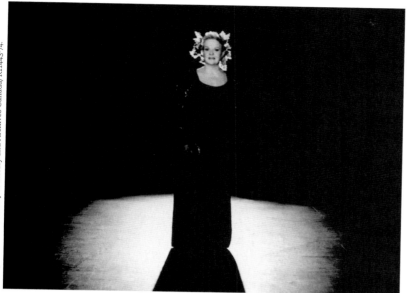

Maureen Forrester, 1999.

1990. Operatic contralto Maureen Forrester is inducted into the Canadian Music Hall of Fame. Her earliest professional engagements included the Opera Guild of Montreal (1953), the Montreal Symphony Orchestra (1953), and the Toronto Symphony Orchestra (1954), where she became known for her remarkable range and perfect pitch. Throughout her career, Forrester gave as many as 120 performances a year on five continents, and performed with virtually every major orchestra and choir in the world. She always maintained a strong connection to Canada, however, performing at home as often as thirty times a year and serving as chairperson of the Canada Council.

Also on This Day

1836.
The Hudson's Bay Company steamer *Beaver*, the first on the Pacific Coast, arrives on the Columbia River, docking at Fort Vancouver (near present-day Portland, Oregon) roughly three months later. After serving Pacific ports for over fifty years, the *Beaver* ran aground off Prospect Point in Stanley Park, Vancouver, in 1888.

BORN ON THIS DAY

physician and heart disease expert Maude Abbott
1869

1945
author and actress Joy Fielding

Hockey Hall of Famer Guy Lapointe
1948

MARCH 19

Timeline: The Legalization of Same-Sex Marriage

June 10, 2003: Ontario
July 8, 2003: British Columbia
March 19, 2004: Québec
July 14, 2004: Yukon
September 16, 2004: Manitoba
September 24, 2004: Nova Scotia
November 5, 2004: Saskatchewan
December 21, 2004: Newfoundland and Labrador
June 23, 2005: New Brunswick
July 20, 2005: Alberta, Prince Edward Island, Nunavut, and the Northwest Territories (under the Civil Marriage Act)

Ian Barrett/The Canadian Press.

René LeBoeuf and Michael Hendricks march in the Montréal Pride Parade, 2003. LeBoeuf and Hendricks were the first gay couple to marry legally in Québec.

2004. A Court of Appeal ruling legalizes same-sex marriage in Québec. Both Ontario and British Columbia had legalized same-sex marriage in 2003, and five more provinces and one territory followed suit before the federal Civil Marriage Act was passed in 2005. This act required that legal definitions for husband and wife be amended to "spouse."

BORN ON THIS DAY

physician Henry Morgentaler 1923

author Ann Elizabeth Carlson 1929

Supreme Court justice John Sopinka 1933

director Burt Metcalfe 1935

actress Rachel Blanchard 1976

20 MARCH

Library and Archives Canada/Yousef Karsh/PA-172723.

Hugh MacLennan, 1947.

1907. Novelist Hugh MacLennan is born in Glace Bay, Nova Scotia. The five-time recipient of the Governor General's Literary Award was deeply influenced by the events of the First World War. He wrote *Barometer Rising* about the Halifax Explosion, which he survived as a ten-year-old child. But he is best known as the first major English-speaking writer to attempt a portrayal of Canada's national character—a central theme in a number of his works, including *Two Solitudes,* whose title has since become emblematic of the divide between French and English Canada.

Also on This Day

1995.
The federal immigration department begins legal proceedings against Erich Tobias, a former Latvian accused of war crimes during the Second World War. In 1957, Tobias had arrived in Canada, where he came under investigation for lying on his immigration papers to cover up mass killings perpetrated in Latvia. Tobias did not stand trial, however; he died months after a 1997 Supreme Court ruling that his case should proceed.

BORN ON THIS DAY

scientist Maud Menten 1879

bush pilot Wilfrid Reid "Wop" May 1896

artist Jack Bush 1909

singer Tommy Hunter 1937

Prime Minister Brian Mulroney 1939

Man in Motion Facts and Figures

Days wheeling: 465
Total distance travelled: 40,075 km
Countries crossed: 34
Continents visited: 4
Average daily distance: 85 km
Average speed: 9 km/hr in the city, 14 km/hr in the country
Hours spent wheeling each day: 8
Number of strokes each day: 30,000
Number of tire changes: 160

Rick Hansen wheeling through the rain in Salem, Oregon, during the Man in Motion World Tour.

1985. Wheelchair athlete Rick Hansen leaves Vancouver on his around-the-globe Man in Motion World Tour to raise money for spinal-cord research. Inspired by the example of his friend Terry Fox, Hansen travelled forty thousand kilometres through thirty-four countries on four continents during the twenty-six-month tour, which raised an impressive $26 million. In 1987, he created the Man in Motion Foundation (now the Rick Hansen Foundation) to continue raising money for research and to help improve the lives of people with disabilities.

BORN ON THIS DAY

1912
journalist, politician, and playwright André Laurendeau

1936
politician Ed Broadbent

1980
singer Deryck Whibley

22 MARCH

© Joel No Runner. Aboriginal Arts & Stories/Historica Canada.

Urban Legends **by Joel No Runner. "Although times have changed, I still have a strong sense of my traditions and heritage," explained No Runner. "The buffalo are extinct, another result of colonization, but my people are still here. That is the message I wanted to portray. There is a new generation of First Nations people that are continuing our traditions. I am a part of that next generation, and I continue my traditions."**

1877. The North-West Territorial Council passes An Ordinance for the Protection of the Buffalo in an attempt to slow the animals' destruction. The act made it illegal to drive buffalo into ravines or pits, or to hunt or kill them for entertainment. The legislation was repealed the following year, however, and within a decade the buffalo was virtually extinct. Later conservation efforts saw the Canadian government purchase a bison herd from Montana, and that herd eventually came to populate Wood Buffalo National Park.

Aboriginal Peoples and the Buffalo

Until the collapse of the herds in the 1880s, buffalo was the primary food source of the Aboriginal peoples of the plains and of the Métis. Additionally, the buffalo hunt was critical to the fur trade activity that supported European settlement.

American policies in the 1860s advocated the extermination of the buffalo as a means to starve Aboriginal peoples onto reservations. The resulting slaughter in the United States and Canada led to the near extinction of the remaining herds, and was a significant factor in the changes to the lives of Aboriginal peoples in Canada.

BORN ON THIS DAY

1931 actor William Shatner

1940 Hockey Hall of Famer Dave Keon

1946 viola player Rivka Golani

1972 figure skater Elvis Stojko

Timeline: The Making of Canada

July 1, 1867: New Brunswick, Nova Scotia, and the Province of Canada (Ontario and Québec) unite to form one dominion.

July 15, 1870: Manitoba and the North-West Territories join Canada.

July 20, 1871: British Columbia joins Canada.

July 1, 1873: Prince Edward Island joins Canada.

June 13, 1898: The Yukon Territory (renamed Yukon in 2003) joins Canada.

September 1, 1905: Saskatchewan and Alberta join Canada.

March 31, 1949: Newfoundland (renamed Newfoundland and Labrador in 2001) joins Canada.

April 1, 1999: The newly created territory of Nunavut comes into being.

National Film Board/Library and Archives Canada/C-006255.

Prime Minister St. Laurent initiates the work of carving Newfoundland's arms.

1949. Royal assent is received for Newfoundland to enter the Dominion of Canada as the tenth and last province through an act of the British Parliament (now called the Newfoundland Act). The terms of union came into effect on March 31, 1949, and the first session of the legislature was held in St. John's on July 13, 1949. Newfoundland's admission was long anticipated. When the Parliament Buildings in Ottawa were reconstructed after the 1916 fire, stone plaques were erected over the entrance to the Peace Tower. There were ten of them—nine bearing the coats of arms of the existing provinces and one left bare, to await the day when Newfoundland joined Canada. On April 1, thirty-three years after those plaques were posted, Prime Minister Louis St. Laurent finally cut the first ceremonial chisel strokes onto the blank stone to signify the province's entry into Confederation.

BORN ON THIS DAY

1934 singer Fernand Gignac

1957 actress Amanda Plummer

1971 model Yasmeen Ghauri

1981 actress Luciana Carro

24 MARCH

©Evan Leeson.

The Legislative Assembly of British Columbia, designed by Francis Mawson Rattenbury.

1935. Celebrated architect Francis Mawson Rattenbury is murdered by his chauffeur, the lover of his second wife, in his native England. Rattenbury had returned to Britain in 1929 after a scandal surrounding his divorce and remarriage. His clients in British Columbia, where he spent most of his career, had begun to shun him due to his egregious treatment of his first wife and their children, and his very public affair with the much younger Alma Pakenham, who would become his second wife. He and Pakenham left Victoria for England, where Rattenbury's finances continued to decline and she took up with their seventeen-year-old chauffeur.

BORN ON THIS DAY

1803 educator Egerton Ryerson

1936 environmentalist David Suzuki

Also on This Day

1975.
A private member's bill (introduced by Sean O'Sullivan) to make the beaver an official symbol of Canada receives royal assent. The beaver is an emblem of Canada older than the maple leaf, and has had a greater impact on Canadian history and exploration than any other animal or plant species. In 2011, Senator Nicole Eaton ignited national controversy when she suggested that the "dentally defective rat" be replaced as the national emblem by the polar bear.

*The Ten Things Canadians Feel Define Canada**

1. The maple leaf
2. Hockey
3. The Canadian flag
4. The beaver
5. The Canadarm
6. Canada Day
7. Peacekeeping
8. Pierre Elliott Trudeau
9. Health care
10. Niagara Falls

*According to a 2008 poll by the Dominion Institute, now Historica Canada

Also on This Day

1951.
Ethel Blondin-Andrew, the first Aboriginal woman elected to the Parliament of Canada (1988), is born in Tulita, Northwest Territories. She held cabinet positions in the governments of both Jean Chrétien and Paul Martin.

How many copies of the Toronto *Globe* did George Brown print for the paper's first week of circulation? See March 5.

Library and Archives Canada/C-003188.

William Lyon Mackenzie King, George Brown, and businessman Peter Larkin en route to the Imperial Conference in London, England, 1923.

1880. Journalist, politician, and Father of Confederation George Brown is shot at the offices of the Toronto *Globe* by George Bennett, a disgruntled former employee. Brown died on May 9, 1880, after the seemingly minor leg wound became infected. A leading Liberal, Brown played an important role in the unification of Canada, as well as in the Charlottetown and Québec Conferences. Though he joined the Great Coalition with Sir John A. Macdonald to promote Confederation, he is still remembered as John A.'s greatest rival and political jousting partner.

BORN ON THIS DAY

Jesuit missionary Jean de Brébeuf
1593

1932
singer Shirley Harmer

Nova Scotia Archives and Records Management, Reference no. 20040026.

A 1921 image of the *Bluenose* by W.R. MacAskill, hand-colourized by Elva MacAskill.

1921. The *Bluenose* is launched in Lunenburg, Nova Scotia. Canada's most famous ship, the schooner was designed to fish the Grand Banks and to race. She held the record for the largest catch of fish brought into Lunenburg, and until her last International Fisherman's Trophy race in 1938, she also held a reputation as one of the fastest ships in the world. The *Bluenose*'s journey came to an unfitting end in 1942, when she was sold to a West Indies trading company; she was wrecked off the coast of Haiti in 1946. Today the schooner is immortalized on the Canadian dime.

Heads or Tails?

Documents dating from 1937, the year the ten-cent *Bluenose* coin was introduced, identify the image on the tails side as a traditional fishing schooner, not the famous *Bluenose*. After some archival research, the Royal Canadian Mint officially recognized the ship on the dime as the true *Bluenose*. The image on the coin, designed by Emanuel Hahn, is based on a 1931 photograph by Wallace MacAskill, and is not a composite of the *Bluenose* and two other ships, as previously believed.

BORN ON THIS DAY

1950 — actor Martin Short

1963 — singer Roch Voisine

Jann Arden performing in Calgary, 2014.

Juno Award–Winning Female Solo Artists of Note

1985: k.d. lang
1987: Rita MacNeil
1992: Alanis Morissette
1995: Susan Aglukark
2001: Nelly Furtado
2003: Avril Lavigne
2005: Feist

1962. Singer-songwriter Jann Arden is born in Calgary. Arden's melancholy yet hopeful adult contemporary pop songs, distinguished by her expressive vocal delivery and introspective lyrics, earned her an international following in the 1990s and 2000s. Her debut album, *Time for Mercy* (1993), contained the haunting single "I Would Die for You" and was certified four times platinum for sales of over four hundred thousand in Canada. The single and its album earned Arden her first two Juno Awards, for best video and best new solo artist.

BORN ON THIS DAY

1952
twin singer-songwriters Richard and Marie-Claire Séguin

1971
actor Nathan Fillion

Library and Archives Canada/Gladwish & Mitchell fonds/C-007869.

Stephen Leacock, ca. 1935.

1944. Humorist, essayist, teacher, political scientist, and historian Stephen Leacock dies in Toronto. The prolific author of literary essays, articles on social issues, and over sixty books was perhaps best known for his 1912 collection, *Sunshine Sketches of a Little Town*. Set in the fictional town of Mariposa (based on Orillia, Ontario, where Leacock owned a home), *Sketches* delves into the business dealings, social life, religion, romance, and politics of a small town with Leacock's own patented brand of humour. His contributions to Canadian literature were so significant that he has been immortalized in a Canada Post stamp and has served as the inspiration for the annual Stephen Leacock Memorial Medal for Canadian Humour Writing.

Selected Recipients of the Stephen Leacock Memorial Medal

1947: Harry L. Symons, *Ojibway Melody*
1955: Robertson Davies, *Leaven of Malice*
1960: Pierre Berton, *Just Add Water and Stir*
1970: Farley Mowat, *The Boat Who Wouldn't Float*
1992: Roch Carrier, *Prayers of a Very Wise Child*
1998: Mordecai Richler, *Barney's Version*
2004: Ian Ferguson, *Village of the Small Houses*
2006: Arthur Black, *Pitch Black*
2007: Stuart McLean, *Secrets from the Vinyl Cafe*
2008: Terry Fallis, *The Best-Laid Plans*
2010: Will Ferguson, *Beyond Belfast*
2011: Trevor Cole, *Practical Jean*
2012: Patrick deWitt, *The Sisters Brothers*
2013: Cassie Stocks, *Dance, Gladys, Dance*
2014: Bill Conall, *The Promised Land: A Novel of Cape Breton*

BORN ON THIS DAY

University of Ottawa chancellor and vice-regal consort Pauline Vanier — 1898

1906 — rower Joseph Wright Jr.

author Jane Rule — 1931

MARCH

Canada's Punchiest Pugilists

Wins/Losses/Draws

1870–1908: George Dixon
65/30/53

1881–1955: Tommy Burns
46/5/8

1883–1956: Sam Langford
167/38/37

1900–1948: Jack Delaney
77/10/2

1907–2004: Jimmy McLarnin
62/11/3

1911–1984: Lou Brouillard
107/29/2

b. 1937: George Chuvalo
73/18/2

1955–2006: Trevor Berbick
49/11/1

b. 1965: Lennox Lewis
41/2/1

1972–2009: Arturo Gatti
40/9/0

b. 1982: Jelena Mrdjenovich
33/9/1

b. 1984: Mary Spencer
118/8/0

George Chuvalo.

1966. The boxing match for the world heavyweight title between Canadian champion George Chuvalo and incumbent Muhammad Ali takes place at Toronto's Maple Leaf Gardens. The fight lasted an impressive fifteen rounds, but in the end, Chuvalo could not defeat the champ and Ali won by unanimous decision. While Chuvalo was not undefeated, he is internationally known for having fought against the world's highest-ranked boxers and never being knocked off his feet.

BORN ON THIS DAY

1933 — poet Jacques Brault

1944 — singer-songwriter Terry Jacks

1959 — mountaineer Barry Blanchard

1968 — singer Sue Foley

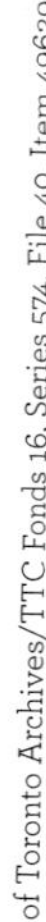

Yonge Street subway construction, 1951.

1954. The Yonge Street subway, the first subway line in Canada, is opened by Ontario premier Leslie Frost, Toronto mayor Allan Lamport, and members of the Toronto Transit Commission at Davisville station. The line ran for 7.4 kilometres between Eglinton and Union stations. Because it was far less expensive than boring a tunnel, the cut-and-cover technique was used to build most of the line. As crowds gathered to watch the construction, a large trench was dug into Yonge Street, utilities relocated, and steel cross members welded into place to support a deck that allowed traffic to return to the street while work proceeded beneath. It proved a major disruption to Toronto's busy main street. TTC chairman William C. McBrien noted in his speech that the Yonge subway was "not the final solution of Toronto's traffic problems. It is only the start of combating this monster."

Subways and Light Rail Systems in Canada

1861: Toronto streetcar system
1954: Toronto Subway
1966: Montreal Metro
1978: Edmonton LRT
1981: Calgary C-Train
1985: Vancouver SkyTrain
2001: Ottawa O-Train

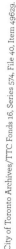

BORN ON THIS DAY

poet Milton Acorn
1923

1960
skier Laurie Graham

Also on This Day

1949.
Newfoundland entered the Dominion of Canada as the tenth province through an Act of Westminster. The first session of the legislature was held in St. John's on July 13. Politician Joseph (Joey) Smallwood, who would go on to be the first premier of the new province, and who fought for years to have Newfoundland join Confederation, won the public over with his willpower, ruthlessness, and courage. In one speech he declared, "We are not a nation. We are a medium-sized municipality . . . left far behind the march of time."

Archives of Manitoba/Winnipeg Collection, Item #1, Neg. 5223.

Machray School in Winnipeg, 1893.

1890. The Manitoba School Act abolishes public funding for separate schools for Catholic students. Members of the French minority, who were most affected, argued that the act violated the agreements under which Manitoba had entered Confederation—specifically, the provision for dual Protestant and Roman Catholic education systems. An amendment to the act in 1897 did not restore separate schools, but it did allow Catholic teachers to be selectively employed and also granted some opportunities for religious instruction within the public schools. Only in the late 1970s were these arrangements amended. Among the Québécois, the Manitoba Schools Question, as the events came to be known, is viewed as a significant loss of French and Catholic rights outside Québec.

BORN ON THIS DAY

composer George Fiala
1922

1968
rapper Maestro Fresh Wes

APRIL

Brianne Ranta.

Near the Hamlet of Repulse Bay, Nunavut, during a fishing derby celebrating Nunavut Day.

1999. Nunavut—which covers roughly two million square kilometres of the eastern Arctic—is declared a new territory, marking Canada's first territorial change since Newfoundland joined Confederation in 1949. With a population made up predominantly of Inuit people (over 80 percent, according to the 2013 census), Nunavut is the only region of Canada to recognize four official languages: Inuktitut, Inuinnaqtun, English, and French. In the Inuit language of Inuktitut, Nunavut translates to "our land."

Also on This Day

1858.
Canada celebrates what is believed to be its first April Fool's Day. In French Canada, the holiday became known as *Poisson d'avril* (or April fish), after a common prank in which a paper fish would be attached to someone's back without the person's notice. The tradition likely originated in France, where clergymen who disliked the change of the start of the calendar year from April 1 to January 1 were often the targets of a similar prank.

BORN ON THIS DAY

1916 actor John Drainie

1921 Hockey Hall of Famer Ken Reardon

AP Photo/Rebecca Blackwell

The CN Tower, lit up for the closing ceremony of the 2015 Pan Am Games.

1975. After more than two years of construction, the final piece of the CN Tower—the steel broadcasting antenna—is bolted into place by helicopter. Built at a cost of $52 million, the tower opened to the public on June 26, 1976. At just over 553 metres tall, the Toronto landmark was the world's tallest free-standing structure until 2010, when it was surpassed by the Burj Khalifa in Dubai. The CN Tower is still the tallest "tower" in the Western Hemisphere.

The Ten Tallest Structures in Canada

1. **CN Tower**, Toronto 553 m
2. **Inco Superstack**, Sudbury 380 m
3. **First Canadian Place**, Toronto 355 m
4. **Commerce Court West**, Toronto 287 m
5. **Trump International Hotel and Tower**, Toronto 277 m
6. **Scotia Plaza**, Toronto 275 m
7. **Aura** (condominiums), Toronto 272 m
8. **One Bloor East**, Toronto 269 m
9. **TD Centre**, Toronto 263 m
10. **Smokestack**, Flin Flon 252 m

BORN ON THIS DAY

politician Lionel Chevrier 1903

1931 author Howard Engel

actress Sharon Acker 1935

1940 figure skater Donald Jackson

APRIL 3

© Bettmann/Corbis.

Allan Dwan holds a mirror for actress Enid Bennett while Douglas Fairbanks looks on, 1922.

1885. Film director Allan Dwan is born in Toronto. Dwan began his career making silent westerns in Hollywood. In 1922, he directed Douglas Fairbanks in *Robin Hood*; the castle for that film was the largest set ever built for the movies up to that time. He also directed two Shirley Temple films, *Heidi* (1937) and *Rebecca of Sunnybrook Farm* (1938), as well as the John Wayne classic *The Sands of Iwo Jima* (1949). Educated as an engineer, Dwan is credited with inventing the dolly shot in 1915.

Also on This Day

1851.
Leading American abolitionist Frederick Douglass visits Toronto to address an anti-slavery crowd of twelve hundred people at the St. Lawrence Hall ballroom.

BORN ON THIS DAY

1876 actress Margaret Anglin

1918 composer Louis Applebaum

1943 musician Richard Manuel

1945 Hockey Hall of Famer Bernie Parent

1982 actress Cobie Smulders

Library and Archives Canada/Duncan Cameron/Duncan Cameron fonds/e007150465.

Prime Minister Louis St. Laurent.

1949. Canada, along with eleven other countries, signs the North Atlantic Treaty—the document establishing the North Atlantic Treaty Organization (NATO)—in Washington, DC. NATO was born in part from concern over the spread of communism, and its creation marked a new era for Canada: it was the country's first involvement in a peacetime military alliance, and it forged closer ties with the United States while distancing Canada from Great Britain. NATO would also bind Canada's trading partners together, providing the potential for beneficial economic collaboration.

NATO Founding Members

Belgium	**Luxembourg**
Canada	**Netherlands**
Denmark	**Norway**
France	**Portugal**
Iceland	**United Kingdom**
Italy	**United States**

BORN ON THIS DAY

1913 Governor General Jules Léger

1925 politician Claude Wagner

1952 figure skater Karen Magnussen

1956 ballet dancer Evelyn Hart

1979 hockey player Roberto Luongo

1987 actress Sarah Gadon

Timeline: The Baby Bonus

1945: Average monthly payment per child aged fifteen and under: $5.94
1978: Refundable Child Tax Credit of $200 per year for families with incomes of $18,000 or less
1988: Tax credit increases to $559 per year for families with incomes of $24,090 or less
1992: Tax-free and income-tested Child Tax Benefit of $85 per month per child up to the age of eighteen

Library and Archives Canada/C-011925.

Jean Talon Visiting Settlers, **by Lawrence Batchelor, ca. 1931.**

1669. The intendant of New France, Jean Talon, introduces the first "baby bonuses" in Louis XIV's name. With the colony's population declining, Talon hoped to encourage growth by offering incentives for early marriage and large families, while assigning penalties for bachelors. Fathers with ten children were awarded three hundred livres (around $5,675 today); those with twelve children received four hundred livres (around $7,569 today). The plan worked: by 1671, there had been as many as seven hundred births.

BORN ON THIS DAY

1830
songwriter and teacher Alexander Muir

1951
author Guy Vanderhaeghe

1970
actress Thea Gill

© Government of Canada. Courtesy of Library and Archives Canada/Department of Communications Fonds/e010937773.

Pierre Trudeau in Winnipeg, undated.

1968. Pierre Trudeau is elected leader of the Liberal Party of Canada at a national leadership convention in Ottawa. He was chosen on the fourth ballot, having defeated several prominent Liberals, including Paul Martin Sr. and Paul Hellyer. On April 20, he was sworn in as Canada's fifteenth prime minister. Trudeau is the country's third-longest-serving prime minister, behind William Lyon Mackenzie King and Sir John A. Macdonald.

The Five Longest-Serving Past Prime Ministers

1. **William Lyon Mackenzie King:** 21 years, 154 days
2. **Sir John A. Macdonald:** 19 years, 1 day
3. **Pierre Trudeau:** 15 years, 166 days
4. **Sir Wilfrid Laurier:** 15 years, 90 days
5. **Jean Chrétien:** 10 years, 39 days

Other end of the scale:
Sir Charles Tupper: 69 days

BORN ON THIS DAY

1884 actor Walter Huston

1955 comedian and writer Cathy Jones

APRIL  7 

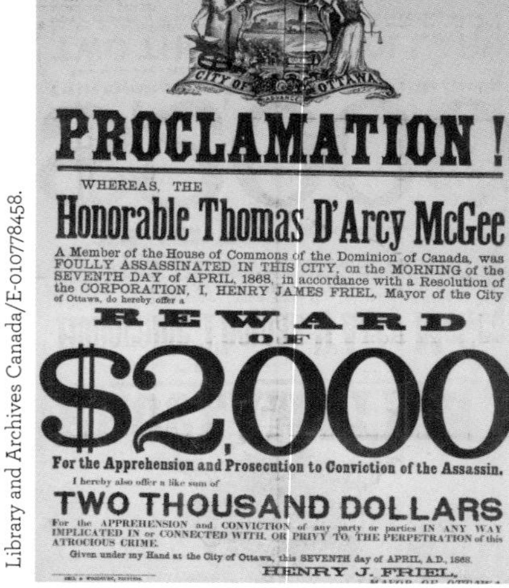

Library and Archives Canada/E-010778458.

A poster advertising a reward for the apprehension of D'Arcy McGee's assassin.

1868. Irish Catholic nationalist and Father of Confederation Thomas D'Arcy McGee is assassinated on Sparks Street in Ottawa on his way home from a parliamentary meeting. McGee had come to Canada from Ireland in 1857 and that same year was elected to the Legislative Assembly of the Province of Canada from Montréal. Although he first worked with George Brown and the Reform Party, he later pursued national interests that brought him into line with Sir John A. Macdonald and the Confederation project. By 1866, he had alienated many Irish voters and was dropped from the cabinet.

It was widely suspected that McGee's killer was an Irish radical. Patrick Whelan was hanged for the crime, though his guilt has since been questioned. McGee was given a state funeral, with a procession witnessed by some eighty thousand in Montréal. He remains the only federal politician assassinated in Canadian history.

Also on This Day

1851.

Publisher and cartoonist

John Wilson Bengough is born in Toronto. At the age of twenty-two, he published the first issue of *Grip*—a satirical magazine best known for its biting political cartoons, including an immortal one of John A. Macdonald.

BORN ON THIS DAY

1908

composer Percy Faith

1927

artist Dorothy Knowles

1983

actor Kyle Labine

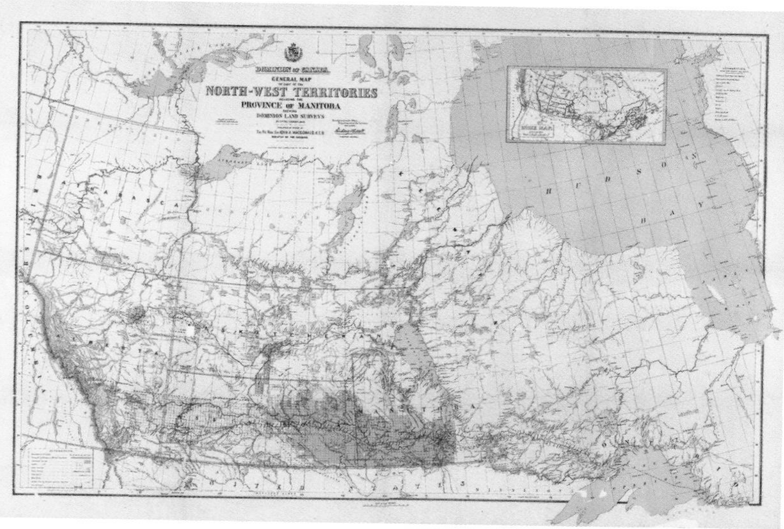

Library and Archives Canada/N-0011621-K.

A map of the North-West Territories, including the province of Manitoba, 1883.

1875. The North-West Territories becomes a political entity. This massive region included all of present-day Yukon, the Northwest Territories, Nunavut, Alberta, and Saskatchewan; most of present-day Manitoba; and much of present-day northern Ontario and northern Québec. It would be governed by an appointed lieutenant-governor and council. The 1875 act that created the territory provided for the gradual addition of elected members to the council as warranted by increases in population.

America's Sweetheart

1893.

Film star Mary Pickford is born in Toronto. Born Gladys Smith, she would become one of the most popular actresses of her day and be immortalized as "America's Sweetheart" for films such as *Coquette* (1929), for which she won an Oscar. At the height of her career, her overseas honeymoon with her new husband, actor Douglas Fairbanks, set off mass hysteria among European fans. But Pickford was no mere celebrity; she also co-founded the United Artists film studio, achieving what no woman in film history had up to that time—starring in, producing, and distributing her own work.

Mary Pickford Select Filmography

1914: *Tess of the Storm Country*
1917: *The Poor Little Rich Girl*
1918: *Stella Maris*
1919: *Daddy-Long-Legs*
1929: *Coquette*

BORN ON THIS DAY

actress and teacher Dora Mavor Moore
1888

1927
senator and first female United Church moderator Lois Wilson

actor J.R. Bourne
1970

APRIL 9

Also on This Day

1995.
Steve Stavro pays $23 million to Harold Ballard Charities as partial payment for Maple Leaf Gardens. The overall cost was $167 million. Maple Leaf Gardens had been the home of the Toronto Maple Leafs for sixty-seven years. Today the former arena is the flagship location of the Loblaws grocery chain. A red circle on the floor among the shelves marks what was once centre ice.

Department of National Defence/Library and Archives Canada/ PA-001439.

The wounded of Vimy Ridge.

1917. On Easter Monday, four Canadian divisions and one British brigade capture Vimy Ridge, near Arras, France. Though they suffered more than 10,000 casualties, including 3,598 dead, it was a brilliant victory for members of the Canadian Corps. Many historians believe that the capture of Vimy gave the Canadian people a new sense of national awareness. In 1936, the Canadian National Vimy Memorial, a majestic tribute to the servicemen of the Canadian Corps, was unveiled at the highest point of the ridge. The monument is inscribed with the names of the 11,285 Canadians who died in France but have no grave. It also bears a dedication—"To the valour of their countrymen in the Great War and in memory of their sixty thousand dead, this monument is raised by the people of Canada."

What monument in Ottawa is the site of commemoration for the fallen without names on Remembrance Day?
See May 25.

BORN ON THIS DAY

1885
Laura Secord candy shop founder Frank O'Connor

1915
Québec premier Daniel Johnson Sr.

1971
racing driver Jacques Villeneuve

Glenn Gould, 1957.

1964. In Los Angeles, pianist, composer, conductor, writer, and broadcaster Glenn Gould gives his last public performance. Despite his stature as one of the most unconventional classical musicians of his day, Gould rejected the concert stage to focus on recording. His celebrated albums, particularly his original reading of Bach's *Goldberg Variations*, won him public acclaim. He would receive numerous awards over the course of his career, including four Grammys (three awarded posthumously), one of which was for lifetime achievement. Since his death in 1982, Gould's reputation has continued to grow, making him one of Canada's most important cultural figures, and one of the world's most admired and studied musicians.

Also on This Day

1919.
In response to Prohibition, Québec holds a referendum on the sale of alcoholic drinks in the province. With spirits already banned, the question posed was whether beer, wine, and cider should also be outlawed. Over 70 percent of Quebecers voted yes to the sale of liquor in the province. While other provinces, including Ontario, went "dry," Québec became known as the "sinkhole" of North America, and tourists flocked to the historic capital city. The provincial government reaped huge profits from the sale of booze.

What significant Act passed in Ontario in 1916? See March 2.

BORN ON THIS DAY

1928 jazz musician Fraser MacPherson

1942 journalist Nick Auf der Maur

1953 Broadcaster and former senator Pamela Wallin

1961 anti-smoking activist Barb Tarbox

Also on This Day

1940.
Vancouver shipyards gear up for war by building corvettes and minesweepers for action in the Battle of the Atlantic. This hard-fought struggle for control of Atlantic shipping routes was the longest continuous battle of the Second World War, and it took the lives of more than four thousand Canadians.

The northern leopard frog.

2000. Environment Minister David Anderson introduces legislation in the House of Commons aimed at protecting Canada's endangered wildlife. The subsequent act (called the Species at Risk Act) listed 233 species at risk of extinction or in need of "special concern," including the northern leopard frog, the burrowing owl, and the bowhead whale. The goal of the legislation was not only to protect existing wildlife and environments but also to recover threatened habitats.

BORN ON THIS DAY

1914 filmmaker Norman McLaren

1914 politician Robert Stanfield

1925 publisher Pierre Péladeau

1934 composer and broadcaster Norma Beecroft

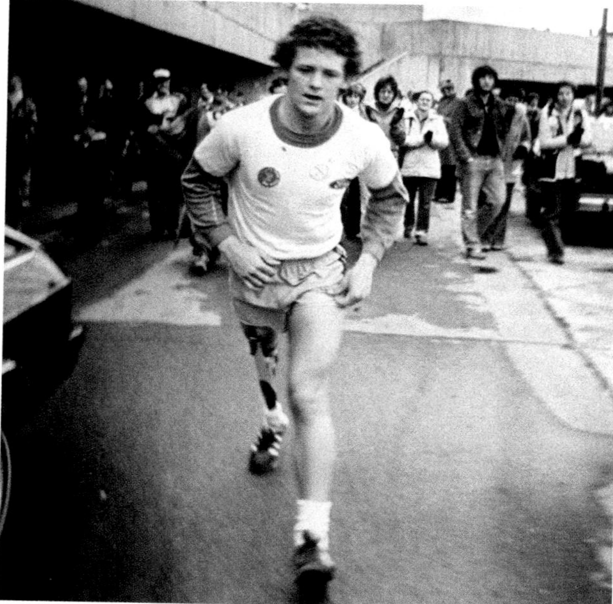
Dick Green/The Canadian Press.

Terry Fox starts his Marathon of Hope in St. John's, Newfoundland.

1980. Terry Fox begins his Marathon of Hope to raise money for cancer research. In 1977, when he was eighteen, Fox had been diagnosed with osteogenic sarcoma (a type of bone cancer), and doctors amputated most of his right leg. Inspired by the story of Dick Traum, an amputee who ran the New York City Marathon in 1976, Fox decided to run across Canada to raise money to help find a cure for cancer. The run ended on September 1 in Thunder Bay, Ontario, after cancer appeared in his lungs. Although he hoped to carry on after treatment, Fox was unable to return to his marathon; he died on June 28, 1981, at the Royal Columbian Hospital in New Westminster, BC, at the age of twenty-two. To this day, millions of Canadians continue to donate to and participate in the annual Terry Fox Run, keeping his memory and his cause alive.

Before the Marathon of Hope

Even as a young boy, Terry Fox was determined to overcome whatever obstacles stood in his way. In grade eight, he decided he wanted to join the basketball team, even though he was still quite short and possessed little natural talent. Hours of practice eventually led to a place on his high school team and later on the junior varsity basketball team at Simon Fraser University. In 1978, not long after he was diagnosed with cancer and had his leg amputated, Terry joined Rick Hansen's wheelchair basketball team, winning three national titles. He brought the same attitude to the Marathon of Hope, logging five thousand kilometres on training runs to prepare for the cross-country journey.

BORN ON THIS DAY

Governor General Lord Durham (John George Lambton) 1792

1944 singer-songwriter John Kay

rock guitarist Pat Travers 1954

1960 *Hockey Night in Canada* sportscaster Ron MacLean

composer and guitarist Erik Mongrain 1980

Man of Many Faces

Grey Owl had an unhappy childhood in his native England, and he withdrew into an imaginary world of books and their romantic depictions of Aboriginal North Americans. As soon as he was able to, he set out for Canada and began remaking himself in the image of these people. But it was his Aboriginal wife who inspired in him the reverence for nature that defined so much of his life. The two beaver kits she convinced him to spare opened his eyes to the beauty of the world around him, and from that day forward, he vowed never to kill another living thing. "Remember," he told packed houses during lecture tours across North America and throughout Britain, "you belong to Nature, not it to you."

Library and Archives Canada/1989-455, e008300732.

Grey Owl sharing his canoe with a beaver in Riding Mountain National Park, Manitoba, 1931.

1938. Conservationist and author Grey Owl dies in Prince Albert, Saskatchewan. Shortly after his death, the *North Bay Nugget* published an article revealing that Grey Owl was a fraud and had no Aboriginal heritage. Born in England as Archibald Belaney, he had emigrated at seventeen and settled in northern Canada. Sometime after his arrival, he began to introduce himself as Grey Owl, falsely claiming to be the son of a Scot and an Apache. His story, as told in his book *Pilgrims of the Wild*, was that his Iroquois wife, Anahareo, had saved the lives of two beaver kits, inspiring him to dedicate himself to the protection of wildlife. He took up this calling with fervour, heading two beaver conservation programs in Manitoba and Saskatchewan. Unfortunately, his contributions to conservation were forgotten for a generation in the uproar over his deception.

BORN ON THIS DAY

Father of Confederation Thomas D'Arcy McGee
1825

1854
poet William Henry Drummond

swimmer and coach Cliff Lumsdon
1931

1949
author Marilyn Bowering

Canadian Department of National Defence/Library and Archives Canada/PA-133348.

Pte. George Pope and Pte. Denis Townsend on the road to Arnhem.

1945. Troops of the First Canadian Army liberate Arnhem, Holland, after two days of fighting. The liberation of the Netherlands by Allied troops had begun in 1944 and lasted through a particularly harsh winter into 1945. When Germany surrendered to the Allies in May 1945, it fell to the Canadians to liberate western Holland, where the Dutch were short of food and fuel. The Canadians, who quickly funnelled relief supplies into the area, were welcomed enthusiastically, and the joyous "Canadian summer" that followed forged deep and long-lasting bonds of friendship between the Dutch and Canadian people.

In His Own Words: Charlie Fielding

Charlie Fielding served in the Second World War with the Royal Canadian Electrical and Mechanical Engineers, attached to the Governor General's Foot Guards. He recalls being stationed in Holland, and bringing food and coal to war-devastated families. "Sixteen years [after the liberation] . . . we were stationed in Germany with the NATO forces, [and] we decided to go and visit the people in Holland, my family and I. When we got there I knocked on the door and it opened. A young man opened the door and I said: 'Does Mr. Verheggan live here?' He says: 'You've got to be Charlie.' I says: 'Well, you must be Peter but you'd never recognize me.' He said: 'Oh yes, I do . . . My family and I always remember you and your crew. You brought us food when we were hungry and coal when we were cold. It was the best Christmas we ever had.'"

—From the *Memory Project*

BORN ON THIS DAY

Governor General Lord Athlone (Alexander Cambridge)
1874

1928
jazz pianist Norm Amadio

actor Lothaire Bluteau
1957

1984
speed skater Charles Hamelin

APRIL 15

Also on This Day

1861.
Confederation poet Bliss Carman is born in Fredericton, New Brunswick. The author of *Low Tide on Grand Pré* (1893), he lived most of his life in the United States and in later years was acclaimed as Canada's poet laureate.

Horst Ehricht/Library and Archives Canada/e002712851.

Mordecai Richler, 1957.

1998. Author Mordecai Richler is awarded the Stephen Leacock Memorial Medal for Canadian Humour Writing for his novel *Barney's Version*. Known for his biting wit and trenchant satire, Richler wrote numerous novels, children's books, and essays. His most recognized works are set in his home turf in the Jewish section of Montréal. Several of Richler's novels are used in the classroom, with *The Apprenticeship of Duddy Kravitz* taught in high schools across Canada.

BORN ON THIS DAY

1800
explorer
James Clark Ross

1841
distiller
Joseph Seagram

1982
actor Seth Rogen

Lt Richard G. Arless/Department of National Defence/Library and Archives Canada/ PA-157021.

Survivors of HMCS *Esquimalt* in Halifax, Nova Scotia, 1945.

1945. The German U-boat *U-190* fires a torpedo and sinks HMCS *Esquimalt* in the approaches to Halifax, believing that the Allied minesweeper had detected its presence. When the *Esquimalt* failed to appear at a scheduled rendezvous with her sister ship, HMCS *Sarnia*, a search was initiated. Sarnia came upon and picked up several survivors, but many subsequently died from exposure to the frigid waters while awaiting rescue. Only twenty-seven of the minesweeper's seventy-one-man crew survived. *Esquimalt* was the last Canadian warship to sink during the Second World War; she went down just three weeks before the war ended. The German U-boat surrendered to Canada on May 11, 1945. Canadian aircraft sank it ceremonially on October 21, 1947, near where it had destroyed the *Esquimalt*.

In His Own Words: Joseph Frank "Tex" Wilson

"I was no sooner in the water than the aftermast of the stern as it was sinking came down and hit me across the back, and took me and the Carley float [life raft] down. I struggled back . . . into the Carley float, and that's where I was for the next six and a half hours.... Sitting in the Carley float was one of the reasons why I was saved. You see, the temperature of the water that [day] was damn near freezing. In the North Atlantic, it always is. If I remember correctly, we started off with about seventeen in . . . and around the Carley float....We only ended up with seven."

Joe Wilson/The Memory Project

Joe Wilson, 1948.

BORN ON THIS DAY

Arctic explorer John Franklin 1786

1827 poet Octave Crémazie

vaudevillian Fifi D'Orsay 1904

1949 jockey Sandy Hawley

APRIL 17

Section 15: The Charter and Equality Rights

"Every individual is equal before and under the law and has the right to the equal protection and equal benefit of the law without discrimination and, in particular, without discrimination based on race, national or ethnic origin, colour, religion, sex, age or mental or physical disability."

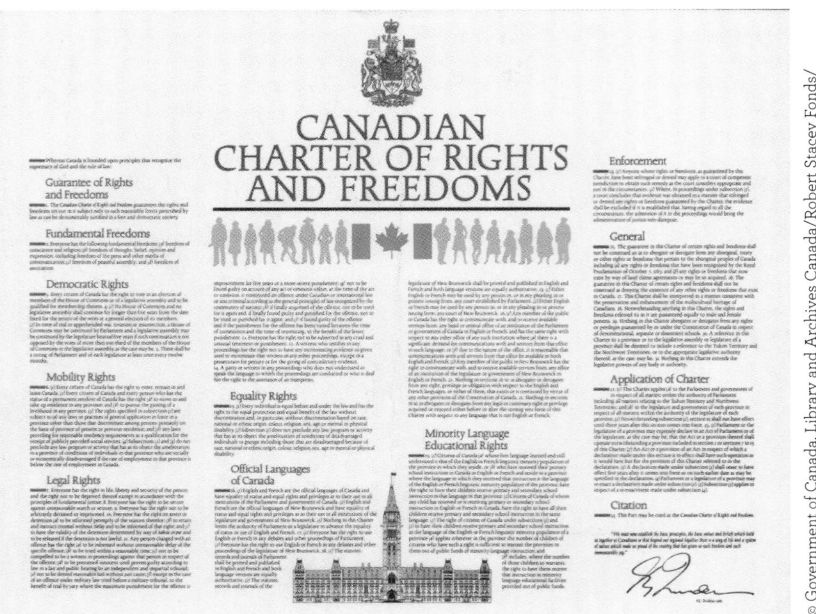

CANADIAN CHARTER OF RIGHTS AND FREEDOMS

Guarantee of Rights and Freedoms

Fundamental Freedoms

Democratic Rights

Mobility Rights

Legal Rights

Equality Rights

Official Languages of Canada

Minority Language Educational Rights

Enforcement

General

Application of Charter

Citation

The Canadian Charter of Rights and Freedoms.

1982. The Canadian Charter of Rights and Freedoms comes into effect. The concept of the Charter had met with controversy early on, with the provinces concerned that it would prevent them from making laws independently. A compromise was brokered between the federal government and the majority of provinces to support an agreement that included a "notwithstanding clause" (a clause allowing the provinces to override some aspects of the Charter under certain conditions). This clause has been employed only a handful of times, including by Québec in 1988 to limit commercial signs in languages other than French, and by Alberta in 2000 to restrict access to same-sex marriage.

BORN ON THIS DAY

educator Marguerite Bourgeoys 1620

field naturalist John Macoun 1831

film producer John Kemeny 1925

singer Bobby Curtola 1943

actress Teri Austin 1959

1946. Jackie Robinson makes his debut with the Montreal Royals, the minor league affiliate of the Brooklyn Dodgers, becoming the first Black professional baseball player in the major leagues. Branch Rickey, president and general manager of the Dodgers, decided that Montréal was a suitable place to introduce Robinson to baseball fans and to begin the process of integrating the major leagues. Robinson stayed with the Royals for the 1946 season and was a crowd favourite, leading his team to the minor league baseball championship.

***Jackie Robinson*, by Christopher Hemsworth.**

Barrier-Breaking Athletes

1948: Norman Kwong:
first Chinese-Canadian professional football player (Calgary Stampeders)

1954: Fred Sasakamoose:
first Aboriginal Canadian to play in NHL (Chicago Blackhawks)

1958: Willie O'Ree:
first Black player in the NHL (Boston Bruins)

1992: Manon Rhéaume:
first woman to play for an NHL team (Tampa Bay Lightning)

2010: Angela James:
one of the first two women, the first openly gay player, and the second Black athlete to be inducted into the Hockey Hall of Fame

2010: Lauren Woolstencroft:
first person in the world to win five gold medals at a single Paralympic Winter Games, in alpine skiing (Vancouver)

BORN ON THIS DAY

Governor General Jacques-Pierre de Taffanel de La Jonquière
1685

1953
actor Rick Moranis

actor Eric McCormack
1963

1982
singer Marie-Élaine Thibert

Also on This Day

2000.
An Alberta judge finds activist Wiebo Ludwig guilty of a 1998 gas-well bombing. The Christian Reformed minister claimed that the wells were responsible for deadly pollution in the northwestern Alberta region of Peace River. Some saw Ludwig as a dangerous environmental terrorist, while others revered him as a folk hero.

©Boomer Jerritt/Picture BC.

A K'omoks First Nation potlatch ceremony, in Comox, British Columbia.

1884. After mounting pressure from missionaries and others, the federal government amends the Indian Act (effective January 1, 1885) to ban the potlatch ceremony of British Columbia's Aboriginal peoples. These highly regulated ceremonies involved feasting, spirit dances, theatrical demonstrations, and the distribution of gifts. Potlatches were held to celebrate, to mourn the dead, and to mark the investiture of chiefs. Although ceremonies continued to take place in contravention of the ban, it was four years before the first person was prosecuted under the law; however, BC chief justice Matthew Begbie ruled against the government, declaring the law unenforceable because it did not define the term "potlatch." The law was repealed in 1951.

BORN ON THIS DAY

1936 playwright Sharon Pollock

1940 poet Frank Davey

1955 author Neil Bissoondath

1981 actor Hayden Christensen

20 APRIL

The Anik-A2 satellite.

1973. The telecommunications satellite Anik A-2 is launched from Cape Canaveral, Florida. With its launch, Canada became the first country in the world to employ geostationary satellites for domestic communications. The Anik satellites, which enabled the CBC to broadcast to the Canadian North for the first time, were stabilized in orbit 35,790 kilometres above the equator by a technique known as spin-stabilization, in which the satellite body spins about its axis for stability and the communications antenna spins in the opposite direction so that it points continually toward earth.

Also on This Day

1976.
Champion horse Big Ben is born in Kalmthout, Belgium. The three-time Canadian show-jumping champ is one of two horses inducted into the Canadian Sports Hall of Fame (the other is Northern Dancer) and was the first horse to win two consecutive world cup titles.

BORN ON THIS DAY

Québec premier Maurice Duplessis 1890

1935 polka king Walter Ostanek

figure skater Toller Cranston 1949

1970 cookbook author and TV host Laura Calder

A True Pioneer

Jennie Trout was a frail woman who struggled throughout her life with nervous anxiety. In the early years of her marriage, her condition was so dire that she decided to try a relatively new medical treatment called electrotherapy. It was this experience that reawakened a childhood dream of a career in medicine. Once she had qualified to practice, she and her friend Emily Amelia Tefft, another graduate of the Woman's Medical College, opened a clinic specializing in electrotherapy for women. Unfortunately, the financial and physical demands of the undertaking took a toll, and Dr. Trout was forced to retire from practice at just forty-one. But she never abandoned her dream of seeing more female doctors, once writing, "I hope to live to see the day when each larger town (at least) in Ont[ario] will have one good true lady physician."

Library and Archives Canada/PA-212242.

Jennie Trout, ca. 1893.

1875. Jennie Trout becomes the first woman licensed to practise medicine in Canada. Born in Scotland, she grew up on a farm near Stratford, Ontario. In 1872, she passed a one-year qualifying course at the Toronto School of Medicine. But no full-time medical program in Canada was willing to admit a female student, so Trout instead studied at the Woman's Medical College in Philadelphia. She received her MD in March 1875 and passed the licensing exams of the College of Physicians and Surgeons of Ontario a month later. She was the only woman authorized to practice medicine in Canada until 1880, when Emily Stowe was also licensed. Dr. Trout later worked toward making the dream of a career in medicine a reality for more women, founding the Women's Medical College in Kingston in 1883.

BORN ON THIS DAY

Senator Keith Davey
1926

1964
swimmer Alex Baumann

Hockey Hall of Famer Ed Belfour
1965

1977
figure skater Jamie Salé

22 APRIL

Library and Archives Canada/Rusins Kaufmanis Collection/cr0017276.

Canadians boycott the Moscow Olympics.

1980. The federal government announces that Canada will join the United States in boycotting the Moscow Olympics over the Soviet invasion of Afghanistan. With more than sixty nations observing the boycott, the Olympics became almost a one-nation show, with the Soviet team collecting eighty gold medals, sixty-nine silver, and forty-six bronze, or more than 30 percent of all medals offered.

Also on This Day

1915.
At the Second Battle of Ypres, Belgium, the Canadian 13th Battalion, despite intense shelling and exposure to chlorine gas, stands firm until reserves are moved up the following day. The French troops, who were directly hit by the gas concentration, had broken and fled.

BORN ON THIS DAY

1875 — Hockey Hall of Famer Harvey Pulford

1905 — author and diplomat Robert Guy Choquette

1959 — actress Catherine Mary Stewart

1975 — racing driver Greg Moore

APRIL

23

Timeline: Aboriginal Supreme Court Rulings

1973: The Supreme Court acknowledges the existence of Aboriginal title in law.
1990: Aboriginal rights, such as the right to subsistence hunting and fishing, are ruled to be protected under the Constitution and cannot be infringed upon.
1997: The court rules that the government has a duty to consult with First Nations on issues concerning Crown land.
1999: Aboriginal band elections are declared open to people living off-reserve.
2014: In the first ruling to grant a declaration of Aboriginal title to a First Nation, the Tsilhqot'in peoples are granted title to land in British Columbia.

© Michael Sunderland.

The Supreme Court of Canada, Ottawa, Ontario.

1999. In a landmark case, *R. v. Gladue*, the Supreme Court of Canada rules that lower courts should consider the backgrounds of Aboriginal offenders as possible mitigating factors and attempt to apply traditional indigenous disciplinary practices, including restorative justice, in sentencing decisions. The defendant in the case, a Cree woman named Jamie Tanis Gladue, had been convicted of manslaughter in the death of her common-law husband and sentenced to three years in prison. The original trial judge ruled her ineligible for alternative discipline because she was not living in an Aboriginal community. The Supreme Court ruled that all Aboriginal offenders are entitled to such considerations, however, and that pre-sentencing reports (prepared by a probation officer), as well as so-called Gladue reports (written by a connection and offering personal and community background on the accused), should be submitted to the judge. Ironically, though this process now bears her name, Gladue's own appeal was denied by the Supreme Court.

BORN ON THIS DAY

Governor General Georges Vanier
1888

1918
poet Margaret Avison

Hockey Hall of Famer Tony Esposito
1943

1986
supermodel Jessica Stam

24 APRIL

Nova Scotia Archives, W.R. MacAskill Collection, 1987-453/3248.

Captain Joshua Slocum on *Spray*.

1895. Nova Scotia–born Joshua Slocum sets out in his small boat, the *Spray*, from Boston, Massachusetts, on his voyage around the world. In 1893, having fallen on hard times in New England, Slocum rebuilt the *Spray*, a derelict oyster sloop, to chase one of the few great marine challenges then remaining. He spent three years, two months, and three days in a boat measuring just under fifty-nine square metres, completing the trip in Newport, Rhode Island, on June 27, 1898. With his arrival, Slocum became the first man to sail around the world alone.

Also on This Day

1779.
The North West Company, a fur-trading consortium that became the chief rival of the Hudson's Bay Company, is established.

BORN ON THIS DAY

composer Violet Archer
1913

1945
composer Doug Riley

fashion designer Linda Lundström
1951

Library and Archives Canada/George Nakash/PA-123482.

Feminist activist Thérèse Casgrain in Montréal, undated.

1940. Québec women are granted the right to vote in provincial elections. Québec was the last province to enfranchise women, as well as the last to allow women to run for office provincially. (Women in the Northwest Territories were not enfranchised until 1951.) In 1916, Manitoba had become the first province to enfranchise women for provincial elections, and women had been able to vote in federal elections since 1918, though this right was afforded to only a segment of the female population. Members of First Nations communities (men and women), as well as those from several ethnic groups, would not receive the vote for many years. Japanese Canadians did not win the vote until 1949.

BORN ON THIS DAY

1923 ballet dancer Melissa Hayden

1927 actress Frances Hyland

THE RIGHT TO VOTE

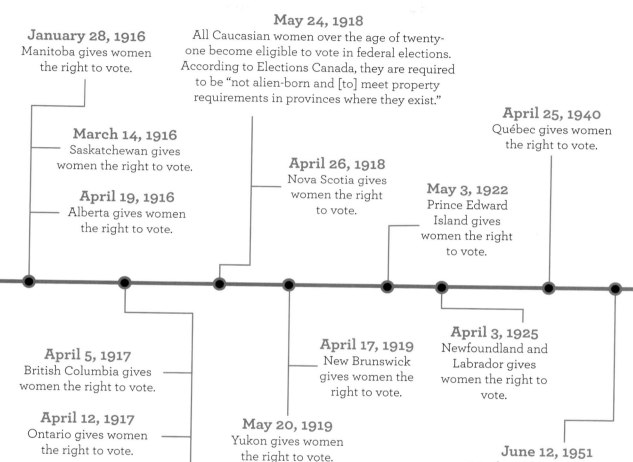

January 28, 1916
Manitoba gives women the right to vote.

March 14, 1916
Saskatchewan gives women the right to vote.

April 19, 1916
Alberta gives women the right to vote.

April 5, 1917
British Columbia gives women the right to vote.

April 12, 1917
Ontario gives women the right to vote.

September 20, 1917
The Military Voters Act gives active and retired women in the armed forces the right to vote; the Wartime Elections Act extends the vote to female relatives of military men.

April 26, 1918
Nova Scotia gives women the right to vote.

May 24, 1918
All Caucasian women over the age of twenty-one become eligible to vote in federal elections. According to Elections Canada, they are required to be "not alien-born and [to] meet property requirements in provinces where they exist."

April 17, 1919
New Brunswick gives women the right to vote.

May 20, 1919
Yukon gives women the right to vote.

May 3, 1922
Prince Edward Island gives women the right to vote.

April 3, 1925
Newfoundland and Labrador gives women the right to vote.

April 25, 1940
Québec gives women the right to vote.

June 12, 1951
Northwest Territories gives women the right to vote.

APRIL 26

© La Presse/Paul-Henri Talbot.

Fidel Castro interviewed by René Lévesque.

1959. Cuban prime minister Fidel Castro visits Montréal. Just months after overthrowing Gen. Fulgencio Batista's regime with an organization of exiled revolutionaries known as the 26th of July Movement, Castro received an enthusiastic welcome in Canada, meeting the crowds with hugs and handshakes upon arrival. He then held a press conference to outline his political policies, during which he was interviewed by several journalists, including René Lévesque, who would later become premier of Québec. Among other things, Castro described his admiration for the Mounties.

The Cuban Missile Crisis

During the Cuban Missile Crisis (October 14–28, 1962), the federal government had to decide whether to comply with an American request to move Canadian forces to a defence status known as Defcon 3. With the approval of Douglas Harkness, the minister of national defence, Canadian units quietly did so, but formal authorization was delayed while cabinet debated.

Disinclined to provoke the USSR and concerned about implications for Canadian policy on nuclear weapons, Prime Minister John Diefenbaker was reluctant to acquiesce. About half of Canada's cabinet ministers remained undecided, but as Soviet ships approached the quarantine zone (a line in the international waters around Cuba where the United States had stationed navy ships), the Harkness position gained support, and on October 25 the Diefenbaker government authorized the Defcon 3 alert.

BORN ON THIS DAY

1904 Roman Catholic cardinal Paul-Émile Léger

1932 Nobel Prize–winning chemist Michael Smith

1942 diplomat Michael Kergin

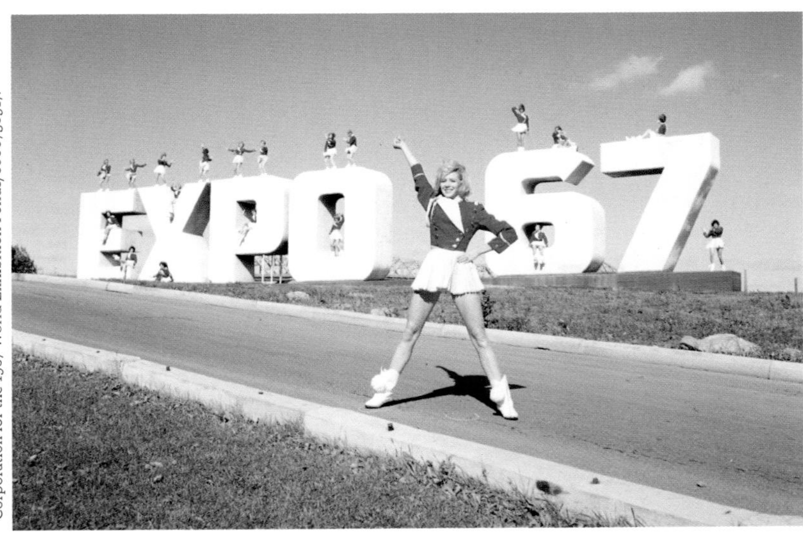

Majorettes around the "Expo 67" sign.

1967. Expo 67 opens in Montréal. It was the highlight of Canada's centennial celebrations, with sixty-two countries participating, along with thousands of private exhibitors and sponsors. The fair was originally awarded to Moscow, but the USSR cancelled in April 1962, allowing Montréal mayor Jean Drapeau to resubmit a bid to host the global event. With the shortened timeline, one of the great challenges was selecting an appropriate site. When Drapeau came up with the idea of enlarging one island in the St. Lawrence River and adding another, his plan was met with skepticism and derision by almost everyone. But he and his engineers persevered, and they soon began the momentous task of filling the river with millions of metric tonnes of rock and earth to create a magnificent and unique locale. The "Universal and International Exhibition" closed on October 29, having hosted more than fifty million visitors from around the world.

If You Build It, They Will Come

Jean Drapeau's plan was to enlarge Île Sainte-Hélène, an island park in the St. Lawrence, and create a wholly new island, called Île Notre-Dame, to become the fairgrounds of Expo 67. Île Sainte-Hélène was enlarged using earth excavated during the construction of the Montreal Metro. The nearby island, Île Notre-Dame, was built from scratch, also using excavated earth from the subway, as well as landfill from other projects. The site cost $40 million to build. The choice of the island locations in the St. Lawrence River also carried historical significance for Canada: as an important trade route and the access point for early explorers, the St. Lawrence symbolizes a link between Canada and the world.

BORN ON THIS DAY

1888 actress Florence La Badie

1939 drummer Jerry Mercer

1959 pianist Louis Lortie

1987 actress Emma Taylor-Isherwood

Also on This Day

1891.
The Canadian Pacific Railway steamer *Empress of India* first arrives in Vancouver, carrying 486 passengers and close to sixteen hundred tonnes of tea, silk, opium, and rice. The steamer continued to make regular trips around the world by way of the Suez Canal until it was sold in 1914 and re-fitted as a hospital ship for Indian troops during the First World War.

© Body Break.

Hal Johnson and Joanne McLeod keeping fit and having fun, undated.

1989. The TV segment *Body Break* first debuts on the CBC. Starring athletes Hal Johnson and Joanne McLeod, the short, informative spots were aimed at giving Canadians tips on healthy living and an active lifestyle. *Body Break*'s energetic hosts have also lent themselves to successful videos, equipment endorsements, and radio shows. The couple married in 1999, and in 2013 they competed on the reality show *The Amazing Race Canada*. Their motto "Keep fit and have fun!" has endured in pop culture.

BORN ON THIS DAY

First Black Victoria Cross winner William Hall
1827

1908
high jumper Ethel Catherwood

singer Ginette Reno
1946

1963
figure skater Lloyd Eisler

29 APRIL

Canada. Dept. of Mines and Technical Surveys/Library and Archives Canada/ C-022991.

Rockslide at Frank, Alberta, 1903.

1903. Eighty-two million tonnes of rock crash down the eastern slope of Turtle Mountain, burying a mine entrance and parts of the town of Frank, Northwest Territories (now Alberta). The Frank Slide swept across approximately 1.6 kilometres, engulfing roads, homes, and farms. While twenty-three men, women, and children were rescued from the rubble, more than ninety people were killed in what is still the country's deadliest rockslide. Turtle Mountain is a naturally unstable landscape, and earthquakes, erosion, and coal mining had, over time, combined to cause the disaster. Turtle Mountain is now monitored daily for any movement.

Historic Rockslides in Canada

Site, Date, Volume (m³), Damage

Rubble Creek, BC, 1855
25 million, unknown

Frank, AB, April 29, 1903
30 million, 90 deaths

Brazeau Lake, AB, July 1933
4.5 million, telephone lines

Hope, BC, January 9, 1965
47 million, 4 deaths, road buried

English Chief River, NT,
October 5, 1985, 7 million, none

BORN ON THIS DAY

1823 — industrialist and philanthropist Hart Massey

1924 — golfer Al Balding

1929 — entrepreneur and environmentalist Maurice Strong

1967 — hockey player Curtis Joseph

APRIL

Also on This Day

1905.
Human rights advocate John Peters Humphrey is born in Hampton, New Brunswick. The first director of the United Nation's Division of Human Rights, he was the principal drafter of the Universal Declaration of Human Rights, which was adopted in 1948.

Which folk singer popularized "Barrett's Privateers" and "Northwest Passage"? See November 29.

York University Libraries, Clara Thomas Archives & Special Collections, Toronto Telegram fonds, ASC05671.

Edith Fowke, photographed by Pete Geddes, at the Mariposa Folk Festival, August 1965.

1913. Folklorist Edith Fowke, an avid collector of folk song recordings, is born in Lumsden, Saskatchewan. After completing university, she moved to Toronto and began travelling throughout Ontario recording folk music. Fowke hosted CBC Radio's *Folk Song Time* from 1950 to 1963, produced several other radio programs, and published more than twenty books on folklore. Her collections, held mostly at the University of Calgary and at York University in Toronto, afford a fascinating glimpse into the lives of working Canadians.

BORN ON THIS DAY

- 1770 — explorer David Thompson
- 1928 — author Hugh Hood
- 1959 — Prime Minister Stephen Harper
- 1959 — actor Paul Gross
- 1971 — singer-songwriter Carolyn Dawn Johnson

MAY

The Five Most Damaging Floods in Canada

Location, Date, Floodwater level, Damages (today's $)

Fraser River, BC, June 1948
7.6 m, $20 million
Winnipeg, MB, April 22, 1950
9.2 m, $125.5 million
Toronto, ON, October 15, 1954
6 to 8 m, $25 million
Winisk, ON, May 16, 1986,
6 km inland, Town completely washed away
Saguenay, QC, July 19, 1996
2 m, $1.5 billion

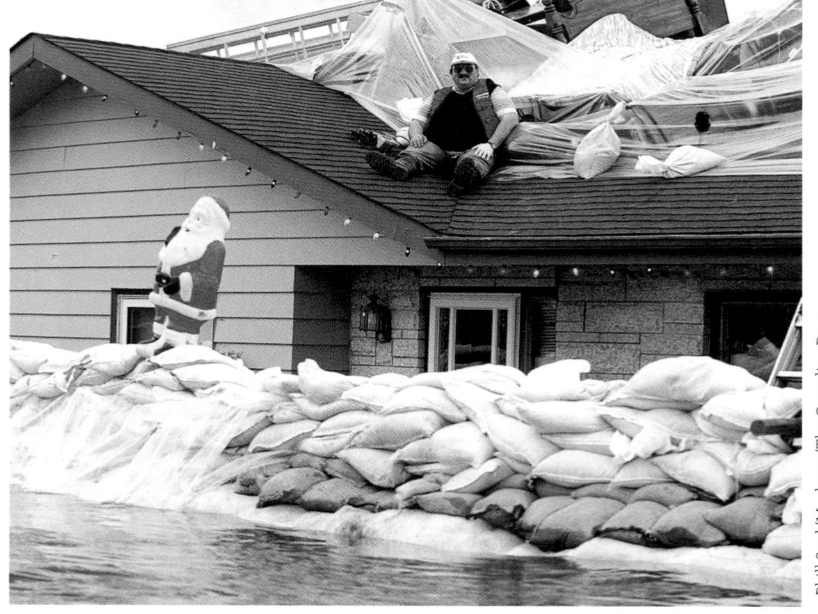

Phill Snel/Macleans/The Canadian Press.

A resident of Winnipeg on the roof of his house during the Red River Flood.

1997. The Red River reaches its peak in the worst flood in southern Manitoba since 1950. Winnipeg was protected by eight million sandbags and the Red River Floodway, a forty-eight-kilometre channel for diverting floodwaters. But a number of other communities, including Grand Forks and East Grand Forks, were inundated by the massive pool of water, which stretched all the way to the American border, devastating parts of North Dakota and Minnesota as well. In Manitoba, some 350 farms were flooded and nearly twenty-eight thousand residents were evacuated. In the aftermath, a joint Canada–US task force was created to help better predict flood risk in the future.

Which year did floodwaters threaten the Calgary Stampede?
See September 2.

BORN ON THIS DAY

1850 Governor General Prince Arthur, Duke of Connaught and Strathearn

1916 actor Glenn Ford

1939 composer Victor Davies

1979 hockey player Jennifer Botterill

Trading at the Hudson's Bay Company post in Coppermine (now Kugluktuk, Nunavut), 1949.

1670. The Hudson's Bay Company (HBC) is founded when King Charles II grants a charter to his cousin Prince Rupert and several partners. HBC's original name was the Governor and Company of Adventurers of England trading into Hudson's Bay. The company was granted wide powers, including exclusive trading rights in the territory traversed by rivers flowing into Hudson Bay. Part of this vast region, named Rupert's Land, would eventually become Manitoba. HBC is the oldest continually operated company in North America.

Also on This Day

1964.
Racehorse Northern Dancer wins the Kentucky Derby. Born in Oshawa, Ontario, on May 27, 1961, Northern Dancer was the first Canadian-bred horse to win the Derby; he also won the Queen's Plate later that same year. Despite a relatively short racing career, he built an enduring reputation for his stamina and his speed. After being retired from racing, he became a highly sought stud horse and is still considered by many racing enthusiasts to be the greatest stud horse in history.

BORN ON THIS DAY

1797 — physician and kerosene inventor Abraham Gesner

ca. 1844 — engineer and inventor Elijah McCoy

1920 — actor William Hutt

1925 — actor John Neville

1966 — executive and politician Belinda Stronach

1980 — skateboarder Pierre-Luc Gagnon

In Flanders Fields

In Flanders fields the poppies blow
Between the crosses, row on row,
That mark our place; and in the sky
The larks, still bravely singing, fly
Scarce heard amid the guns below.

We are the Dead. Short days ago
We lived, felt dawn, saw sunset glow,
Loved and were loved, and now we lie
In Flanders fields.

Take up our quarrel with the foe:
To you from failing hands we throw
The torch; be yours to hold it high.
If ye break faith with us who die
We shall not sleep, though poppies grow
In Flanders fields.

Library and Archives Canada/C-046284.

Lt.-Col. John McCrae and his dog, Bonneau, 1914.

1915. Physician, poet, and soldier John McCrae of Guelph, Ontario, writes the famous poem "In Flanders Fields." He is said to have composed it in twenty minutes during the Second Battle of Ypres, when Germans launched the first gas attacks of the war. During the bloody battle, McCrae's friend Alexis Helmer was killed in action, a loss that in part inspired the poem. "In Flanders Fields" was first published in December 1915 in the British magazine *Punch*. Within months, it became the most popular poem of the First World War. Its evocative use of the symbol of poppies blooming from the churned earth led to the tradition of using poppies as a sign of remembrance for those killed in service.

BORN ON THIS DAY

Father of Confederation Adams Archibald 1814

1881 Hockey Hall of Famer Joe Hall

opera singer Léopold Simoneau 1916

1926 curler Matt Baldwin

singer and actress Irenee (Irene) Byatt 1926

THE TORONTO STAR 100 1892–1992

TUESDAY May 5, 1992

Hundreds riot downtown after anti-racism protest

The front page of the May 5, 1992, issue of the *Toronto Star*.

1992. A daytime demonstration against the acquittal of police officers in the Rodney King case in Los Angeles descends into a nighttime riot on Toronto's Yonge Street. The two hundred or so demonstrators grew to more than a thousand and became increasingly belligerent, in what would later be called the Yonge Street Rebellion. While protest leaders attempted to keep activities peaceful, some demonstrators engaged in looting and vandalism, causing the media to decry the "America-style violence" of the young Black men. The riot did, however, prompt some Canadians to examine the root causes of Black frustration.

Notable Riots in Canada

September 7, 1907:
Asiatic Exclusion League Riot, Vancouver
August 16, 1933:
Christie Pits Riot, Toronto
March 17, 1955:
Richard Riot, Montréal
October 7, 1969:
Murray-Hill Riot, Montréal
August 7, 1971:
Gastown Riot, Vancouver
June 9, 1993:
Stanley Cup Riot, Montréal
April 20, 2001:
3rd Summit of the Americas Riot, Québec City
June 26–27, 2010:
G20 Summit Riot, Toronto
June 15, 2011:
Stanley Cup Riot, Vancouver

BORN ON THIS DAY

1928 trumpeter Maynard Ferguson

1954 speed skater and cyclist Sylvia Burka

1957 skier Kathy Kreiner

1977 actress Emily Perkins

Also on This Day

1893. Arctic explorer and ornithologist J. Dewey Soper is born in Guelph, Ontario. He helped determine the nesting grounds of the blue goose (more commonly called the snow goose), the result of a six-year search on Baffin Island that earned him the nickname "Blue Goose Soper." The Soper River on Baffin Island was named after him.

AP/The Canadian Press.

Ron Turcotte rides Secretariat during the ninety-ninth Kentucky Derby.

1973. New Brunswick–born jockey Ron Turcotte rides the legendary horse Secretariat to a record-setting victory (1 minute, 59.4 seconds) in the Kentucky Derby, the annual race at Churchill Downs in Louisville, Kentucky. Secretariat was the first Triple Crown winner in twenty-five years, and Turcotte became the first jockey in seventy-one years to ride Kentucky Derby–winning horses in consecutive years (he won the race on Riva Ridge in 1972). His strength as a jockey was often credited to his early years labouring as a lumberjack in New Brunswick. His career ended tragically on July 13, 1978, when he broke his back and was left partially paralyzed after falling from his horse at the Belmont track.

BORN ON THIS DAY

1796
explorer William Cormack

1915
dancer Betty Farrally

1938
figure skater Barbara Wagner

6 MAY

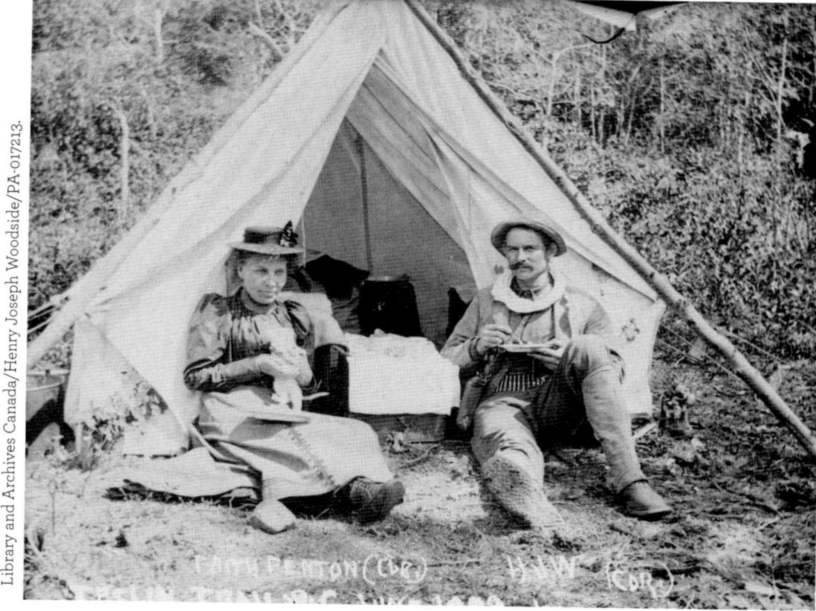

Faith Fenton and H.J. Woodside, correspondents with the Yukon Field Force, in Teslin Trail, British Columbia.

Timeline: There's Gold in Them Thar Hills

1851: Queen Charlotte Islands (Haida Gwaii), BC
1858: Fraser River Gold Rush, BC
1860: Cariboo Gold Rush, BC
1869: Omineca Gold Rush, BC
1896: Klondike Gold Rush, Yukon/Alaska

1898. The Yukon Field Force (YFF), consisting of 203 volunteers, leaves Ottawa for Dawson City, Yukon, to help the North-West Mounted Police (NWMP) under Sir Sam Steele maintain order during the Klondike Gold Rush. The YFF was composed of 191 men and 12 officers drawn from all three branches (cavalry, artillery, and infantry) of the Permanent Force of the Canadian Militia. Women played important roles as nurses and prison matrons in both the YFF and the NWMP from the earliest days of their involvement in the North. Faith Fenton, Canada's first female newspaper columnist, accompanied the YFF's nurses to the Yukon to cover the gold rush for the *Globe*. Half of the YFF force was withdrawn in September 1899, and the remainder, restyled as the Yukon Garrison, left a year later.

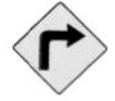
In which Canadian river was gold first discovered? See August 17.

BORN ON THIS DAY

1918 composer Godfrey Ridout
1972 hockey player Martin Brodeur
1979 skeleton racer Jon Montgomery
1982 gymnast Kyle Shewfelt
1986 actor Tyler Hynes

Also on This Day

1787. Jacques Viger, the first mayor of Montréal, is born in that city. He began his career in municipal administration, conducted a census in 1825 (to gather the details of his fellow citizens' lives), and was elected mayor in 1833, a year after the city was incorporated.

The Department of National Defence/Library and Archives Canada/PA-114617.

VE Day celebrations on Sparks Street in Ottawa.

1945. Germany capitulates unconditionally to the Allies at 2:41 a.m. local time in Reims, France. The First Canadian Army immediately moved forward to liberate the last German-held areas in the western Netherlands, including the great cities of Amsterdam and Rotterdam. "Every village, street and house," reported the headquarters of the 1st Canadian Infantry Division, "was decked with red, white and blue Dutch flags and orange streamers." VE (Victory in Europe) Day celebrations began on May 7, but they're now officially commemorated on May 8. When victory was declared, a two-day riot broke out in Halifax. Several thousand servicemen looted and vandalized the city's downtown, where the effects of wartime constraints were severely felt. VJ (or Victory over Japan) Day would be achieved on August 14 with the surrender of the Japanese, effectively ending the Second World War.

BORN ON THIS DAY

1893 hockey coach and manager Frank J. Selke

1894 politician George Drew

1939 Nobel Prize–winning biochemist Sidney Altman

1951 pianist Janina Fialkowska

1992 actor Alexander Ludwig

Gilles Villeneuve practising for the Grand Prix in Watkins Glen, New York, 1979.

Also on This Day

1818.
Father of Confederation Leonard Tilley is born in Gagetown, New Brunswick. Tilley actively promoted railway development, Confederation, and—unsuccessfully—Prohibition.

1982. Auto racer Gilles Villeneuve is killed in a qualifying session for the Grand Prix of Belgium, following a collision with another car at a speed of 225 km/h. In his brief career, Villeneuve was Canada's finest high-speed racer. In all, he started in sixty-seven Grand Prix races, winning six and appearing on the podium thirteen times. Montréal's Grand Prix circuit has been named for him. Decades later, Formula One watchers in Europe still rate Villeneuve high on the list of the all-time best drivers. His son, Jacques Villeneuve, carried on his legacy, becoming the first North American to win the Formula One racing championship in 1997.

BORN ON THIS DAY

"O Canada" lyricist and judge Adolphe-Basile Routhier
1839

1912
author and historian George Woodcock

author and activist Naomi Klein
1970

1976
singer-songwriter Martha Wainwright

Also on This Day

1992.
Methane gas escapes from the coal seam of the Westray Mine in Plymouth, Nova Scotia, causing an explosion and trapping twenty-six miners, none of whom survived. A public inquiry concluded that the mine had been badly mismanaged and the disaster could have been avoided. The mine was later dismantled and permanently sealed.

Library and Archives Canada/Orlando Scott Goff/R13796-2.

Gabriel Dumont, ca. 1886.

1885. Fewer than 350 Métis and First Nations, led by Louis Riel and Gabriel Dumont, resist Maj.-Gen. Frederick Middleton and his 800-man force for four days at Batoche, Saskatchewan, during the North-West Rebellion. The rebellion was the culmination of the discontent of the Métis, First Nations, and white settlers with the federal government, which governed the region from afar without representation in Ottawa. At the battle, the Métis were drawn out of their rifle pits by a frontal attack. Over twenty-five men from each side were killed. Riel surrendered a few days later, while Dumont fled to the United States. Batoche is now a National Historic Site.

BORN ON THIS DAY

- 1896 — Academy Award–winning art director Richard Day
- 1909 — fiddler and band leader Don Messer
- 1914 — country singer Hank Snow
- 1928 — figure skater Barbara Ann Scott
- 1956 — actress Wendy Crewson
- 1965 — Hockey Hall of Famer Steve Yzerman

10 MAY

McCord Museum/M15949.18.

St. Ann's Market, Montreal, 1839, **by James Duncan.**

1844. The capital of Canada is moved from Kingston, Canada West (formerly Upper Canada), to Montréal, Canada East (formerly Lower Canada), over fears that Kingston's location made it overly vulnerable to American attack. With 44,591 inhabitants, Montréal was a booming city with a rising merchant class. But in 1857, the capital was relocated once more—this time to Ottawa. The final city was chosen by Queen Victoria because it was the only significant settlement on the border of Canada East and Canada West, and it was connected to the Grand Trunk Railway and American rail networks, making it a desirable location ready for growth.

Also on This Day

1929.
Author Antonine Maillet is born in Bouctouche, New Brunswick. She is especially known and praised for using Acadian themes in her writing, and is also highly celebrated in France. Her major works include *La Sagouine* and *Pélagie-la-Charrette*, which charts the return home of the Acadian people after their expulsion.

Why were the Acadians expelled from the East Coast in 1755? See July 28.

BORN ON THIS DAY

1863 explorer James Tyrrell

1929 author Peter C. Newman

1965 supermodel Linda Evangelista

Also on This Day

1943.
Skier Nancy Greene is born in Ottawa. She was Canada's top ski racer through the 1960s, winning gold and silver medals at the 1968 Winter Olympics and overall world cup titles in 1967 and 1968. Her total of thirteen world cup victories is a Canadian record.

Tom Hanson/The Canadian Press.

Nisga'a leaders outside the Senate chamber on Parliament Hill.

2000. The Nisga'a Final Agreement, British Columbia's first modern land claim agreement, comes into effect. After years of negotiations, the historic agreement-in-principle with Canada and BC had been signed and ratified on March 22, 1996, by the Nisga'a peoples. The agreement included the transfer of nearly two thousand square kilometres of Crown land to the Nisga'a nation, the creation of Bear Glacier Provincial Park, a significant measure of self-government for the Nisga'a, and the establishment of a massive water reservation. The landmark agreement was the first in BC to constitutionally enshrine an Aboriginal peoples' right to self-government.

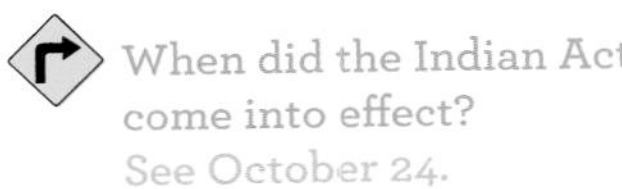

When did the Indian Act come into effect?
See October 24.

BORN ON THIS DAY

1918
author Sheila Burnford

1927
comedian Mort Sahl

1982
actor Cory Monteith

Bill Becker/The Canadian Press.

Farley Mowat, undated.

1921. Environmentalist, activist, and author Farley Mowat is born in Belleville, Ontario. A passionate environmentalist and one of Canada's most widely read writers, Mowat often wrote about the natural world, and particularly offered a portrait of the beautiful and complex Canadian North. One of his most famous works, *Never Cry Wolf,* based on his own experiences studying Arctic wolves, is credited with altering the negative perception of these animals as vicious killers. While he was sometimes criticized for straying from hard facts in his accounts, he is praised for shedding light on serious environmental issues and the plight of the Inuit, and for bringing about substantive changes of policy in Ottawa. Mowat's books have been translated into fifty-two languages and have sold more than seventeen million copies in more than forty countries around the world.

Notable Works of Farley Mowat

1952: *People of the Deer*
1955: *The Regiment*
1957: *The Dog Who Wouldn't Be*
1961: *Owls in the Family*
1963: *Never Cry Wolf*
1967: *The Polar Passion*
1979: *And No Birds Sang*
1987: *Woman in the Mists: The Story of Dian Fossey and the Mountain Gorillas of Africa*
1998: *The Farfarers: Before the Norse*
2006: *Bay of Spirits: A Love Story*

BORN ON THIS DAY

Kid in the Hall Bruce McCulloch
1961

1970
golfer Mike Weir

A Canadian Icon

An excerpt from "The Hockey Sweater" was featured on the five-dollar bill from 2002 until the new polymer fives were released in November 2013. Alongside an illustration of children playing hockey, skating, and tobogganing was the introductory sentence of Carrier's most enduring story: "The winters of my childhood were long, long seasons. We lived in three places—the school, the church and the skating rink—but our real life was on the skating rink."

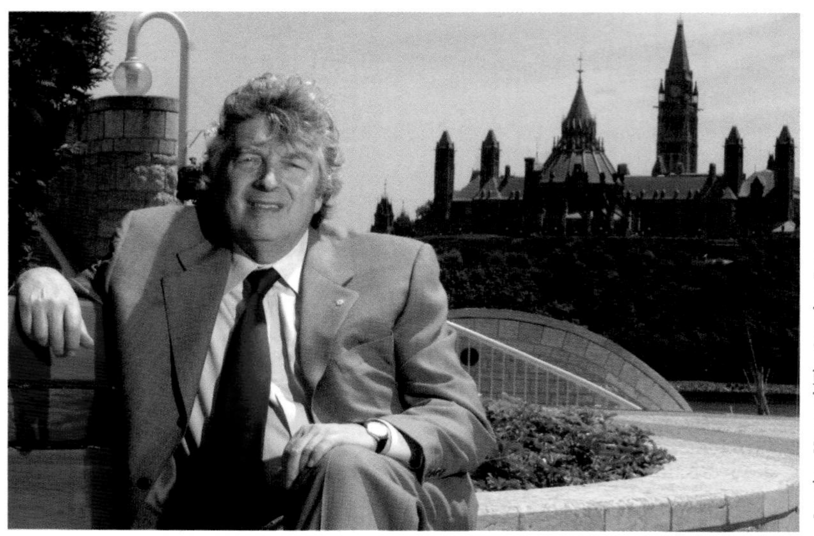

Jonathan Hayward/The Canadian Press.

Roch Carrier in Hull, Québec.

1937. Poet and storyteller Roch Carrier is born in Beauce, Québec. Carrier's career in Québec and abroad was established by the work *La Guerre, Yes Sir!* (1968), a surreal nightmare vision of Québec's Second World War conscription crisis. His most famous piece, however, was "The Hockey Sweater" (originally published as a short story), in which a young Ste-Justine boy receives a Toronto Maple Leafs sweater from Eaton's instead of a Montreal Canadiens sweater, and as a result is ostracized by other children. Based on a childhood recollection, the story grew from a CBC Radio request that Carrier reflect on the culture and desires of Québec, which at the time was swept up with separatist sentiment and debate about the future of the province within Canada. In 1980 the story was made into an animated short film that has been seen by millions around the world, and in 1984 it was published as a children's book that quickly became a modern classic.

BORN ON THIS DAY

1904 poet Earle Birney

1936 dancer Patricia Beatty

The Canadian Press/Kelowna Daily/Courier Darren Handschuh

Canadian rocker Tom Cochrane, performing at Skyreach Place in Kelowna, BC, in 1999.

1953. Tom Cochrane, the popular Canadian singer-songwriter, is born in Lynn Lake, Manitoba, a community of approximately 675 residents. Cochrane started his music career as a solo artist before he joined the group Red Rider in the 1980s. The group released seven increasingly popular albums in the years between 1980 and 1989, achieving US radio success with *Neruda* (1983, inspired in part by Chilean poet Pablo Neruda) and scoring Canadian hits with such songs as "Human Race," "Boy Inside the Man," and "Big League." He later achieved significant international success under his own name with *Mad Mad World* (1991). Led by the international top-ten anthem "Life Is a Highway," the album sold more than two million copies worldwide, earned Cochrane a Grammy Award nomination, and resulted in a sweep of major trophies at the 1992 Juno Awards.

Also on This Day

1914.
Oil is discovered in Turner Valley, southwest of Calgary. This was the first major natural gas and oil field discovered in Alberta, and it ushered in the province's oil age.

BORN ON THIS DAY

Prime Minister Frederick William Borden
1847

1929
goaltender Lorne John "Gump" Worsley

hockey player Jayna Hefford
1977

Timeline: Significant Strikes in Canada

1872: Toronto Printers' Strike and the Nine-Hour Movement
1904: CPR Workers' Strike
1919: Winnipeg General Strike
1925: Davis Day Coal Miners' Strike, NS
1937: Québec Textile Mill Workers' Strike
1938: Bloody Sunday, Vancouver
1946: Stelco Strike, Hamilton, ON
1949: Asbestos Strike, Asbestos, QC
1978: Inco Strike, Sudbury, ON
1996: GM Strike, Oshawa, ON

The Archives of Manitoba/Foote 1690, N2756.

The Winnipeg General Strike, at Portage and Main Street.

1919. A general strike is called by the Winnipeg Trades and Labour Council. Within hours, an eerie calm had descended on the streets of Winnipeg: streetcars and delivery wagons sat idle as some thirty thousand tradesmen, labourers, and city and provincial employees walked off the job, leaving the city paralyzed. Workers sought better collective bargaining opportunities, better wages, and the improvement of often dreadful working conditions. The strike lasted forty-two days and exposed bitter class divisions in Canadian society. The strikers returned to work on June 26, following pressure from the government and the Citizen's Committee, a group of a thousand influential manufacturers, bankers, and politicians who had declared the strike a conspiracy to fuel fears of communism and block conciliation. It was North America's first general strike.

BORN ON THIS DAY

1770 politician and brewer Ezekiel Hart

1906 astronomer Robert Petrie

1914 Hockey Hall of Famer Walter "Turk" Broda

1923 architect Ron Thom

1978 actress Caroline Dhavernas

1981 baseball player Justin Morneau

Library and Archives Canada/PA-021904.

Charles Hays (far left) on a train platform with (from right to left) D'Arcy-Tate, W. Deet, Alfred W. Smithers, A.B. Atwater, 1910.

1856. Charles Hays, president of the Grand Trunk Pacific Railway, is born in Rock Island, Illinois. He came to Canada in 1896 as general manager of the Grand Trunk Railway (GTR), becoming president in 1909. He also created its subsidiary, the Grand Trunk Pacific Railway. Under his directorship, the GTR suffered intense labour strife, and one of Wilfrid Laurier's ministers described Hays as heartless, cruel, and tyrannical. In April 1912, he went down with the *Titanic* when it sunk in the North Atlantic.

Which Canadian ship capsized with a crew of 29 in 1975? See November 10.

The Titanic *and Canada*

After the sinking of the *Titanic*, the White Star Line dispatched four Canadian ships to begin retrieval efforts. Canadian ships recovered 328 of the 337 bodies found by all ships, with 119 of those people buried at sea. A number of those who died aboard the *Titanic* are buried in various Halifax cemeteries, their graves marked with plain granite headstones paid for by the White Star Line. Charles Hays's body was recovered on April 26; he was identified by a number of papers on his person and a watch engraved with his name. He was buried in Montréal. In 1997 Canadian director James Cameron retold the story of the *Titanic* in what would become an all-time box-office champion with worldwide receipts in excess of $2.1 billion.

BORN ON THIS DAY

astronaut Dafydd "Dave" Williams
1954

1961
Kid in the Hall Kevin McDonald

triathlete Simon Whitfield
1975

1977
hockey player Jean-Sébastien Giguère

Coronation Park

On May 22, 1939, the monarchs attended a celebration near Toronto's Coronation Park. As they drove by, First World War veterans and schoolchildren lining the road placed shovelfuls of soil on the roots of 123 maple trees. The road led to Coronation Park, which has at its centre a royal oak planted in honour of King George VI. Surrounding the oak are other trees, including maples, representing veterans of the First World War, the Fenian Raids, the North-West Rebellion, and the South African War. Later more trees were added to honour Second World War veterans.

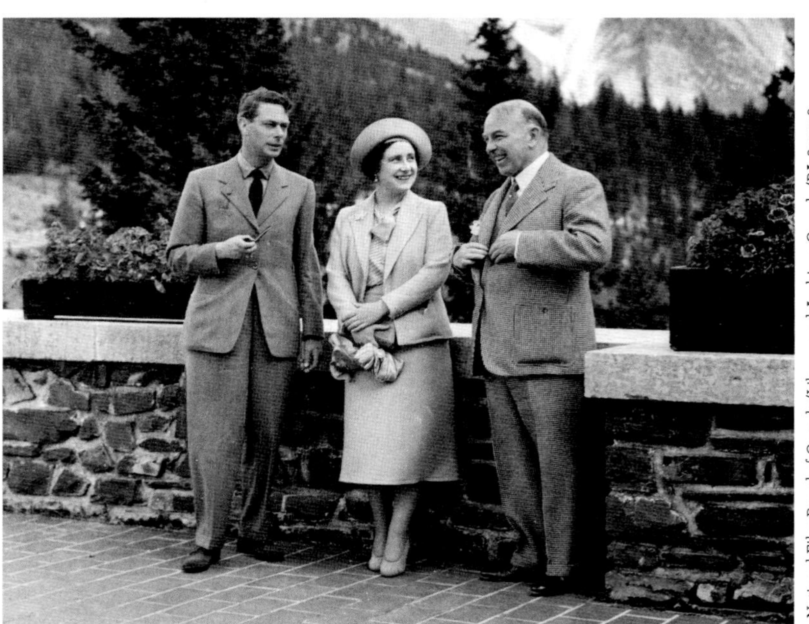

National Film Board of Canada/Library and Archives Canada/PA-802278.

Queen Elizabeth, King George VI, and William Lyon Mackenzie King at the Banff Springs Hotel.

1939. King George VI and Queen Elizabeth arrive in Canada for a state visit, the first reigning monarchs to visit any Commonwealth country. The extensive tour was planned to solidify Canadian support for Britain on the eve of the Second World War and included a visit to Toronto's Coronation Park, site of a memorial created in honour of both George VI's coronation and Canadian war veterans. During her stay, Queen Elizabeth was asked whether she was English or Scottish and famously replied, "Since we reached Québec, I've been Canadian." She made her last visit to Canada fifty years later, at the age of eighty-nine.

BORN ON THIS DAY

writer Anna Jameson

1794

1898

Group of Seven artist A.J. Casson

The Department of National Defence/Library and Archives Canada/PA-022751.

Officers of the first French Canadian battalion to be formed under conscription, undated.

1917. Prime Minister Robert Borden announces the introduction of conscription. By late 1916, the relentless human toll of the First World War and the terrible casualties at the front in Europe had left Canadian commanders overseas in desperate need of reinforcements. Borden believed it essential to assist the men in the trenches, and though he had promised not to introduce conscription, he decided that compulsory service was necessary. To pass the controversial Military Service Act, he approached the Liberal leader, Sir Wilfrid Laurier, about forming a coalition government. Laurier, who believed Québec would never agree to conscription (French Canadians were among the measure's fiercest opponents), refused, but Borden was able to put together a loose alliance of individual parliamentarians to get the act through. In 1917, he was returned to power in a bitterly contested election.

The imposition of conscription on reluctant French Canadians was a particular failure and bitterly divided the country along French–English lines. Over the Easter weekend of 1918, anti-conscription riots in Québec City left four civilians dead.

Did You Know?

The Borden government helped ensure its 1917 election victory by passing legislation designed to enfranchise likely supporters. The Military Voters Act extended the vote to men and women serving overseas, while the Wartime Elections Act allowed the wives, mothers, and sisters of servicemen to vote.

All conscientious objectors and immigrants who had come from enemy countries within the previous fifteen years were disenfranchised.

Of the 404,395 men eligible for conscription, 380,510 applied for an exemption.

Approximately 125,000 conscripted men were eventually enlisted; of those, only 24,132 went overseas.

BORN ON THIS DAY

politician Gordon O'Connor 1939

hockey player Marty McSorley 1963

hockey player Vicky Sunohara 1970

singer-songwriter Chantal Kreviazuk 1974

MAY

19

The Ten Largest National Parks in Canada

Park; Location; Area (km2); Founded

1. **Wood Buffalo;** Alberta and Northwest Territories; 44,778; 1922
2. **Quttinirpaaq Nunavut;** 37,775; 1988
3. **Nahanni;** Northwest Territories; 30,000; 1976
4. **Sirmilik;** Nunavut; 22,252; 1999
5. **Kluane;** Yukon; 22,061; 1972
6. **Auyuittuq;** Nunavut; 19,089; 1976
7. **Ukkusiksalik;** Nunavut; 20,880; 2003
8. **Tuktut Nogait;** Northwest Territories; 18,181; 1996
9. **Aulavik;** Northwest Territories; 12,200; 1992
10. **Wapusk;** Manitoba; 11,475; 1996

City of Edmonton Archives/EA-10-1939.

Banff, 1909: Looking north across the Bow River with Mather's skating rink in the foreground and Mount Norquay in the background.

1911. The world's first national parks service, Canada's Dominion Parks Branch, is established under the authority of the Department of the Interior. James B. Harkin, the first commissioner, served from 1911 to 1936. During his tenure, ten national parks were established: Elk Island (1913), Mount Revelstoke (1914), Thousand Islands (1914), Point Pelee (1918), Kootenay (1920), Wood Buffalo (1922), Prince Albert (1927), Riding Mountain (1930), Georgian Bay Islands (1930), and Cape Breton Highlands (1936). Prior to the creation of the Dominion Parks Branch, Canada had set aside several areas of land for public use, the first being what is now Banff National Park, in 1885. Now known as Parks Canada, the agency celebrates Canada's natural and cultural heritage.

BORN ON THIS DAY

1908 track athlete Percy Williams

1925 actor Guy Provost

1926 philosopher and poet Francis Sparshott

1977 voice actress Kelly Sheridan

20 MAY

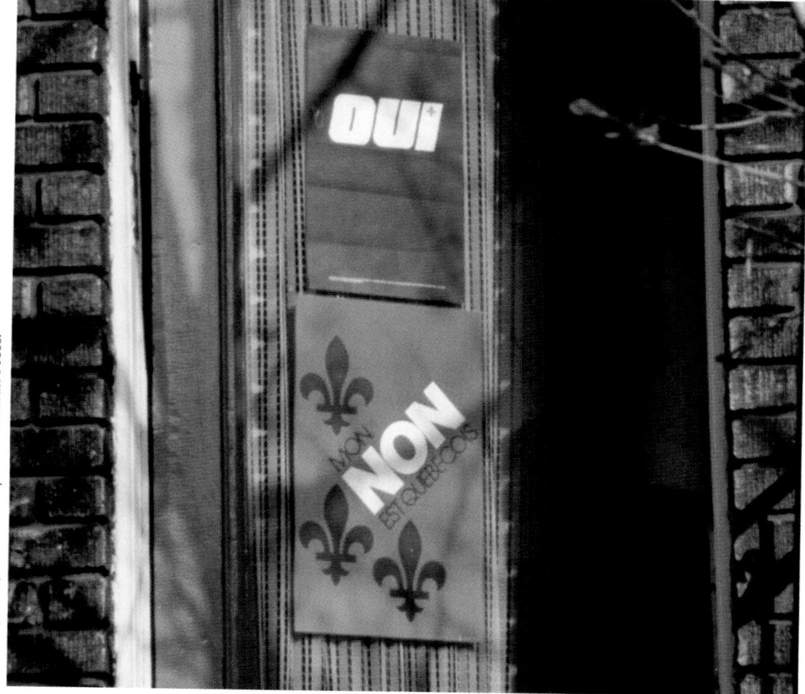

Boris Spremo/Toronto Star/The Canadian Press.

Posters displayed during the Québec referendum.

Asking the Nation

In its history, Canada has staged only three nationwide plebiscites:

September 29, 1898: National referendum on Prohibition: 51.3% in favour

April 27, 1942: Canadian conscription plebiscite: 64.1% in favour

October 26, 1992: National referendum on the Charlottetown Accord: 45.7% in favour

1980. A referendum on sovereignty-association is held in Québec, thus honouring the promise the Parti Québécois government had made in 1976 to hold a referendum before taking steps to separate from Canada. Québec voters were asked to provide their government "a mandate to negotiate" an agreement giving the province political independence while still retaining its economic ties to the rest of Canada. After an often emotional campaign, voters rejected the proposal by a margin of 60 to 40 percent. Debate over Québec's constitutional status would arise again during discussions surrounding the Meech Lake and Charlottetown Accords (1987 and 1992, respectively), culminating in a similar referendum in 1995. This one was much more narrowly won by the pro-federalist (or No) side, with a majority of just 50.58 percent.

BORN ON THIS DAY

feminist and educator Eliza Ritchie
1856

1940
figure skater and politician Otto Jelinek

hockey player Stan Mikita
1940

1949
actor Dave Thomas

Other Notable Works by Moshe Safdie

Habitat, built in Montréal for Expo 67

Major addition—the Jean-Noël Desmarais Pavilion—to the Montreal Museum of Fine Arts (1991)

Expansion of Ottawa City Hall (1994)

Library Square, Vancouver Public Library—with DA Architects (1995)

New Terminal 3 at Ben Gurion International Airport in Tel Aviv, Israel—with Skidmore, Owings and Merril; Karmi Architects; and Lissar Eldar Architects (2004)

Yad Vashem Holocaust History Museum in Jerusalem, Israel (2005)

New Terminal 1 at Lester B. Pearson Airport in Toronto—with Airport Architects Canada (2007)

United States Institute of Peace Headquarters in Washington, DC (2011)

Crystal Bridges Museum of American Art in Bentonville, AR (2011)

Kauffman Center for the Performing Arts in Kansas City, MO (2011)

Outside the National Gallery of Canada, undated.

1988. The new National Gallery of Canada, designed by famous architect Moshe Safdie, officially opens in Ottawa. While curators had been collecting artwork since 1880, it was not until 1913 that Parliament adopted an act to incorporate the National Gallery and appoint a board of trustees. After more than a century of occupying borrowed space, the gallery was finally given a home in its present location on Sussex Drive. Today its collections contain 36,000 works of art, as well as 125,000 images held in the Canadian Museum of Contemporary Photography.

BORN ON THIS DAY

1887 first Aboriginal senator James Gladstone (Akay-na-muka)

1917 actor Raymond Burr

22 MAY

A pair of vintage duelling pistols.

1838. In Verdun, Lower Canada (now Québec), lawyer Robert Sweeny shoots and kills Maj. Henry Warde in the last fatal duel recorded in Canada. Duelling was a formal armed combat between two people in the presence of witnesses, to settle differences or a point of honour. Causes varied and were often trivial. In this case, Major Warde had committed the error of sending a love letter to Mrs. Sweeny. Duels were recorded in New France as early as 1646; the last known duel in what is now Canada occurred in 1873 in St. John's, Newfoundland—an ultimately harmless shootout in which the seconds had loaded the pistols with blanks.

Also on This Day

1970.
The Vancouver Canucks join the National Hockey League for a price of $6 million. Their first game—which they lost to the Los Angeles Kings—was on October 9 of that year. The team won its first playoff series in 1982, defeating the Calgary Flames and advancing to (but ultimately losing) the Stanley Cup finals against the New York Islanders.

BORN ON THIS DAY

1851 politician and chocolate company co-founder Gilbert White Ganong

1883 Hockey Hall of Famer Tommy Phillips

1940 actor Michael Sarrazin

1942 actress Barbara Parkins

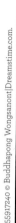

1958 singer-songwriter Lisa Dalbello

Timeline: The Komagata Maru *Incident*

May 23, 1914: The *Komagata Maru* anchors at Vancouver.
June 1, 1914: Officials refuse to allow passengers to disembark, with the exception of twenty men who'd previously resided in Canada.
June 23, 1914: Twelve hundred Vancouver residents demand the government expel the ship.
July 6, 1914: The British Columbia Court of Appeal upholds Canada's "continuous journey" policy.
July 17, 1914: Passengers refuse to allow the ship to move from the harbour. At night, police and immigration officers attempt to board the *Komagata Maru* but are chased off.
July 23, 1914: Prime Minister Robert Borden orders *HMCS Rainbow* to escort the *Komagata Maru* from Canadian waters.
September 29, 1914: Indian police kill twenty *Komagata Maru* passengers near Calcutta during a conflict in which officers try to force the passengers onto a train bound for Punjab.

Vancouver Public Library/16639.

Baba Gurdit Singh (left) and other passengers on board the *Komagata Maru*, 1914.

1914. The ship *Komagata Maru* arrives in Vancouver carrying at least 337 Sikh immigrants, about 12 Hindu immigrants, and approximately 27 Muslim immigrants—all British subjects of Indian origin. The ship was not allowed to dock, however, and most of the passengers were detained on board. At the time, East Indians were kept out of Canada by an order-in-council requiring them to come to the country by continuous passage from their homeland—despite the fact that no steamship line provided that service. Passengers on the *Komagata Maru* waited for two months while immigration officials manoeuvred to keep them out of court and their leaders negotiated departure terms. The ship was finally forced out of Vancouver on July 23. It sailed for Calcutta, where it was met by police suspicious of the passengers' politics. Twenty passengers were killed after fighting broke out when some resisted arrest. The affair strengthened Indian nationalist feeling, but it did not significantly soften Canadian immigration law.

BORN ON THIS DAY

1928

singer-songwriter Pauline Julien

1929

singer and restaurateur Joso Špralja

1937

singer-songwriter Jacqueline Lemay

24

MAY

GRAND
CAMP FIRE
AND CIRCUS
OF SPORTS
In Aid of
The Great War Veterans'
Home
LANSDOWNE PARK
On Victoria Day
May 24th, 1917
CANADIAN AT YPRES

Library and Archives Canada/1983-28-518.

A poster advertising a Victoria Day campfire, 1917.

1902. Victoria Day is observed as a legal holiday for the first time. Prime Minister Wilfrid Laurier designated May 24, Queen Victoria's birthday, as the date for the holiday, which had been celebrated unofficially in Canada since before Confederation. Today it marks the birthdays of Queen Victoria and Queen Elizabeth II. In 1952, the date was changed to the first Monday preceding May 25. Quebecers, whose attitude to the British monarchy is complex, enjoy the holiday under the name of *Journée nationale des patriots* (National Patriots' Day).

Also on This Day

1930.
Wildlife artist and naturalist Robert Bateman is born in Toronto. Among the world's most celebrated wildlife artists, he is also known for raising awareness of vanishing habitats and endangered species.

BORN ON THIS DAY

1900 athlete and politician Lionel Conacher

1933 author Marian Engel

1938 actor Tommy Chong

1948 poet Lorna Crozier

1975 speed skater Marc Gagnon

MAY 25

© Michael Sunderland.

The Tomb of the Unknown Soldier, Ottawa.

2000. The body of a Canadian soldier killed in France is exhumed near Vimy Ridge, the first major battle at which Canadian troops from all branches of service fought as a combined force. The body was later carried to the National War Memorial in Ottawa by an RCMP horse-drawn gun carriage and interred at a ceremony memorializing the twenty-eight thousand Canadian soldiers who have died in battle but have no known grave. Each year, Remembrance Day ceremonies are held at this site—the Tomb of the Unknown Soldier—and Canadians deposit their poppies to pay their respects. The headstone that had originally marked the grave of the unknown soldier in France is now on display at the Canadian War Museum.

Also on This Day

1963.
Actor and comedian Mike Myers is born in Scarborough, Ontario. Myers has played numerous memorable characters during his career in film and television, including the lead in *Wayne's World* and its sequel, and the title character in the *Austin Powers* film series. He also voiced the titular character in the *Shrek* film franchise.

BORN ON THIS DAY

1879
financier and politician Lord Beaverbrook (Max Aitken)

1900
poet Alain Grandbois

1935
author W.P. Kinsella

26 MAY

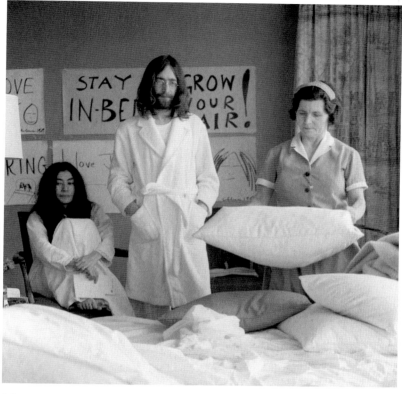

Charles Ley/Mirrorpix/The Canadian Press.

John Lennon and Yoko Ono take a break from their bed-in.

1969. Music legend John Lennon and his wife, Yoko Ono, arrive in Montréal and check into the Queen Elizabeth Hotel, beginning their second celebrated Bed-In for Peace. During their week-long stay, which was in part a protest against the Vietnam War, the couple met with famous guests, such as psychologist Timothy Leary, poet Allen Ginsberg, and Québec separatist Jacques Larue-Langlois. The legacy of the events was the song "Give Peace a Chance," which was written and recorded that week.

Also on This Day

1874.
The Dominion Elections Act gets royal assent. This legislation required that all votes be cast on the same day, introduced the secret ballot, and eliminated property qualifications for candidates. In 1948, the last of the property ownership requirements for voting were also abolished.

BORN ON THIS DAY

Senator Muriel McQueen Fergusson
1899

actor Jay Silverheels
1912

opera singer Teresa Stratas
1938

author Aritha van Herk
1954

archer Lucille Lessard
1957

Portage in the Park

Portaging remains common practice, especially in Canada's national and provincial parks. The portage is a path by land around an interruption in a water route. The first such trails around waterfalls and rapids were blazed by moose and adopted by Aboriginal peoples, who carried light birchbark canoes across them. Later, voyageurs navigating the fur trade routes portaged crafts laden with heavy goods, sometimes at their peril. Portage des Morts, in Ontario's Quetico Provincial Park, is named for a voyageur crushed to death by the weight of his own canoe.

Which notable Canadian painter disappeared in Canoe Lake in 1917? See July 8.

Courtesy Laurentiu Florea.

Lookout at Algonquin Park.

1893. The Ontario government creates Algonquin Park, Canada's first provincial park. Covering 7,630 square kilometres across the southern edge of the Canadian Shield, between Georgian Bay and the Ottawa River, the park consists mainly of Precambrian granites smoothed and gouged by ice sheets that receded ten thousand years ago. While the land was used for hunting and fishing by the Aboriginal peoples from whom it takes its name, it did not see large-scale settlement until loggers arrived in the 1800s, seeking to harvest its large white pine trees. The park was established to create a wildlife sanctuary and protect the headwaters of five major rivers that pool there. Algonquin Park is home to countless rivers, thousands of lakes, and stunning wildlife, including a large population of moose and black bears, and over two hundred bird species.

BORN ON THIS DAY

actress Lucile Watson
1879

1933
broadcasting entrepreneur Ted Rogers

singer-songwriter Bruce Cockburn
1945

1971
model Monika Schnarre

28 MAY

The Dionne Quintuplets with their parents, nurse, and guardian, 1939.

> *Also on This Day*
>
> **1944.** Singer-songwriter Rita MacNeil is born in Big Pond, Nova Scotia. Known as Cape Breton's first lady of song, MacNeil recorded many popular tunes, including "Home I'll Be," "Working Man," and "Flying on Your Own." When she died in 2013, flags in Cape Breton Island flew at half-mast.

1934. The Dionne Quintuplets are born to Oliva and Elzire Dionne in Corbeil, Ontario. Annette, Emilie, Yvonne, Cecile, and Marie were the first quintuplets to survive for more than a few days. This miracle, along with the poverty of their French Canadian parents and a controversy over their guardianship, made them the sensation of the 1930s. Fearing private exploitation, the Ontario government removed the girls from their parents and placed them in a specially built hospital under the care of Dr. Allan Roy Dafoe, who had delivered them. Oliva Dionne fought a nine-year battle to regain custody of his daughters. In the interim, they became the country's biggest tourist attraction and a $500-million asset to the province. Three million people trekked to "Quintland" to watch the babies at play behind a one-way screen. It wasn't until 1987 that another set of quints was born in Canada.

In spite of the millions made by the province, the Dionnes discovered that their trust fund contained only $800,000 when they gained access to it at the age of twenty-one. In 1998, the surviving three sisters (Annette, Cecile, and Yvonne) sued the government of Ontario for the lost money and received $4 million in compensation for their exploitation as children.

BORN ON THIS DAY

comedian Johnny Wayne
1918

1947
cartoonist Lynn Johnston

Also on This Day

1970.
The Hudson's Bay Company receives a Canadian charter, transferring its headquarters from London to Winnipeg. Its head offices are now in Toronto, and it remains the oldest chartered company in the world.

Library and Archives Canada/Royal Canadian Mounted Police/e003894952.

The *St. Roch* arriving in Vancouver, 1954.

1950. The RCMP ship *St. Roch* reaches Halifax after passing through the Panama Canal from Vancouver. A wooden schooner powered by sails and a diesel engine, she was the first ship to circumnavigate North America. The *St. Roch* had been launched in North Vancouver in May 1928 for RCMP operations in the Arctic, whose crushing sea ice she was built to withstand. Her expeditions and presence would strengthen Canadian claims of Arctic sovereignty. In 1954, the city of Vancouver purchased the *St. Roch*, and the federal government declared her a National Historic Site in 1962. Today the ship is in dry dock at the Vancouver Maritime Museum.

BORN ON THIS DAY

actress Beatrice Lillie
1894

1896
dancer Lillian Powell

TV host Roy Bonisteel
1930

1948
actor Nick Mancuso

Fred Chartrand/The Canadian Press.

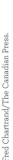

David Milgaard with his mother, Joyce, outside the Supreme Court of Canada, 1999.

1969. Sixteen-year-old David Milgaard is arrested in Prince George, British Columbia. The arrest came after police were tipped off by Milgaard's friend Albert Cadrain. Eight months later, Milgaard was convicted of murdering nursing student Gail Miller in Saskatoon and sentenced to life in prison. He served twenty-three years before the Supreme Court of Canada recommended a new trial, based on reviewed evidence and recanted testimony. Saskatchewan chose not to prosecute Milgaard again, and he was released. In 1997, DNA evidence cleared his name, and the Saskatchewan government formally apologized for his wrongful conviction. These events inspired the Tragically Hip's 1992 song "Wheat Kings."

Also on This Day

1961.
Over 254 millimetres of rain falls in less than one hour near Buffalo Gap, Saskatchewan. In duration, this was the greatest flash flood in Canadian history.

BORN ON THIS DAY

1890
physicist John Stuart Foster

1946
Royal Canadian Air Farce member Don Ferguson

1947
golfer Jocelyne Bourassa

1959
curler Randy Ferbey

Corey Hart Discography

1983: *First Offense*
1985: *Boy in the Box*
1986: *Fields of Fire*
1988: *Young Man Running*
1990: *Bang!*
1991: *The Singles*
1992: *Attitude & Virtue*
1996: *Corey Hart*
1999: *Jade*
2014: *Ten Thousand Horses*

Corey Hart.

How many hit singles did Bryan Adams's album *Reckless* include? See November 5.

1962. Corey Hart, a popular Canadian singer-songwriter, is born in Montréal. Hart rocketed onto the music scene in 1983 with the release of the international hit "Sunglasses at Night" from the album *First Offense*. Two years later, he released a second album, *Boy in the Box*, which sold one million copies in Canada alone, equalling a mark established by Bryan Adams's *Reckless*. The record included Hart's biggest hit, "Never Surrender," which won the 1985 Juno Award for single of the year. Between 1984 and 1990, Hart sold over ten million records and earned nine US top-forty *Billboard* hits.

BORN ON THIS DAY

1865
astronomer Clarence Chant

1903
Hockey Hall of Famer Tiny Thompson

JUNE

Also on This Day

1875.
Construction begins on the Canadian Pacific Railway. The "first sod" on the main line was turned near present-day Thunder Bay, Ontario. On November 7, 1885, the last spike was driven home at Craigellachie, British Columbia, completing the Confederation dream of a transcontinental railway.

Alanis Morissette performing on stage, 1995.

1974. Singer-songwriter and performer Alanis Morissette is born in Ottawa. Morissette wrote her first song at age nine and released her first (independent) single at eleven. She was originally known as a mall-touring teen idol and later appeared as a regular on the syndicated TV series *You Can't Do That on Television*. Morissette rocketed up the charts with her major label debut, the dance-pop album *Alanis*, for which she received the 1992 Juno Award for most promising female vocalist. By 1995, she had moved toward angst-driven alternative rock with the album *Jagged Little Pill*, which sold an astounding thirty-three million copies worldwide. The following year, at age twenty-one, Morissette won four Grammy Awards, including one for album of the year.

Which Canadian singer started performing in her family's restaurant when she was twelve?
See December 17.

BORN ON THIS DAY

1823 geologist Henry Hind

1941 actor Richard Donat

Library and Archives Canada/William Rider-Rider/PA-001654.

Capt. Billy Bishop.

1917. First World War pilot William Avery "Billy" Bishop is carrying out an early morning raid on a German airfield near Estourmel, France, when he discovers and destroys several aircraft on the ground. He received the Victoria Cross for this solo attack—making him the first Canadian airman to be accorded the honour. His last major action of the First World War was on June 19, 1918, when he claimed five enemy aircraft. Over the course of the war, Bishop was the top-scoring Canadian and imperial ace, and was credited with seventy-two victories. After the war, he and fellow fighter pilot W.G. Barker started a short-lived commercial flying enterprise.

A Selection of Billy Bishop's Awards

- Victoria Cross
- Order of the Bath (Companion)
- Distinguished Service Order
- Military Cross
- Distinguished Flying Cross
- 1914–15 Star
- Canadian Volunteer Service Medal
- War Medal 1939–1945
- King George V Silver Jubilee Medal
- King George VI Coronation Medal
- Queen Elizabeth II Coronation Medal
- British War Medal
- Victory Medal with MID
- Canadian Efficiency Decoration with Bar
- *Legion d'honneur* (Chevalier)
- *Croix de guerre* (with two bronze palms)

BORN ON THIS DAY

track-and-field athlete Jane Bell
1910

1935
author Carol Shields

figure skater Robert Paul
1937

1950
actress Joanna Gleason

Library and Archives Canada/James Peters/C-018957.

First ford of Loon Lake, the site of Sam Steele's battle.

1885. The Battle of Loon Lake, the last engagement of the North-West Rebellion, takes place at Steele Narrows, Saskatchewan. It was an encounter between the Scouts, a North-West Mounted Police (NWMP) unit under the command of Sam Steele, and about 150 Cree warriors led by Big Bear. Several Scouts were wounded, and some warriors were killed, including Woods Cree chief Cut Arm. Steele Narrows is now a National Historic Site.

BORN ON THIS DAY

1924 actress Colleen Dewhurst

1926 politician Flora MacDonald

1927 economist Sylvia Ostry

1954 singer-songwriter Dan Hill

THE NORTH-WEST REBELLION

December 16, 1884
Louis Riel sends a petition to the government listing Métis grievances and demands.

March 19, 1885
The Métis form the Provisional Government of Saskatchewan.

March 26, 1885
A force of North-West Mounted Police is routed by the Métis under Gabriel Dumont at Duck Lake, Saskatchewan, marking the outbreak of the North-West Rebellion.

March 30, 1885
Two hundred Cree, Stoney, and Métis fighters under Chief Poundmaker ransack Battleford, North-West Territories.

April 2, 1885
Wandering Spirit and other Cree fighters in Chief Big Bear's band kill nine white men at Frog Lake, Saskatchewan.

April 24, 1885
Gen. Frederick Middleton engages Gabriel Dumont's Métis at Fish Creek, North-West Territories; the battle is a stalemate.

May 9, 1885
The Métis effectively resist General Middleton's forces for three days at Batoche, Saskatchewan, until drawn out of their rifle pits by a concerted attack.

June 3, 1885
NWMP officers commanded by Sam Steele meet Cree forces led by Big Bear at Steele Narrows, North-West Territories.

July 2, 1885
Big Bear surrenders at Fort Carlton. He is sentenced to three years in prison for treason.

November 16, 1885
Louis Riel is hanged for treason at the Regina jail.

National Archives of Canada/William James Topley, PA-012854/The Canadian Press

Department of National Defence/Library and Archives Canada/1964-114-NPC.

Canada vs. the United States during the Inter-Allied Games at Pershing Stadium in Paris, France, 1919.

1838. The first recorded baseball-type game in North America is played in Beachville, Upper Canada (near Woodstock, Ontario). The game—between teams from the townships of Oxford and Zorra—featured five bases and took place on a square field in a pasture. It predated, by eight years, the establishment of Alexander Cartwright's New York Knickerbocker Base Ball Club and the "New York game," which fielded nine players. The first Canadian baseball team was the Young Canadians of Hamilton, Ontario, which was formed in April 1854.

Also on This Day

1948.
Golfer Sandra Post is born in Oakville, Ontario. Canada's first professional female golfer, she won US$521,735 between 1968 and 1983—more prize money than any other Canadian golfer, male or female, had won to that time.

BORN ON THIS DAY

1894 singer La Bolduc (Mary Travers)

1948 author Margaret Gibson

5 JUNE

Ron Poling/The Canadian Press.

Joe Clark in his Parliament Hill office, 1976.

1939. Politician Charles Joseph Clark is born in High River, Alberta. Clark became the leader of the federal Progressive Conservative (PC) Party and leader of the official opposition in 1976. In the 1979 federal election, the PCs won a minority government and Clark became Canada's sixteenth prime minister, the youngest person and first native westerner to hold the office. He served as prime minister until March 1980 and later as a senior minister in the PC government under Prime Minister Brian Mulroney, who succeeded him as party leader in 1983.

Born on This Day

1939.

Playwright and novelist Margaret Hollingsworth is born in London, England, in 1939. Hollingsworth came to Canada in 1968 and settled in Thunder Bay before moving on to Vancouver. Her work touches on themes of immigration and feminism and has captured the attention of several awards panels. She was a finalist for the Governor General's Award for *War Babies* in 1984 and received a Chalmers and Dora Mavor Moore Award for *Ever Loving* in 1980.

BORN ON THIS DAY

1894 — press baron Roy Thomson

1939 — playwright Margaret Hollingsworth

1986 — actress Amanda Crew

Also on This Day

1944.
Canadians storm ashore at the Juno Beach sector of the French coast in one of the most successful operations on D-Day—which was a turning point in the Second World War. The Canadian forces suffered 18,444 casualties during the Normandy campaign, but the operation led to the liberation of Europe from Nazi occupation.

Library and Archives Canada/C-038862.

Shawnadithit, the last surviving member of the Beothuk.

1829. Shawnadithit, the last member of the now extinct Beothuk tribe of Newfoundland, dies of tuberculosis. She was captured, along with her mother and sister, by English furriers in 1823 and taken to St. John's. When her mother and sister both died of tuberculosis, Shawnadithit was brought to live in the home of planter John Peyton. In 1828 she was moved to the Beothuk Institution at St. John's, where her skills with a pencil and sketchbook allowed her to create drawings of the Beothuk community that are a valuable record of her people.

As a result of European encroachment, slaughter, and diseases to which they had no natural resistance, the Beothuk rapidly declined in numbers following contact, dwindling to a mere few hundred by the mid-eighteenth century.

BORN ON THIS DAY

1920 singer and actor Jan Rubes

1935 author Joy Kogawa

Provincial Archives of Alberta/A3459.

Louise McKinney of the Famous 5.

1917. Louise McKinney is elected to the Legislative Assembly of Alberta, making her, with Roberta MacAdams of Calgary, one the first women elected to a legislature in Canada or the British Empire. In 1928, McKinney was one of the Famous 5—the five women who petitioned the court for the right to hold public office in what is commonly known as the Persons Case. The case began at the Supreme Court, which decided, after weeks of debate and argument, that women were not "persons" who could hold office as Canadian senators.

Also on This Day

1866.
About a thousand Fenians, members of various Irish nationalist organizations, cross the American border and occupy Pigeon Hill in Missisquoi County, Canada East. Canadian forces arrived the following day, and the Fenians, running low on weapons and supplies, surrendered.

BORN ON THIS DAY

Prime Minister John Turner
1929

1988
actor Michael Cera

hockey player Milan Lučić
1988

Also on This Day

1542.
After a difficult winter, explorer Jacques Cartier sets off for France from Charlesbourg-Royal, the first French settlement in North America. He and four hundred others had attempted to establish a permanent colony near present-day Cap-Rouge, Québec, but harsh weather, scurvy, and conflicts with the local Aboriginal peoples doomed the venture to failure. Cartier never returned to the New World.

What landmark compensation deal came into effect in 2007? See September 19.

Provincial Archives of Alberta/GR1989.0516/595#1.

Lieutenant-Governor Ralph Steinhauer at an Alberta Agriculture Hall of Fame presentation in Edmonton, 1974.

1905. Ralph G. Steinhauer, the first Aboriginal person to serve as lieutenant-governor of a Canadian province, is born in Morley, Alberta. A full-treaty member of the Cree tribe, Steinhauer was educated at the Brandon Indian Residential School. His varied career included establishing a farm on the Saddle Lake reserve, which he cultivated for over fifty years. He also founded the Indian Association of Alberta and was president of the Alberta Indian Development Corporation.

BORN ON THIS DAY

1921 actress Alexis Smith

1965 curler Joan McCusker

9 JUNE

© Alan Light.

Michael J. Fox at the Emmy Awards, 1988.

1961. Actor, producer, and author Michael J. Fox is born in Edmonton, Alberta. Fox began acting at a young age, appearing in such Canadian television shows as *The Beachcombers*. He achieved fame with the character Alex P. Keaton on the American sitcom *Family Ties* (1982–89)—a role that earned him one Golden Globe and three Emmy Awards. Fox became a major film star in the 1980s, most notably with the role of Marty McFly in the *Back to the Future* films. In 1998, he revealed that he had been diagnosed with Parkinson's disease in 1991. Despite the challenges caused by the debilitating illness, he has continued to act and has been a leading advocate for stem-cell research through the Michael J. Fox Foundation for Parkinson's Research.

Can you name the person who traversed thirty-four countries in a wheelchair to raise money for spinal-cord research?
See March 21.

BORN ON THIS DAY

Bluenose captain Angus Walters 1882

author Louise Maheux-Forcier 1929

journalist Steve Paikin 1960

actress Gloria Reuben 1964

FAMOUS CANADIAN COMEDIC ACTORS

Dan Aykroyd:
The Blues Brothers; Ghostbusters

John Candy:
Cool Runnings; Spaceballs; Planes, Trains and Automobiles

Jim Carrey:
Ace Ventura: Pet Detective; The Truman Show; Bruce Almighty

Michael Cera:
Arrested Development; Youth in Revolt; Juno; Scott Pilgrim vs. the World

Mike Myers:
Wayne's World; Austin Powers; Shrek

Leslie Nielsen:
Airplane!; The Naked Gun; Due South

Catherine O'Hara:
Beetlejuice; The Nightmare Before Christmas; Best in Show

Seth Rogen:
Knocked Up; The 40-Year-Old Virgin; Pineapple Express; The Interview

Martin Short:
Three Amigos; Innerspace; The Santa Clause 3: The Escape Clause

Nia Vardalos:
My Big Fat Greek Wedding; Connie and Carla

Mike Myers (far left and centre) in *Austin Powers*, with co-star Heather Graham (right).

The BAnQ Vieux-Montreal/Harvey Majeau/Fonds Harvey Majeau/P243.

Premier Jean Lesage.

1912. Québec premier Jean Lesage is born in Montréal. He led the Québec government during the Quiet Revolution, a period of profound change in the collective lives of the Québécois. As Québec Liberal leader and later as premier, Lesage completely reformed government through a program of social and political change, including the rooting out of patronage and corruption. Among his projects was the nationalization of the province's private electrical utilities under Hydro-Québec and education reforms that saw the public school system, formerly controlled by the Catholic Church, moved to the Ministry of Education.

Also on This Day

1947.
President Harry Truman begins a two-day visit to Ottawa, where he addresses Parliament. "Canada and the United States have reached the point where we no longer think of each other as 'foreign' countries," he declared in his speech. "We think of each other as friends, as peaceful and cooperative neighbors on a spacious and fruitful continent." Truman was the first American president to make a state visit to the country.

BORN ON THIS DAY

author Saul Bellow
1915

1918
actor Barry Morse

politician Preston Manning
1942

1968
actress Susan Haskell

The Johnny Bright Incident

In 1951, while playing for Drake University in Iowa, Bright was the victim of an on-field assault by Oklahoma A&M player Wilbanks Smith. The assault came to be known as the Johnny Bright Incident. In what was widely believed to be a racially motivated attack, Bright was knocked unconscious three times in the first seven minutes of play, with Smith landing one blow that broke Bright's jaw. The incident led to new rules against rough play, and contributed to making protective face guards a mandatory piece of equipment in college football.

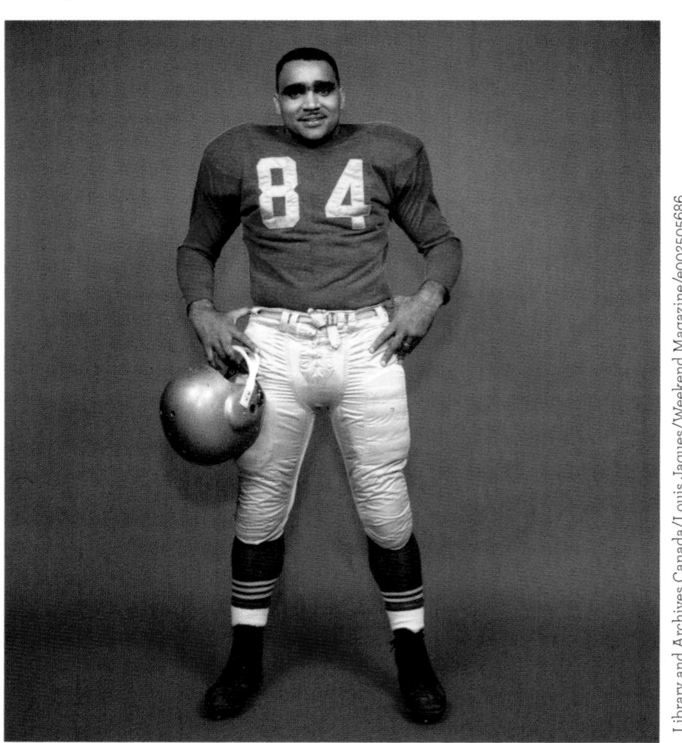

Library and Archives Canada/Louis Jaques/Weekend Magazine/e002505686.

Johnny Bright, 1958.

1930. Football player Johnny Bright, the first Black person to win a major football award in Canada, is born in Fort Wayne, Indiana. Bright turned down an opportunity to play for the Philadelphia Eagles in 1952, signing instead with the Calgary Stampeders to begin a thirteen-year CFL career. As an exceptional linebacker and fullback with the Edmonton Eskimos, he won the Schenley Award as Canada's outstanding player in 1959. Bright retired in 1964, having scored 71 touchdowns and amassed 10,909 yards rushing in 1,969 carries.

BORN ON THIS DAY

1945
children's author Robert Munsch

1963
curler Sandra Schmirler

© Daniel Kerray.

Christine Sinclair (middle) and her teammates return home with their Olympic medals, 2012.

1983. Christine Sinclair, one of Canada's most renowned soccer players, is born in Burnaby, British Columbia. As captain of the Canadian women's soccer team for the 2012 London Olympics, Sinclair led the team to a bronze medal, Canada's first in a traditional team sport at the summer games since 1936. But the medal was not without controversy, and Sinclair was suspended for four Fédération Internationale de Football Association (FIFA) games for comments she made after Canada's heart-breaking semifinal loss to the United States. To date, Sinclair is Canada's all-time leading scorer and third all-time career international scorer.

Also on This Day

1850.
Journalist, lawyer, engineer, and athlete James Creighton is born in Halifax, Nova Scotia. Creighton is credited with organizing the first recorded indoor hockey match, in Montréal, and has been dubbed "the father of organized hockey." The only claim he made, however, was that he had the honour of being the captain of the first regular hockey club formed in Canada.

BORN ON THIS DAY

TV host Mike Bullard
1957

1959
Kid in the Hall Scott Thompson

The Cremation of Sam McGee

There are strange things done in the midnight sun
By the men who moil for gold;
The Arctic trails have their secret tales
That would make your blood run cold;
The Northern Lights have seen queer sights,
But the queerest they ever did see
Was that night on the marge of Lake Lebarge
I cremated Sam McGee.

—Robert W. Service

Library and Archives Canada/013494.

The Yukon Hotel, ca. 1898.

1898. An act of Parliament makes Yukon a separate territory. The territory's name comes from the Gwich'in word *Yu-kun-ah*, for the "great river" that drains most of its area. Lying in the northwestern corner of Canada's continental mainland, Yukon is isolated by rugged mountains. Historically, it is associated with the great Klondike Gold Rush, and its character has been captured in the works of Robert W. Service, the Bard of the Yukon, in lasting treasures like "The Shooting of Dan McGrew" and "The Cremation of Sam McGee."

BORN ON THIS DAY

1931 poet Jay Macpherson

1972 fiddler Natalie MacMaster

14 JUNE

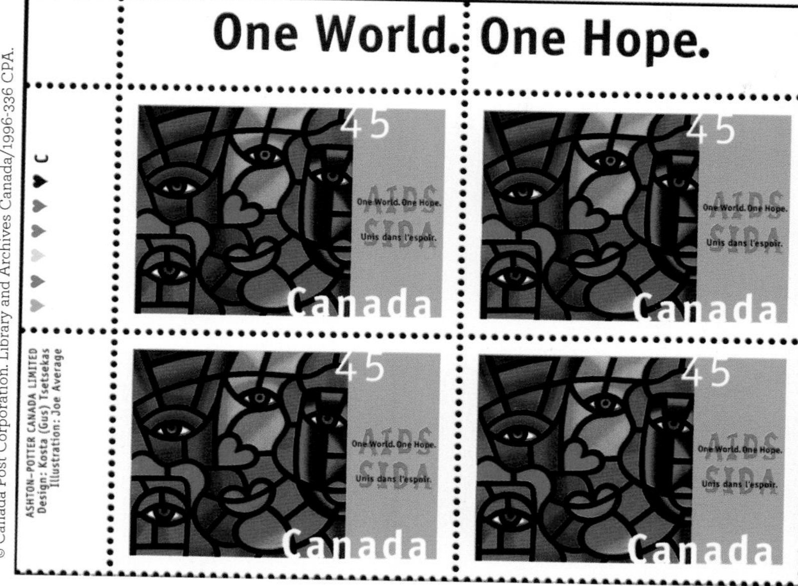

"AIDS—One World, One Hope" stamp, issued by Canada Post in 1996.

1997. The Centers for Disease Control in the United States reported a 19 percent reduction in AIDS deaths over the previous year, the first decline since the outbreak of the epidemic. The decrease was the result of a new antiretroviral therapy called HAART (highly active antiretroviral therapy). Medical advances have steadily lowered the AIDS mortality rate in Canada, from 1,764 in 1995 to fewer than 400 in 2013.

AIDS in Canada

The 1980s saw the emergence of the HIV/AIDS epidemic, which would have a devastating impact on Canada's gay community. Throughout the decade, gay men felt that their health was being ignored by the medical establishment and the government, and increasingly they took matters into their own hands. As the crisis escalated, the movement became more organized and politically proactive. In 1983, AIDS Vancouver became Canada's first AIDS service organization, offering care to those with HIV or AIDS. Many others were to follow. Another watershed moment came in 1988, with the establishment of AIDS Action Now (AAN), a group that adopted direct action as a means of pressuring governments to take meaningful steps to address the crisis.

BORN ON THIS DAY

architect Arthur Erickson 1924

1947 dancer Vanessa Harwood

Timeline: Josiah Henson

1828–29: Tries to buy his freedom.
1829: Is taken to New Orleans. to be sold along with his wife and four children.
1830: Escapes with his family to Canada.
1841: Purchases two hundred acres of land with business partners.
1842: Establishes the British-American Institute, providing general education and trade-labour instruction to members of the community.
1849: Publishes his autobiography, *The Life of Josiah Henson, Formerly a Slave, Now an Inhabitant of Canada.*
1883: Dies in Dresden, ON.

Uncle Tom's Cabin Historic Site.

Nancy Gambril Henson and Josiah Henson.

1789. Josiah Henson, an enslaved American who escaped to Canada and founded a settlement for fugitives from slavery, is born in Charles County, Maryland. In 1829, Henson, his wife, and their four children were taken to New Orleans to be sold as slaves. They fled to Upper Canada, reaching the Niagara Peninsula in October 1830. The family settled near Dresden, in what is now Ontario, where Henson established the Dawn community in 1834. Built on two hundred acres of land, Dawn was centred around the British-American Institute—a school Henson founded to help refugees from slavery get educated and become self-sufficient. Harriet Beecher Stowe acknowledged Henson's 1849 memoirs as a source for her anti-slavery novel, *Uncle Tom's Cabin.*

BORN ON THIS DAY

1809
poet François-Xavier Garneau

1875
skiing legend Herman "Jackrabbit" Smith-Johannsen

1920
retailer Sam "The Record Man" Sniderman

16 JUNE

J.M. Harrison, © Natural Resources Canada/Geological Survey of Canada.

Churchill Falls, Labrador.

1972. The Churchill Falls Generating Station opens in Labrador, despite many protests. Taking more than seven years to complete, the project employed more than thirty thousand people and cost $950 million. The acrobatic river drops 66 metres before plummeting another 75 metres over the falls and a further 158 metres through Bowdoin Canyon. The generating station is 24 kilometres downstream from the falls. It is one of the largest single-site hydroelectric projects in the world.

Also on This Day

1984.
John Turner wins the leadership of the Liberal Party, defeating Jean Chrétien. He dissolved Parliament after being sworn in and, after less than three months in office, lost the 1984 election in a landslide to Brian Mulroney's Progressive Conservatives.

BORN ON THIS DAY

Prime Minister Arthur Meighen
1874

1952
singer-songwriter Gino Vannelli

JUNE

Canadian Bridge Disasters

May 26, 1896: Fifty-five streetcar passengers perish during celebrations for Queen Victoria's birthday on the Point Ellice Bridge in Victoria, BC. One span of the bridge collapsed, taking a loaded streetcar with it.

August 29, 1907: Seventy-five workmen die during the construction of the Québec Bridge.

June 29, 1864: A Grand Trunk train with 538 passengers is unable to stop for an open swing bridge over the Richelieu River. The train plunges into the gap and the coaches pile on top of one another; ninety-nine people are believed to have died.

September 11, 1916: Thirteen men are killed during late-stage construction of the Québec Bridge.

August 10, 1966: The Heron Road Bridge collapses in Ottawa, killing nine.

September 30, 2006: The De la Concorde overpass collapses in Laval, Québec; five members of the same family are killed.

The Second Narrows Bridge collapse.

1958. Seventy-nine workers plunge into Burrard Inlet when two of the spans of Vancouver's Second Narrows Bridge, then under construction, collapse. Eighteen workers were killed, and one diver died during the rescue. Factors in the failure were complex, and included questionable steel quality and lax engineering practices. Stompin' Tom Connors paid tribute to the fallen in his song "The Bridge Came Tumblin' Down." In 1994, the bridge was renamed the Ironworkers Memorial Second Narrows Crossing.

BORN ON THIS DAY

1881
boxer Tommy Burns

1917
politician Duff Roblin

1930
politician Rosemary Brown

© Laval Bouchard/BAnQ Montreal/E6, S7, SS1, P664017.

Marie-Claire Kirkland-Casgrain, a lawyer and politician who was instrumental in advocating for Bill 16.

1964. Québec's Bill 16 comes into effect, permitting women to enter legal contracts without the consent of their husbands. Prior to this, a married woman essentially had the legal status of a minor; she was dependent on her husband's approval. Bill 16 was part of a larger set of social reforms enacted in Québec under the Lesage government during the 1960s. This so-called Quiet Revolution also included the establishment of the Québec Pension Plan and an overhaul of the education system.

Timeline: The Changing Legal Status of Women in Canada

1929: Women are recognized as persons for purposes of appointment to the Senate.

1982: Bertha Wilson is the first woman appointed to the Supreme Court of Canada.

1970s: Most provinces pass Matrimonial Property Acts to provide for the equal division of assets on dissolution of marriage.

1984: Legislation providing redress for victims of sexual harassment is introduced into Canada's Labour Code.

1985: The Indian Act is amended so that women no longer lose their treaty and Aboriginal rights as a result of marriage.

1988: The Supreme Court strikes down Canada's abortion law.

1989: In a landmark ruling (Brooks v. Canada Safeway Ltd.), the Supreme Court overturns the 1978 Bliss decision, which had found that pregnancy discrimination did not qualify as discrimination based on sex.

BORN ON THIS DAY

artist Laura Muntz Lyall
1860

1947
actress Linda Thorson

figure skater Kurt Browning
1966

Also on This Day

1888.
Artist Frank (Franz) Johnston is born in Toronto. A founding member of the Group of Seven, Johnston was noted for his atmospheric landscape paintings, including *Batchawana Falls* and *Fire-swept, Algoma.*

Which painter is buried on the grounds of the McMichael Canadian Art Collection?
See January 29.

The Royal Canadian Mounted Police/Library and Archives Canada/ PA-201150.

North-West Mounted Police officers in front of the Regina town station, 1895.

1903. Two years before Saskatchewan becomes a province, Regina is incorporated as a city. It saw significant growth over the course of the twentieth century, becoming not only the capital but also the commercial and financial centre of the province.

Regina was named by Princess Louise in honour of her mother, Queen Victoria (*regina* is Latin for "the reigning queen"), but like so many Canadian cities and towns, it has its origins in Aboriginal culture. At one point, the fledgling town was known as Pile of Bones, after the massive mounds of buffalo bones gathered by Cree hunters (they believed herds of living buffalo would return to the area to visit the bones). In Cree, the name was *Oskana-Ka-asateki,* or "the bones are piled high together," which was later incorrectly pronounced as *Wascana*. In Regina today, that name lives on in a lake, a public park, and even an electoral district.

BORN ON THIS DAY

1815 — artist Cornelius Krieghoff

1841 — North-West Mounted Police commissioner George Arthur French

1902 — bandleader Guy Lombardo

1950 — comedy writer Rosie Shuster

© Bruce Allen.

Anne Murray, undated.

1945. Singer Anne Murray is born in Springhill, Nova Scotia. As Canada's most successful pop performer of the 1970s, she gained fame internationally for her recording "Snowbird." First recorded on her second album, *This Way Is My Way* in 1969, "Snowbird" was re-released the following year for the American market as the B-side of a single, with "Bidin' My Time" on the other side. The single sold more than one million copies in 1970, making Murray the first Canadian woman to have a gold record in the United States. The recipient of multiple music awards, she was inducted into the Canadian Music Hall of Fame in 1993.

Also on This Day

1830.
Physician William Canniff is born in Thurlow, Upper Canada (now Ontario). He would go on to produce the first Canadian textbook on pathology and to found the Canadian Medical Association.

Which famous East Coast female singer died in 2013? See May 28.

BORN ON THIS DAY

colonizer Lord Selkirk (Thomas Douglas)
1771

1857
hydroelectricity advocate Adam Beck

JUNE

21

Also on This Day

1900.
Broadcasting pioneer and inventor Edward Samuel Rogers Sr. is born in Toronto. At just thirteen, Rogers won a contest for building the best amateur radio in Ontario. In his twenties, he developed the Rogers Batteryless radio and founded the radio station CFRB. He died in 1939, and although Rogers Communications was not established until much later, he is considered the founder of the company, which was headed by his son, Edward Samuel "Ted" Rogers Jr., until his death in 2008.

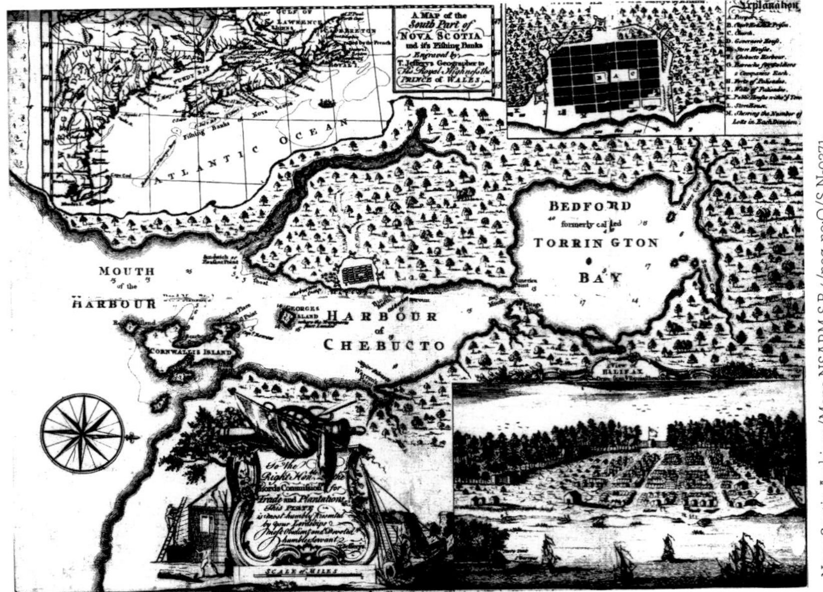

Nova Scotia Archives/Maps NSARM S.B.4/neg. no:O/S N-0371.

A map of Halifax, 1750.

1749. Modern Halifax is founded in the summer of 1749, when the newly appointed governor, Edward Cornwallis, arrives in Chebucto harbour with 2,567 settlers. Work began immediately on the port town, which replaced Annapolis Royal as the capital of Nova Scotia. Initially named Chebucto, it was renamed Halifax in honour of George Dunk, 2nd Earl of Halifax and president of the Board of Trade and Plantations. The city's founding established a strong British foothold in Nova Scotia.

Which tragedy occurred in Halifax in 1917?
See December 6.

BORN ON THIS DAY

1826 Governor General Lord Dufferin (Frederick Temple Blackwood)

1923 author and publisher Jacques Hébert

1941 actor and comedian Joe Flaherty

1942 First Nations activist Jeannette Lavell

Wayne Glowacki/Winnipeg Free Press/The Canadian Press.

Elijah Harper during the Meech Lake Accord negotiations.

1990. Manitoba and Newfoundland refuse to ratify the Meech Lake Accord, an agreement designed to bring Québec into the "constitutional family" along with all the other provinces. In 1985, the federal government and the provinces began discussing ways of revising the Constitution. The government of Québec proposed a package first to address the province's distinctiveness within the country, and then to enhance the relationship of all the provinces to the federal government. The provinces initially agreed to the package—which became known as the Meech Lake Constitutional Accord of 1987—but to become law, it had to be ratified by Parliament and the legislatures of all ten provinces. Opposition soon emerged from Elijah Harper, an Aboriginal member of the Legislative Assembly of Manitoba, who was frustrated with the disregard of Native issues, and from Newfoundland premier Clyde Wells, who objected to the "distinct society" status for Québec and to what he believed was the diminishment of Newfoundland's standing in Parliament. This led to the death of the accord one day before its planned passage.

Who Was Elijah Harper?

Elijah Harper was best known for the role he played in scuttling the Meech Lake Accord. He refused to give his consent because he was dismayed that Aboriginal Canadians had not been consulted with or recognized in the constitutional discussions. His efforts to delay the vote in the Manitoba legislature until the deadline for ratification had passed effectively quashed the accord. As a result, he was named the Canadian Press newsmaker of the year for 1990. The first Aboriginal member of the Manitoba legislature, Harper also served as the minister for northern affairs. From 1993 to 1997, he represented the riding of Churchill in the federal Parliament.

BORN ON THIS DAY

1952 actor Graham Greene

1970 singer-songwriter Steven Page

1971 curler Marcel Rocque

JUNE 23

Also on This Day

1990.
On his second attempt at the Liberal Party leadership, Jean Chrétien wins the job by a large margin on the first ballot. He became prime minister in 1993 and held the office for more than a decade, making him one of the longest-serving prime ministers in Canadian history.

The Air India memorial in Toronto.

1985. The worst terrorist act in Canadian history occurs when a bomb is detonated on Air India Flight 182 from Toronto to Mumbai via London. The plane was destroyed over the Atlantic Ocean off the coast of Ireland, killing all 329 passengers and crew. Police believed that the attack was the work of Sikh extremists. Charges were laid against Vancouver resident Inderjit Singh Reyat, who pleaded guilty to manslaughter and was sentenced to five years in prison. On the twenty-fifth anniversary of the bombing in 2010, Prime Minister Stephen Harper offered an apology to the families of those killed. In his remarks, he stated that the federal government's treatment of the families' need for answers had been characterized by "administrative disdain."

BORN ON THIS DAY

Hockey Hall of Famer Fred "Cyclone" Taylor
1884

1909
politician David Lewis

curler Ed Werenich
1947

1976
actress Emmanuelle Vaugier

24 JUNE

Library and Archives Canada/C-070448.

Calixa Lavallée, undated.

1880. "O Canada" is first performed at a Québec City banquet attended by the governor general, the Marquess of Lorne. Originally called "Chant national," the anthem was composed by Calixa Lavallée with lyrics by Adolphe-Basile Routhier. It first became popular as a patriotic anthem of French Canadians and only later spread across Canada in various English-language versions, the best known of which was written by Robert Stanley Weir in 1908. One hundred years after it was first performed, "O Canada" was officially proclaimed the country's national anthem in Ottawa on July 1, 1980. Its lyrics, which have seen minor amendments over the years, continue to breed controversy to this day, with some groups arguing that the anthem should be secularized (reverting from "God keep our land, glorious and free" to the original "O Canada, glorious and free"), and others insisting that the line "all thy sons command" be changed to "all of us command" (a modernized version of the original "thou dost in us command").

O Canada

O Canada!
Our home and native land!
True patriot love in all thy
sons command.
With glowing hearts we see thee rise,
The True North strong and free!
From far and wide, O Canada,
We stand on guard for thee.
God keep our land glorious and free!
O Canada, we stand on guard for thee.
O Canada, we stand on guard for thee.

O Canada! Terre de nos aïeux,
Ton front est ceint de fleurons glorieux!
Car ton bras sait porter l'épée,
Il sait porter la croix!
Ton histoire est une épopée
Des plus brillants exploits.
Et ta valeur, de foi trempée,
Protégera nos foyers et nos droits.
Protégera nos foyers et nos droits.

BORN ON THIS DAY

inventor
Thomas Ahearn
1855

1911
opera singer
Portia White

figure skater
Barbara Underhill
1963

Canadian Writers from the LGBT Community

Marie-Claire Blais: *La Belle bête*; *Le Sourd dans la ville*
Dionne Brand: *Land to Light On*; *In Another Place, Not Here*; *At the Full and Change of the Moon*
Wayson Choy: *The Jade Peony*; *Paper Shadows: A Chinatown Childhood*
Douglas Coupland: *Generation X: Tales for an Accelerated Culture*; *All Families Are Psychotic*; *Worst. Person. Ever.*
Timothy Findley: *The Wars*; *Pilgrim*; *The Piano Man's Daughter*
Tomson Highway: *Kiss of the Fur Queen*; *Dry Lips Oughta Move to Kapuskasing*
Ann-Marie MacDonald: *Fall on Your Knees*; *The Way the Crow Flies*; *Goodnight Desdemona (Good Morning Juliet)*
David Rakoff: *Fraud*; *Don't Get Too Comfortable*; *Half Empty*
Sinclair Ross: *As for Me and My House*; *Sawbones Memorial*
Jane Rule: *Desert of the Heart*; *Lesbian Images*; *Outlander*
Shyam Selvadurai: *Funny Boy*; *Cinnamon Gardens*

Michel Tremblay.

1942. Playwright and novelist Michel Tremblay is born in Montréal. His first widely produced play, *Les Belles-soeurs* (1965), offered a renewed vision of the working-class neighbourhood where he was born. It was considered a watershed piece of Canadian theatre at the time, and since then Tremblay has won several prizes and distinctions for his vast catalogue of work, including the Governor General's Award in 1999. In 1991, he was appointed a knight of the *Ordre national du Québec*.

How is Dionne Brand triply marginalized? See January 7.

BORN ON THIS DAY

National Ballet of Canada founder Celia Franca
1921

1941
director Denys Arcand

General Roméo Dallaire
1946

1963
author Yann Martel

Department of National Defence/Lieutenant B.J. Gloster/Library and Archives of Canada/PA-129092.

Pte. Helen Brymer and Pte. Dorothy Lowry check a car battery at a garage in England, 1944.

1941. The Department of National Defence announces the establishment of a women's corps for the army. The Canadian Women's Army Corps (CWAC) permitted women to enlist as active members of the military during the Second World War. Thousands of women were employed in a multitude of roles both at home and overseas, including as clerks, drivers, cooks, and telephone operators. Throughout the war, approximately fifty thousand women served in the army, navy, and air force, and another forty-five hundred served as nursing sisters.

Timeline: Women in the Military

1885: Canadian women first served as nurses in the North-West Rebellion.

1892: Twelve Canadian nursing sisters served overseas in the South African War.

1908: Georgina Fane Pope became the first matron of the Canadian Army Medical Corps.

1914–18: Nearly three thousand nursing sisters served in Canada, England, France, Belgium, and around the Mediterranean during the First World War.

1939: Hundreds of nurses rushed to enlist with the outbreak of the Second World War.

1941: In addition to CWAC, the Royal Canadian Air Force Women's Division and the Women's Royal Canadian Naval Service were created.

What year did Air Canada hire its first female pilot? See February 13.

BORN ON THIS DAY

Prime Minister Robert Borden
1854

1906
artist Marian Scott

Kid in the Hall Mark McKinney
1959

Also on This Day

1922.
Scientist, limnologist, environmentalist, and teacher Richard Vollenweider is born in Zurich, Switzerland. He would help set the limit for phosphorus loading to the Great Lakes, thus avoiding severe eutrophication of the world's largest supply of fresh water. In 1986 Vollenweider was awarded the Tyler Prize (considered equivalent to a Nobel Prize in environmental science), and in 1987 he earned the Naumann-Thiennemann Medal from the International Limnological Society.

Library and Archives Canada, Acc. No. 1970-188-31 W.H. Coverdale Collection of Canadiana.

Her Most Gracious Majesty, Queen Victoria, 1859.

1860. North America's oldest continuously run horse race, the Queen's Plate, is first held at Toronto's Carleton Track. On April 1, 1859, the Toronto Turf Club petitioned Queen Victoria to grant a trophy for a race in what is now Ontario. She assented, and the race began the following year. It was open to all horses bred in Upper Canada that had not yet won money, and it offered an initial prize of fifty guineas. Today the purse is a million dollars.

BORN ON THIS DAY

1862
vaudeville performer May Irwin

1885
Group of Seven artist Arthur Lismer

1967
synchronized swimmer Sylvie Fréchette

Around the conference table during the negotiations over the Treaty of Versailles.

1919. The Treaty of Versailles, the peace settlement imposed on Germany after the First World War, is signed. The settlement divided and redistributed the German empire, and imposed substantial reparations. Prime Minister Robert Borden's mission for the negotiations was to achieve recognition for Canada's sixty thousand war dead. He fought for, and won, separate Dominion representation at the peace conference and individual signatures on the treaty, greatly increasing Canada's presence on the world stage.

The Treaty of Versailles

The Treaty of Versailles is often seen as a catalyst for the rise of Hitler's Third Reich and the outbreak of the Second World War. The military restrictions and economic reparations exacted as punishment for Germany's role in the First World War were severe: demilitarization of the Rhineland; vast territorial reduction; comprehensive restrictions on Germany's armed forces; and the demand for steep financial reparations, which became untenable during the Great Depression. All were legally justified under what is now known as the War Guilt Clause, which forced Germany to admit responsibility for starting the war.

BORN ON THIS DAY

- 1937 golfer George Knudson
- 1940 actress Marilyn Lightstone
- 1941 Governor General David Johnston
- 1990 actress Jasmine Richards

29

1864. In one of Canada's worst train disasters, a Grand Trunk Railway (GTR) train plunges off the Beloeil Bridge into the Richelieu River near St-Hilaire, Québec, killing ninety-nine people and injuring a hundred. Many passengers were newly arrived German and Polish immigrants. At the time of the incident, the GTR was debt-ridden and unable to upgrade its equipment.

Which president of the Grand Trunk Railway was a passenger on the *Titanic*?
See May 16.

Library and Archives Canada/A. Bazinet/C-003286.

A scene from the Beloeil Bridge accident.

BORN ON THIS DAY

1930
actress and senator Viola Léger

1959
actress Kate Lynch

1981
hockey player Cherie Piper

RAILWAY DISASTERS IN CANADA

1910
A CPR train derails near Sudbury, ON, killing forty-three people.

1947
Two passenger trains collide near Dugald, MB, killing thirty-one passengers and crew.

1950
A train carrying Canadian troops en route to Korea collides with a passenger train outside Canoe River, BC, killing twenty-one soldiers and crew.

1986
A passenger train and a freight train collide west of Edmonton, AB, killing twenty-three people and injuring ninety-five.

2000
Over forty people are rushed to hospital when a passenger train crashes into a rail yard in Miramichi, NB.

2012
A train derails while switching tracks outside Burlington, ON. Three crew members die and forty-five passengers are injured.

2013
A train with seventy-two oil tankers left unattended rolls downhill toward the town of Lac-Mégantic, QC. The train derails and the ensuing explosions raze the town, killing forty-seven people.

Paul Chiasson/The Canadian Press

Also on This Day

2001.
Some fifteen hundred so-called Duplessis Orphans receive an apology from the government of Québec and a fault-free offer of compensation. In the 1940s and 1950s, the Québec government (then led by Premier Maurice Duplessis) had arranged for thousands of healthy orphaned or abandoned children to be declared mentally incompetent. These children were sent to psychiatric hospitals, which received greater federal subsidies than orphanages. Once institutionalized, the children often suffered physical or sexual abuse, and some were subjected to lobotomies and electroshock. As compensation for those years of trauma, each orphan received a lump sum of $10,000 and an additional $1,000 for each year spent in an asylum, for a total of roughly $25,000 per person.

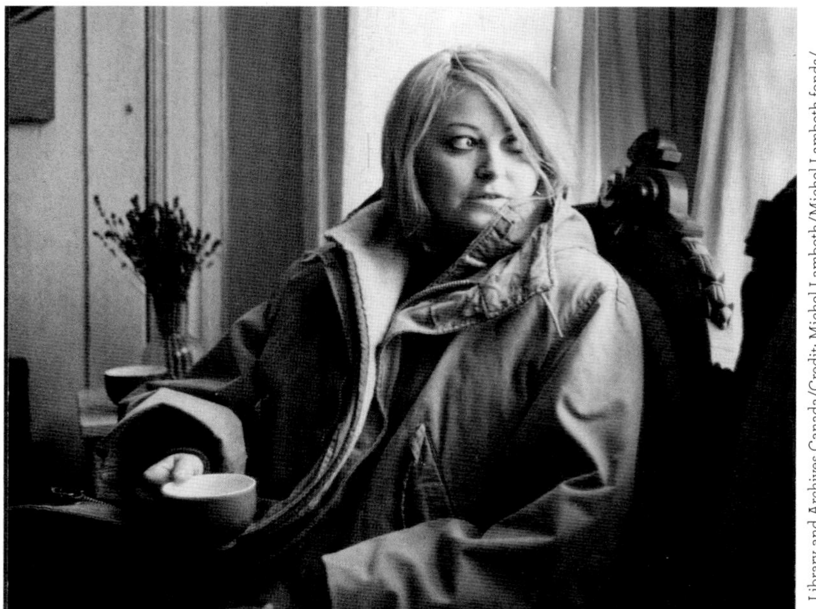

Library and Archives Canada/Credit: Michel Lambeth/Michel Lambeth fonds/e010955309.

Joyce Wieland, ca. 1960.

1931. Artist Joyce Wieland is born in Toronto. Wieland's 1971 exhibition at the National Gallery of Canada, *True Patriot Love,* was the institution's first major show devoted to a living Canadian woman artist. Challenging accepted hierarchies within the arts, Wieland worked with a variety of media, including cartoons, knitwear, and in the case of the exhibit's signature piece, *Arctic Passion Cake,* a beautifully decorated cake. She drew inspiration from history, politics, and the environment. Wieland died in 1998, but she is still remembered as one of Canada's foremost modern artists.

BORN ON THIS DAY

1948 singer Murray McLauchlan

1952 playwright and actor Morris Panych

1960 writer David Frum

1975 actress Angela Tong

JULY

ROBERTSON SCREWS

The Robertson screw was invented by Canadian industrialist P.L. Robertson. The screw's square socket keeps the screwdriver in place, allowing it to be used one-handed. These humble screws are a common sight in Canada, but they're less common south of the border.

In Québec, a *tête carrée*, or "square head," is a derogatory term for an anglophone.

The Model T Ford contained more than seven hundred Robertson screws. Using these screws saved about two hours of work per car.

Henry Ford attempted to get an exclusive licence to the Robertson screw. When Robertson turned him down, Ford switched to Phillips screws.

Other Canadian Robertsons include Barenaked Ladies singer Ed Robertson, author Robertson Davies, and news anchor Lloyd Robertson.

Dreamstime/getstock.com

When one American was introduced to the Robertson screw, he said, "That's what they're called! I used to work in a warehouse, and we called them crowbar screws. We'd curse every time we got crates from Canada . . . [because] we needed to use crowbars to break the crates apart."

Library and Archives Canada/C-005812.

"Confederation! The Much-Fathered Youngster," by John Wilson Bengough.

Cartier and Confederation

Confederation resulted from years of negotiations led by numerous individuals, among them the prime minister of the Province of Canada, George-Étienne Cartier. Cartier leveraged his railway and militia connections to bring French Canada, Manitoba, and British Columbia into the newly united country. As John A. Macdonald quipped about his compatriot to biographer Joseph Pope, "But for him confederation could not have been carried."

1867. John A. Macdonald becomes the first prime minister when the Dominion of Canada—consisting of the Province of Canada (divided into Ontario and Québec), Nova Scotia, and New Brunswick—comes into existence. The union wasn't born out of revolution or a sweeping outburst of nationalism. Rather, it was created in a series of negotiations and meetings, culminating in several major conferences: the Charlottetown and Québec Conferences of 1864, and the London Conference of 1866–67. Unification was driven by the need for economic expansion and the ever-looming threat of American invasion.

In what year did John A. Macdonald become an alderman?
See January 11.

BORN ON THIS DAY

1942 actress Geneviève Bujold

1952 actor Dan Aykroyd

1967 actress Pamela Anderson

1977 hockey player Jarome Iginla

Also on This Day

1979.
Astronomer Carlyle Smith Beals dies in Ottawa. He was made Dominion Astronomer in 1946, and he held the position until his retirement in 1964. In this role, Beals initiated a highly successful program to identify and study meteorite craters in Canada.

Library and Archives Canada/O.B. Buell/C-001873.

Chief Big Bear.

1885. Plains Cree chief Big Bear (Mistahimaskwa) surrenders at Fort Carlton, in what is now Saskatchewan. By the 1870s, Big Bear had emerged as the headman of about sixty-five lodges. He was concerned with the disappearance of the buffalo, the increasing numbers of European settlers, and the impossible treaty conditions that seemed to ensure perpetual poverty and the destruction of his people's way of life. Big Bear advocated peaceful negotiation, but the government's refusal to confer with him led some of his followers to take up arms. As a result, he was convicted of treason and sentenced to three years in prison.

BORN ON THIS DAY

physicist Harriet Brooks
1876

1948
actor Saul Rubinek

actor and wrestler Bret Hart
1957

1971
author Evelyn Lau

3 JULY

Patent and Copyright Office/Library and Archives Canada/PA-030926.

Town of Pugwash, Nova Scotia, 1910.

1957. Scientists from around the world gather in Nova Scotia for the first meeting of the Pugwash Conference. At the height of the Cold War, philanthropist and financier Cyrus Eaton invited the scholars to his hometown of Pugwash, Nova Scotia, to discuss strategies for nuclear disarmament. Born from a manifesto written by Albert Einstein and Bertrand Russell in 1955, the conference was rooted in the idea that scientists could play a significant role in establishing world peace. The Pugwash Conference has continued to grow annually, with participants assisting in the development of both the Treaty on the Non-Proliferation of Nuclear Weapons (1968) and the Anti-Ballistic Missile Treaty (1972).

Also on This Day

2014.
Eugenie Bouchard of Westmount, Québec, becomes the first Canadian women's singles tennis player to reach a Grand Slam final after defeating Romania's Simona Halep at Wimbledon. She also made it to the semifinals of both the Australian Open and the French Open that same year.

BORN ON THIS DAY

author Rohinton Mistry
1952

1969
musician Kevin Hearn

actor
Brandon Jay McLaren
1981

Library and Archives Canada/Charles A. Aylett/C-014090.

Tom Longboat, 1907.

1886. Distance runner Tom Longboat is born in Ohsweken, Ontario, on the Six Nations of the Grand River reserve. Longboat was widely popular in his day, and was an internationally recognized sports hero. He won the Boston Marathon in record time in 1907, and set a new fifteen-mile world record of 1:18:10 in 1912. He also served as a dispatch runner in France during the First World War. When he advocated for greater control of his career, however, his manager, Tom Flanagan, decried him for laziness and insubordination. Flanagan's criticisms, later seen as veiled racism, were circulated by the press, but Longboat's responses were rarely published. Flanagan then sold Longboat's contract—"like a racehorse," as the runner put it.

In a message to the press—February 6, 1909, Longboat said, "I do not like the idea of doing all the work and somebody else getting all the credit for winning my victories. Do you think that Flanagan could make me run if I do not want to? I can get along without assistance and if any of these other runners want to race me they will have to make arrangements with me, and no one else."

Tom Longboat—
Selected Races Won

1906—Around the Bay Road Race
1906, 1907, 1908—Toronto Ward's Island Marathon
1907—Boston Marathon
1909—World's Professional Marathon Championship
1918—Canadian Corps Dominion Day competitions

BORN ON THIS DAY

distiller and businessman Hiram Walker
1816

1915
medical physicist Harold Elford Johns

5 JULY

© Cupids Legacy Centre.

The village of Cupids, Newfoundland.

1610. John Guy and a boatload of settlers depart from Bristol, England, and land at Cupers Cove (now Cupids), Newfoundland, where they establish the first English settlement in what is now Canada. The pioneers built their settlement from scratch, including defences, dwelling houses, a storehouse, a sawmill, a grist mill, and a brewhouse. They also sought to establish a trade in furs with the Beothuk. Despite the threat from pirates and the fact that the colony did not make a profit for its investors in England, some settlers remained, and a number of other colonies were established on the island, including Harbour Grace in 1617 and Ferryland in 1621. After French attacks in 1697, the settlement shifted from its original location to one farther along Cupids harbour. The location of Guy's original settlement was lost to the sands of time for nearly three hundred years.

 When did the last member of the Beothuk tribe die? See June 6.

The First French Settlement

In June 1604, about one hundred men arrived at the mouth of the river dividing present-day New Brunswick and Maine. There, on a small island they called Île Ste. Croix, they established the beginnings of a permanent French settlement in North America. Though they'd been guided to the island by the Etechemin (Passamaquoddy) people, the French settlers—including their leader, Pierre Du Gua de Monts, and cartographer Samuel de Champlain—were poorly prepared for the harsh winter. They lasted only one year on the island before moving the colony across the Bay of Fundy. That second settlement—near present-day Annapolis Royal, Nova Scotia—would lead to the establishment of the New France colonies. Île Ste. Croix is now an International Historic Site.

BORN ON THIS DAY

1918
broadcaster René Lecavalier

1943
singer-songwriter, musician, and producer Robbie Robertson

Clayoquot Sound

Aboriginal peoples from the Nuu-chah-nulth (Nootka) First Nation have resided in the Clayoquot Sound area for at least two millennia. All the region's forests were licensed in the 1950s to two forest companies; nearly one-quarter of the timber in the sound has since been logged. In 1993, the BC government established a logging zone amounting to 62 percent of the Crown land in Clayoquot Sound. Protected areas totalled just 33 percent. Public outcry over this plan resulted in a summer of protest that made international headlines. In late 1994, the Nuu-chah-nulth and the provincial government signed an interim agreement providing for local Aboriginal review of logging plans in the sound. More than 60 percent of Clayoquot's old-growth forest is now protected.

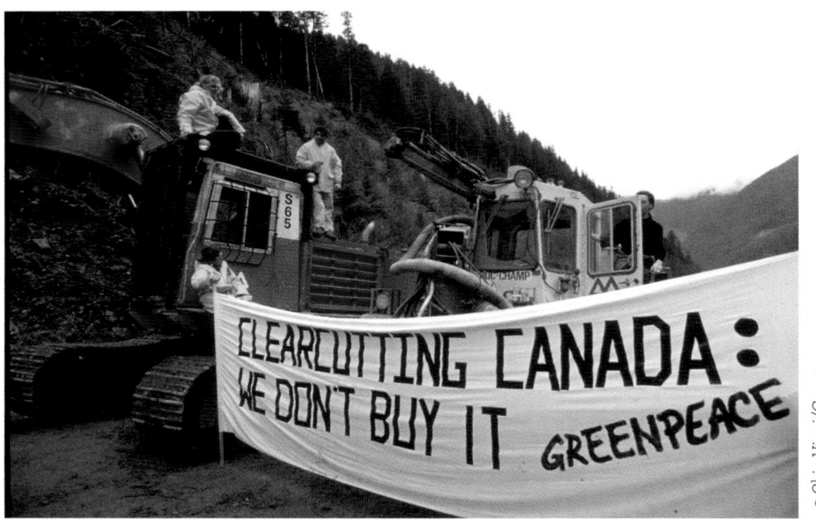

A road blockade by Greenpeace activists at Clayoquot Sound, British Columbia.

1993. The first arrests are made during protests opposing the clear-cut logging of Clayoquot Sound, on the west coast of Vancouver Island. Protestors began blockading roads on July 5, 1993, and continued their efforts throughout the summer. Logging company Macmillan Bloedel Ltd. obtained a court injunction prohibiting the blockades, and the RCMP began charging violators with criminal contempt. Over the course of the five-month protest, more than eight hundred demonstrators, from the thousands who had gathered, were arrested, tried, and convicted in the Supreme Court of British Columbia. In January 2000, the entire sound, including part of the Pacific Rim National Park Reserve, was designated a UNESCO Biosphere Reserve.

BORN ON THIS DAY

businesswoman and civil rights activist Viola Desmond
1914

1921
professor and politician Allan MacEachen

broadcaster Peter Mansbridge
1948

1952
water-skier George Athans Jr.

J.P. Moczulski/The Canadian Press.

Luc Plamondon accepts an award at the Canadian Songwriters Hall of Fame gala, 2011.

2001. A Parliament Hill tribute concert for lyricist and producer Luc Plamondon attracts an audience of ten thousand people. Plamondon produced some of Québec's most famous pop hits in the 1970s, including *"J'ai rencontré l'homme de ma vie," "En écoutant Elton John," "La Chanteuse straight,"* and *"Pars pas sans me dire bye-bye."* In the late 1970s and 1980s, he devoted himself to writing musicals and modern rock operas, including *Starmania,* which depicted the pitfalls of stardom and premiered at the *Palais des congrès de Paris* in 1979. Plamondon's songs were also popularized by singers such as Céline Dion and Monique Leyrac.

Also on This Day

1967.
The first Order of Canada appointments are announced. The honourees include author Hugh MacLennan, soldier and humorist Gregory Clark, neurosurgeon Dr. Wilder Penfield, opera singer Pierrette Alarie, and Montreal Canadiens legend Maurice Richard.

BORN ON THIS DAY

Hockey Hall of Famer Joe Sakic
1969

actress Cree Summer
1969

curler Jennifer Jones
1974

Portrait of the Artist as a Young Man

Perhaps the most popular Canadian artist of the early twentieth century, Tom Thomson was born near Claremont, Ontario, on August 5, 1877. From a young age, Thomson dabbled with various art forms, including music, but he decided to pursue a career as an artist in the early 1900s. In 1906, he attended the Central Ontario School of Art and Industrial Design (the precursor to today's Ontario College of Art and Design University), and there he developed his technique as a painter. His growing maturity as an artist and distinct style were evident by 1913, with one of his first major works, *A Northern Lake* (based on a sketch he completed while in Algonquin Park). In the years that followed, he became closely associated with painters who would form the Group of Seven, including A.Y. Jackson, Franklin Carmichael, and Lawren Harris, whose works he inspired. By the time of his death in 1917, Thomson was a celebrated artist, renowned for his majestic natural landscapes.

Library and Archives Canada/1981-254 NPC.

Tom Thomson, undated.

1917. Artist Tom Thomson disappears at Canoe Lake, Ontario, and his body is discovered eight days later. An early inspiration for what became the Group of Seven, Tom Thomson was perhaps the most influential and enduringly popular Canadian artist of the early part of the twentieth century. He left behind a large collection of works, including about fifty canvases and over three hundred sketches. His paintings *The West Wind* (1917) and *Jack Pine* (1916–17) are familiar Canadian icons, and his renderings of Algonquin Park have become synonymous with our image of the Canadian landscape. The suspicious circumstances surrounding his death have since become fodder for writers, amateur sleuths, and serious scholars.

How many major rivers pool in Algonquin Park? See May 27.

BORN ON THIS DAY

1933 — Supreme Court chief justice Antonio Lamer

1948 — children's entertainer and writer Raffi Cavoukian

1960. In a miraculous rescue, seven-year-old Roger Woodward is pulled from the waters of the Niagara River after having plunged over the Horseshoe Falls. The boy had been out for a boat ride with his older sister, Deanne, and a family friend, James Honeycutt, when the engine failed and the boat capsized. Honeycutt, the only passenger without a life jacket, went over the falls and was killed. Deanne was rescued just metres from the cusp, but Roger was carried over by the current and plunged into the depths below, where his life jacket brought him up to the surface. He was picked up by the *Maid of the Mist II* and made history as the youngest person ever to go over the falls and survive.

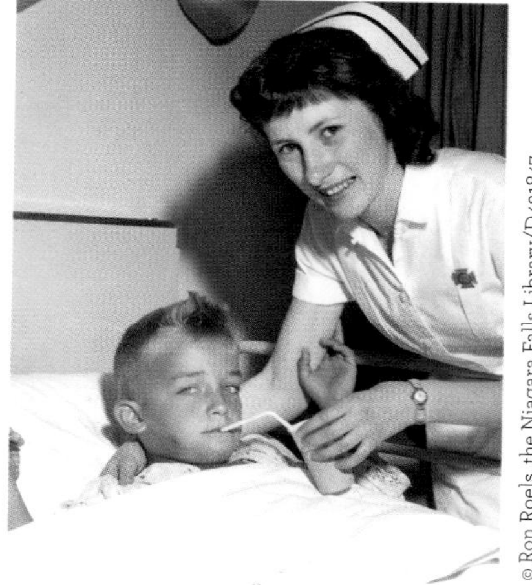

Roger Woodward with nurse Eleanor Weaver after his trip over the Horseshoe Falls.

Early Niagara Falls Daredevils

While "stunting" is now prohibited by the Niagara Parks Commission, there is a long history of individuals tempting fate at the falls. Tragically, some would perish, but these are a few tales of success:

June 30, 1859: Jean François Gravelet (known as the Great Blondin) is the first person to cross the Niagara River gorge on a tightrope.

October 24, 1901: Sixty-three-year-old Annie Taylor is the first recorded person to survive a plunge over Niagara Falls in a barrel.

July 25, 1911: Former circus-man Bobby Leach took his turn in a steel barrel, breaking both kneecaps and his jaw but surviving. He needed six months in hospital to recover from his injuries.

July 4, 1928: Jean Lussier of Québec draws large crowds when he goes over the falls in a six-foot rubber ball containing oxygen tubes.

BORN ON THIS DAY

1845 — Governor General Gilbert Elliot (4th Earl of Minto)

1927 — Hockey Hall of Famer Red Kelly

1953 — dancer and choreographer Margie Gillis

1954 — businessman and TV personality Kevin O'Leary

10

A poster by graphic artist Christopher Hemsworth captures the spirit of Joe Shuster as represented in Historica Canada's *Heritage Minute*.

1914. Cartoonist Joe Shuster is born in Toronto. Along with writer Jerry Siegel, Shuster created what is arguably the comic book world's most famous hero, Superman. In the original version of the comic, Superman's mild-mannered alter ego, Clark Kent, worked for the *Daily Star*, which was patterned after the *Toronto Daily Star*. The newspaper's name was later changed to the *Daily Planet*. In 1938, Shuster and Siegel sold Superman for $130 to the company that published Action Comics, but they failed to copyright the character. They were paid to draw the series as staffers until 1947, when they were fired after suing for a more equitable percentage of royalties and the rights to both Superman and Superboy. Before the release of the first Superman movie, which starred Christopher Reeve and made more than $80 million, DC Comics agreed to restore Shuster and Siegel's creator credits and pay each of them a lifetime stipend that eventually reached $30,000 a year.

Comic Book Canadiana

Superman is only one in a long line of unforgettable characters to come from the fertile imaginations of Canadian comic book artists and graphic novelists. From postwar favourites like Nipper and Jasper the Bear to more modern incarnations like Scott Pilgrim and the Patterson family of *For Better or for Worse*, Canadians have contributed a great deal to the comic landscape. Even iconic real-world figures like Louis Riel and strongman Louis Cyr have been given the graphic novel treatment, while Kate Beaton's popular webcomic, *Hark! A Vagrant*, takes a lighter look at Canadian history.

BORN ON THIS DAY

1946 — Royal Canadian Air Farce founding member Roger Abbott

1952 — musician and broadcaster Kim Mitchell

11 JULY

Shaney Komulainen/The Canadian Press.

Canadian soldier Patrick Cloutier and Mohawk warrior Brad Laroque during the standoff at Oka, Québec.

1990. A standoff begins at Oka, Québec, when police attempt to storm a barricade erected by the Mohawk people of Kanesatake, assisted by supporters from the nearby communities of Kahnawake and Akwesasne. The blockade was designed to halt the expansion of a golf course on land claimed by the Mohawk, which included a traditional burial ground. The Oka Crisis escalated throughout the seventy-eight-day siege and was resolved only after the army was called in. Mohawk warriors surrendered to soldiers on September 26. The golf course expansion was cancelled and the land purchased by the federal government, but it still has not been transferred to the Kanesatake community.

Timeline: The Oka Crisis

1718: King Louis XV grants land outside Montréal to the St. Sulpice Seminary; the Sulpicians later sell pieces of the land to settlers. Mohawk inhabitants petition for rights to the land.

1961: The city of Oka builds a nine-hole golf course on disputed land, despite efforts by the Mohawk of Kanesatake to have construction stopped. The Mohawk continue to fight their land claim.

March 1990: After the Oka mayor announces an extension of the golf course, the Mohawk establish a barricade on the site of the proposed development.

July 11, 1990: Sûreté du Québec (SQ) officers storm the barricades with tear gas, concussion grenades, and assault rifles. One officer is killed, and police retreat. Both sides establish roadblocks. The Mohawk blockade Mercier Bridge outside of Montréal.

August 20, 1990: The Canadian army takes over from the SQ. Tensions rise around Oka and Montréal, where anti-Mohawk protests have already turned racist and violent. The so-called Oka Crisis receives intense national media attention. Violent confrontations occur, with protestors complaining of siege-like conditions.

September 26, 1990: After the federal government purchases the disputed land and the Mercier Bridge blockade is dismantled, the last Kanesatake protestors surrender to soldiers.

1993: Alanis Obomsawin releases the documentary *Kanehsatake: 270 Years of Resistance*, filmed from inside the crisis.

December 19, 1994: The Mohawk of Kanesatake and the federal government sign a memorandum of understanding to begin negotiations to settle grievances.

BORN ON THIS DAY

1949 — guitarist and composer Liona Boyd

1984 — actress Serinda Swan

People and Events You Probably Learned about from Pierre Berton

The Klondike Gold Rush
The Battle of Vimy Ridge
The building of the Canadian Pacific Railway
The War of 1812
The Great Depression
The Dionne Quintuplets

Pierre Berton leaning on a train during the filming of *The National Dream*.

1920. Journalist, historian, and media personality Pierre Berton is born in Whitehorse, Yukon. Berton was among Canada's best-known writers and was particularly well regarded as a popularizer of Canadian history. He brought his highly readable narrative style to essential nation-building events, including the War of 1812, Vimy Ridge, and the creation of the Canadian Pacific Railway. One of his first important books was *Klondike* (1958), an account of the Klondike Gold Rush of 1896–99. The son of a gold-seeker who grew up in Dawson amid the debris of the stampede for gold, Berton had lived for years in the long shadow of the events he retold in this book.

BORN ON THIS DAY

1849 physician, writer, and educator William Osler

1930 actor and writer Gordon Pinsent

1939 journalist, author, and activist Michele Landsberg

1954 skier Dave Irwin

1961 actress Camilla Scott

1979 speed skater Cindy Klassen

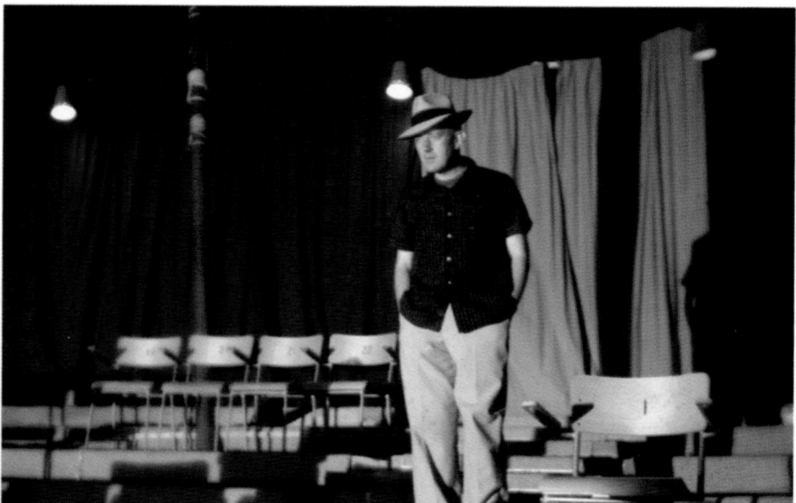

Alec Guinness after a rehearsal at the Stratford Festival.

1953. The Stratford Festival opens its first season with Alec Guinness in *Richard III* and Irene Worth in *All's Well That Ends Well*. The festival resulted from the efforts of Stratford journalist Tom Patterson, who had formed a local committee to explore the prospects for an annual drama festival in his hometown on the banks of the Avon, west of Toronto. His real motive was to find a way to save Stratford's dying economy. Despite his limited knowledge of theatre, Patterson won a grant of $125 from the Stratford city council to seek artistic advice about mounting the event. Rehearsals took place in an old barn besieged by mating sparrows and falling eggs. Over the years, some of Canada's greatest theatre actors have graced the stages of Stratford, among them Christopher Plummer, Kate Reid, William Hutt, Colm Feore, and Martha Henry.

Notable Stratford Alumni

Len Cariou: roles included Prospero in *The Tempest* (1982)
Megan Follows: roles included Juliet in *Romeo and Juliet* (1993)
Paul Gross: roles included title role in *Hamlet* (2000)
Eric McCormack: roles included Demetrius in *A Midsummer Night's Dream* (1989)
Al Waxman: roles included Willy Loman in *Death of a Salesman* (1997)

BORN ON THIS DAY

1932
astrophysicist Hubert Reeves

1934
writer, journalist, and radio host Peter Gzowski

Also on This Day

1912.
Educator and literary critic Northrop Frye is born in Sherbrooke, Québec. The author of several important works, including *Fearful Symmetry*, *Anatomy of Criticism*, and *The Great Code*, Frye gained international recognition for his literary theories.

NWT Archives/Henry Busse/N-1979-052-2769.

Judge J.H. Sissons sits at his desk in the 1950s.

1892. Judge Jack Sissons is born in Orillia, Ontario. As first judge of the Territorial Court of the Northwest Territories, Sissons took "justice to every man's door" by aircraft and dogsled. He travelled approximately sixty-four thousand kilometres in a twice-yearly circuit, holding trials in remote communities. Several of his decisions relating to hunting rights, Aboriginal marriage, and adoption practices became legal landmarks. He was a legend to the Inuit people and was called *Ekoktoegee*, "the one who listens to things."

BORN ON THIS DAY

1918
labour leader
Grace Hartman

1938
architect and professor
Moshe Safdie

15 JULY

1870. Three years after Confederation, the Manitoba Act comes into effect, creating Canada's fifth province. The British government had transferred Rupert's Land and the North-Western Territory to the newly formed nation of Canada the previous year, dispatching a lieutenant-governor and land surveyors to the region. That had set off concerns among the Métis inhabitants of the Red River Colony about the influx of Anglo-Protestant immigrants; established settlers, meanwhile, feared for their land rights under a new Canadian government. Led by Louis Riel, the Métis mounted a rebellion and, in December 1869, declared a provisional government to negotiate terms for entering Confederation. The resulting agreement—the product of discussions with Sir George-Étienne Cartier and Sir John A. Macdonald in Ottawa—became the basis for the Manitoba Act.

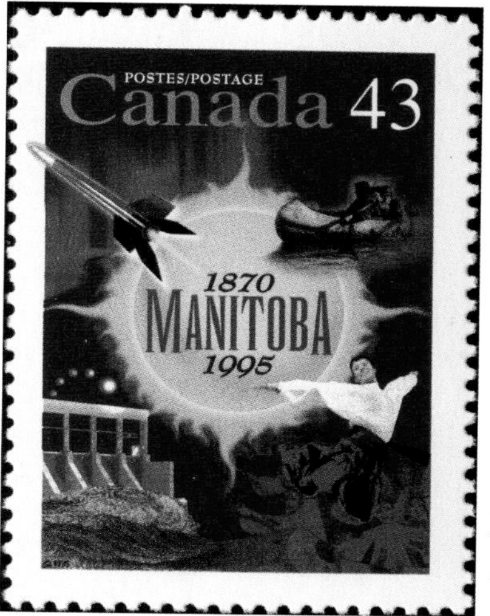

"Manitoba 1870–1995," a commemorative stamp issued by Canada Post.

Also on This Day

1918.
Physicist Bertram Neville Brockhouse is born in Lethbridge, Alberta. Brockhouse pioneered a technique for aiming a beam of neutrons at a target material in order to glean information about that material's atomic structure. He was a co-winner (with American Clifford G. Shull) of the Nobel Prize in Physics in 1994.

BORN ON THIS DAY

1940
movie producer and director Denis Héroux

1961
actress Lolita Davidovich

Library and Archives Canada/1996-282-7.

***The Coming of the Loyalists*, 1783, by Henry Sandham.**

1783. The British Crown announces that American Loyalists who supported the British cause during the Revolutionary War will receive land grants to settle in Canada. More than nineteen thousand such Loyalists had served Britain in special provincial militias. They fought for various reasons, including personal loyalty to the Crown and a fear that revolution could bring chaos to America. Between forty and fifty thousand of these Loyalists settled north of the American border. Ethnically, they were diverse, and many were recent immigrants. White Loyalists brought sizable contingents of slaves with them. Free Blacks and escaped slaves who had fought in the Loyalist corps also came, as did as many as two thousand Aboriginal allies (mainly Six Nations Iroquois from New York). Loyalists were instrumental in establishing educational, religious, social, and governmental institutions.

Who were among the first settlers of Nova Scotia in 1784? See July 26.

Richard Pierpoint

Richard Pierpoint was among the thousands of Black Loyalists who came to Canada after the American Revolution. Born in Bondu (now Senegal) around 1744 and formerly enslaved, he settled in Niagara after 1783. During the War of 1812, Pierpoint petitioned the military for the creation of an all-Black unit, and Captain Runchey's Company of Coloured Men was formed. Also known as the Coloured Corps or the Black Corps, the unit was instrumental during the Battle of Queenston Heights, and Pierpoint himself served as a private from September 1812 to March 1815. After the war, he petitioned the lieutenant-governor for aid in returning to Africa, but his request was ignored and he remained in Upper Canada. There, he is said to have become a leader in his community, helping formerly enslaved Black people through the Underground Railway before he died around 1837.

BORN ON THIS DAY

1661
explorer Pierre Le Moyne d'Iberville

1946
diplomat Louise Fréchette

1948
violinist, violist, and conductor Pinchas Zukerman

St. Boniface Cathedral on July 22, 1968.

1972. Manitoba's newly rebuilt St. Boniface Cathedral, a centre of worship for the local Franco-Manitoban population, is dedicated after having been destroyed by a fire in 1968. Six churches have stood on the site since the first was built in 1818. Twice the building was destroyed by fire—in 1860, when it burned to the ground, taking all of the mission's historical records with it, and in 1968, when flames destroyed many of the cathedral's features, including the rose window. The modern 1972 structure was built within the surviving historic walls and façade. An empty stone ring in the façade shows where the rose window was once displayed.

Also on This Day

1976.
The opening ceremony for the Montreal Olympics takes place. At the close of the games on August 1, Canada was in twenty-seventh place overall, with no gold medals—an unfortunate first for a host country.

BORN ON THIS DAY

1896 Hockey Hall of Famer Wilfred "Shorty" Green

1935 actor Donald Sutherland

1942 writer and actress Gale Zoë Garnett

1956 Hockey Hall of Famer Bryan Trottier

JULY 18

Also on This Day

1926.
Author Margaret Laurence is born in Neepawa, Manitoba. Laurence was best known for her novels set in Manawaka, a fictional small Manitoba town, including *The Stone Angel* and *The Diviners*. A two-time winner of the Governor General's Award, she was a member of the Order of Canada and a co-founder of the Writers' Trust of Canada.

© Mike Gericke.

Another postal strike, 2011.

1968. A nationwide postal strike begins when twenty-four thousand workers walk off the job. The strike was mainly the result of wage grievances, and the disruption lasted twenty-two days, until August 9, 1968, when deliveries resumed with news of a pay increase. In 1970, rotating twenty-four-hour walkouts, which were also motivated by wage grievances, again secured an increase. Since 1965, the Canadian Union of Postal Workers has been involved in about twenty major disputes.

BORN ON THIS DAY

1911
actor, director, and writer Hume Cronyn

1933
composer, writer, and educator R. Murray Schafer

1950
politician and educator Jack Layton

19 JULY

Atom Egoyan, undated.

1960. Internationally acclaimed filmmaker Atom Egoyan is born in Cairo, Egypt, to Armenian parents. As a child, Egoyan moved with his family to Victoria, British Columbia, an experience in cultural displacement that he has often cited as a profound influence on his life and work. Egoyan studied at the University of Toronto, where he became intensely involved in campus theatre and, like David Cronenberg before him, made his first films. Egoyan's rise in the world of international film was solidified with the release of *The Sweet Hereafter,* which premiered at the 1997 Cannes Film Festival, where it won several prizes. The film—a critical (if not a box office) success—also won eight Genie Awards in Canada and was nominated for two Oscars at the 1998 Academy Awards. He is known as one of the most influential Canadian cinematic voices.

Also on This Day

2013.
A thunderstorm strikes Toronto, felling the silver maple tree that is said to have inspired Alexander Muir's 1867 poem-turned-song "The Maple Leaf Forever." Crowds later gathered to take pictures, collect leaves, and mourn the historic tree.

How many Genie awards did filmmaker David Cronenberg's *Naked Lunch* win?
See November 22.

BORN ON THIS DAY

hockey player and coach Dick Irvin
1892

1950
cyclist Jocelyn Lovell

curler Jan Betker
1960

Also on This Day

1811.
James Bruce, 8th Earl of Elgin, is born in London, England. As governor general, he negotiated the 1854 Reciprocity Treaty between British North America and the United States. He is also credited with implementing the policy of responsible government in Canada.

City of Vancouver Archives/AM1535-: CVA99-541.

Celebrating Confederation Day on Cambie Street in Vancouver, 1917.

1871. British Columbia enters Confederation as Canada's sixth province. After 1867, the British colony on the west coast had debated whether it should join the new federation of eastern provinces known as Canada. In 1871, BC voters agreed to enter the Dominion of Canada on the condition that the federal government build a transcontinental railway to link it with the eastern provinces. The government agreed, but the new province waited—rather impatiently at times—for nearly fifteen years before the Canadian Pacific Railway reached the southwest coast. The union with Canada was an unhappy one at first. The new province ran heavily into debt; the cost of governing a large mountainous area with few people was very high, and revenues from resource users were low. It was not until the early twentieth century, following the construction of the Panama Canal, that British Columbia experienced its first economic boom since the Cariboo Gold Rush in the early 1860s.

BORN ON THIS DAY

1950
actress Tantoo Cardinal

1971
actress Sandra Oh

21 JULY

Marshall McLuhan and students, 1973.

1911. Communication theorist Marshall McLuhan is born in Edmonton, Alberta. A professor of English at the University of Toronto, McLuhan gained international fame during the 1960s for his studies of the effects of mass media on thought and behaviour. He popularized the idea that technology has a profound effect on our lives, culture, and history. McLuhan thought of himself as a grammarian studying the linguistic and perceptual biases of mass media. His oft-quoted statement "The medium is the message" became a mantra for decoding the appeal and impact of mass media in the modern era. His contribution to the field of communications has been compared to the work of Darwin and Freud for its universal significance.

Also on This Day

1836.
Canada's first railway, the Champlain and Saint Lawrence Railroad, officially opens. Operations began on July 25. The railway heralded a revolutionary change in Canadian transportation history.

BORN ON THIS DAY

Nobel Prize–winning chemist Rudolph A. Marcus
1923

1926
director and producer Norman Jewison

actor Art Hindle
1948

What Canadian city holds the Guinness World Record for largest parking lot? See October 8.

Alex Trebek, host of *Music Hop*, 1963.

1940. Television personality Alex Trebek is born in Sudbury, Ontario. He began his career as a news, weather, and sports broadcaster for CBC radio and television, and had his first gig as quizmaster for the show *Reach for the Top* from 1966 until 1973. In 1984, he became host of the American trivia game show *Jeopardy!* It was by far his most notable role, earning him numerous Emmy Awards for outstanding game show host. In 2014, Trebek set a Guinness World Record for hosting 6,829 episodes of *Jeopardy!*—the most game show episodes hosted by the same presenter (same program), surpassing the previous record holder, Bob Barker of *The Price Is Right*.

BORN ON THIS DAY

1820
politician Oliver Mowat

1941
Triple Crown jockey Ron Turcotte

1973
singer-songwriter Rufus Wainwright

LET'S MAKE IT A TRUE DAILY DOUBLE

Alex Trebek, as host of *Jeopardy!*

The recipient of an "immaculate" education, this popular TV host attended Jesuit schools as a child and went to boarding school at Ottawa's Oblates of Mary Immaculate before earning a degree in philosophy from the University of Ottawa.

"Who is Alex Trebek?"

Trebek summoned the strength of Hercules and snapped this ankle tendon, named after a Greek hero, when he chased a woman who was later arrested for robbing his hotel room in 2011.

"What is the Achilles tendon?"

Trebek got his start in the US in 1973 when fellow Canadian Alan Thicke, who had worked at the CBC as a writer on this long-running country music show, suggested Trebek for the NBC game show *The Wizard of Odds*.

"What is *The Tommy Hunter Show*?"

Although Will Ferrell immortalized Trebek in parodies on *Saturday Night Live*, Trebek's own favourite impersonation is done by this *SCTV* star. (Hint: rhymes with "blue jean heavy.")

"Who is Eugene Levy?"

Trebek carried a torch for this country when it hosted the Olympics in 1996, and was so smitten he became a naturalized citizen in 1998.

"What is the United States?"

23

Also on This Day

1885.
Financier Izaak Walton Killam is born in Yarmouth, Nova Scotia. In 1901, he joined the Union Bank of Halifax as a clerk. He went on to manage the London office of Lord Beaverbrook's Royal Securities, reputedly becoming Canada's wealthiest man. He left his entire fortune to his wife, Dorothy Killam, who carried out her husband's wishes by donating the greater part of their wealth to institutions that continue to support education, scientific research, and artistic ventures across Canada.

La Presse.

Jean-Paul Desbiens (centre) receives an award from the magazine *Liberté*, 1961. He is flanked by Jacques Godbout on the left and Gérard Pelletier on the right.

2006. Jean-Paul Desbiens, teacher, philosopher, writer, and journalist, dies in Château-Richer, Québec. Better known by the pseudonym Frère Untel, or Brother Anonymous, Desbiens was a member of the Catholic order of Marist Brothers and an activist for education reform. His 1960 book, *Les insolences du Frère Untel* (The Impertinences of Brother Anonymous), which denounced the failures of Québec's education system, became closely associated with the Quiet Revolution. But in 1961, Desbiens was removed from the debate by his superiors and sent off to Europe, where he studied theology and philosophy. Upon his return to Québec in 1964, he joined the ministry of education and became one of its chief architects of reform.

BORN ON THIS DAY

1961
author and comedian André Ducharme

1968
director Shawn Levy

Ed Mirvish Estate.

Ed Mirvish in front of the Ed Mirvish Theatre in Toronto, undated.

1914. Theatrical producer and entrepreneur Ed Mirvish is born in Colonial Beach, Virginia. His family moved to Toronto in 1923, and Mirvish eventually bought a series of stores around Bloor and Bathurst Streets, where he later opened the beloved discount emporium Honest Ed's. In 1963, he bought the historic Royal Alexandra Theatre in Toronto, saving it from demolition. With his son, David, he became a dominant force in Canadian theatre. In 1993, he and David opened the Princess of Wales Theatre, which was the first privately owned and financed theatre to be built in Canada since 1907. The Princess of Wales famously housed the Cameron Mackintosh production of *Miss Saigon*, the most expensive show in Canadian theatre up to that time.

Also on This Day

1967.
During a state visit for Expo 67, French president Charles de Gaulle proclaims, "Vive le Québec libre!" to a cheering crowd in front of Montréal's city hall, lending legitimacy to the Québec separatist slogan. After Prime Minister Lester Pearson went on television to tell de Gaulle that his statements were "unacceptable to the Canadian people and its government," the French president cut short his trip and went home.

BORN ON THIS DAY

actor, writer, and Squamish chief Dan George
1899

1917
composer, conductor, and arranger Robert Farnon

actress Anna Paquin
1982

Also on This Day

1930.
Opera singer Maureen Forrester is born in Montréal. She sang as a soprano until she was seventeen, and later became known as one of the world's leading contraltos. Her career spanned five decades and brought her international prominence. Forrester also served as chair of the Canada Council for the Arts.

Jacques Boissinot/The Canadian Press.

Bloc Québécois leader Lucien Bouchard at an election rally in Québec, 1993.

1990. The newly created Bloc Québécois (BQ), led by former Progressive Conservative cabinet minister Lucien Bouchard, unveils its separatist program in Montréal. Formed by a group of Québec MPs who left the Progressive Conservative and Liberal parties after the failure of the Meech Lake Accord, the BQ was established to promote Québec's interests and sovereignty in the House of Commons. It became an official political party in June 1991. The party's first major test came in 1992, when members campaigned against and ultimately contributed to the defeat of the Charlottetown Accord. The BQ was led by Bouchard until he left to become leader of the provincial Parti Québécois and premier of Québec in January 1996.

BORN ON THIS DAY

1905 — social activist and politician Grace MacInnis

1936 — actor August Schellenberg

1939 — politician and businesswoman Catherine Callbeck

1957 — skier Steve Podborski

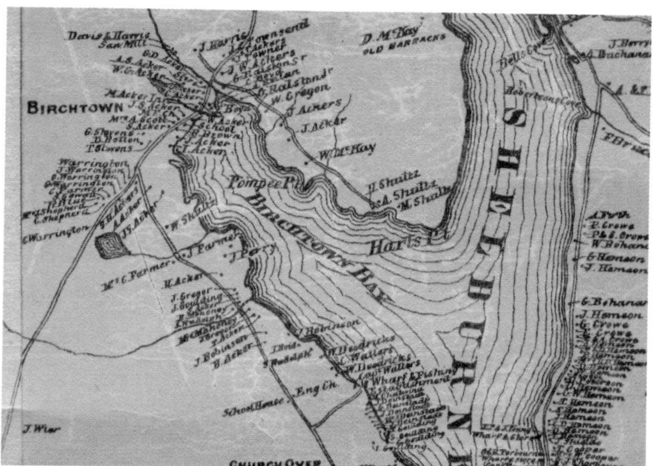

Nova Scotia Archives Map Collection/Topographical Township Map of Shelburne County.

This 1882 map of Birchtown, Nova Scotia, shows the names of property owners and local landmarks, including the church, school, store, and sawmill.

1784. Black Loyalists are among the first settlers in Shelburne, Digby, Chedabucto, and Halifax, Nova Scotia. Following the American Revolution, more than three thousand emancipated and free-born Black people came to the Maritimes, mostly Nova Scotia, to seek freedom from their slaveholders and to secure land and provisions promised by the British government. Most of these people, sometimes called the Black Loyalists, received a smaller grant than expected or nothing at all. Nearly half of them initially went to Shelburne; they subsequently founded a new settlement on less desirable land across the harbour and established their own community, called Birchtown. Anti-Black hostility reached a boiling point on July 26, 1784, as hundreds of disbanded white soldiers accused free Blacks of stealing jobs by working for intolerably low wages. The resulting race riot—the first recorded in North American history—continued in Shelburne for at least ten days; attacks against Blacks in Birchtown continued for a least a month.

Africville

Founded in the mid-eighteenth century, Africville was an African Canadian village located north of Halifax on the southern shore of Bedford Basin. Early settlers of the area may have included African people held as slaves and Jamaican Maroons (i.e., escaped slaves) resettled by the British. Black refugees from the War of 1812 and their descendants established a settlement at Africville in the 1840s. Settlers purchased land and the community prospered, though without help from the city of Halifax, which collected taxes from residents but did not provide essential services such as paved roads, running water, public transportation, garbage collection, and adequate police protection. After the city decided in 1962 to tear down the "dilapidated" structures in Africville under the guise of "urban renewal," land was expropriated and homes unceremoniously demolished. Displaced inhabitants found that the promised "home for home" deals did not materialize and compensation was inadequate. Many believe anti-Black racism was behind these decisions. This sad chapter in Canadian history was given due recognition when Africville was designated a National Historic Site in 1996, and in 2010 Halifax mayor Peter Kelly apologized for the community's destruction.

BORN ON THIS DAY

astrophysicist Frank Hogg
1904

1928
politician, lawyer, and businessman Peter Lougheed

pianist Angela Hewitt
1958

In His Own Words: Peter Chisholm

Peter Chisholm was sent to Korea as a lieutenant with the Royal Canadian Engineers (RCE), arriving just prior to the July 27, 1953, armistice. His work there was important in preparing South Korea for peace, as he marked and fenced minefields, helped establish the Demilitarized Zone, and removed bodies.

"The next morning, after the truce had been signed … our troop position was just southwest of Hill 355, and Hill 355, as a feature, sort of extended almost directly west, and the Chinese locations, west of Hill 355, were four hills referred to as Matthew, Mark, Luke, and John … And I don't know which one of the hills it was on, but when we got up at first light, on the twenty-seventh of July, the Chinese had erected a banner—it must have been two or three hundred metres long, bright blue—and we could readily read the lettering on it from where we were. And what the lettering said—excuse me—was 'Don't f*ck up the peace, boys.'"

— From the *Memory Project*

Fred Joyce/The Memory Project.

Canadian soldiers in Tokyo, after the announcement that the Korean War armistice has been signed.

1953. An armistice ends three years of combat in the Korean War. Canada had sent some twenty-seven thousand soldiers, sailors, and airmen to fight in Korea; more than five hundred lost their lives. The last Canadian soldiers left Korea in 1957. Upon their return home, veterans were not initially recognized for their war service, as the Korean conflict was described as a UN "police action." It was not until 1991 that the government established the Canadian Volunteer Service Medal for Korea. For this reason, and because it is often overshadowed by Canada's participation in the two world wars, the Korean War has been described as the "forgotten war."

Which war was known as "the engineer's war"? See December 18.

BORN ON THIS DAY

1934 equestrian Jim Elder

1942 singer-songwriter and folklorist Édith Butler

1949 actor Maury Chaykin

28 JULY

McCord Museum/VIEW-14851.

***Expulsion of the Acadians*, painting by Henri Beau, copied for Robert Glasgow, 1914–15.**

1755. British lieutenant-governor Charles Lawrence and the Nova Scotia Council decide to deport the French-speaking Acadians after delegates refuse to swear an oath of allegiance to Britain. The oath would have removed the Acadians' neutral status in the long-running battle for control of the region between the French and the English. The people who became known as the Acadians began to settle in present-day Nova Scotia with the 1604 founding of Port-Royal, a small, vibrant colony on the Annapolis River. The community hoped to avoid military backlash by not taking sides between the two great colonial powers. But their neutral stance ended with the *Grand Dérangement* (Great Upheaval), when approximately ten thousand Acadians from present-day Nova Scotia, New Brunswick, and Prince Edward Island were displaced. An unknown number perished from hunger, disease, and exposure during the expulsion, and ships full of exiles sank at sea.

Evangeline

Sometimes, historical fiction brings greater awareness of important events to the public consciousness. *Evangeline: A Tale of Acadie* (1847), a narrative poem by American writer Henry Wadsworth Longfellow, is one such example. The poem describes a young Acadian, Evangeline, searching for her lost love, Gabriel, during the Great Upheaval. Although the accuracy of certain historical details has since come into question, the poem was immensely popular in the United States and abroad, even among nineteenth-century Acadians, who regarded it as symbolic of the struggle of their ancestors.

BORN ON THIS DAY

1936 jazz artist Jim Galloway

1936 football player Russ Jackson

1970 figure skater Isabelle Brasseur

1971 speed skater Annie Perreault

Also on This Day

1874.
Politician James Woodsworth, the first leader of the Co-operative Commonwealth Federation, is born in Etobicoke, Ontario. He is credited with contributing to the creation of Canada's social security system. In 1922, he stated, "I submit that the Government exists to provide for the needs of the people, and when it comes to choice between profits and property rights on the one hand and human welfare on the other, there should be no hesitation whatsoever in saying that we are going to place the human welfare consideration first and let property rights and financial interests fare as best they may."

Morten Hvaal/AP/The Canadian Press.

Lewis Mackenzie behind an armoured personnel carrier at Sarajevo Airport.

1992. Canadian UN peacekeepers under Maj.-Gen. Lewis MacKenzie begin to withdraw from the Sarajevo Airport, having turned the facility over to the French relief force on July 28. At the end of the Cold War and with the breakup of Yugoslavia, Bosnia and Herzegovina was experiencing internal strife and ethnic conflict. In the mid-1990s, the UN sent peacekeeping forces to the area, including a large contingent of Canadians, to aid in bringing stability. Success was mixed. Since early July, the Canadians had been guarding the airport to permit safe arrival of humanitarian aid—including food and medical supplies—as well as undertaking dangerous missions to save local civilians caught in the crossfire. Canada's brave efforts in Sarajevo in July 1992 made international headlines.

BORN ON THIS DAY

actor Lloyd Bochner
1924

1938
broadcaster Peter Jennings

30 JULY

National Film Board of Canada/Chris Lund/Library and Archives Canada/1971-271 NPC.

Consulting a roadmap for the Trans-Canada Highway, 1952.

1962. British Columbia opens Rogers Pass to highway traffic, a major landmark in the construction of the Trans-Canada Highway. Public agitation for a national road began as early as 1910, but more than half a century elapsed before the highway was completed. Canadians could now drive (using ferry services on both coasts) from St. John's, Newfoundland, to Victoria, British Columbia—though more than three thousand kilometres was still unpaved and detours were sometimes necessary. Work had started in the summer of 1950 with an infusion of $150 million of federal funds provided for in the Trans-Canada Highway Act (1949). Finished in 1971, the highway ultimately cost over $1 billion. At almost eight thousand kilometres, it is among the world's longest national highways.

Also on This Day

1941.
Singer-songwriter Paul Anka is born in Ottawa. Anka became famous in the 1950s for writing and singing such teen favourites as "Diana" (his first number-one hit) and "Lonely Boy." He also wrote the theme for Johnny Carson's *Tonight Show.*

What has been described as the first all-weather road to cross the Arctic Circle?
See August 18.

BORN ON THIS DAY

1922
publisher Jack McClelland

1949
composer, pianist, and educator Alexina Louie

1971
comedian and actor Tom Green

Also on This Day

1932.
Canadian track-and-field athlete Duncan McNaughton wins an Olympic gold medal in high jump. American Bob Van Osdel, who took home the silver, was a close friend who actually coached McNaughton to his win. When McNaughton's medal was stolen in 1933, Van Osdel—by then a dentist—is said to have made a replica with a cast of his silver medal.

The Canadian Press.

Dr. Hawley Crippen after his arrest, being led away by Insp. Walter Dew.

1910. Wanted criminal Dr. Hawley Harvey Crippen, a homeopathic physician from Michigan, is arrested on the Canadian Pacific liner SS *Montrose* near Rimouski, Québec. Dr. Crippen was charged with murder in England after his wife's body was found under their cellar floor. He'd moved his lover into his home soon after reporting his wife's supposed death in California. Sensing something was amiss, a detective questioned Dr. Crippen, who soon after fled with his lover to Antwerp, where they sailed for Canada. The good doctor and his paramour, Ethel "Le Neve" Neave, posed as father and son on board the ship. Suspicious, the ship's captain wired its owners, who in turn informed British authorities that the fugitive might be on board. Dr. Crippen was the first murderer to be caught with the aid of wireless communication. He was hanged for his crime at Pentonville Prison, in England.

BORN ON THIS DAY

1928 director and screenwriter Gilles Carle

1966 curler Kevin Martin

1970 actress Amanda Stepto

1971 actress Christina Cox

AUGUST

THE CANADA GOOSE

There are at least eleven different species of Canada goose. The smallest, the cackling goose, weighs about 2 kilograms and lives in the Arctic. The largest, the giant Canada goose, weighs around 7 kilograms.

The Canada goose seems to have adapted to living alongside humans. In suburban areas, the geese are safe from both natural predators and hunters. There are currently at least seven million Canada geese in North America, and although half a million are killed in Canada each year by hunters, their numbers are stable or increasing.

Canada Goose is a successful brand of Canadian-made winter parkas and other outdoor clothing. The coats have become so popular that they're frequently counterfeited. The company now sews holograms into its garments to prove their authenticity.

A half a million years ago, the Canada goose settled in Hawaii, where it evolved into a giant species that seems to have been on its way to becoming flightless. The bird was hunted to extinction soon after humans arrived on the islands. A smaller descendant, the Hawaiian goose (more commonly called the nene), is the official state bird of Hawaii.

The collective noun for geese is gaggle; when flying close together they are called a plump.

The Canada goose has a long lifespan. A number of wild birds have lived for over thirty years.

Gerald R. Ford Presidential Library/A5764-9A.

President Ford signing the final act of the Conference on Security and Co-operation in Europe (the Helsinki Accords) on August 1, 1975. Trudeau is at the table, seventh from left.

1975. The Helsinki Accords are signed by a number of countries, including Canada. The accords were meant to reduce Cold War tensions between the West and the Eastern Bloc (as Albania, Bulgaria, Czechoslovakia, East Germany, Hungary, Poland, Romania, the Soviet Union, and Yugoslavia were then known). The Cold War began at the close of the Second World War and became publicly known because of the actions of a Soviet cipher clerk named Igor Gouzenko.

Why did Prime Minister Diefenbaker commission the top-secret construction of an underground safe house? See December 14.

The Gouzenko Affair

The Gouzenko Affair started on September 5, 1945, when Igor Gouzenko, a cipher clerk at the Soviet embassy in Ottawa, stuffed over a hundred documents into his clothes and attempted to turn the sensitive information over to the *Ottawa Journal* and then to the Ministry of Justice. He was rebuffed by both. Prime Minister Mackenzie King did not act until Soviet agents ransacked the Gouzenkos' apartment. Gouzenko and his family were granted political asylum and the story was kept secret until February 1946, when an American journalist leaked it. Gouzenko's documents revealed that the Soviets, allies of the West during the Second World War, had spies in key agencies of the Canadian government. The accused spies were soon arrested. The Soviets were the new enemies, and the Cold War was on.

BORN ON THIS DAY

1793 — singer and actress Eva Tanguay

1876 — actor Arthur Hill

AUGUST 2

The Douglas Treaties

- **Teechamitsa Tribe:** Country lying between Esquimalt and Point Albert
- **Kosampsom Tribe:** Esquimalt Peninsula and Colquite Valley
- **Swengwhung Tribe:** Victoria Peninsula, South of Colitz
- **Chilcowitch Tribe:** Point Gonzales
- **Whyomilth Tribe:** Northwest of Esquimalt Harbour
- **Che-ko-nein Tribe:** Point Gonzales to Cedar Hill
- **Ka-ky-aakan Tribe:** Metchosin
- **Chewhaytsum Tribe:** Sooke
- **Sooke Tribe:** Northwest of Sooke Inlet
- **Saanich Tribe:** South Saanich
- **Saanich Tribe:** North Saanich
- **Queackar Tribe:** Fort Rupert
- **Quakeolth Tribe:** Fort Rupert
- **Saalequun Tribe:** Nanaimo

In exchange for signing the treaties, the individual Aboriginal communities received payments of blankets calculated in pounds sterling. They were also promised the right to hunt and fish as before and the continued use of their villages and fields. Most of British Columbia's land was never formally purchased from residing Aboriginal groups.

Library and Archives Canada/1971-109 NPC.

A view of Victoria, ca. 1870.

1862. Victoria, British Columbia, is incorporated as a city. The site was chosen for settlement around 1843 by James Douglas, chief factor at the Hudson's Bay Company at Fort Vancouver (present-day Vancouver, Washington), and it became HBC's western headquarters in 1849. Between 1850 and 1854, Douglas, as governor of BC, concluded fourteen treaties—the so-called Douglas Treaties—with local Aboriginal groups to secure title to land in the vicinity of Victoria. However, translation problems likely caused misunderstandings about the meaning of these documents, and evidence exists that some of the Aboriginal leaders involved believed they were negotiating peace treaties, not selling their land.

BORN ON THIS DAY

movie producer Jack Warner
1892

1932
Hockey Hall of Famer Leo Boivin

pianist, composer, and conductor André Gagnon
1939

1948
politician, lawyer, and author Bob Rae

Library and Archives Canada/Canada invents/ISBN 1894379233/P. 82/ NLC-10064.

A Ganong storefront in Québec, 1934.

1877. Chocolate manufacturer and politician Arthur Ganong is born in St. Stephen, New Brunswick. He worked in the family chocolate business, and according to legend, he and a company employee began placing long pieces of chocolate in a protective wrapping to take along on fishing trips. The company would go on to introduce, in 1910, the first individually wrapped chocolate bar in North America.

Other Notable Canadian Food Inventions

1894:
Red Rose Tea, New Brunswick

1918:
Habitant Pea Soup, Québec

1923:
Jos Louis Snack Cake, Québec

1924:
Red River Cereal, Manitoba

1939:
Coffee Crisp, Nova Scotia

1982:
Breton Crackers, Ontario

BORN ON THIS DAY

Governor General Lord Aberdeen (George Hamilton-Gordon)
1847

1915
politician, businessman, and Nisga'a Tribal Council founder Frank Calder

Hockey Hall of Famer Marcel Dionne
1951

AUGUST 4

Canadian War Museum/George Metcalf Archival Collection/19940081-004.

A Toronto streetcar recruiting for the No. 1 Construction Battalion.

1914. Britain declares war on Germany, launching the First World War. On June 28, Archduke Franz Ferdinand of Austria had been assassinated by Serb nationalist Gavrilo Princip, leading to hostilities between Austria-Hungary and Serbia that drew in other regional powers, including Russia and Germany. As Russia mobilized against the Austro-Hungarian invasion of Serbia, Germany invaded neutral Belgium and Luxembourg. Britain issued an ultimatum to withdraw from Belgium. When Germany ignored the ultimatum, which expired on August 4, the British Empire, including Canada, was at war.

Canada and the Great War

Start: July/August 1914
End: November 11, 1918
Canada's total population: 8 million
Canadians who served (men and women): 630,000
Canadians who went overseas: 425,000
Canadians killed: 60,661
Canadians wounded: 172,000

BORN ON THIS DAY

1921 — Hockey Hall of Famer Maurice "Rocket" Richard

1931 — curler Ernie Richardson

The BAnQ Vieux-Montreal/P66, S9, P21.

Camillien Houde returning after his internment in Fredericton, 1944.

1940. Camillien Houde, the mayor of Montréal, is arrested by the RCMP and the Québec Provincial Police for sedition. Houde had issued a statement urging "the population" not to take part in compulsory registration for military service, part of the National Resources Mobilization Act. This act gave the federal government the ability to enlist the property and services of Canadians for home defence. Houde viewed this as a conscription measure, and he felt the government of Mackenzie King had reneged on its promise not to draft Canadians. At least fifty thousand Montréalers welcomed Houde triumphantly after his release from internment on August 18, 1944, and he was quickly re-elected mayor, a position he held comfortably through elections in 1947 and 1950.

Also on This Day

1907.
Rodeo cowboy Herman Linder is born in Darlington, Wisconsin. He would go on to produce rodeo shows, including one at Expo 67 in Montréal, and eventually would come to be known as the King of the Cowboys at the Calgary Stampede.

What natural disaster almost prevented the 2013 Calgary Stampede? See September 2.

BORN ON THIS DAY

1918 National Ballet School of Canada founder Betty Oliphant

1968 singer-songwriter Terri Clark

1981 skier Erik Guay

Also on This Day

1969.
During practice for an aerobatic show at the annual regatta in Kelowna, British Columbia, a US navy jet causes a sonic boom that shatters windows over an eight-block area of downtown.

Muskoxen in the Canadian Arctic.

1992. The creation of Aulavik National Park on Banks Island, Northwest Territories, is announced. Founded on the westernmost island of the Arctic Archipelago, along the Thomsen River valley, Aulavik is an Inuvialuktun name that means "where people travel." The Thomsen River valley is the most productive area in the world for muskoxen, and the Lower Thomsen River is a designated migratory bird sanctuary, home to a large population of Brant geese. Access to the park is by charter aircraft from Inuvik, about eight hundred kilometres southwest.

BORN ON THIS DAY

1820
businessman, politician, and diplomat Donald A. Smith

1845
Governor General the Marquess of Lorne (John Douglas Sutherland Campbell)

1946
singer-songwriter Carole Pope

7 AUGUST

Library and Archives Canada/Albert Almon/PA-051546.

Anna Swan and her husband Martin Van Buren Bates, ca. 1878.

A Canadian Giant

Known as the Cape Breton Giant, Angus MacAskill was born in Scotland in 1825 and grew up in St. Ann's, Nova Scotia. He reportedly grew to be 2.36 metres (7 feet 9 inches) tall and weighed 193 kilograms (425 pounds). He toured as a curiosity, but later made his living as a farmer and businessman back in St. Ann's. MacAskill died in 1863. The Giant Angus McAskill Museum on Cape Breton houses his chair, bed, clothing, and other custom-sized artifacts.

1846. Giantess Anna Swan is born in Mill Brook, Nova Scotia. Measuring 2.31 metres (7 feet 6 inches), she was a star attraction of P.T. Barnum's American Museum in New York. Having joined Barnum when she was just sixteen years old, the intelligent, well-spoken Swan was paid $1,000 a month and provided with a private tutor so she could continue her studies. In 1871, she married a giant from Kentucky named Martin Van Buren Bates, who built them a customized house in Ohio with soaring ceilings and made-to-measure furniture.

BORN ON THIS DAY

author Deborah Ellis

1960

1965

figure skater Elizabeth Manley

AUGUST 8

Also on This Day

1944.
Premier Maurice Duplessis returns to power in the Québec provincial election, narrowly defeating the sitting premier, nationalist Adélard Godbout. Duplessis easily held his position for the next fifteen years, becoming known as *le Chef*—"the chief."

Josh McCulloch/Picture BC.

Vancouver's downtown skyline, modern day.

What ship carrying over 370 British subjects of Indian origin arrived in Vancouver in 1914 but was forced to return to India after a two-month stalemate?
See May 23.

1887. The Vancouver Electric Illumination Company starts up its steam-powered generating plant, illuminating fifty-three streetlights and about three hundred lights in private homes and offices. The recent completion of the Canadian Pacific Railway was associated with a rapid pace of change in Vancouver and a significant population boom that saw the city grow from one thousand inhabitants in 1887 to fourteen thousand by 1891. The Vancouver Electric Illumination Company was a precursor for BC Hydro, which was formed by the province in 1962 and soon after began developing the hydroelectric potential of the Peace and Columbia Rivers.

BORN ON THIS DAY

1938
composer and teacher Jacques Hétu

1947
Hockey Hall of Famer Ken Dryden

1948
Assembly of First Nations national chief Georges Erasmus

9 AUGUST

Ronny Jacques/Library and Archives Canada/R3133-664-1-F.

Paul-Émile Borduas, 1946.

1948. Written primarily by painter Paul-Émile Borduas and signed by fifteen Québécois artists and intellectuals, including Jean-Paul Riopelle, the *Refus global* (Total Refusal) manifesto is launched. The manifesto was a by-product of Borduas's surrealist-inspired Automatistes movement, which called for the abandonment of the artistic to the subconscious. *Refus global* also challenged the traditional values of Québec—advocating liberation and spontaneity in art and life—and called for an expansion of Québec society into international thought. Borduas lost his job as a teacher at Montréal's *École du meuble* as a result of the manifesto, and by January 1949 more than a hundred newspaper and magazine articles had condemned it.

Also on This Day

1988.
In a move that left hockey fans stunned, owner Peter Pocklington trades Wayne Gretzky of the Edmonton Oilers to the Los Angeles Kings for Jimmy Carson, Martin Gélinas, three first-round draft picks, and millions of dollars in cash.

Which artist challenged Québec's post-war conservatism? See March 12.

BORN ON THIS DAY

1934 author Graeme Gibson

1942 comedian and director David Steinberg

1950 Trivial Pursuit co-creator Chris Haney

1964 Hockey Hall of Famer Brett Hull

Notable Canadian Physicians

Sir Frederick Banting: Discovered insulin with his assistant, Charles Best, and their colleagues
Dr. Norman Bethune: Surgeon, inventor, and political activist; renowned in the People's Republic of China
Dr. Gustave Gingras: Dedicated to helping individuals with physical disabilities
Kahkewaquonaby: Probably the first Aboriginal person to become a medical doctor in Canada
Sir William Osler: Physician, writer, and educator
Dr. Wilder Penfield: Neurosurgeon who developed a surgical treatment for epilepsy
Dr. Emily Howard Stowe: Canada's first openly practising female doctor
Dr. Lucille Teasdale: One of the first female surgeons in Canada; devoted to improving health care in Uganda

Library and Archives Canada/1986-7-255.

Mohawk chief Oronhyatekha, painted by Henry Wentworth Acland, 1860.

1841. Physician and fraternal order administrator Oronhyatekha (Burning Cloud) was born on the Six Nations reserve near Brantford, in what is now Ontario. While not the first Aboriginal person to be accredited as a medical doctor, Oronhyatekha was perhaps the first to practise in Canada and, later, was the first supreme chief ranger of the new Independent Order of Foresters (IOF), a fraternal benefit organization with origins in Britain. At Oronhyatekha's death in 1907, the IOF had over 250,000 members worldwide and more than $10 million in liquid assets.

BORN ON THIS DAY

1865 artist James Wilson Morrice

1979 singer Matt Mays

11 AUGUST

An ice sheet remnant between Qikiqtarjuaq and Cape Dyer on Baffin Island, Nunavut.

1576. While searching west of Greenland for a passage to Asia, explorer Martin Frobisher sails into the bay that would later bear his name, in modern-day Nunavut. Believing it to be a passage of water dividing Asia to the north and America to the south, he named it Frobisher Strait, and that's how it appeared on maps until 1861, when American mariner Charles Francis Hall explored the area and discovered that it was, in fact, a bay.

Also on This Day

1922.
Author Mavis Gallant is born in Montréal. Considered one of the world's finest writers of short fiction, she was known for collections such as *Montreal Stories* and *Home Truths*, which earned her a Governor General's Literary Award in 1981.

BORN ON THIS DAY

1930 actor and television host Paul Soles

1960 actress, singer, and dancer Cynthia Dale

1966 skeleton racer Duff Gibson

1968 singer-songwriter Veda Hille

Frank Gunn/The Canadian Press.

Prime Minister Brian Mulroney signing the North American Free Trade Agreement with Trade Minister Michael Wilson.

1992. Trade Minister Michael Wilson concludes negotiations for a draft North American Free Trade Agreement (NAFTA) between Canada, the United States, and Mexico. NAFTA came into effect on January 1, 1994, creating a huge free trade zone of about 370 million people by reducing the barriers to commerce and investment and making businesses exempt from various government regulations. The agreement resulted in increased trade between the three countries.

Also on This Day

1914.

Songwriter Ruth Lowe is born in Toronto. At sixteen, she was a "song plugger," playing piano in Toronto music stores to promote sheet music. She began performing in nightclubs as part of a two-piano team, and later joined various musical groups. After her husband's sudden death, Lowe wrote her first hit song, "I'll Never Smile Again." It was covered by many artists, among them Frank Sinatra and the Ink Spots. Another of her songs, "Put Your Dreams Away (For Another Day)," became Sinatra's closing theme for many years.

What came before NAFTA? See March 17.

BORN ON THIS DAY

1904

curler Ken Watson

1956

singer Bruce Greenwood

1978

hockey player Hayley Wickenheiser

13 AUGUST

1535. The word "Canada" first appears in the journals of Jacques Cartier after he sails past Anticosti Island in the Gulf of St. Lawrence. Two Aboriginal youths are said to have pointed out the route to a nearby village they called *kanata* (likely Stadacona, the Iroquoian village located at the present-day site of Québec City). *Kanata* was simply the Iroquoian word for "village" or "settlement," but Cartier adopted the name "Canada" for the entire area controlled by Chief Donnacona. Cartier documented his impressions of the "Kingdom of Canada," identifying the mouth of the St. Lawrence River as the "way to and the beginning of . . . the route to Canada." By 1547, maps designated all land north of the St. Lawrence River as "Canada."

Library and Archives Canada/1953-24-31.

Jacques Cartier, undated.

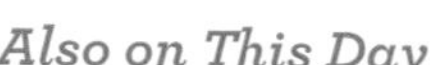

Also on This Day

1900.
Pioneer director and filmmaker Gordon Sparling is born in Toronto. He would go on to create the Canadian Cameo series of short films, which were Canada's first major films with sound.

Which explorer was also known as the Father of New France? See January 15.

BORN ON THIS DAY

Hockey Hall of Famer "Bullet" Joe Simpson
1893

1941
actress Erin Fleming

Hockey Hall of Famer Bobby Clarke
1949

AUGUST 14

Also on This Day

1935.
Lucile Wheeler, winner of Canada's first Olympic medal in skiing (a bronze at Cortina d'Ampezzo, Italy, in 1956), is born in Montréal. In 1958, after winning both the downhill and the giant slalom titles at the Alpine World Ski Championships, she was inducted into the Canadian Olympic Hall of Fame and Canada's Sports Hall of Fame.

Library and Archives Canada © Mr. Brian Johannesson.

Members of the Winnipeg Falcons hockey team en route to the Olympics in Belgium.

1920. Among Canada's delegates to the 1920 Summer Olympics in Antwerp were the Winnipeg Falcons, one-time underdogs who became the top hockey team in Canada. The Falcons Hockey Club, made up almost entirely of players of Icelandic descent, faced discrimination in its early days and was barred from Winnipeg's hockey leagues. Just before the First World War began, the team had been gaining momentum and was accepted into the city's senior league. Most eligible players enlisted, and two teammates were killed in action. After the war, the team reassembled and went on to win the Allan Cup, securing their place at the Olympics. The team travelled back to Europe, this time to represent Canada on the ice and to win the first-ever gold medal in Olympic ice hockey.

BORN ON THIS DAY

1860
author and wildlife artist Ernest Thompson Seton

1972
makeup artist Jay Manuel

1976
actor Steve Braun

15 AUGUST

Library and Archives Canada/e011073127.

Oscar Peterson with his sister Daisy, undated.

1925. Jazz pianist and composer Oscar Peterson, whose numerous awards include a Grammy for lifetime achievement, is born in Montréal. Few jazz musicians were recorded more extensively, and even fewer Canadian musicians would enjoy the same level of international fame. Among Peterson's best-known compositions was his *Canadiana Suite*, comprising jazz themes inspired by cities and regions of Canada. A life-like sculpture of Peterson at his piano—a tribute to the legendary musician, who passed away in 2007—was unveiled by the Queen and the Duke of Edinburgh outside the National Arts Centre in Ottawa in 2010.

Which pianist and composer hated performing live? See April 10.

Oscar Peterson: Select Awards

1975: Grammy Award, Best Jazz Performance, Group, for *The Trio*

1978: Inducted into the Juno Hall of Fame

1978: Grammy Award, Best Jazz Performance, Soloist, for *The Giants*

1979: Grammy Award, Best Jazz Instrumental Performance, Soloist, for *Oscar Peterson Jam—Montreux '77*

1980: Grammy Award, Best Jazz Instrumental Performance, Soloist, for *Oscar Peterson and the Trumpet Kings—Jousts*

1987: Juno Award, Best Jazz Album, for *If You Could See Me Now*

1990: Grammy Awards, Best Jazz Instrumental Performance, Soloist, and Group, for *The Legendary Oscar Peterson Trio Live at the Blue Note*

1991: Grammy Award, Best Jazz Instrumental Performance, Group, for *Saturday Night at the Blue Note*

1992: Governor General's Performing Arts Award

1993: Glenn Gould Prize

1997: Grammy Award for Lifetime Achievement

1997: International Jazz Hall of Fame Award

2000: UNESCO International Music Prize

2008: Canadian Songwriters Hall of Fame Legacy Award

BORN ON THIS DAY

Arctic mariner Robert Bartlett
1875

1948
singer, actress, and songwriter Patsy Gallant

actress Natasha Henstridge
1974

2000. Prime Minister Jean Chrétien is hit with a pie while attending a meet-and-greet with local residents in Prince Edward Island. The lone protestor was able to slip past RCMP security to approach the prime minister. Calling himself a member of the PEI Pie Brigade, he claimed to be protesting a variety of issues, including poverty and the sale of genetically engineered foods in Canada. He was arrested and charged with assault. Making light of the incident, Chrétien quipped that PEI had "developed a funny way of serving pie these days."

Who was Canada's twentieth prime minister? See November 4.

Jean Chrétien, "Pie" Minister, by Aislin, 2000.

In His Own Words: Aislin

Terry Mosher (pen name Aislin), the Montreal Gazette's well-known political cartoonist, captured the moment when Chrétien transformed from prime minister into "pie" minister. "In 2000, a lone protestor slipped by Jean Chretien's RCMP security guards and planted a cream pie in the prime minister's face," Aislin explained. "Initially, Chrétien was not happy about this, so I drew this caricature with him pondering how to clean up the mess. (Note the play on words regarding his adversary, Paul Martin). Jean Chrétien was very easy to caricature from any angle. Here he is instantly recognizable without us even able to see his face."

BORN ON THIS DAY

1954 — director James Cameron

1972 — TV and radio host George Stroumboulopoulos

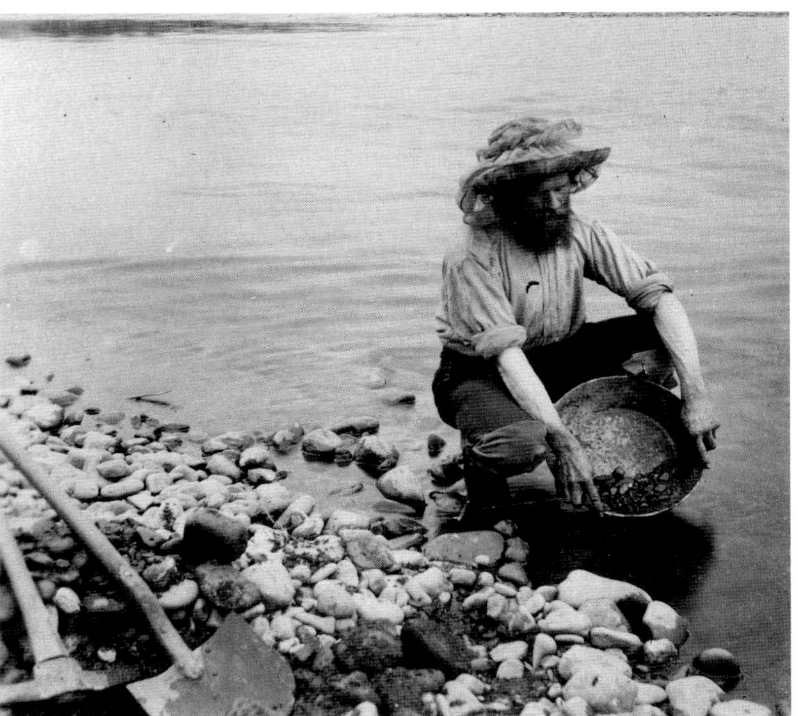

Library and Archives Canada/C-005389

Panning for gold in the Klondike, ca. 1897.

1896. George Washington Carmack, Keish (better known as Skookum Jim Mason), and Káa Goox (Dawson Charlie) discover gold on Bonanza Creek (then known as Rabbit Creek), a tributary of the Klondike River. From 1897 to 1899, tens of thousands stampeded north for the Klondike Gold Rush. The discovery of gold and the influx of people led to the establishment of Dawson City in 1896 and the creation of the Yukon Territory in 1898.

Born on This Day

1964.
Guitarist and songwriter Colin James is born in Regina in 1964. His major label debut, a self-titled album in 1988, featured the hit songs "Five Long Years," "Why'd You Lie," and "Voodoo Thing." Known for blending pop, rock, and swing, Colin James has won a string of JUNO Awards, including Single of the Year for "Just Came Back" (1991), Male Vocalist of the Year (1995 and 1996), and Best Blues Album for *National Steel* (1998).

BORN ON THIS DAY

astronaut and biomedical engineer Robert Thirsk

1953

1963

actor and filmmaker Don McKellar

AUGUST 18

Also on This Day

1849.
In an important moment in the history of race relations in Canada, Edwin Larwill, a virulent segregationist, challenges Rev. William King to a debate. Larwill opposed King's proposal to establish the Elgin Settlement for escaped slaves from the United States. Although King was reportedly booed and hissed at during the debate, Larwill ultimately lost political support for his anti-Black position. The Elgin Settlement, also called Buxton, was eventually built on a tract of land in what is now southwestern Ontario and was for many the last stop on the Underground Railroad.

© Erica Thompson.

The Dempster Highway, just before the Yukon–Northwest Territories border.

1979. The Dempster Highway officially opens in Flat Creek, Yukon. Twenty years earlier, as part of Prime Minister John Diefenbaker's Roads to Resources Program, construction began on what has been described as the first all-weather road to cross the Arctic Circle. The highway was named after Insp. William J.D. Dempster of the RCMP, who served thirty-six of his thirty-seven years on the force at various posts in the Yukon. Upon completion, the Dempster Highway—which stretches from just east of Dawson City to Inuvik—added 730 kilometres of road trip possibilities in Canada.

Which "conductor" lived in St. Catharine's, Ontario? See March 10.

BORN ON THIS DAY

1893
composer and conductor Sir Ernest MacMillan

1932
British Columbia premier Bill Bennett

1977
singer-songwriter Régine Chassagne

Ministry of National Defence/Library and Archives Canada/PA-171080.

Landing craft en route to Dieppe, France, during Operation Jubilee, August 19, 1942.

1942. Canadian and British troops raid the French port of Dieppe. Operation Jubilee was the first Canadian Army engagement in the war, and it was meant to test the Allies' ability to launch amphibious assaults against German-controlled ports. The disastrous raid lasted only nine hours, but of the nearly five thousand Canadian soldiers involved, more than nine hundred were killed and almost two thousand taken prisoner.

In His Own Words: David Mann

David Mann served with the Royal Regiment of Canada as runner for the reserve platoon. He landed at Puys, called "Blue Beach," one of the initial landing sites of Operation Jubilee, and was ultimately wounded and unable to get off the beach.

"There was very little beach. There was a seawall and then a cliff, a very steep cliff, and that's what we were up against. And grenades and shellfire [were] just pouring at us. And you could see a whole line of people lined up in front of the seawall just where they fell. They fell when they hit the beach actually. They were just like shooting fish in a barrel."

BORN ON THIS DAY

1928 sculptor Qaqaq Ashoona

1948 singer-songwriter Susan Jacks

1969 actor Matthew Perry

Clarifying the Clarity Act

The Clarity Act defines the requirement for clarity set out by the Supreme Court of Canada in its ruling on Québec secession. It states that among other things, a constitutional amendment is required if a province is to secede from Canada. A provincial referendum can lead to negotiation with federal government but does not in itself satisfy the requirements for secession. Furthermore, the act declared that the House of Commons alone has the power to decide on the clarity of any question being posed in a referendum. When enacted in 2000, the Clarity Act met with opposition from Québec sovereignists, but overall, it was favourably received across the country.

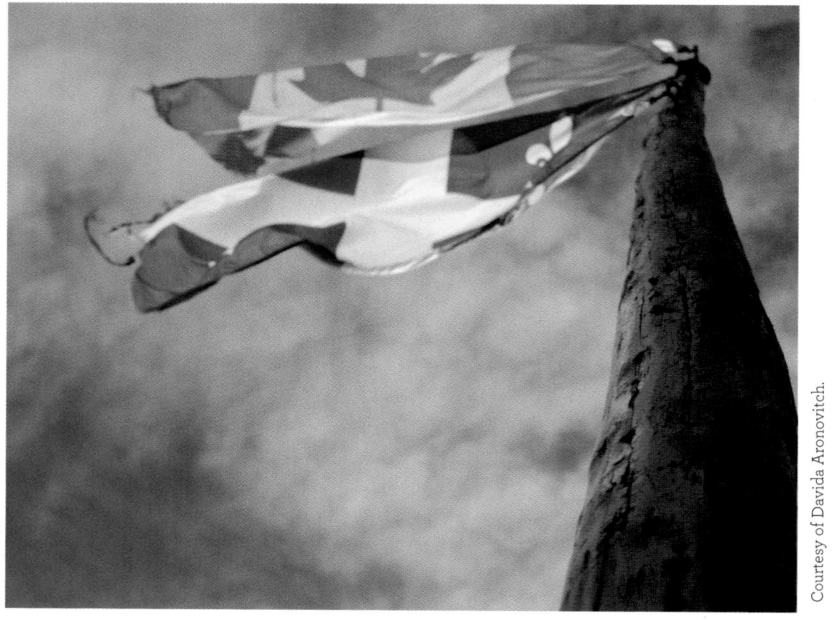

Courtesy of Davida Aronovitch.

The flags of Canada and Québec share a pole in Gaspé.

1998. The Supreme Court rules that Québec cannot separate from Canada without first negotiating the terms of secession with the federal government and the other provinces. Both the government of Québec and the government of Canada declared this ruling a victory, as the legal reasoning allowed for numerous interpretations. In 2000, largely in response to the court's ruling, the federal government passed the Clarity Act, which defined what constitutes a clear question and a clear majority in any future referendum on secession.

BORN ON THIS DAY

1930 — conductor and pianist Mario Bernardi

1957 — swimmer Cindy Nicholas

21 AUGUST

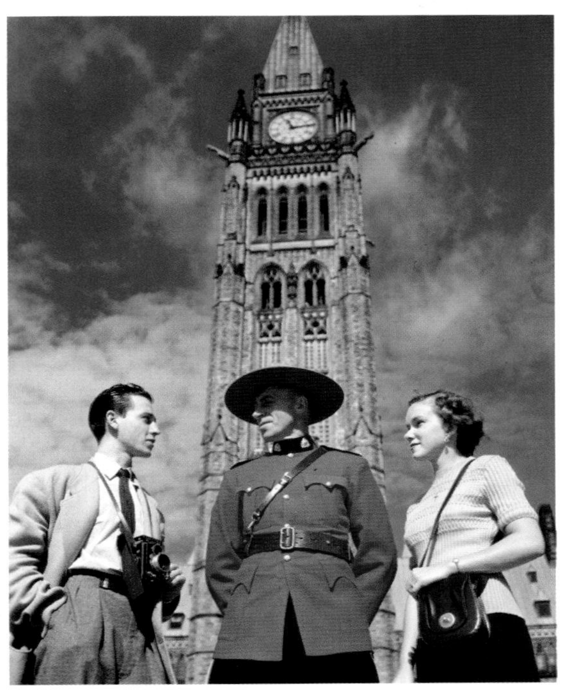

Two people speak with an RCMP officer in front of the Peace Tower in Ottawa, 1949.

1860. Police officer Aylesworth Bowen Perry is born in Violet, Ontario. As commissioner of the North-West Mounted Police (the forerunner of the RCMP), he transformed the force from a romantic part of frontier lore into a legitimate national police force. He is known for modernizing equipment and methods, and was in charge when the headquarters moved from Regina to Ottawa in 1920. That same year, Perry was responsible for reorganizing the NWMP and the Dominion Police into the Royal Canadian Mounted Police. The RCMP is the world's only national, federal, provincial, and municipal policing body.

Also on This Day

1871.
Treaty No. 2 is concluded between the Crown and the Chippewa peoples, also known as the Ojibwa, opening a tract of land in what is now southwest Manitoba and part of southeast Saskatchewan to immigration and settlement.

BORN ON THIS DAY

1912 — Hockey Hall of Famer Hector "Toe" Blake

1956 — actress Kim Cattrall

1967 — actress Carrie-Anne Moss

AUGUST 22

1992. The country's premiers emerge from discussions about the text of the Charlottetown Accord, which ultimately recognized Québec as a distinct society, gave all provinces a veto on changes to national institutions, and established a new Senate. The agreement was finalized on August 28 and subsequently put to a referendum. Despite being endorsed by every provincial premier and a number of influential political groups, the accord was rejected by Canadian voters in the midst of an era marked by high anti-government sentiment.

***Poker Game*, by Aislin, 1991.**

In His Own Words: Aislin

"Here I have cartooned Canadian prime minister Brian Mulroney and Québec premier Robert Bourassa in the midst of a tense poker game, actually an allegory for the ongoing difficult negotiations between Canada and Québec over myriad matters," explained Aislin (Terry Mosher) of his 1991 editorial cartoon for the *Montreal Gazette*. "In fact, the two were fast friends. However, that never got in the way of them each looking for an advantage in bargaining for their respective domains."

BORN ON THIS DAY

1827 — businessman and politician Ezra Butler Eddy

1915 — scientist James Hillier

1958 — actor Colm Feore

The Ogopogo stamp issued by Canada Post as part of the Legendary Creatures series in 1990.

1926. The name Ogopogo—a palindrome from a popular music-hall song—was first used in Vernon, British Columbia, to refer to the legendary beast the Salish people called *N'ha-a-itk*, meaning "sacred creature of the water" or "snake in the lake." Perhaps Canada's most famous water monster, Ogopogo is said to live in Lake Okanagan and is variously described as having a horse-shaped head and a serpent-like neck.

Cryptids in Canada

Windigo: Cree and Ojibwa legends state that the Windigo is a spirit that can take possession of vulnerable persons and cause them to engage in various types of antisocial behaviour, including cannibalism.

Sasquatch: A mysterious ape-like creature said to roam remote regions of the Pacific Northwest, the sasquatch appears in Aboriginal myths and was reported in the journals of early explorers. Sightings have persisted to modern day. As recently as 2006, claims of sasquatch sightings have been made in Deschambault Lake, Saskatchewan, and Flin Flon, Manitoba.

Cadborosaurus ("Caddy"): A long-necked, horse-headed creature reportedly seen in British Columbia waters and named after Cadboro Bay, near Victoria.

BORN ON THIS DAY

publisher William Southam
1843

1960
actor Chris Potter

politician Martin Cauchon
1962

In His Own Words: Alex Colville

"In the field, of course, it was not feasible to do big canvases or anything like that. So I did watercolours and drawings, and I think most of the war artists worked in that way. Then we had periods in London, often of some weeks or perhaps months occasionally, when we were working on doing big things from sketches that we had done in the field ... So it was what would be a kind of literary equivalent to a person being a kind of reporter—with a division or whatever—and later writing a book or a long article in a capital city, kind of gathering together what he had done. For me, it was work. If you're a writer or a painter, your material is life as you see it being lived and that's it. You get to work and do it."

Department of National Defence/Lieutenant Barney J. Gloster/Library and Archives Canada/PA-206003.

Lieut. Alex Colville, war artist, with the 3rd Canadian Infantry Division in Germany, 1945.

1920. Painter Alex Colville is born in Toronto. Colville joined the army and was sent to Europe as a war artist in 1944. He returned to Canada late in 1945 and worked in Ottawa on paintings based on his sketches and watercolours until his demobilization in 1946. His later works represented his immediate, intimate environment and reflected a world that was at once joyful and disturbing. The $1.29-million sale of *Man on Verandah* in 2010 set a new record for a work by a living artist in Canada. Colville passed away on July 16, 2013, leaving a lasting legacy as one of Canada's pre-eminent artists. Among his admirers is Hollywood director Wes Anderson, who included a tribute to Colville's *To Prince Edward Island*, his famous binocular painting, in his film *Moonrise Kingdom*.

BORN ON THIS DAY

1922 journalist and Québec premier René Lévesque

1942 artist Tony Hunt

1972 skier Jean-Luc Brassard

25 AUGUST

Library and Archives Canada/Miscellaneous collection/PA-022208.

The Victoria Bridge in Montréal.

1860. The Prince of Wales presides over a ceremony officially opening the Victoria Bridge, which spans the St. Lawrence River at Montréal. Work had begun on July 20, 1854. At nearly three kilometres and with twenty-four ice-breaking piers, it was the first bridge to span the St. Lawrence River and was considered one of the engineering wonders of its day.

Also on This Day

1873.
One of the deadliest storms ever recorded in Canada ravages the Maritimes and Newfoundland after having reached the coast of Nova Scotia the previous day. The cyclone destroyed over a thousand ships and left more than five hundred people dead.

What musical artist paid tribute to the people killed in Vancouver's Second Narrows Bridge collapse?
See June 17.

BORN ON THIS DAY

1910
actress Ruby Keeler

1921
author and journalist Brian Moore

1941
playwright Carol Bolt

1944
publisher and author Conrad Black

AUGUST 26

Also on This Day

1875.
Author and future governor general John Buchan is born in Perth, Scotland. A prolific writer, Buchan penned more than one hundred books, including the 1915 suspense novel *The Thirty-Nine Steps*, which director Alfred Hitchcock turned into a film in 1935.

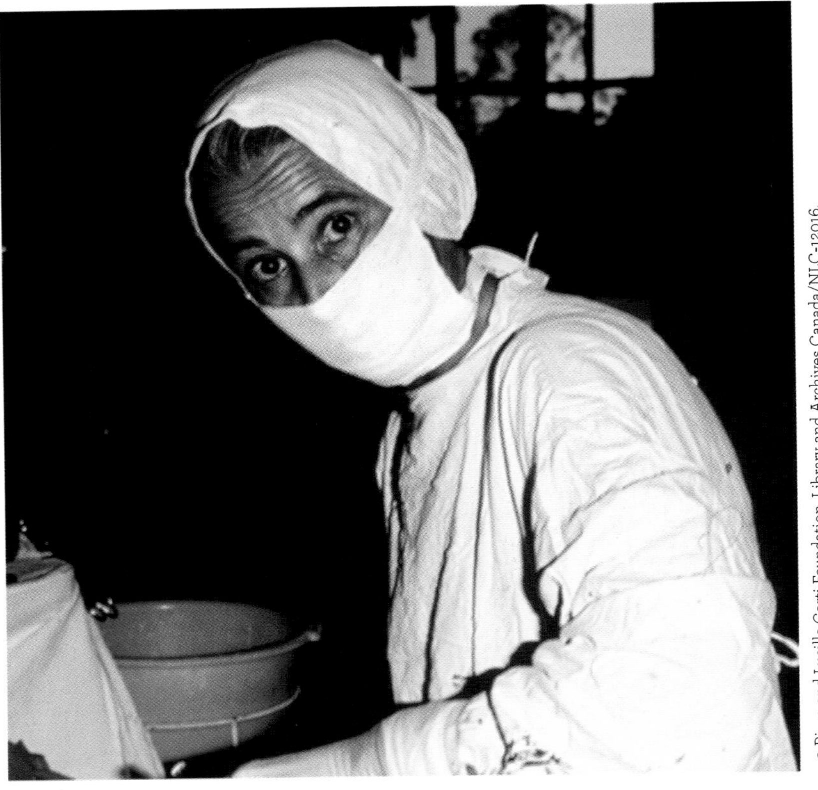

Dr. Lucille Teasdale performing surgery, undated.

1987. Dr. Lucille Teasdale receives the Frederic Newton Gisborne Starr Award, the highest award granted by the Canadian Medical Association, for her devotion to the people of Uganda. Teasdale had travelled to Uganda in 1961 with a fellow doctor, Piero Corti, whom she married later that year. Together, they began transformative work at St. Mary's Hospital Lacor. The pair remained devoted to their practice during years of civil war and unrest in the country. Over the course of her career, Teasdale performed more than thirteen thousand operations. In 1985, she discovered she was HIV-positive, likely having contracted the illness by performing surgery on infected soldiers. After an eleven-year battle with HIV/AIDS, Lucille Teasdale passed away in 1996.

BORN ON THIS DAY

paleontologist Alice Evelyn Wilson
1881

1910
surgeon Jessie Catherine Gray

musician Peter Appleyard
1928

1957
athlete Rick Hansen

Adventurers Thomas W. Wilby and Jack Haney.

1912. Sponsored by the REO Motor Car Company, Thomas Wilby and Jack Haney begin the first cross-Canada motor trip in Halifax, Nova Scotia. Wilby was a journalist and Haney an REO mechanic and driver. Though long stretches of the journey were made by rail or ferry where roads were non-existent, the REO is said to have covered a distance of about sixty-seven hundred kilometres. The trip lasted fifty-two days, ending in Victoria, British Columbia.

Also on This Day

1873.
Modern dance pioneer Maud Allan is born in Toronto. Allan—who was influenced by her musical mentor, Ferruccio Busoni, and by German expressionism—choreographed more than fifty dances, most notably *The Vision of Salomé*.

BORN ON THIS DAY

1926 — singer Juliette "Our Pet" Cavazzi

1973 — actor, director, and choreographer Cory Bowles

1976 — actress Sarah Chalke

AUGUST 28

Also on This Day

1965.
Singer-songwriter Shania Twain is born in Windsor, Ontario (as Eilleen Regina Edwards). Twain was raised in Timmins and on the nearby Mattagami First Nation reserve, and later in Sudbury, where she was singing publicly by age eight. In the late 1980s, she worked as a solo lounge entertainer at a Huntsville, Ontario, resort to support herself and her younger siblings after her parents were killed in a car accident. Twain saw moderate success with her first self-titled album, but her career took off after her marriage to producer Robert John "Mutt" Lange. Often referred to as the Queen of Country Pop, she is the most commercially successful female country artist of all time and was the first female artist to have three consecutive albums sell over ten million copies in the United States.

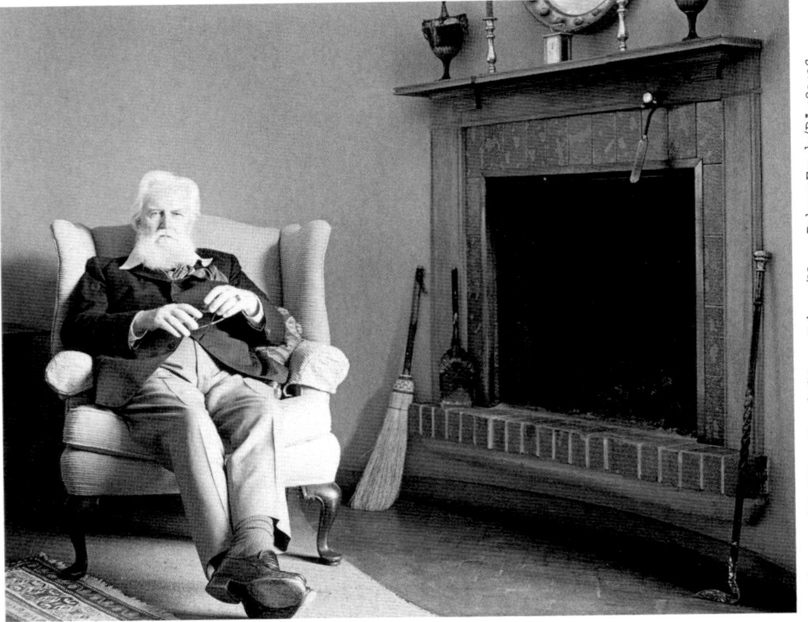

©Library and Archives Canada/Harry Palmer/Harry Palmer Fonds/PA-182426.

Robertson Davies, 1984.

1913. Writer, journalist, actor, and professor Robertson Davies is born in Thamesville, Ontario. An outstanding essayist, award-winning playwright, and brilliant novelist, Davies is known for his numerous works, including *Leaven of Malice* (1954), which won the Stephen Leacock Memorial Medal for Humour, and *Fifth Business* (1970), the first novel of the Deptford Trilogy. The latter work depicts characters in roles roughly corresponding to Jungian archetypes—an illustration of Davies's belief that things of the spirit are more important than worldly concerns.

BORN ON THIS DAY

1938 Prime Minister Paul Martin

1952 actor Guy Nadon

1969 actor Jason Priestley

1988 gymnast Rosannagh "Rosie" MacLennan

Department Natural Resources/Library and Archives Canada/PA-020614.

A scene from the Quebec Bridge disaster.

1907. During construction, the Quebec Bridge, spanning the St. Lawrence River near Québec City, collapses, killing seventy-five of its eighty-six workers. The impact was so significant that people as far as ten kilometres away thought an earthquake had struck. Blame for the tragedy was placed on American engineer Theodore Cooper, who'd made grave errors in design and faulty load calculations. After another deadly collapse in 1916—when a span being hoisted into place fell into the river below, killing thirteen—the bridge was finally completed in 1917.

Also on This Day

1899.
Pioneer, author, and botanist Catharine Parr Traill dies in Lakefield, Ontario. Like her sister Susanna Moodie, she recorded her experiences as a settler. She collected her letters to family members and friends back in Suffolk, England, into *The Backwoods of Canada* (1836), which remains an important source of information about pioneer life in the country.

BORN ON THIS DAY

1933
artist, writer, and philosopher Sorel Etrog

1959
astronaut Chris Hadfield

John Goddard/The Canadian Press.

Rosemary Brown, 1973.

1972. Social worker and activist Rosemary Brown is elected to the Legislative Assembly of British Columbia, becoming the first Black woman in Canada to be a member of a Canadian legislature. A founding member of the Vancouver Status of Women Council, Brown was encouraged by her colleagues to enter provincial politics. Her role as a politician was a natural progression from her activism in the 1960s, when she was an outspoken advocate against sexism and racism. She once stated, "To be black and female in a society which is both racist and sexist is to be in the unique position of having nowhere to go but up!"

Who Was Rosemary Brown?

Born in Kingston, Jamaica, in 1930, Rosemary Brown immigrated to Canada in 1951 to pursue post-secondary education. In 1972, she won her seat in the Vancouver-Burrard riding as a member of the New Democratic Party (NDP). She later ran for the leadership of the national party, finishing a close second to Ed Broadbent, who would become a long-time NDP leader. After retiring from the BC legislature in 1988, Brown continued to be politically active on the international stage. She received numerous honours, including the Order of British Columbia (1995), the Order of Canada (1996), and the United Nations Human Rights Fellowship (1973). She died in 2003, and her life-long commitment to ending discrimination was commemorated on a national scale when Canada Post issued a stamp in her honour.

Which accessory gave its name to a battle for minority language rights?
See March 4.

BORN ON THIS DAY

1896
actor Raymond Massey

1935
theatre director and producer Bill Glassco

1976
model Gabriel Aubry

31 AUGUST

Geddy Lee of Rush and television host Jeanne Beker.

1984. "The nation's music station," MuchMusic, begins airing. Its French-language counterpart, MusiquePlus, would follow on September 2, 1986. In its early years, MuchMusic was largely devoted to music videos, with on-camera "VJs" (video jockeys) serving the function of DJs. The first video aired on the station was a short from the 1920s featuring American jazz composer and pianist Eubie Blake. The second was Rush's "The Enemy Within." Though entertainment news and reality television programming have become the mainstays of MuchMusic, the station continues to help establish and advertise new trends in popular music (and fashion) in Canada.

Memorable MuchMusic Programs

Countdown
Egos and Icons
Electric Circus
Fromage
Intimate & Interactive
MuchEast
MuchWest
Outlaws & Heroes
The Power Hour
R.S.V.P.
RapCity
Spotlight
Too Much 4 Much
The Wedge

BORN ON THIS DAY

Hockey Hall of Famer Jean Béliveau — 1931

1932 — journalist Allan Fotheringham

Poet, editor, and author Dennis Lee — 1939

SPACE CAPTAINS

According to creator Gene Roddenberry, one of the inspirations for *Star Trek* was the 1956 film *Forbidden Planet*. The captain in that film was played by Leslie Nielsen, who was born in Regina, Saskatchewan. In the film, Nielsen's character confronts the brilliant Dr. Morbius, played by fellow Canadian Walter Pidgeon, born in Saint John, NB.

Two more Canadian space captains featured in the original series of *Battlestar Galactica*. Ottawa-born Lorne Greene played Commander Adama. His enemies, the Cylons, were led by Baltar, played by John Colicos of Montréal. It wasn't Colicos's first appearance as a space villain—he had previously played a Klingon commander on *Star Trek*.

The voice for the HAL 9000 computer in the film *2001: A Space Odyssey* was provided by Winnipeg-born actor Douglas Rain. The film's director, Stanley Kubrick, thought the Canadian "had the kind of bland mid-Atlantic accent we felt was right for the part."

On March 13, 2013, Chris Hadfield became the first Canadian to have a real-life space command when he took over the International Space Station. Before returning to earth, Hadfield attracted attention with his microgravity performance of David Bowie's song "Space Oddity."

Montréal-born William Shatner was famous for playing James T. Kirk, captain of the *USS Enterprise*, on the TV show *Star Trek*. He wasn't the only Canadian on board. James Doohan, who played Scotty, the ship's engineer, was born in Vancouver.

Inventor and entrepreneur Elon Musk obtained Canadian citizenship through his Canadian-born mother and spent two years studying at Queen's University in Kingston. His company SpaceX has built a number of rockets and space capsules. When the Dragon cargo capsule travelled to the International Space Station, Chris Hadfield tweeted photos of it docking with the aid of the Canadarm2.

SEPTEMBER

SEPTEMBER 1

Also on This Day

1910.
All-around athlete and track-and-field star Hilda Strike is born in Montréal. At the 1932 Olympic Games in Los Angeles, she crossed the finish line of the 100-metre dash at the same moment as Stanislawa Walasiewicz, also called Stella Walsh, an American resident competing for Poland. The judges awarded Walsh the gold medal and Strike the silver. When Walsh was murdered during a robbery in 1980, it was discovered that she was intersex, casting doubt on the legitimacy of her medals in women's competitions. Although there were calls for the International Olympic Committee to award Strike the gold medal in Walsh's place, this never happened.

C.M. Tait/Molson Archives Collection/Library and Archives Canada / PA-139521.

The inaugural celebration of Alberta's entry into Confederation.

1905. Alberta and Saskatchewan enter Confederation as Canada's eighth and ninth provinces. Alberta was named after Queen Victoria's daughter, Princess Louise Caroline Alberta, while Saskatchewan was named for the Saskatchewan River, which the Cree called *Kisiskatchewani Sipi*, or "swift-flowing river." Both provinces were carved out of the greater North-West Territories and created as rapid population growth led to increased demand for control over local matters, including taxes.

BORN ON THIS DAY

1915
children's author Barbara Smucker

1922
actress Yvonne De Carlo

1923
business magnate Kenneth Thomson

1926
poet, playwright, and professor James Reaney

1941
poet Gwendolyn MacEwen

Courtesy of Glenbow Archives/NA-5495-12.

Guy Weadick twirling rope around sailors on board the *Empress of Scotland*, ca. 1921.

1912. The Calgary Stampede—the brainchild of American cowboy Guy Weadick—is held for the first time. The inaugural stampede parade was watched by many thousands of spectators and featured rodeo competitors, the Duke and Duchess of Connaught and their daughter Princess Patricia, and nearly two thousand Aboriginal peoples in full regalia. Prizes totalling $16,000 were provided for the rodeo events, which included bucking horse riding, fancy roping, and trick riding. The show-stopper was an electrifying bronco ride by twenty-four-year-old Tom Three Persons on the famously unrideable Cyclone. In spite of its success, the stampede was not repeated until after the First World War, in August 1919, when a Great Victory Stampede was held.

The Stampede After the Flood

When southern Alberta suffered massive floods in June 2013, the Calgary Stampede grounds were directly affected by the rising Elbow and Bow Rivers. Calgary and many surrounding communities were evacuated, and the city declared a state of emergency. With the stampede due to begin in just two weeks, a small crew of employees remained at Stampede Park to push water away from electrical substations, helping to prevent further damage. Over the next days, workers and volunteers cleaned up the grounds, vowing that the stampede would go on "come hell or high water." Downtown Calgary re-opened on July 2 and Calgary Transit was up and running on July 3, just in time for the scheduled start of the Stampede on July 5. More than one million visitors attended that year.

BORN ON THIS DAY

1964 — actor Keanu Reeves

1965 — world heavyweight champion boxer Lennox Lewis

SEPTEMBER 3

> *Also on This Day*
>
> **1810.**
> Artist Paul Kane is born in Mallow, Ireland. He was known for his paintings of western landscapes and his depictions of Aboriginal peoples. His work was influenced by American artist George Catlin, who predicted that European expansion would destroy Aboriginal ways of life.

Toronto Star Archives/getstock.com

William Lyon Mackenzie King with Sir William Mulock, 1940.

1939. In anticipation of the Second World War, the Wartime Prices and Trade Board is established. It was created to ensure that the social and economic conditions of the First World War—including inflation that often resulted in social unrest and demands for higher wages—would not return. But the board was ineffective in holding back inflation until August 1941, when it became the responsibility of the Ministry of Finance. Its powers were then enormously expanded as Prime Minister Mackenzie King announced a price freeze and the "stabilization" of wages and salaries. The board was not without its critics, but its major achievement—a mere 2.8 percent rise in prices between October 1941 and April 1945—was proof of its effectiveness.

BORN ON THIS DAY

Québec governor Lord Dorchester (Guy Carleton)
1724

1916
Hockey Hall of Famer Doug Bentley

sculptor Armand Vaillancourt
1929

1963
author Malcolm Gladwell

Courtesy of Library and Archives Canada/1983-30-62.

A war effort poster, ca. 1939.

SEPTEMBER 4

Mario Beauregard/CPI/The Canadian Press.

The Montreal Museum of Fine Arts is located on Sherbrooke Street in Montréal.

1972. The Montreal Museum of Fine Arts is robbed of $2 million worth of paintings and other art objects. In the early morning hours, armed thieves entered the museum through a skylight, binding and gagging guards before making off with a stash of jewels and eighteen paintings. The stolen artworks included pieces by French Romantic painter Eugène Delacroix and English landscape artist Thomas Gainsborough, as well as *Landscape with Cottages*, a rare work by Rembrandt worth an estimated $1 million at the time. The crime has yet to be solved. It remains the largest art heist in Canadian history.

BORN ON THIS DAY

1908
film director Edward Dmytryk

1972
tennis player Daniel Nestor

1985
bobsledder Kaillie Humphries

FAMOUS HEISTS IN CANADIAN HISTORY

September 10, 1904:
American outlaw Bill Miner and two accomplices pull off Canada's first train robbery, acquiring $7,000 and a revolver near Mission, BC.

March 1, 1966:
Ken "The Flying Bandit" Leishman and his partners in crime pose as airline employees and make off with $400,000 of gold bullion from the Winnipeg airport. Leishman was later arrested; he managed to escape from prison but was soon recaptured.

September 19, 1967:
Québec bank robber Monica "Machine Gun Molly" Proietti meets her demise during a dramatic Montréal robbery. After knocking over a credit union, Proietti set off on a high-speed police chase that ended in her fatal shooting.

February 7, 2007:
Thieves make off with approximately $6 million worth of jewels taken from the safes of a north Toronto gem store. Police said the crafty burglars cut the shop's phone lines, disconnecting its security system from an alarm.

SEPTEMBER 5

Norse Settlement in Newfoundland

In 985 or 986, an Icelandic flotilla set out to colonize southwest Greenland. Trader Bjarni Herjolfsson sailed late to join the group but was driven off course by stormy weather. It is believed that his journey led him to what is now Newfoundland, Labrador, Baffin Island, and possibly as far south as Maine, making him the first European to sight the eastern coast of North America. Explorer Leif Ericsson subsequently retraced this journey, surveying three regions that he named Helluland (likely the area from the Torngat Mountains to Baffin Island), Markland (central Labrador), and Vinland (a region farther south, where the Norse set up camp). Further expeditions followed, all led by members of Ericsson's family. Settlements in Newfoundland, including the one at L'Anse aux Meadows, remained but a few years and were relatively small. The distant and often treacherous journey to North America made it less appealing to settlers than Europe, where more products could be obtained. This fact, combined with confrontations with local Aboriginal peoples, may have led to a short-lived presence of the Norse on the continent.

Village life at L'Anse aux Meadows, Newfoundland.

1978. Two Canadian sites are among the first twelve spots given World Heritage status at UNESCO meetings in Washington, DC. Newfoundland's L'Anse aux Meadows National Historic Site was chosen for its cultural significance: it is the first authentic Norse site found in North America. Nahanni National Park Reserve in the Northwest Territories was designated for its natural splendour: the wilderness of rugged mountains is crossed by the twisting South Nahanni River, which crashes through three immense canyons, plummets over Virginia Falls, and rushes past boiling hot springs, icy caves, and seething rapids.

BORN ON THIS DAY

United Church of Canada minister Lydia Gruchy
1894

1916
comedian Frank Shuster

skier Dave Murray
1953

1959
screenwriter Graham Yost

6 SEPTEMBER

Courtesy of CBC Still Photo Collection.

La Famille Plouffe **was a popular series on both French and English television in the 1950s.**

1952. Canada's first television station, CBFT (Radio-Canada) in Montréal, begins transmitting. Among the first programs aired were the film *Aladdin and His Lamp*, cartoons, and news. The station broadcast both French and English programming; the English-language station, CBLT in Toronto, began operations two days later. The first English broadcast accidentally displayed the station ID slide upside down and backwards before airing a puppet sketch and a weather report. At the time, television was available to only 26 percent of the population, but by 1954 the number had increased to 60 percent and Canada ranked second in the world in live television production.

Also on This Day

1814.
Sir George-Étienne Cartier is born in Saint-Antoine-sur-Richelieu, Lower Canada (present-day Québec), to a wealthy family of grain exporters and millers. A key architect of Canada's unification, Sir George-Étienne Cartier led Québec into Confederation and was also responsible for negotiating the entry of Manitoba and British Columbia.

What pivotal role did Cartier play in Confederation?
See July 1.

BORN ON THIS DAY

Father of Confederation Alexander Galt
1817

1932
entrepreneur Frank Stronach

Governor General Michaëlle Jean
1957

Courtesy of Library and Archives Canada/George P. Roberts/C-000733.

The Charlottetown Conference, Prince Edward Island.

Also on This Day

2012.
The government declares that it has closed the Canadian embassy in Tehran and expelled all Iranian diplomats from Canada. Among Ottawa's cited reasons for breaking ties were Iran's foreign policy, its violations of human rights, and its nuclear program.

1864. The Charlottetown Conference adjourns after delegates from the colonies of New Brunswick, Nova Scotia, and Prince Edward Island agree in principle to join a federal union with the Province of Canada rather than create a single Maritime union. Along with the Québec Conference (1864) and the London Conference (1867), this meeting established terms that were incorporated into the British North America Act, 1867. The new country came into being on July 1 of that year.

BORN ON THIS DAY

1927

Supreme Court justice Claire L'Heureux-Dubé

Supreme Court chief justice Beverley McLachlin

1943

1979

singer-songwriter, violinist, and composer Owen Pallett

8 SEPTEMBER

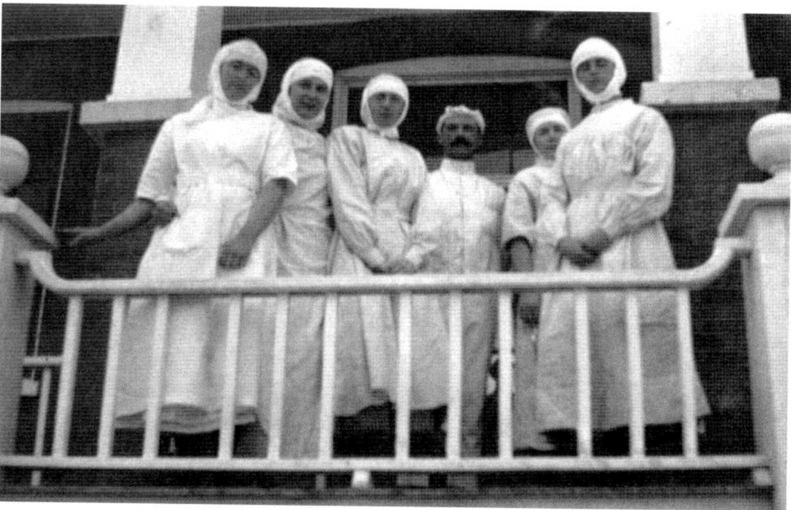

Courtesy of Glenbow Archives/NA-1422-7.

Nurses at an isolation hospital in Lloydminster, Saskatchewan.

1918. Canada's first civilian outbreak of Spanish influenza is reported, setting off an epidemic that would last for one year. The virus arrived with soldiers returning home from service overseas. Worldwide, the Spanish flu outbreak of 1918–19 was one of the most devastating pandemics in human history. In Canada, it killed about fifty thousand at a time when the country's population numbered less than nine million. Restrictions such as service closures, quarantines, and the wearing of masks in public were put in place to stop the spread of the disease. Canadians generally complied, but they defied the federal government's request that First World War victory celebrations be postponed until December 1. The Spanish influenza strain remained active in Canada until the mid-1920s.

Spanish Influenza Mortality Rates

Worldwide: estimated 25 million deaths
Canada: approximately 50,000 deaths, or 4.5% of the population; several Aboriginal communities lost nearly their entire population
Ontario: 8,700 deaths
Saskatchewan: 5,000 deaths
Alberta: 4,000 deaths
Manitoba: 4,000 deaths

BORN ON THIS DAY

1871 car manufacturer Robert Samuel McLaughlin

1937 broadcaster Barbara Frum

1965 curler Marcia Gudereit

1987 skier Alexandre Bilodeau

Also on This Day

1965.
Simon Fraser University opens in Burnaby, just east of Vancouver. Named for the explorer who surveyed the eponymous Fraser River, the university was designed by Canadian architects Arthur Erickson and Geoffrey Massey. Its initial enrolment was approximately twenty-five hundred; today, it has three campuses and is home to over thirty thousand students.

Which runner attended Simon Fraser University? See April 12.

Marilyn Bell in her Lakeshore Swimming Club jacket.

1954. Sixteen-year-old Marilyn Bell becomes the first person to swim across Lake Ontario. Bell swam 51.5 kilometres from Youngstown, New York, to a breakwater off Toronto's western shore (near what is now Marilyn Bell Park) in twenty hours and fifty-nine minutes. A war of words between the *Toronto Star* and *Toronto Telegram* reporters who were covering the event came to real blows while Bell was in the water fighting lamprey eels and choking on oil slicks. Her feat captured national attention and earned her the nickname the First Lady of the Lake. Later she became the youngest person to swim both the English Channel and the Strait of Juan de Fuca.

BORN ON THIS DAY

1894
union leader and politician Humphrey Mitchell

1975
singer Michael Bublé

10 SEPTEMBER

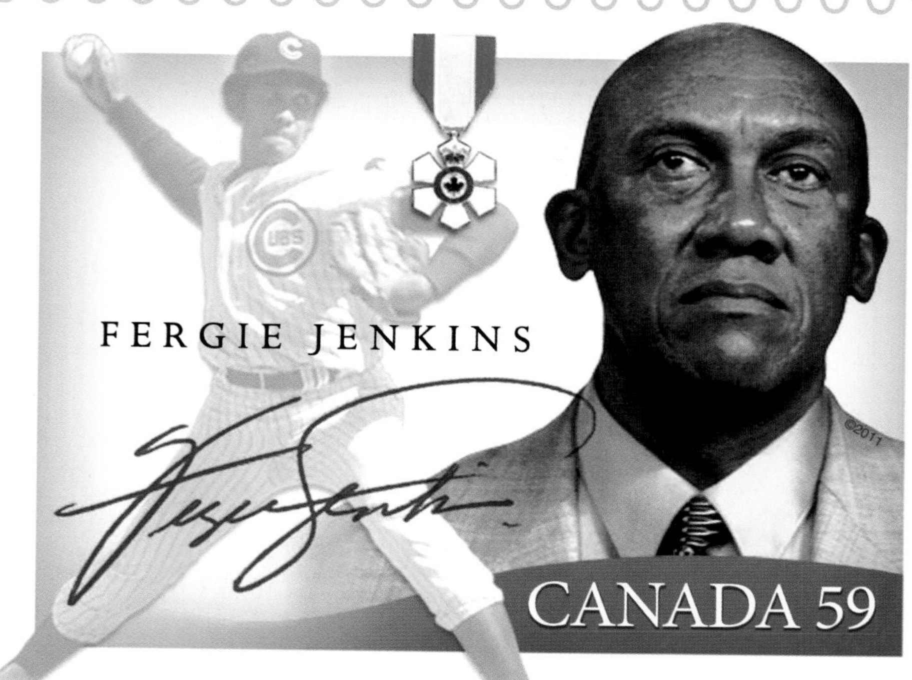

Canada Post Corporation/Library and Archives Canada/4276598.

This Fergie Jenkins stamp was issued in February 2011.

1965. Canadian pitcher Ferguson "Fergie" Jenkins makes his Major League Baseball debut with the Philadelphia Phillies against the St. Louis Cardinals. He later joined the Chicago Cubs, and in 1967, he began a six-year string of twenty or more wins per season. Released by the Cubs prior to the 1984 season, Jenkins had amassed a remarkable record that included 284 wins, 3,192 strikeouts, and a strikeout-to-walk ratio of 3.20. In 1991, he became Canada's first inductee into the American Baseball Hall of Fame.

BORN ON THIS DAY

1948 author and mental health advocate Margaret Sinclair Trudeau Kemper

1955 dancer, choreographer, and director James Kudelka

Also on This Day

1939. Canada declares war on Germany, officially entering the Second World War. With the 1931 passage of the Statute of Westminster, which made Canada an independent nation, it was the first time the country had declared war on another nation on its own.

SEPTEMBER  11 

Also on This Day

2001.
Approximately three thousand individuals, including at least twenty-four Canadians, are killed when the World Trade Center and the Pentagon are attacked by the Al-Qaeda terrorist group. A hijacked plane that crashed in a Pennsylvania field also contributed to the death toll. The impact of these events in the United States continues to be felt across the globe. As a neighbouring country, Canada responded with compassion as well as strategic support, most notably through Operation Yellow Ribbon, during which Canadian airports accepted more than two hundred flights filled with thousands of passengers originally bound for the United States.

Courtesy of City of Toronto Archives, Fonds 1244, Item 1356.

A horse-drawn streetcar in Toronto, 1892.

1861. Toronto's first streetcar route starts operating. This first route stretched from the historic St. Lawrence Market along Yonge Street to the Yorkville Town Hall. The fleet of horse-drawn Haddon Car trams were an improvement upon previous transportation methods, but they were far from ideal. They couldn't handle heavy loads, and the horses were expensive and required frequent rest periods. They also polluted the streets. The electric railway, invented in 1879 and introduced to Canada in the 1880s, would revolutionize streetcar operations.

 **When did the first subway line open in Canada?** See March 30.

BORN ON THIS DAY

1862

Governor General Lord Byng of Vimy (Julian Byng)

1919

artist Daphne Odjig

1920

political organizer and journalist Dalton Camp

12 SEPTEMBER

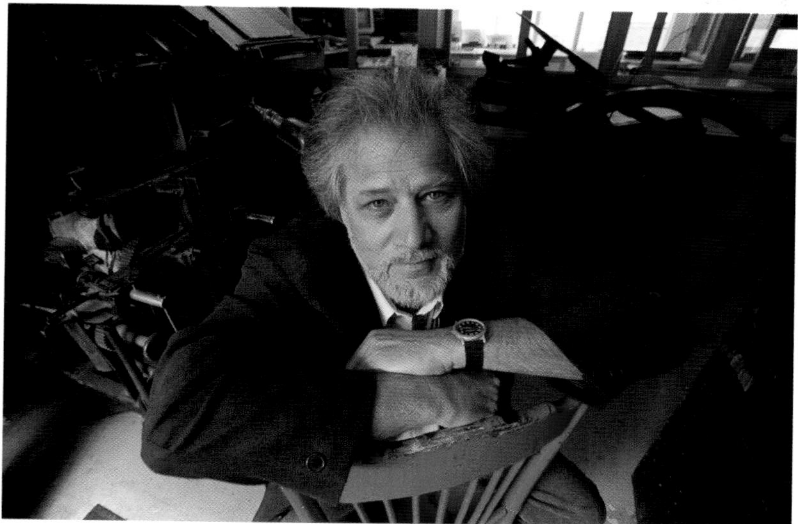

Canadian Press/Kevin Frayer.

Canadian author Michael Ondaatje poses in an old print room at Coach House Press in Toronto, on April 20, 1999.

1943. Acclaimed author, poet, and filmmaker Michael Ondaatje is born in Colombo, Sri Lanka (then known as Ceylon). He immigrated to Canada in 1962, studying at the University of Toronto and eventually teaching at Western University in London, Ontario, and York University in Toronto. Ondaatje published his first poetry collection in 1967. His most famous novel is *The English Patient* (1992), which won the Governor General's Award and was a co-winner of the Booker Prize; the film version received nine Academy Awards, including one for best picture. He is considered one of Canada's most celebrated living authors.

Also on This Day

1906.
Swimwear designer and businesswoman Rose Marie Reid is born in Cardston, Alberta. Reid developed flattering bathing suits and was known for turning swimwear into a fashion item. Her creative innovations included tummy control panels. Reid's business thrived in the 1950s but declined in the following decade; she eventually left the company after refusing to design bikinis.

BORN ON THIS DAY

1914 — aviator Janusz "The Great Zura" Zurakowski

1937 — boxer George Chuvalo

SEPTEMBER 13

Did You Know?

The British victory at the Plains of Abraham brought about the defeat of a significant French stronghold in New France and foreshadowed the eventual British control of what would become Canada.

Governor Pierre de Rigaud de Vaudreuil surrendered New France to a British invasion force in Montréal on September 8, 1760.

The Treaty of Paris, signed on February 10, 1763, officially ceded New France to Britain.

The American Revolution indirectly resulted from the removal of France as a North American power, since colonists no longer needed the protection of the British military.

An aerial view of the Plains of Abraham, modern day.

1759. In the early morning hours, British soldiers scale the cliffs near Québec City and overpower French troops guarding a path, allowing Gen. James Wolfe to lead forty-five hundred soldiers onto the Plains of Abraham. When the French general, Louis-Joseph de Montcalm (the Marquis de Montcalm), learned of their landing, he attacked hastily and quickly fell to Wolfe's forces. Both commanding officers died from wounds sustained during the battle. It was a pivotal moment in the Seven Years' War and in the history of Canada, and it led to the surrender of Québec City to the British. The French never recaptured Québec and effectively lost control of New France in 1760. At the end of the war, in 1763, France surrendered many of its colonial possessions—including Canada—to the British.

BORN ON THIS DAY

Governor of Canada Lord Sydenham (Charles Poulett Thomson)

1799

1941

singer-songwriter and producer David Clayton-Thomas

14 SEPTEMBER

Dr. Elizabeth Bagshaw, one of Canada's first female doctors, 1968.

1936. Nurse Dorothea Palmer is arrested in Eastview, Ontario, for distributing contraceptives and information on birth control. An 1892 amendment to the Criminal Code made the advertisement, sale, or disposal of birth control punishable by a two-year prison term unless an accused could prove that the "public good" was served. This was the claim made by Palmer's lawyers, and she was ultimately acquitted of all charges.

Canada's first birth control clinic, the Hamilton Planned Parenthood Clinic, was run for more than thirty years by Dr. Elizabeth Bagshaw. After the Depression, Dr. Bagshaw began to speak more openly about her work at the clinic, explaining, "There was no welfare and no unemployment payments, and these people were just about half-starved because there was no work, and for them to go on having children was a detriment to the country. They couldn't afford children if they couldn't afford to eat." Dr. Bagshaw's clinic didn't become legal until 1969, when access to birth control was finally decriminalized.

Birth Control in Canada

Early supporters of birth control in Canada were generally educated men and women. Some were inspired by the ideals espoused by the Social Gospel movement and by feminism. In the 1920s, Canadians more widely began to question the 1892 law, and family size among informed couples in higher socio-economic brackets was shrinking. But high birth rates persisted among the less educated and lower-income families. Following the Second World War and the onset of the baby boom, public acceptance of birth control increased rapidly. The advent of the pill in 1960 was a key advancement. In 1963, birth control groups, led by activists Barbara and George Cadbury, formed an organization called the Canadian Federation of Societies for Population Planning (now known as the Planned Parenthood Federation of Canada). Following the decriminalization of contraception in 1969, a variety of public and privately owned programs emerged to help provide services.

BORN ON THIS DAY

journalist, publisher, and philanthropist Floyd Chalmers
1898

1904
Olympic canoeing gold medallist Frank Amyot

actor Callum Keith Rennie
1960

Department of National Defence/Library and Archives Canada/1964-114-NPC.

Dressing the wounded in a trench during the Battle of Courcelette.

1916. The 22nd Battalion from Québec, the 25th from Nova Scotia, and the 26th from New Brunswick capture Courcelette, France, during the Somme Offensive of the First World War. The Canadian Corps had launched its attack to capture the ruined remains of the village from the Germans. Rather than wait for their army's artillery bombardment to end, the Canadians walked behind a "creeping" barrage that steadily advanced across German lines—keeping enemy soldiers in their dugouts until the Canadians were on top of them and ready to fight. After another week of fighting, the Battle of Flers-Courcelette officially ended on September 22. It was a victory, but it came at a terrible cost—the Canadian Corps lost more than seven thousand soldiers.

BORN ON THIS DAY

1901

ballet director, choreographer, and teacher Gweneth Lloyd

1907

writer and actress Fay Wray

1962

actor Scott McNeil

16 SEPTEMBER

Royal Canadian Mounted Police, "Depot" Division, Regina, Saskatchewan
Recruit Training - Troop 17 -74/75
September 23, 1974 to March 3, 1975
Front Row J.L. Graham; S/M W.D. Pomfret; Supt. E.R. Madill; C/Supt. H. Tadeson; Supt.W.F. MacRae; Major D.E. Toole; Cpl. K.F.G. Wilkens; H.A. Phyllis
Second Row C.M.Lafosse; S.E. MacNeil; B.A. MacDonald; J.M. Whidden; D.G. Courtney; P.R. Painter; S.E. Lowden; R.M. Russell; K.L. Somers
Third Row S.A. Merinuk; C.J. Smith; C.A. Marshall; J.P.M. Potvin; D.I. Burns; T.G. Kivissoo; M.I.L.D. Wright; P.S. Moisse; S.H. Sullivan; D.L. Pohorelic
Fourth Row J.E. Giergon; G.E. Mortensen; C.L. Joyce; A.V. Pritchard; B.J. Woods; M.L.D.Pilotte; B.A. Glassman; B.K. Hosker; B.J. Morris

Troop 17, the first female troop in the RCMP.

1974. The first female officers from Troop 17 are sworn in by the Royal Canadian Mounted Police. From this point forward, women were recruited into the force as constables and underwent the same training as their male counterparts. Since the early 1900s, women had been allowed to serve as lab technicians and fingerprinters, but not as officers. They would rise through the ranks in the 1980s and 1990s. In December 2006, Beverley Ann Busson (one of the original members of Troop 17) was appointed commissioner. She was the first woman to hold the force's highest rank. It was only in recent years, however, that the RCMP permitted female officers to wear pants and boots instead of skirts and pumps.

Also on This Day

1842.
The first Baldwin–La Fontaine cabinet is formed in the Province of Canada. Louis Hippolyte La Fontaine and Robert Baldwin were both lawyers who, motivated by idealism and a strong sense of duty, took up politics at a young age. Together, they worked to convince the British government that legislative power should reside in the hands of the colony's elected representatives. Their partnership led to the development of responsible government across the country.

Which system of government was sparked in part by the Rebellions of 1837? See December 5.

BORN ON THIS DAY

1919 writer Laurence Peter

1921 physicist and educator Ursula Franklin

1958 actress Jennifer Tilly

SEPTEMBER 17

Militia Courts

1760: Amid the threat of famine and social upheaval, the British military seeks to maintain order in its newly conquered territory of Canada.

1760s: French Canadian militiamen are empowered to act as police and as intermediaries between the British regime and the people. Militia officers are asked to act as judges of "militia courts." Most people prefer these to the British court-martial system. Militia courts apply the pre-Conquest civil code.

1763: The Treaty of Paris brings an end to the military courts but makes no commitment to maintaining the French civil code.

1774: The Quebec Act restores the use of French law in private and civil matters.

No. 4 QUÉBEC, Palais de Justice.
Editeurs, Pruneau & Kirouac, Québec.

Courtesy of BAnQ Vieux-Montreal/P186, S9, P261.

Québec courthouse, ca. 1900.

1764. James Murray, the governor of Britain's newly acquired Province of Québec, establishes a system of civil courts, introducing English law to the territory. This followed a period of military rule that had been implemented by Britain during the Seven Years' War (although French laws still governed everyday matters during that time). After France ceded Québec to Britain in the Treaty of Paris, the province's court system was converted to English law. This held sway until the passage of the Quebec Act, which re-established French civil law in 1774. British law remained in place for criminal cases.

BORN ON THIS DAY

1914
shoe manufacturer
Thomas Bata

1979
movie director
Neill Blomkamp

1984
alpine racer
John Kucera

18 SEPTEMBER

Courtesy of Nikkei National Museum/Reggie Yasui collection/2010.26.26.

An Asahi player at bat at Vancouver's Powell Street Grounds, ca. 1939.

1941. Members of the Asahi baseball team play their last game in Vancouver. Within months they, like other Japanese Canadians, had been shipped to internment camps to wait out the war. Before the Second World War, the Asahi team was legendary in Vancouver. Formed in 1914, the team joined the Vancouver International League in 1918, and later played at the top of the Pacific Northwest League for five consecutive years, from 1937 to 1941. The players developed their own strategic brand of baseball, called "brain ball," featuring precise bunts, stealthy base running, and squeeze plays. A source of pride for the Japanese community in Canada, the team earned applause from people of all cultures. The players' unique skills were recognized in 2003, when the team was inducted into the Canadian Baseball Hall of Fame.

Also on This Day

1895.
Prime Minister John Diefenbaker is born in Neustadt, Ontario. He served as prime minister from 1957 to 1963, and was the only Conservative leader between 1935 and 1979 to take the party to an election victory, a feat he repeated three times—although only once with a majority of seats.

BORN ON THIS DAY

1861 journalist and women's rights activist Ella Cora Hind

1888 writer and conservationist Archibald Belaney (Grey Owl)

1903 Hockey Hall of Famer Frederick Joseph "Bun" Cook

1923 Supreme Court justice Bertha Wilson

1933 Hockey Hall of Famer and coach William "Scotty" Bowman

1950 Hockey Hall of Famer Darryl Sittler

Residential Schools in Literature

Indian School Days
by Basil H. Johnston (1988)
Sisters: A Play
by Wendy Lill (1991)
Kiss of the Fur Queen
by Tomson Highway (1998)
Porcupines and China Dolls
by Robert Arthur Alexie (2009)
Indian Horse
by Richard Wagamese (2012)

***Keeper of the Voice*, by Métis artist Nicole Paul.**

2007. A landmark compensation deal for former residential school students comes into effect. The agreement established a truth and reconciliation commission and included $2 billion in compensation for former pupils, along with a separate fund to address claims of sexual or serious physical and psychological abuse. The following year, Prime Minister Stephen Harper issued an apology on behalf of the government of Canada. In partnership with the nation's churches, the government had created the residential school program in the 1880s; at its peak, it included eighty institutions in every province and territory. Around 150,000 First Nations, Inuit, and Métis children were removed from their families, often forcibly, to attend these residential schools, where the common objective was assimilation. A host of social problems resulted from the physical, sexual, and mental abuse that was inflicted upon students. The last residential school remained open until 1996.

BORN ON THIS DAY

1940 folk singer, guitarist, and broadcaster Sylvia Tyson

1984 actor Kevin Zegers

20 SEPTEMBER

Courtesy of the © Hamilton Spectator.

Lincoln Alexander after his win in the riding of Hamilton West.

1985. Lincoln Alexander is sworn in as Ontario's twenty-fourth lieutenant-governor. He was the first Black person to hold a vice-regal position in Canada. Born to West Indian immigrant parents—his mother was from Jamaica, his father from St. Vincent—Alexander grew up in an Ontario where people of African descent faced discrimination that was more widespread than today, though it could occasionally be overcome. When he joined the Royal Canadian Air Force (RCAF) in 1942, that branch of the armed forces was only beginning to accept non-whites into service. (There was no formal policy preventing their enlistment, but the practice was common.) Alexander served as a corporal until 1945. He entered politics in 1965, and in 1968 became the first Black Canadian to sit in the House of Commons. He was re-elected four times, serving a total of twelve years. When he died on October 19, 2012, Alexander was honoured with a provincial state funeral. The following year, the Legislative Assembly of Ontario declared January 21 Lincoln Alexander Day.

Timeline: Lincoln Alexander

1942: Joins the RCAF, a branch of the armed forces that informally restricted non-whites from entering active service

1953: Receives a degree from Osgoode Hall Law School

1968: Becomes the member of Parliament for the Ontario riding of Hamilton West (re-elected four times)

1980: Resigns as member of Parliament to become chairman of the Ontario Workers' Compensation Board

1985: Sworn in as Ontario's twenty-fourth lieutenant-governor

1991: Begins first of five terms as chancellor of the University of Guelph

1992: Becomes a Companion of the Order of Canada and a member of the Order of Ontario

BORN ON THIS DAY

First Nations leader Phil Fontaine
1944

1951
Hockey Hall of Famer Guy Lafleur

Five-time Olympic rowing medallist Lesley Thompson-Willie
1959

SEPTEMBER

Notable SCTV Alumni

John Candy
Robin Duke
Joe Flaherty
Eugene Levy
Andrea Martin
Rick Moranis
Catherine O'Hara
Tony Rosato
Martin Short
Dave Thomas

The Everett Collection/Canadian Press.

The cast of *SCTV*. Left to right: Andrea Martin, Joe Flaherty, John Candy, Martin Short, and Eugene Levy.

Which Canadian funny-man starred in *Family Ties*?
See June 9.

1976. The first episode of the breakout comedy show *SCTV* airs. Named for the fictional Second City television station, the media satire series played off the original Second City, a comedy cabaret that opened in Chicago in 1959. The show was written and performed by some of Canada's most successful artists, including John Candy, Catherine O'Hara, and Martin Short. It aired across Canada and the United States until 1983, producing over 110 hours of programming and garnering thirteen Emmy nominations. The show continues in syndication around the world.

BORN ON THIS DAY

Hockey Hall of Famer Howie Morenz
1902

1967
Barenaked Ladies drummer Tyler Stewart

22 SEPTEMBER

Courtesy of © Newfoundland Archives/SANL 1.502.151.

The Bowring's Ladies Championship Crew during the Royal St. John's Regatta, 1949.

1818. The first official, organized regatta race is held in St. John's, Newfoundland. The Royal St. John's Regatta is a series of rowing races over a 2.45-kilometre course in fixed-seat shells carrying six oarsmen. When the Prince of Wales visited St. John's in 1860, he offered one hundred pounds to the winner. In 1901, a crew from Outer Cove set a time of 9:13.75, establishing a record that was not broken until 1981. (The current record, 8:51.32, was set in 2007.) Although there were years when no regatta was held—on the death of King George IV in 1830, for example, and through the First World War—it is believed to be the oldest continuing sporting event in North America. Regatta Day, celebrated on the first Wednesday of August, is a statutory holiday for the city of St. John's.

Also on This Day

1877.
Treaty Number 7 (more commonly known as the Blackfoot Treaty) is signed by the Siksika, Kainai (Blood), Piikani (Peigan), Tsuu T'ina (Sarcee), and Stoney peoples at Blackfoot Crossing in southern Alberta. By this treaty, the First Nations established peaceful relations with the Crown and opened up a large tract of territory to railway development in return for promises of reserve land, payments, and annuities.

Which familiar ship was designed for fishing and racing? See March 26.

BORN ON THIS DAY

women's rights activist Louise McKinney
1868

1901
Nobel Prize–winning physiologist Charles B. Huggins

actress Tatiana Maslany
1985

Also on This Day

1946.
Movie and television producer and director Anne Wheeler is born in Edmonton. Her works include *Bye Bye Blues* and *The War Between Us* (both set during the Second World War), and she also directed episodes of *This Is Wonderland* and *Da Vinci's Inquest.*

Manon Rhéaume, 2013.

1992. Goalie Manon Rhéaume becomes the first woman to play professional hockey in the NHL when she hits the ice for the Tampa Bay Lightning in an exhibition game against the St. Louis Blues. A native of Lac-Beauport, Québec, Rhéaume played twenty-four professional games with seven other male-dominated teams in her career. With the Atlanta Knights of the International Hockey League, she made history as the first woman to play in a regular-season professional game. Rhéaume also helped lead Canada to a silver medal when women's hockey became an Olympic event in 1998.

 **Who is considered the "Wayne Gretzky of Women's Hockey"?**
See December 22.

BORN ON THIS DAY

actor Walter Pidgeon
1897

1906
diplomat
Charles Ritchie

24 SEPTEMBER

1988. Ben Johnson wins a gold medal at the Seoul Olympics with a world-record time of 9.79 seconds in the 100-metre final. The triumph was short lived, however, as Johnson tested positive for performance-enhancing drugs soon after. Olympic officials confiscated his medal, erased his record, and suspended him from competition for two years. He was also eventually stripped of his previous world record, set in 1987 at the World Championships. At a 1989 government investigation into drugs in sport, Johnson and his coach, Charlie Francis, both admitted that he and other athletes had systematically used steroids, beating drug tests by stopping for a set period before a race. Francis was banned from coaching for life. After serving the mandatory two-year suspension, during which time he counselled young people against the use of drugs, Johnson returned to competition in January 1991. He was later banned for life by the International Amateur Athletics Federation (IAAF) when his testosterone levels were found to be too high in 1993. Since then, several other prominent sprinters have faced accusations of drug use.

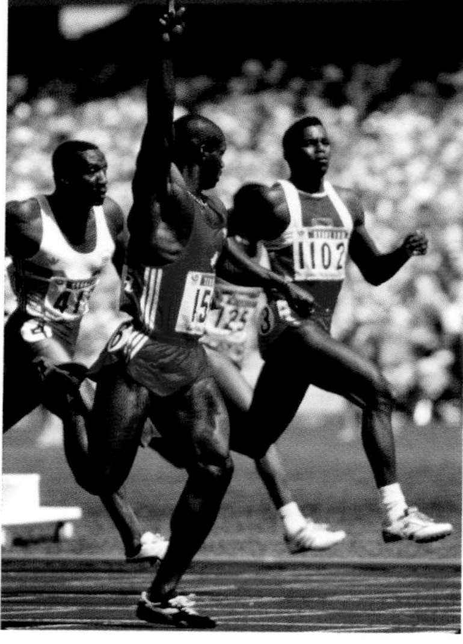

Ben Johnson winning the 100-metre final at the Seoul Olympics.

Also on This Day

1950.
Dense smoke from forest fires burning in British Columbia and Alberta is observed as far away as Nunavut. The smoke even travelled over Ontario and into Ohio and New York. Known as the Great Smoke Pall, the plume disrupted flights, created blackout conditions in some cities, and forced Toronto to turn on the street lamps at midday. Some concerned citizens thought the brown clouds were the result of a nuclear attack.

BORN ON THIS DAY

actor Phil Hartman
1948

1960
singer-songwriter and producer Amy Sky

actress and writer Nia Vardalos
1962

Vive le français!

Number of Canadians outside of Québec who speak French at home (rounded to the nearest hundred):

Ontario: 595,900
New Brunswick: 245,400
Alberta: 74,200
British Columbia: 69,500
Manitoba: 42,600
Nova Scotia: 34,400
Saskatchewan: 14,900
Prince Edward Island: 5,500
Newfoundland and Labrador: 4,300
Yukon: 1,700
Northwest Territories: 1,300
Nunavut: 500

Courtesy of ColourCanada.com.

The Franco-Ontarian flag.

1975. The Franco-Ontarian flag is raised for the first time at the University of Sudbury. The flag was created at Laurentian University by Gaétan Gervais, a historian, and Michel Dupuis, a student. It is divided into two halves: on one side is the fleur-de-lis, symbolizing the Francophonie, and on the other the trillium, symbolizing Ontario. The green colour represents summer, and the white winter. While the flag was quickly adopted within the Franco-Ontario community, it was not officially recognized by the provincial government until 2001. In 2010, September 25 was named Franco-Ontarian Day in the province, to celebrate the important contributions the community has made to Ontario's history and culture dating back to the 1600s. The francophone population in the province now numbers about six hundred thousand.

North-West Mounted Police commissioner James Macleod

1836

1933

singer-songwriter, guitarist, and rancher Ian Tyson

BORN ON THIS DAY

26 SEPTEMBER

Courtesy of © Maclean's Magazine.

John Bayne Maclean and Horace Hunter with a copy of the *Financial Post*, 1947.

1862. Publisher John Bayne Maclean, who founded a vast assortment of magazines, including *Chatelaine* and *Maclean's*, is born in Crieff, Canada West (now Ontario). Maclean was a teacher, a reporter, and the financial editor of the Toronto *Mail* before founding a highly successful trade magazine, *Canadian Grocer*, in 1887. It was followed by an array of similar magazines, making him Canada's leading producer of trade publications. This solid base allowed him to found wider-interest publications, such as the *Financial Post* (1907), the *Farmer's Magazine* (1910), *Mayfair* (1927), and *Chatelaine* (1928). As well, he purchased *Canadian Homes and Gardens* (1925) and *Busy Man's Magazine* (1905), the latter of which became his namesake *Maclean's* in 1911. By the 1930s, his company had become Canada's leading magazine publisher and had branches in the United States and Great Britain.

Also on This Day

1826.
The settlement that developed into Bytown (now Ottawa) is founded. The community was established as a home for contractors and labourers engaged in building the Rideau Canal and was named for Lt.-Col. John By, builder of the canal.

BORN ON THIS DAY

1946 writer, actor, and composer John Gray

1984 tennis player Frank Dancevic

"Squatters" in Stanley Park

Stanley Park is primarily known as a scenic escape for Vancouver-area residents and tourists, but it's also part of land that was occupied by Aboriginal peoples for millennia. In the 1860s, after the establishment of the Moodyville and Hastings sawmills, it became the site of a year-round settlement for Aboriginal and non-Aboriginal families. But when the land became a park in 1888, residents were labelled "squatters" and began to be forced out. Despite resistance, most families were gone by 1931, except for siblings Tim and Agnes Cummings, who remained in the park until their deaths in the 1950s.

Philip Tims/Vancouver Public Library/5.

A group of sightseers at the Hollow Tree, 1904.

1888. Stanley Park, the largest of Vancouver's two hundred or so parks, is opened. The space was originally home to the Tsleil-Waututh (Burrard), Musqueam, and Squamish peoples, and was named for Canada's sixth governor general, Lord Frederick Stanley. Over the years, Stanley Park has been home to many important activities, including a 1935 Mother's Day mass demonstration to abolish relief camps. It was also the site of military training for some three hundred members of the Canadian Women's Army Corps during the Second World War.

BORN ON THIS DAY

1943
singer-songwriter Randy Bachman

1972
cyclist and speed skater Clara Hughes

1984
singer-songwriter Avril Lavigne

28 SEPTEMBER

Courtesy of Jonathan Hayward/The Canadian Press.

Mourners waiting to pay their respects to the late Pierre Trudeau in the Hall of Honour, Parliament Hill.

2000. Politician, writer, and lawyer Pierre Elliott Trudeau dies in Montréal. Tens of thousands of people paid their respects while he lay in state at Parliament Hill. His casket was then returned to Montréal by train. Thousands of Canadians lined the route as Trudeau's body made its slow journey to his hometown, where it was greeted by thousands more mourners. A state funeral was held at Notre-Dame Basilica on October 3, and was attended by three thousand mourners, including Jean and Aline Chrétien, Fidel Castro, Jimmy Carter, and Prince Andrew. Trudeau held power for fifteen years, making him one of the nation's longest-serving prime ministers. He is remembered for negotiating Canada's constitutional independence from Britain and establishing a new constitution with an entrenched Charter of Rights and Freedoms. He also put in place a language law that made Canada officially bilingual. In and out of office, he was a controversial figure with strong supporters and equally strong critics.

BORN ON THIS DAY

1955 academic and politician Stéphane Dion

1990 actress Kristen Prout

IN HIS OWN WORDS: PIERRE TRUDEAU

"There's no place for the state in the bedrooms of the nation."

—Speaking about the decriminalization of homosexuality in 1967

"Of course a bilingual state is more expensive than a unilingual one—but it is a richer state."

—Extolling the virtues of multiculturalism in 1968

"We peer so suspiciously at each other that we cannot see that we Canadians are standing on the mountaintop of human wealth, freedom and privilege."

—From his 1980 New Year's message to Canadians

"We must now establish the basic principles, the basic values and beliefs which hold us together as Canadians so that beyond our regional loyalties there is a way of life and a system of values which make us proud of the country that has given us freedom and such immeasurable joy."

—From the citation for the Charter of Rights and Freedoms, 1981

"Some things I never learned to like. I didn't like to kiss babies, though I didn't mind kissing their mothers. I didn't like to slap backs or other parts of the anatomy. I liked hecklers, because they brought my speeches alive. I liked supporters, because they looked happy. And I really enjoyed mingling with people, if there wasn't too much of it."

—From his memoirs, published in 1993

29 SEPTEMBER

2004. The Montreal Expos play their last game at the Olympic Stadium before moving to Washington, DC, and being renamed the Washington Nationals. The Expos were defeated 9–1 by the Florida Marlins in front of more than thirty thousand fans. Established in 1969, the Expos were the first Canadian team in Major League Baseball. Between 1979 and 1983, they attracted over two million fans annually, and in that period they had the best overall winning percentage (.548) in the National League. The team remained competitive through the late 1980s and early 1990s, but attendance dropped substantially, putting the Expos under financial pressure. Principal owner Charles Bronfman sold the team to a consortium of Québec businessmen in 1991, after rejecting several offers from buyers who would have moved the Expos out of Montréal. But the team continued to be one of the least successful in the major leagues, both on the field and in ticket sales, making the move to Washington inevitable. After the Expos' relocation, the club's mascot, Youppi, was adopted by the Montreal Canadiens.

Courtesy of City of Montréal Archives/VM94-Y-25-304-037.

Youppi, the Montreal Expos mascot.

Also on This Day

1962.
Alouette 1, Canada's first satellite, is launched by NASA. Its mission—to study earth's upper atmosphere, which many believed held the key to better long-range communications—lasted ten years. *Alouette 1* was the first satellite built by a country other than the US or the USSR. Its name means "skylark" in English.

What were the Montreal Expos named after?
See April 27.

BORN ON THIS DAY

1953 — director and screenwriter Jean-Claude Lauzon

1970 — comedian Russell Peters

Also on This Day

1940.
Track-and-field athlete Harry Jerome is born in Prince Albert, Saskatchewan. He was the first man to hold simultaneous world records in the 100-yard and 100-metre events.

Who was the first Canadian woman in space?
See January 30.

Photograph: © Victor Zelentsov. Courtesy of NASA.

Laliberté in a Russian Sokol spacesuit.

2009. Cirque du Soleil founder Guy Laliberté becomes the first Canadian space tourist, taking part in a mission he hoped would increase awareness of the need for global water conservation. The fire-breathing, accordion-playing, and stilt-walking street performer had built Cirque du Soleil from a small band of Québec buskers and street musicians into an organization of international repute. When his massively successful franchise celebrated its twenty-fifth anniversary in 2009, Laliberté—who donned a red clown nose before blast-off—perhaps felt he needed a new challenge. His cheering supporters broke into a chorus of Elton John's "Rocket Man" upon hearing that his ship had entered orbit. The twelve-day round trip to the *International Space Station* came with a price tag of US$35 million.

BORN ON THIS DAY

1813

surgeon, fur trader, and explorer John Rae

1939

actor, director, and singer Len Cariou

1944

writer, sound poet, and editor bpNichol

OCTOBER

THE HOCKEY PUCK

Hockey pucks are kept in a freezer or ice cooler to reduce bounciness during the game. They're changed after every two minutes of playing time. The NHL uses an average of twenty-five to thirty pucks per game.

Early hockey pucks were square blocks of cherrywood. Eventually, someone had the idea of cutting a rubber lacrosse ball into thirds and using the middle section as a puck. The first round pucks appeared in the 1800s, and were developed by the Victoria Hockey Club of Montréal.

In 2012, Swedish player Alexander Wennberg scored by carrying the puck across the goal line in his pants. Wennberg didn't realize the puck was there, and it fell out as he crashed the net. The goal was considered legal.

Canada is one of four major producers of hockey pucks. The others are Russia, the Czech Republic, and China.

Hockey pucks are made of vulcanized rubber. The puck is nicknamed a *biscuit*, and to "put a biscuit in the basket" means to score a goal. In 1978, the song "Rubber Biscuit" was a hit for the Blues Brothers, an R & B band featuring comedians John Belushi and Ottawa-born Dan Aykroyd.

NASA astronauts learn how to move large objects in microgravity by manipulating a "two-ton hockey puck" over a special floor that's similar to a giant air hockey table. But astronauts use real hockey pucks too—in January 2013, Chris Hadfield dropped the ceremonial first puck for a Maple Leafs home opener from the International Space Station.

Courtesy of City of Ottawa Archives/MG393/CA03072-002/Newton.

Prime Minister Louis St. Laurent with Ottawa mayor Charlotte Whitton, 1954.

1951. Charlotte Whitton becomes Canada's first female mayor of a major city. During her time as Ottawa's mayor, she championed women's equality in the workplace while paradoxically opposing more liberal divorce laws and criticizing married women who worked. Whitton is best remembered as Ottawa's flamboyant and outspoken mayor during the 1950s and 1960s, but she also had significant accomplishments earlier in her career, including twenty years spent as founding director of the Canadian Council on Child Welfare (known today as the Canadian Council on Social Development), where she relentlessly advocated for professional standards in the care of juvenile immigrants and neglected and dependent children.

Also on This Day

1961.
Reach for the Top first airs on the CBC affiliate station CBUT in Vancouver. The show pitted teams of high school students against each other in rousing battles of trivia. The French version of the show, *Génies en herbe*, aired on Radio-Canada from 1973 to 1997. An adapted version of the French-language show was also aired in recent years, and a competition based on *Reach for the Top* still takes place in Canadian schools.

Which quiz-master was born in Sudbury, Ontario? See July 22.

BORN ON THIS DAY

1926 — cartoonist Ben Wicks

1943 — singer-songwriter, actress, and broadcaster Angèle Arsenault

1967 — Hockey Hall of Famer Geraldine Heaney

Also on This Day

1955.
The overhauled Unemployment Insurance Act comes into effect. The revised act, among other changes, extended the minimum benefit period from six to fifteen weeks and reduced the maximum period from one year to thirty-six weeks.

Library and Archives Canada/1991-35-21.

The Nova Scotia House of Assembly meets for the first time in the Halifax courthouse.

1758. The first elected assembly in what is now Canada meets in Halifax, marking the beginning of representative government in the country. The twenty-two assembled members had been elected on July 31 by votes from British Protestant male landowners over the age of twenty-one. Although representative government was new to Canada, elected assemblies did exist in Britain and New England before 1749, when Halifax was founded by Edward Cornwallis. In fact, the British government had instructed Cornwallis to set up an elected assembly in the new settlement. But he didn't think the time was right and refused. In early 1758, a group of irate settlers sent a representative to London to petition for an elected assembly, and their request was approved, with the Lords of Trade writing, "His Majesty's subjects (great part of whom are alleged to have quitted the Province on account of the great discontent prevailing for want of an Assembly) may no longer be deprived of that privilege, which was promised to them by His Majesty, when Settlement of this Colony was first undertaken."

BORN ON THIS DAY

physicist Robert Boyle

1883

1946

actor Eric Peterson

3 OCTOBER

Courtesy of Library and Archives Canada/E. Espèrence/PA-030192.

Canada's first contingent in Gaspé Bay, off Québec.

1914. The first contingent of Canadian troops sails for England following the outbreak of the First World War months earlier. The largest convoy ever to cross the Atlantic, it comprised nearly thirty-three thousand troops aboard thirty-one ocean liners escorted by Royal Navy warships. Also sailing in this convoy were soldiers from the British colony of Newfoundland, which was still separate from Canada at the time.

Also on This Day

1882.
Artist and writer Alexander Young (A.Y.) Jackson is born in Montréal. As a leading member of the Group of Seven, Jackson helped to remake the visual image of Canada; as a sparkling storyteller, he ensured the Group's notoriety. Soon after moving to Toronto in the fall of 1913, Jackson began sharing his studio with a shy, uncertain painter named Tom Thomson. The two became firm friends, to their mutual advantage: Jackson taught Thomson aspects of technique, while Thomson taught Jackson about the Canadian wilderness. Eager to experience Thomson's north country, Jackson went to Canoe Lake in Algonquin Park in February 1914. There he found not only excellent painting country but also an image of Canada. His experience resulted in the iconic painting *The Red Maple.*

BORN ON THIS DAY

1956 — actor and director Hart Bochner

1973 — actress and producer Neve Campbell

1981 — actress Amanda Walsh

Also on This Day

1869.
The Saxby Gale sweeps up the Bay of Fundy, causing death and destruction along New Brunswick's coast and the inner reaches of Minas Basin and Chignecto Bay. The tropical cyclone was named for Stephen Martin Saxby, a naval officer and the author of *Saxby's Weather System* (1864), who had predicted the storm in a letter to the *London Standard* and *London Press* almost a year earlier. He based his prediction on uncommonly high tides caused by the position of the moon.

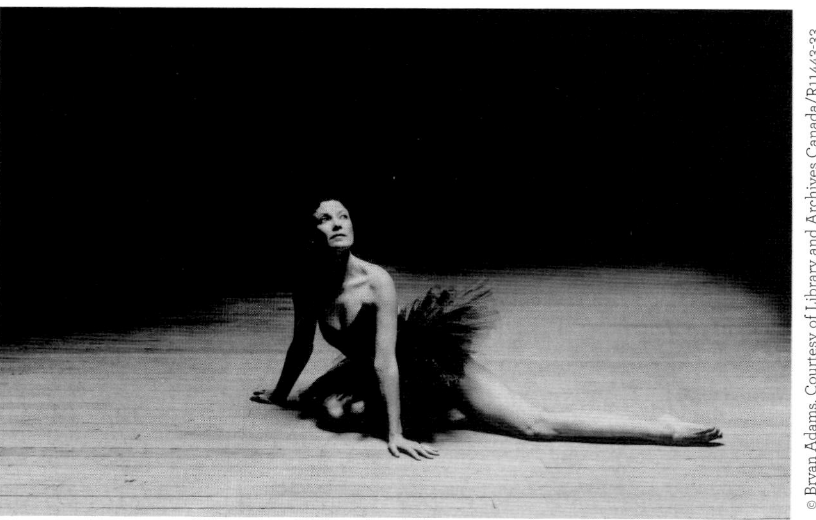

© Bryan Adams. Courtesy of Library and Archives Canada/R1443-33.

Karen Kain, 1999.

1997. In Winnipeg, dancer Karen Kain gives the last performance of her cross-country tour with the National Ballet of Canada before retiring from her twenty-five-year career as a ballerina. Kain began training at the National Ballet School when she was just eleven; after making her debut in the role of the Swan Queen in the 1971 production of *Swan Lake*, she was quickly promoted to the rank of principal dancer. She was known for her versatile technique and impressive ability in both classical and contemporary works. She often partnered with fellow Canadian dancer Frank Augustyn; the pair, known as the Gold-Dust Twins, became Canada's favourite dance couple. Kain rejoined the National Ballet of Canada in 1998 as artist-in-residence and became artistic director in 2005.

BORN ON THIS DAY

statesman Louis-Hippolyte La Fontaine
1807

1934
author Rudy Wiebe

5 OCTOBER

Marc Garneau, 2000.

1984. Marc Garneau becomes the first Canadian in space during the STS-41G mission of the US space shuttle *Challenger*. During this mission, Garneau was tasked with testing the "space vision system," which was designed to help astronauts manoeuvre robotic devices such as the Canadarm. Over the course of his three flights, he logged more than 677 hours in space. In 2001, Garneau was named president of the Canadian Space Agency, a position he held until 2005, when he resigned to run for political office. In 2008, he was elected the member of Parliament for the Montréal riding of Westmount–Ville-Marie.

Who was the first Canadian in space? See January 30.

Highlights of Garneau's Career

1984: Appointed an Officer of the Order of Canada
1989–1992: Serves as Deputy Director of the Canadian Astronaut Program
1992: Reports to the Johnson Space Center in Houston, Texas, for mission specialist training
1996 and 2000: Serves as Mission Specialist 2 on board the *Endeavour*
2001: Appointed Executive Vice President of the Canadian Space Agency and later that year is appointed its president
2003: Promoted to Companion of the Order of Canada
2005: Resigns from the Canadian Space Agency to run for federal office
2006: Runs in the federal general election but loses to the candidate for the Bloc Québécois
2008: Wins a seat in the House of Commons in the Westmount–Ville-Marie riding
2011: Narrowly re-elected
2012: Announces his intention to run for Liberal Party leadership
2013: Drops out of the leadership race in support of Justin Trudeau's bid

BORN ON THIS DAY

author Marie-Claire Blais
1939

Hockey Hall of Famer Mario Lemieux
1965

Hockey Hall of Famer Patrick Roy
1965

OCTOBER

The Rainiest Months on Record

Alberta: 213 mm, Eckville South, June 1970
British Columbia: 489 mm, Ucluelet, October 1967
Manitoba: 217 mm, Riding Mountain Park, September 1975
New Brunswick: 179 mm, Alma, April 1962
Newfoundland and Labrador: 173 mm, St. John's, August 1876
Northwest Territories: 91 mm, Ennadai Lake (now in Nunavut), September 1972
Nova Scotia: 239 mm, Halifax, September 1942
Ontario: 264 mm, Harrow, July 1989
Prince Edward Island: 164 mm, Charlottetown, September 1942
Québec: 172 mm, Barrage des Quinze, August 1932
Saskatchewan: 179 mm, Willmar, July 1984
Yukon: 91 mm, Quiet Lake, July 1972

The Tragically Hip in concert at Calgary's Jubilee Auditorium, 2009.

1992. The Tragically Hip releases its wildly successful third album, *Fully Completely*. The album produced a number of hit songs, including "Fifty Mission Cap," based on the true story of Toronto Maple Leafs player Bill Barilko; "Courage (for Hugh MacLennan)," about the celebrated author; "At the Hundredth Meridian," a place marking the longitude that roughly divides Western and Central Canada; and "Wheat Kings," which tells the story of David Milgaard's wrongful conviction in Saskatchewan. The album was certified diamond in 2007 for sales of more than one million copies and is considered one of the all-time greatest rock albums in Canada.

BORN ON THIS DAY

1769 army officer and colonial administrator Isaac Brock

1866 inventor Reginald Fessenden

© Bryan Adams/Library and Archives of Canada/R11443-115.

Adrienne Clarkson, 2004.

1999. Broadcaster and author Adrienne Clarkson is sworn in as Canada's twenty-sixth governor general. She was the second woman and the first Chinese Canadian to hold the office. She was also the first governor general without either a military or a political background, having spent most of her career hosting a variety of shows for the CBC. Clarkson is credited with transforming the vice-regal position.

Also on This Day

1763.
The Royal Proclamation is issued by King George III, setting the western boundary of British settlement following the Seven Years' War. The Proclamation stated that Aboriginal title had existed and continued to exist; it also established the constitutional framework for the negotiation of treaties with the Aboriginal inhabitants of large sections of Canada. All land was considered Aboriginal land until ceded by treaty, which could only be annexed by the Crown.

Who was Canada's first female Governor General?
See December 23.

BORN ON THIS DAY

1786 politician and lawyer Louis-Joseph Papineau

1923 artist Jean-Paul Riopelle

1953 actress and playwright Linda Griffiths

1979 actors Shawn and Aaron Ashmore

OCTOBER 8

The World's First Pacemaker

1958.
A Swedish doctor successfully implants the world's first pacemaker, a Canadian invention. In 1949, electrical engineer John A. Hopps of Winnipeg had devised a prototype of the machine alongside Dr. Wilfred Bigelow and Dr. John Callaghan at the Banting Institute in Toronto. That first machine had to be plugged into a wall outlet and provided electric shocks to the heart through a wire inserted in the jugular vein. Today's pacemakers are implanted right in the patient's body; some even include microprocessors that can monitor a person's activity levels and adjust the heartbeat accordingly.

What hand-held, portable, two-way radio transceiver was invented in 1937? See October 22.

City of Edmonton Archives/EA-10-2715.

Jasper Avenue in Edmonton, looking east, 1904.

1904. Edmonton is incorporated as a city. As the provincial capital (a status it gained in 1905, when the Province of Alberta was formed), it has become increasingly multicultural and is often referred to as the Gateway to the North, because of its strategic location between the highly productive farmlands of central Alberta and the resource-rich northern hinterland. Edmonton is also the gateway to the West Edmonton Mall—which has over eight hundred shops, an indoor amusement park, and a wave pool. It is the largest mall in North America, and it also holds the Guinness World Record for the largest parking lot.

BORN ON THIS DAY

1864
artist Ozias Leduc

1929
dancer Lois Smith

1956
entrepreneur and TV personality Arlene Dickinson

9 OCTOBER

1867. In a great act of heroism, sealing captain and sailing master William Jackman throws himself into the icy waters off Labrador and single-handedly rescues eleven of twenty-seven people stranded on a foundering ship called the *Sea Clipper*. When rescuers finally arrived to assist, they brought a dory and a rope. The sea proved too rough for the dory, however, so Jackman tied the rope around his waist, swam to the boat, and tied the other end to the rail. With the rope and the extra hands on shore he swam out sixteen more times, over the course of two hours, to bring the remaining men and women to safety.

A stamp featuring William Jackman, issued by Canada Post as part of the Legendary Heroes series, 1992.

Another Daring Rescue

Abigail Becker is remembered as the Heroine of Long Point for a courageous rescue on Lake Erie. On November 24, 1854, a raging storm caused a schooner to founder on a sandbar. The captain and crew did not dare venture into the rough waters of the surf until Becker, in spite of an inability to swim, waded shoulder-high into the frigid waves and persuaded the men to swim toward her. This heroic act was generously praised by the crew and even by Queen Victoria, who sent Becker a handwritten note, along with fifty pounds. The Heroine of Long Point would go on to assist six other shipwrecked sailors in her life.

BORN ON THIS DAY

anti-slavery activist, journalist, and publisher Mary Ann Shadd
1823

1955
writer, director, and producer Linwood Boomer

tennis player Carling Bassett-Seguso
1967

OCTOBER  

Also on This Day

1863.
Weightlifter Louis Cyr is born in Saint-Cyprien-de-Napierville, Québec. The strongman's feats included lifting a 250-kilogram weight with one finger and holding two driving horses to a standstill, one tied to each of his massive arms. In 1895, Cyr lifted a platform holding eighteen men weighing a combined 1,967 kilograms. He spent several years touring with the Ringling Brothers and Barnum and Bailey, and later opened a tavern in Montréal. Cyr died of Bright's disease in 1912, at the age of forty-nine.

Courtesy of Tom Hanson/The Canadian Press.

The Dalai Lama greets Rohahes Iain Phillips, a Mohawk elder, while William Commanda, an Algonquin elder, looks on.

1980. His Holiness the fourteenth Dalai Lama, Tenzin Gyatso, arrives in Canada for a seventeen-day visit. Canada had admitted 228 individuals under the 1971–72 Tibetan Refugee Program—a response to the Dalai Lama's appeal to the international community to accept Tibetan refugees from Chinese occupation. During his visit, the spiritual and worldly leader of the Tibetan people met with Prime Minister Paul Martin and Governor General Edward Shreyer. In 2006, he was awarded honorary Canadian citizenship while visiting Vancouver to open the Dalai Lama Center for Peace and Education.

BORN ON THIS DAY

1819
Governor General Charles Stanley Monck

1966
skier Karen Percy

1974
hockey player Chris Pronger

11 OCTOBER

same potential in achieving fame and fortune as children of single birth."

* * *

"PERHAPS IT'S because I'm getting old and grumpy but I notice that I'm more bothered by noise than ever before. We live in an upper duplex, not far from a busy thoroughfare.

"Is there anything I can do to escape from all the racket?"

IT'S NOT so much that you're growing old and grumpy but that the noises are becoming more numerous and louder. That's part of the price we must pay for a bustling, highly mechanized society.

Short of moving to a quieter place, there are some anti-noise measures you can take:

Put down wall-to-wall carpeting and install acoustic tiles on your ceilings. Use long, wide, thick drapes on your windows. All these are excellent noise mufflers.

Adjust your telephone so it'll ring more softly. Install a more gentle doorbell. Oil the hinges on your doors. Typewriters vibrate less when placed on a thick piece of foam rubber.

Equip your high-fi, radio or TV with earphones so that if only one person is listening, others in the house won't be disturbed.

If you're bothered by noises from outside your home—such as barking dogs, no muffler cars, trucks rumbling by late at night, all-night parties next door—you can make use of the protection afforded by the law. Discuss it with the officer in charge of your district police station.

'Undignified' highway post kept out of Queen's Park

There'll be no black and white highway guardrail posts crossing the floor of the Ontario Legislature.

That was the ruling by Speaker Donald Morrow yesterday after Clerk of the Legislature Rod Lewis spotted Leo Bernier (PC—Kenora) lugging a five-foot experimental fibreglass post towards the legislative chamber.

Bernier intended to present the post to Highways Minister George Gomme while the House was in session to demonstrate its value as a substitute for cedar posts.

But Lewis felt this would offend the dignity of the House and the Speaker agreed.

So, like a sentinel on guard, the post is standing outside the chamber and during the budget debate next week, Bernier will get a chance to invite Gomme to look at it.

A firm in Bernier's home town of Hudson makes the posts.

some way of making its ceasefire order stick.

The crisis also led to revitalization of the 130-man truce organization to pro-

HEAVY EXPLOSIONS

General Bull said heavy explosions were heard north of Tiberias, there was in-

tolerate here this monstrous cynicism and deliberate falsification?" Fedorenko asked.

Last night's session of the

from Arab soil.

U.S. ambassador Arthur Goldberg made the point that the "quasi-judicial" nature of the council made it

A page from the *Toronto Star*, showing an advertisement for the Company of Young Canadians, 1967.

1969. The Company of Young Canadians (CYC), a government volunteer agency that offers social improvement programs across the country, is accused of harbouring terrorists and communist agitators. That week, the city of Montréal had seen rioting in the wake of a police strike. Amid frenzied finger-pointing, the city's executive committee issued a statement accusing members of the CYC of belonging to the Front de libération du Québec (FLQ), making Molotov cocktails, using their printing press to produce agitation propaganda, and planning protest marches. While the allegations were not proven, and no federal inquiry was launched, the group was eventually abolished by the government in 1976.

Notable Company of Young Canadians Alumni

Lloyd Axworthy, former minister of foreign affairs; **Gilles Duceppe,** Bloc Québécois leader; **Georges Erasmus,** former national chief, Assembly of First Nations; **Phil Fontaine,** former national chief, Assembly of First Nations; **Barbara Hall,** former mayor of Toronto; **Maurice Strong,** businessman and environmentalist

What federal act was put in place to deal with the October Crisis?

See October 16.

BORN ON THIS DAY

1929 — architect and planner Raymond Moriyama

1984 — actress Martha MacIsaac

Also on This Day

1962.
Typhoon Freda hits Vancouver around midnight, with winds greater than one hundred kilometres per hour. The storm lasted about four hours, killing seven people and blowing down nearly a fifth of all the trees in Stanley Park.

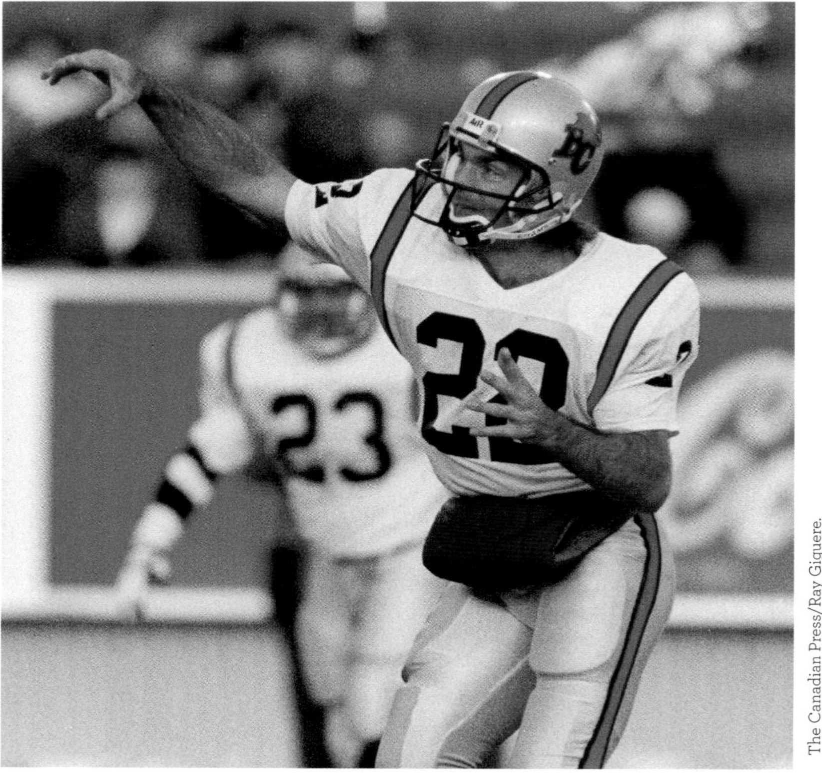

The Canadian Press/Ray Giguere.

Quarterback Doug Flutie of the BC Lions unloads a long bomb in Calgary in 1991.

1991. Quarterback Doug Flutie of the BC Lions breaks Warren Moon's Canadian Football League (CFL) record for yards passing in a season with a 582-yard performance in an overtime loss to the Edmonton Eskimos. Winner of the prestigious Heisman Trophy, Flutie began his career in the NFL in 1985, when he was drafted by the Los Angeles Rams. In 1990 he moved to the CFL, signing with the BC Lions. After being traded to the Calgary Stampeders, Flutie helped his team win the 1992 Grey Cup.

BORN ON THIS DAY

1909
poet Dorothy Livesay

1955
singer-songwriter Jane Siberry

1971
curler Atina Ford

13 OCTOBER

Library and Archives Canada/e010952223.

***Brock Entering Queenston*, 1812, by J.D. Kelly and A.H. Hider.**

1812. In a critical battle of the War of 1812, British and Canadian soldiers defeat a much larger American force at Queenston Heights, Ontario. The soldiers from Canada included Captain Runchey's Company of Coloured Men, a contingent made up largely of Black soldiers, as well as a force of Six Nations warriors led by Mohawk chief John Norton. The Battle of Queenston Heights was both a victory and a loss for the British and Canadian forces, as it resulted in the death of Gen. Isaac Brock. In total, three hundred Americans were wounded or killed, and almost another thousand taken prisoner. British troops lost only twenty-eight men and saw seventy-seven wounded.

Also on This Day

1993.
Michael Smith wins the Nobel Prize in Chemistry for developing a system for editing genetic DNA sequences using site-directed mutagenesis. This process allows biologists to make intentional and directed changes to the DNA sequence of a gene. He donated the prize money to a variety of projects, including the advancement of women in scientific careers and research on schizophrenia.

BORN ON THIS DAY

journalist and author William Kirby

1817

1820

geologist John Dawson

OCTOBER 14

Courtesy of Library and Archives Canada/Duncan Cameron/Duncan Cameron fonds/PA-114542.

Left to right: Paul Martin Sr., Lester B. Pearson, and Louis St. Laurent in Ottawa after Pearson's Nobel Peace Prize win.

1957. Lester B. Pearson is awarded the Nobel Peace Prize for resolving the Suez Crisis. Pearson, then secretary of state for external affairs, had proposed the first United Nations peacekeeping force as means of easing the British and French out of Egypt in 1956. When disagreements over control of the Suez Canal—which connected the Mediterranean and Red Seas, giving the West easier access to Middle Eastern oil—grew heated, Pearson's plan was implemented. By the end of 1956, British and French troops had completely withdrawn from Egypt. The crisis not only garnered Pearson the distinguished prize but also gave Canadians a favourable opinion of peacekeeping. In 1958, Pearson won the leadership of the federal Liberal party, and he became prime minister after the fall of John Diefenbaker's Conservatives in 1963.

BORN ON THIS DAY

1887

sculptor Frances Loring

1927

conductor, arranger, and choral editor Elmer Iseler

1985

actor Daniel Clark

THE SUEZ CRISIS 1956

July 26
Egyptian president Gamal Abdel Nasser nationalizes the Suez Canal Company, which is jointly owned by French and British interests. Built by Egyptian workers, the canal is a main route for oil travelling to Britain from the Middle East. If Nasser blocked the flow of that oil, he could damage the British economy.

October 29
After diplomatic efforts fail to effect change over the summer, France and Britain, along with their ally Israel, secretly plot to attack the region without informing the United States, Canada, and other NATO allies. Israeli forces advance to the canal as part of a ploy designed to give Britain and France an excuse to invade and regain control. The two European powers respond by ordering both Israel and Egypt to withdraw.

October 31
Britain and France begin bombing the canal zone when Egypt does not retreat. Britain's tactics go against US calls for peaceful resolution, which causes a rift between the two powerful nations. Canada's secretary of state for external affairs, Lester Pearson, works behind the scenes with colleagues at the United Nations and develops the idea for the UN's first large-scale peacekeeping force.

November 4
Fifty-seven UN states vote in favour of Pearson's idea. British and French paratroops ignore the vote.

November 6
A cease-fire is called at midnight.

November 15–16
The first United Nations Emergency Force (UNEF) arrives in Egypt and immediately enters the canal area. Pearson's solution allows Britain, France, and Israel to withdraw their forces without giving the appearance of having been defeated. The UNEF, under the command of Canadian general E.L.M. Burns, is in place by late November. British and French troops depart the region by the end of the year, and Israeli forces leave the following spring.

Also on This Day

1954.
Hurricane Hazel strikes Toronto. The storm dumped an estimated 300 million tonnes of rain on the city, submerging streets, washing out bridges, and resulting in enormous human tragedy. More than eighty people were killed, and nearly two thousand families were left homeless. The total cost of the destruction was estimated to be as much as $100 million (more than $1 billion today).

Where did Canada's most damaging flood take place? See May 1.

A page from *La Presse*, 1899.

Courtesy of McCord Museum/C571.1.

1884. The first issue of the French-language newspaper *Le Nouveau Monde*—renamed *La Presse* just a few days later—is published in Montréal by William-Edmond Blumhart. The paper was created by conservative francophones who were dissatisfied with Prime Minister John A. Macdonald and the support he received from *Le Monde*, a rival newspaper edited by journalist and politician Hector-Louis Langevin. In 1896, the paper's circulation was 14,000. By the time of its centennial, in 1984, circulation had grown to 225,000 during the week and 323,000 on Saturdays.

BORN ON THIS DAY

1701
founder of the Sisters of Charity St. Marguerite d'Youville

1908
economist John Kenneth Galbraith

1933
philosopher and author Leonard Peikoff

BACK BACON

Toronto was home to one of the country's earliest and largest meatpackers, the William Davies Company, which, according to lore, is the source of the city's nickname, Hogtown. But an 1898 article in the Toronto *Globe* claimed that the nickname actually referred to the greedy reputation of the city's residents and the way Toronto affairs dominated provincial politics.

The William Davies Company is credited with inventing peameal bacon. Butchers rolled trimmed pork loin in peameal to preserve it for the long trip to England. Peameal bacon is still popular in Canada—although today the coating is actually cornmeal.

In the United States, Canadian bacon is a type of back bacon that is cooked and ready to eat. This is not generally sold in Canada.

William Davies died at the age of ninety on a trip through the United States. He stepped out of his car to relieve himself and was butted by an angry goat.

Canadian Bacon was a 1995 comedy directed by Michael Moore about a US–Canadian war. It was the last of John Candy's films to be released. A war between the two countries is also the basis for the 1999 film *South Park: Bigger, Longer & Uncut*. Its song "Blame Canada" received an Oscar nomination for best original song.

When the CBC asked for more Canadian content in the comedy series *SCTV*, Rick Moranis and Dave Thomas created Bob and Doug McKenzie, two stereotypical Canadian "hosers." Although Bob and Doug were intended to mock the Canadian content requirements, they became hugely popular in both Canada and the US. The characters spent much of their onscreen time drinking beer and cooking back bacon.

OCTOBER

Library and Archives Canada. Courtesy of Library and Archives Canada/ Duncan Cameron fonds/ e010858585.

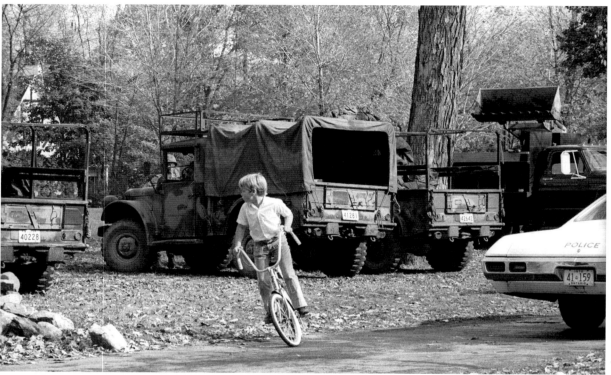

Troops are stationed in Montréal as part of the War Measures Act. 1970.

Also on This Day

1870.
Aeronautical engineer Wallace Turnbull is born in Saint John, New Brunswick. He would go on to build the first wind tunnel in Canada and to invent the variable-pitch propeller.

1970. The federal government invokes the War Measures Act, allowing it to suspend civil liberties while dealing with the October Crisis. Soon, tanks roamed Montréal streets and soldiers in full battle gear raided homes looking for members of the Front de libération du Québec (FLQ), which sought to advance an extremist agenda for Québec sovereignty and socialism. Three days earlier, reporters had asked Prime Minister Pierre Trudeau how far he would go in his efforts to stop the terrorist group. Trudeau gave his now famous, cold-eyed response: "Just watch me."

BORN ON THIS DAY

1927

physician and medical researcher James Fraser Mustard

1946

typographer, author, and poet Robert Bringhurst

1981

actress Caterina Scorsone

17 OCTOBER

Photograph: © Jon Sturge. Courtesy of The Mercer Report.

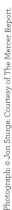

Rick Mercer in the graffitied Toronto alleyway where he delivers his weekly "rants" on the *Rick Mercer Report*.

Rickisms

"I like to think of myself as an equal opportunity offender."

"Do the unexpected. Take twenty minutes out of your day [and] do what young people all over the world are dying to do: vote."

"I didn't come out of the womb ranting, but chances are I heard a few good ones while I was in there."

1960. Satirist, comedian, screenwriter, and actor Rick Mercer is born in St. John's, Newfoundland. One of Canada's foremost political and social commentators, he began his career on the CBC in the early 1990s, working on *This Hour Has 22 Minutes*. This led to the launch of his popular sitcom *Made in Canada* in 2003 and, the following year, the current affairs show now known as the *Rick Mercer Report* (*RMR*). From his "Talking to Americans" segment on *This Hour Has 22 Minutes* to his trademark "rants" on *RMR*, Mercer has added thought-provoking humour to the Canadian political landscape. He is also active in social causes and was credited with inspiring many young adults to vote in the 2011 federal election. In 2006, after a trip to Africa, Mercer co-founded the Spread the Net campaign. The campaign has provided over two and a half million insecticide-treated bed nets to vulnerable families in Africa.

BORN ON THIS DAY

1948 actress Margot Kidder

1963 actor, writer, and producer Norm Macdonald

OCTOBER 18

A plaque ceremony to honour the Famous 5, 1938. (Front row, left to right: Mrs. Muir Edwards, daughter-in-law of Henrietta Muir Edwards; Mrs. J.C. Kenwood, daughter of Judge Emily Murphy; Mackenzie King; Mrs. Nellie McClung. Back row, left to right: Senators Iva Campbell Fallis and Cairine Wilson.)

Courtesy of the National Film Board of Canada/Eugene M. Finn/Library and Archives Canada/C-054523.

In what year were women first elected to a legislature in Canada? See June 7.

1929. The Judicial Committee of the Privy Council rules that women are legally "persons" and therefore can hold seats in the Canadian Senate. This reversed a Canadian Supreme Court ruling, which excluded women from public office—an exclusion the Privy Council called "a relic of days more barbarous than ours." The so-called Persons Case was brought forward after strenuous lobbying by the Famous 5—Emily Murphy, Henrietta Muir Edwards, Nellie McClung, Louise McKinney, and Irene Parlby. The Persons Case recognized women as eligible candidates for appointment to the Senate, paved the way for Cairine Wilson to become the first female senator in 1930, and was instrumental to the women's rights movement in Canada.

BORN ON THIS DAY

1932

broadcaster and politician Iona Campagnolo

1946

composer, conductor, and saxophonist Howard Shore

1977

soccer player Paul Stalteri

19 OCTOBER

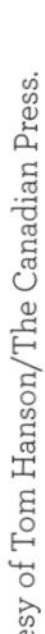
Courtesy of Tom Hanson/The Canadian Press.

Treasury Board President Lucienne Robillard responds to questions about the federal court decision on pay equity.

1999. The Federal Court of Canada rules against the government in a fifteen-year-old pay equity dispute. The settlement cost about $3.2 billion, most of which was paid out to female workers and retirees. The case found its way to the Federal Court when the government appealed a 1998 decision by the Canadian Human Rights Tribunal, which had accepted a complex pay equity method supported by the Public Service Alliance of Canada and the Canadian Human Rights Commission.

Also on This Day

1987. Panicked stockholders sell off millions of shares at the New York Stock Exchange, causing the worst single-day percentage drop on the Dow Jones Industrial Average in history and triggering stock market crashes around the world. The Black Monday crash was eerily close to the October 24 anniversary of the 1929 crash that ushered in the Great Depression. Its impact was felt in Canada, where the Toronto Stock Exchange 300 Index dropped a record 407.2 points and suffered a total loss of $37 billion. The TSE wouldn't surpass its pre-crash peak until August 1993.

BORN ON THIS DAY

swimmer Marilyn Bell
1937

1977
director Jason Reitman

Also on This Day

1873.
Author and suffragist Nellie McClung is born in Chatsworth, Ontario. She became active in the Woman's Christian Temperance Union before publishing her first novel, the bestselling *Sowing Seeds in Danny*. McClung fought for many reforms, including female suffrage and factory safety legislation. She was also a proponent of forced sterilization in an era when the pseudo-science of eugenics was sweeping the globe and was instrumental in the passing of highly controversial eugenics legislation in Alberta in 1928. This legislation would stand until the Conservative government of Peter Lougheed abolished it in 1972.

Courtesy of Library and Archives Canada/C-078979.

A team from the boundary commission marks the 49th parallel, 1861.

1818. The Convention of 1818 establishes the boundary between British North America and the United States as a line from the farthest northwest part of Lake of the Woods to the 49th parallel and then west to the Rocky Mountains. This resolved a long-standing frontier dispute between Great Britain and the United States. In 1846, the Oregon Treaty extended the 49th parallel to the Pacific Ocean and left Vancouver Island to the British. After the treaty was signed, both nations sent out working parties to map the frontier. The maps were adopted by both governments at the final joint meeting of the boundary commission in 1870. Although the 49th parallel is sometimes used to reference the entire border, in fact Manitoba, Saskatchewan, and Alberta are the only provinces entirely north of that line.

BORN ON THIS DAY

1904 — politician and father of socialized medicine Tommy Douglas

1910 — Ontario lieutenant-governor Pauline McGibbon

1961 — wilderness survival expert Les Stroud

1963 — astronaut Julie Payette

21 OCTOBER

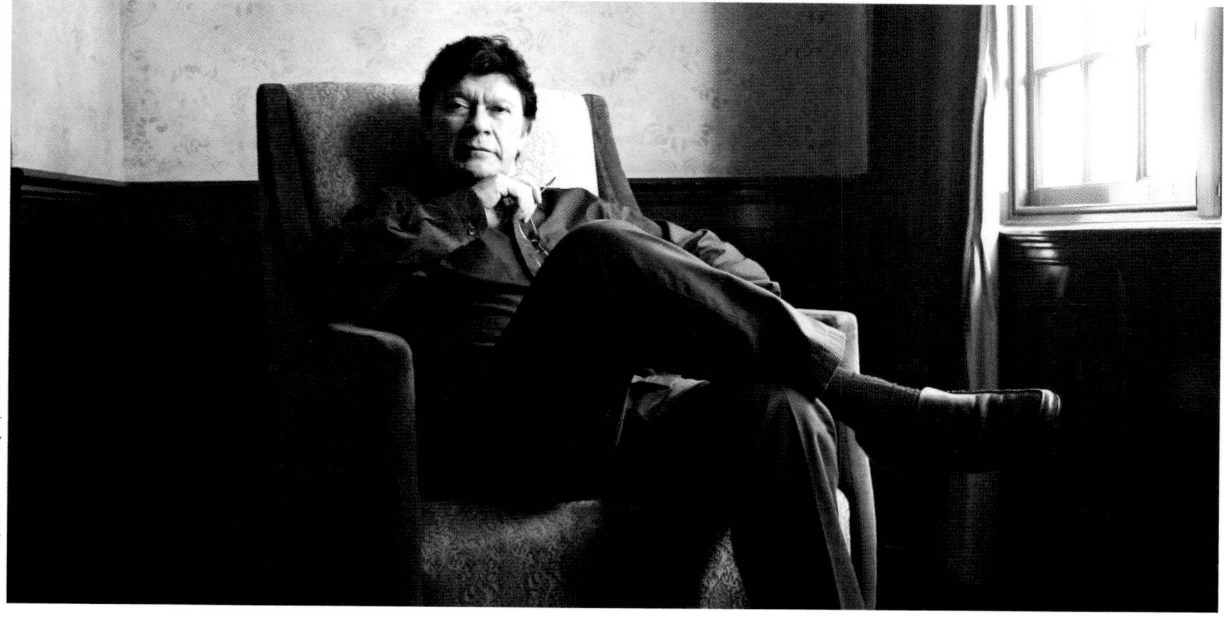

Courtesy of Adrian Wyld/The Canadian Press.

Robbie Robertson, 2005.

1988. Robbie Robertson's self-titled album is certified gold in the United States. Sales of the album—by one of Canada's best-known guitarists, singer-songwriters, and producers—exceeded two hundred thousand copies in Canada, and Robertson garnered Juno Awards for male vocalist of the year, album of the year, and (with Daniel Lanois) producer of the year. Of Mohawk and Jewish heritage, Robertson rose to fame during the 1960s as a member of the Canadian-American rock group The Band, for which he wrote several classic songs, including "The Weight," "The Night They Drove Old Dixie Down," and "Up on Cripple Creek." His later albums, including *Music for the Native Americans* and *Contact from the Underworld of Redboy*, featured collaborations with other Aboriginal musicians and have been credited with increasing the recognition of Aboriginal music in mainstream markets.

Select Robbie Robertson Discography

1987: *Robbie Robertson*
1991: *Storyville*
1994: *Music for the Native Americans*
1998: *Contact from the Underworld of Redboy*
2011: *How to Become Clairvoyant*

BORN ON THIS DAY

1954 politician Brian Tobin

1975 rapper Shane "Madchild" Bunting

OCTOBER 22

Notable Canadian Communications Inventions

1937: the Walkie-Talkie
1949: the pager
1972: computerized Braille
1996: the 56k modem
1999: the BlackBerry

Library and Archives Canada/PA-117883.

Employees of the G.N.W. Telegraph Company Messenger Service pose on the steps of their Montréal office, 1900.

Which broadcasting pioneer won a contest at age thirteen for building the best amateur radio in Ontario?
See June 21.

1846. The first telegraph company in Canada is established. The Toronto, Hamilton, Niagara, and St. Catharines Electro-Magnetic Telegraph Company transmitted the first message from Toronto to Hamilton on December 19, 1846. The telegraph profoundly altered nineteenth-century life, offering a faster means of communication. Developments in communication moved at a rapid pace—on December 12, 1901, Italian inventor Guglielmo Marconi proved that electrical signals could be transmitted without wires when he received the world's first radio transmission at Signal Hill in Newfoundland.

BORN ON THIS DAY

1951
author Elizabeth Hay

1952
modern dancer and choreographer Peggy Baker

1969
musician Stuart Chatwood

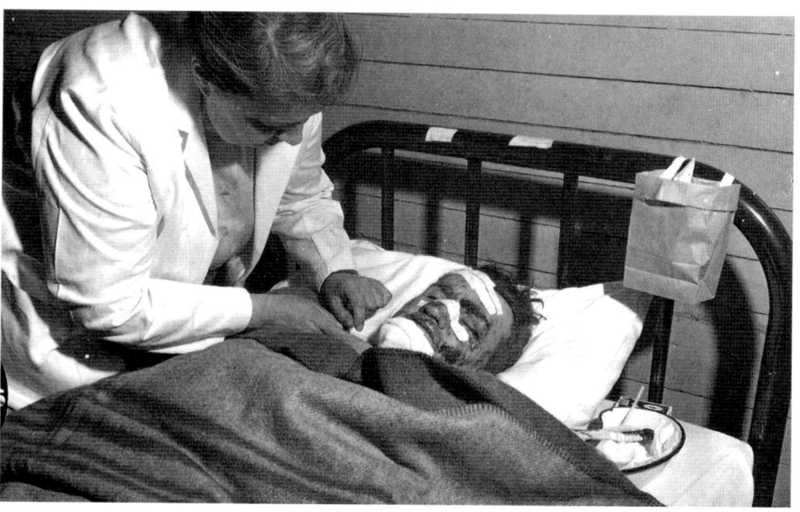

Nova Scotia Archives/Maurice Crosby fonds, 1997-254/005 #41.1.

A Springhill Mine survivor is tended to by a nurse in hospital.

1958. A so-called bump (underground earthquake) at a coal mine in Springhill, Nova Scotia, results in the death of seventy-four miners and the rescue of a hundred, some from levels as deep as 3,960 metres, the deepest rescue ever conducted in Canada. Inspired by the disaster, American folksinger Peggy Seeger and British singer Ewan MacColl composed "The Ballad of Springhill." With its haunting lyrics—"When the earth is restless, miners die / bone and blood is the price of coal"—the song captured the hardscrabble life of the coal miner and was performed by groups like the Dubliners, U2, and Peter, Paul and Mary. While the disaster was not the first to affect Springhill—424 people lost their lives in mining accidents between 1881 and 1969—the 1958 collapse ended the community's time as a large-scale mining town.

Coal-Mining Disasters in Canada

May 13, 1873: Drummond Colliery Disaster (Nova Scotia)
May 3, 1887: No. 1 Esplanade Mine Disaster (British Columbia)
June 19, 1914: Hillcrest Mine Disaster (Alberta)
July 25, 1917: Dominion No. 12 Colliery Explosion (Nova Scotia)
January 23, 1918: Allan Shaft Explosion (Nova Scotia)
December 6, 1938: Sydney Mines Disaster (Nova Scotia)
January 14, 1952: MacGregor Mine Explosion (Nova Scotia)
February 24, 1979: Glace Bay Disaster (Nova Scotia)
May 9, 1992: Westray Coal Mine Explosion (Nova Scotia)

BORN ON THIS DAY

politician Onésime Gagnon
1888

1976
actor Ryan Reynolds

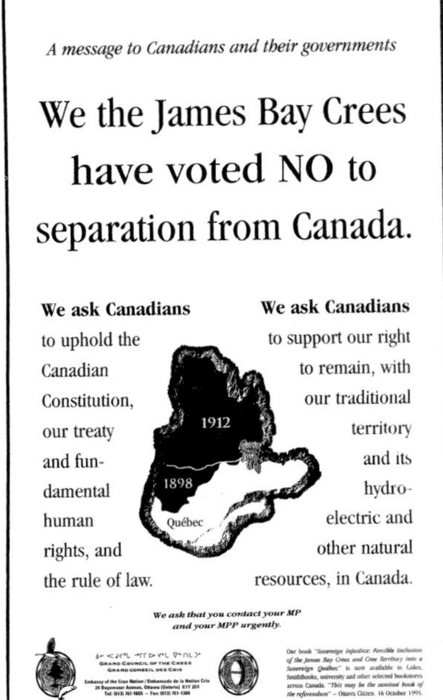

A message to Canadians and their governments

We the James Bay Crees have voted NO to separation from Canada.

We ask Canadians to uphold the Canadian Constitution, our treaty and fundamental human rights, and the rule of law.

We ask Canadians to support our right to remain, with our traditional territory and its hydro-electric and other natural resources, in Canada.

We ask that you contact your MP and your MPP urgently.

Grand Council of the Crees
Grand Conseil des Cris

A full-page notification in the *Toronto Star*.

1995. In the lead-up to Québec's second referendum on sovereignty, the James Bay Cree hold their own referendum, arguing that they too have the right to decide whether their territory will remain a part of Canada should Québec vote to separate. An overwhelming 96 percent voted in favour of staying within the country. A similar referendum was held by the Inuit of Northern Québec on October 26, and it also resulted in a vote to stay. The intense political climate surrounding Québec's sovereignty debate spurred many Aboriginal peoples to speak out for their right to determine their own future—and that of Canada.

Aboriginal Self-Government

The Indian Act of 1876 removed traditional systems of governance and imposed regulations on Aboriginal peoples and their communities. To this day, Canadian law continues to have more authority over Aboriginal rights and the occupation of Aboriginal lands. Some Aboriginal peoples formalized their relationships with the provincial and federal governments through self-government agreements. By 2012, there were eighteen of these agreements involving thirty-two communities in Canada.

BORN ON THIS DAY

1908 — geophysicist John Tuzo Wilson

1929 — football player, businessman, and Alberta lieutenant-governor Norman Kwong

1946 — Steppenwolf drummer Jerry Edmonton

1986 — rapper, singer-songwriter, and actor Aubrey "Drake" Graham

25 OCTOBER

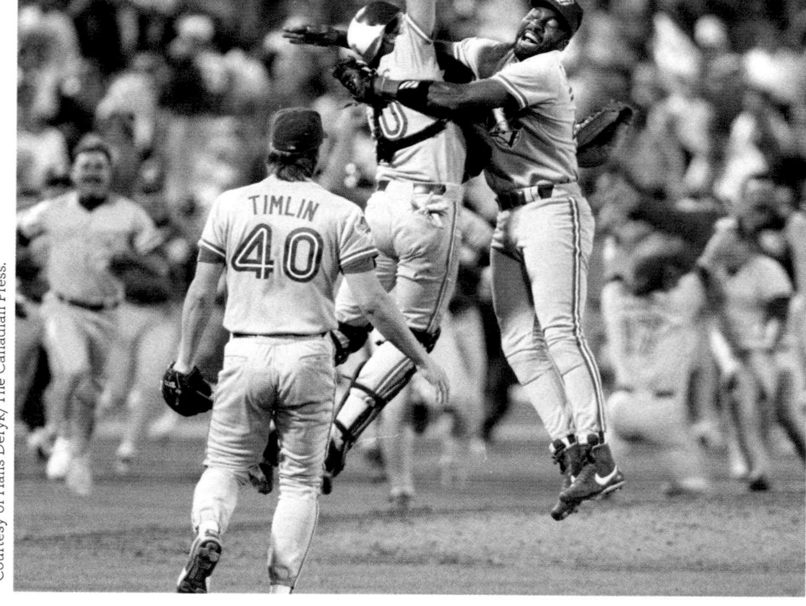

Courtesy of Hans Deryk/The Canadian Press.

Joe Carter and Pat Borders celebrate the Blue Jays' World Series win.

1992. The Toronto Blue Jays are welcomed home by cheering fans after defeating the Atlanta Braves to become the first team from outside the United States to win Major League Baseball's World Series. The following season, the Jays became the first team since the 1977–78 New York Yankees to repeat as champions, defeating the Philadelphia Phillies in six games. Joe Carter hit a three-run home run in the final inning of the sixth game in a dramatic series-winning play.

Also on This Day

1854.
Maj.-Gen. James Thomas Brudenell, the 7th Earl of Cardigan, leads an English cavalry brigade at the Battle of Balaklava in the Crimean War. More than half of his men were killed or wounded in the infamous Charge of the Light Brigade. Canadian Alexander Dunn received the Victoria Cross for bravery that day, the first ever awarded to a Canadian.

Which city can take pride in having had the first Canadian baseball team?
See June 4.

BORN ON THIS DAY

1802 strongman Jos Montferrand

1902 author Leslie McFarlane

1962 director and producer David Furnish

1970 singer-songwriter Ed Robertson

The Boys of Pine Street

Over the course of the First World War, sixty-nine Canadians were awarded the Victoria Cross, a medal reserved for those who demonstrate exceptional bravery. Amazingly, three of the recipients lived on Pine Street in Winnipeg.

During the Battle of Passchendaele, **Lt. Robert Shankland** led his men to a forward position and then made his way alone through the battlefield to deliver crucial information about his company's position to battalion headquarters before returning to his men at the front.

Caught alone in a trench, **Corp. Leo Clarke** was under attack from enemy soldiers. Though wounded by a bayonet strike to the knee, he managed to kill eighteen Germans and take another prisoner. Unfortunately, he was killed by a falling shell in 1916.

Sgt.-Maj. Frederick William Hall was posthumously awarded the medal for giving his life to save that of a fellow soldier during the Second Battle of Ypres in April 1915. He was in the process of lifting up the wounded man when he was struck in the head and killed.

In 1925, Pine Street in Winnipeg was renamed Valour Road in recognition of these three brave young men who served.

Courtesy of the Departmentof National Defence/Library and Archives Canada/PA-002107.

Wounded Canadian soldiers are transported to an aid post during the Battle of Passchendaele.

1917. Over muddy terrain, soldiers of the Canadian Corps begin their attack during the First World War's bloody Passchendaele offensive in Belgium. After weeks of fighting and more than 15,600 casualties, the Canadians finally seized Passchendaele on November 6, 1917. Nine Victoria Crosses were awarded to Canadians after the battle, including one to Lt. Robert Shankland, whose "courage and splendid example inspired all ranks and coupled with his great gallantry and skill undoubtedly saved a very critical situation."

BORN ON THIS DAY

1965 actress Kelly Rowan

1970 actor Trevor White

Photograph: © Michael Reichmann. Courtesy of CBC Still Photo Collection.

Gilles Vigneault, 1967.

1928. Gilles Vigneault, singer-songwriter, poet, and publisher, is born in Natashquan, Québec. Vigneault was instrumental in the revitalization of the *chanson* and the popularization of Québécois culture on the international stage. His rousing song "Mon Pays" (1964) sealed his popularity at home and abroad. The song, which speaks to the experience of living in Québec during the harsh winter, has become a Québécois anthem. A vocal proponent of Québec culture, Vigneault was profoundly affected by the October Crisis of 1970. He became a devoted sovereigntist, and his music took a more political turn. His "*J'ai planté un chêne*" was the theme song of the Parti Québécois during the 1976 provincial election.

Selected Discography of Gilles Vigneault

1962: *Gilles Vigneault*

1965: *À la Comédie-Canadienne*

1966: *Mon pays*

1973: *Pays du fond de moi*

1976: *J'ai planté un chêne*

1978: *Les quatre saisons de Piquot*

1982: *Combien de fois faut-il parler d'amour*

1987: *Les îles*

1992: *Le chant du portageur*

1996: *C'est ainsi que j'arrive à toi*

2003: *Au bout du coeur*

2014: *Vivre debout*

BORN ON THIS DAY

1915
movie producer Harry Saltzman

1946
director and producer Ivan Reitman

William Hutt Selected Filmography

1957: *Oedipus Rex* (feature film)
1960: *Macbeth* (TV movie)
1960: *There Was a Crooked Man* (feature film)
1962: *Cyrano De Bergerac* (TV movie)
1968: *The Fixer* (feature film)
1974: *The National Dream: Building the Impossible Railway* (TV miniseries)
1979: *The Shape of Things to Come* (feature film)
1982: *The Elephant Man* (TV movie)
1983: *The Wars* (feature film)
1984: *Covergirl* (feature film)
1998: *Emily of New Moon* (TV series)
2003: *The Statement* (feature film)
2006: *Slings and Arrows* (TV series)
2008: *The Trojan Horse* (TV miniseries)

In what year did the Stratford Festival open its first season? See July 13.

Photograph: David Hou. Courtesy of the Stratford Festival Archives.

***The Tempest*, starring William Hutt as Prospero, 2005.**

2005. Actor William Hutt gives his last Stratford Festival performance, as Prospero in Shakespeare's *The Tempest*. Hutt had joined the Stratford Festival in 1953, its inaugural year, and had a long relationship with the company, even serving as festival director. He played nearly every great Shakespearean role, touring with the festival around the world and appearing in several films and TV series. Hutt passed away in 2007 but is still remembered as one of Canada's foremost classical actors.

BORN ON THIS DAY

1599
founder of the Ursuline Order in New France Marie de l'Incarnation

1953
businessman Pierre Boivin

1963
actress Lauren Holly

29 OCTOBER

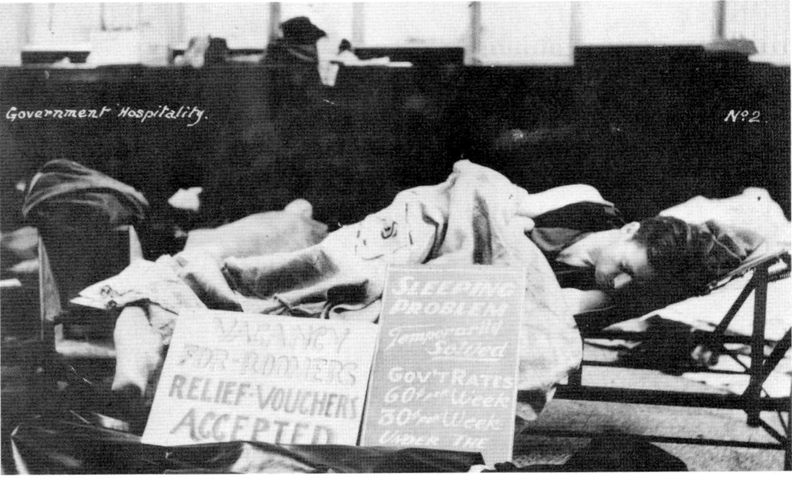

During the Stock Market Crash.

1929. New York's stock market crash, commonly called Black Tuesday, ushers in the Great Depression, a social and economic disaster that left millions of Canadians unemployed, hungry, and often homeless. The Depression had a severe effect on Canada during what became known as the Dirty Thirties, when widespread job losses triggered the birth of social welfare and a variety of populist political movements. With aid funds in short supply, local governments refused to assist single homeless men, and so the federal government instead established unemployment relief camps.

Did You Know?

Most historians and economists cite the stock market crash as a leading cause of the Great Depression.

From the stock market's peak in 1929 to mid-1930, the fifty most active Canadian stocks fell on average to less than half their market value. Shareholders in the Canadian Pacific Railway lost more than $60 million.

Depression economics led to the political downfall of Prime Minister R.B. Bennett, who was elected in 1930. With unemployment rates still high, the Conservatives were defeated in 1935.

Joblessness remained high until the Second World War, when massive state expenditures finally reduced unemployment.

BORN ON THIS DAY

opera singer Jon Vickers
1926

1953
Hockey Hall of Famer Denis Potvin

figure skater Jessica Dubé
1987

OCTOBER  30

Also on This Day

1995. Québec holds its second sovereignty referendum. The No side won with a 50.58 percent majority, with 93.5 percent of eligible voters casting a ballot. Following the vote, there was considerable controversy relating to the large number of "spoiled" ballots, the enumeration of eligible voters, and other issues. Premier Jacques Parizeau resigned from office and Lucien Bouchard assumed the leadership of the Parti Québécois. Even before becoming premier, Bouchard announced his intention to conduct another referendum on separation in 1997.

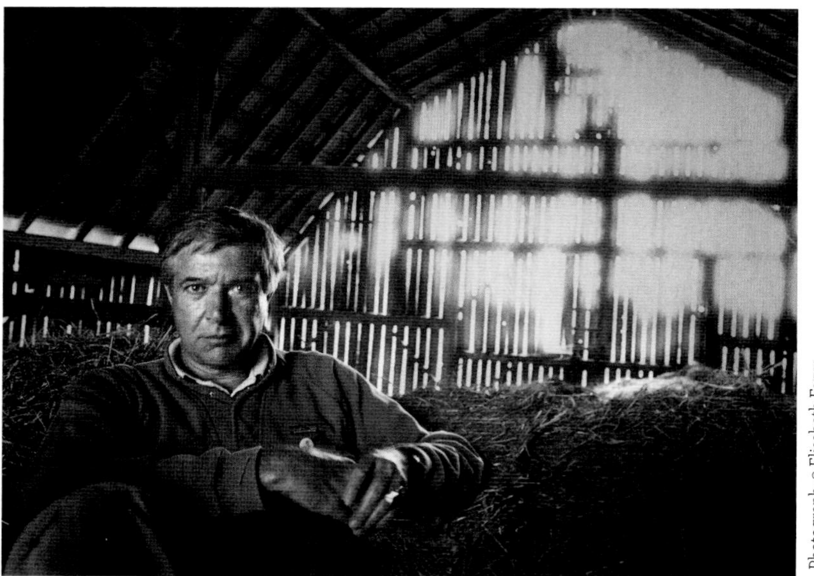

Timothy Findley, undated.

1930. Author and actor Timothy Findley is born in Toronto. A charter member of the Stratford Festival, he later won acclaim for his novels, which included the Governor General's Award–winning *The Wars*, as well as *Not Wanted on the Voyage* and *The Piano Man's Daughter*. Findley's first two novels, *The Last of the Crazy People* and *The Butterfly Plague*, were originally published in Britain and the United States, after being rejected by Canadian publishers. Mental illness, gender, and sexuality are recurring themes in his works. The influence of Jungian psychology can be most clearly seen in *Pilgrim*, Findley's second-to-last novel, in which Carl Jung is featured as a character.

BORN ON THIS DAY

1891 golfer Ada Mackenzie

1962 dancer Rex Harrington

31 OCTOBER

Courtesy of Library and Archives Canada/1933-145.

A portrait of Marguerite Bourgeoys, 1653.

1982. Marguerite Bourgeoys, founder of the *Congrégation de Notre-Dame de Montréal,* is canonized, making her the first Canadian woman to be declared a saint. In 1640, Bourgeoys had joined a non-cloistered congregation of teachers attached to a convent in Troyes, France. She sailed for Canada in 1653, and in 1658 opened a girls' school in a Montréal stable. She spent her last two years in meditation and prayer, and was already revered as a saint by the colonists when she died in 1700. The Notre-Dame-de-Bon-Secours Chapel, which she rallied the colonists to build, was rebuilt in 1771, but the ruins of the original chapel remain.

Also on This Day

1950.
Actor John Candy is born in Toronto. Candy was a regular on *SCTV*, creating and playing such characters as Johnny LaRue and Yosh Schmenge. He also starred in a number of major films, including *Spaceballs*, *Uncle Buck*, and *Planes, Trains and Automobiles*. He died of a heart attack in 1994, when he was just forty-three years old.

BORN ON THIS DAY

hockey and lacrosse player Édouard "Newsy" Lalonde

1887

1912

explorer and archaeologist Graham Rowley

actor Justin Chatwin

1982

NOVEMBER

SNOWSHOES

Snowshoes work by distributing the wearer's weight over a greater area. Larger snowshoes can support a heavier person and allow for walking over softer snow. Smaller shoes are better for breaking a trail.

Aboriginal peoples developed a wide range of snowshoes. One of the largest is the Cree hunting snowshoe, which is more than six feet long.

Snowshoes were adopted by the French and then the British. They were used in the Seven Years' War, which featured two different conflicts, in 1787 and 1788, called the Battle on Snowshoes.

The snowshoe hare is found across Canada and the northern United States. It's named for its large, fur-covered hind feet, which allow it to travel easily over snow.

The classic snowshoe is made from an ash frame filled with a webbing of caribou hide. It has a long tail, which helps keep it from turning from side to side. It resembles a wooden tennis racket and in French is even called a *raquette de neige*, or "snow racket."

In recent years, recreational snowshoes have seen a surge in popularity. Modern versions are smaller and lighter than the traditional snowshoe, and can be used for hiking or running over packed snow.

1 NOVEMBER

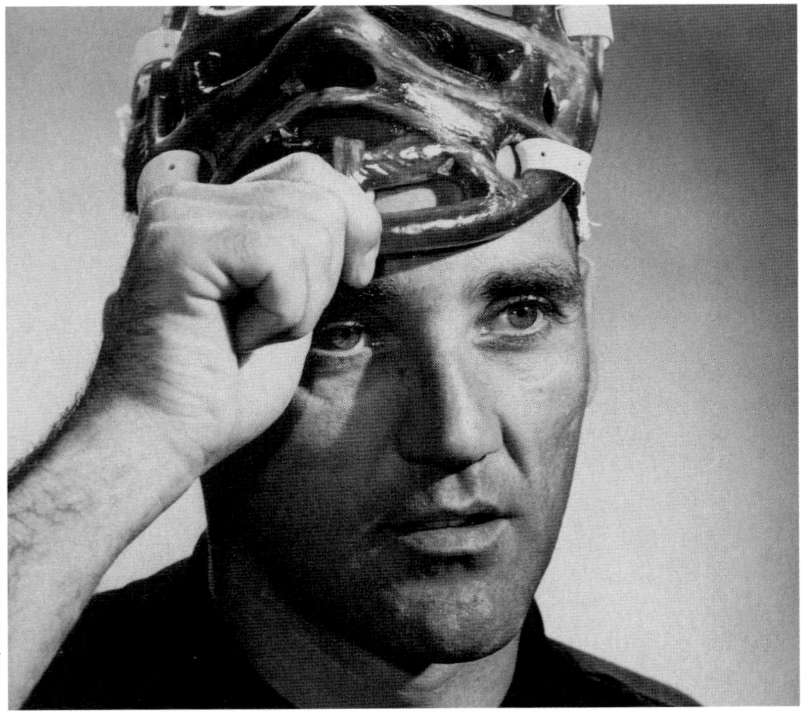

Library and Archives Canada/PA-195211.

Jacques Plante, 1960.

1959. After a backhand shot by New York Ranger Andy Bathgate cuts his face, Montreal Canadiens goaltender Jacques Plante gets stitched up in the dressing room of Madison Square Garden. When he returned to the ice, Plante was wearing a mask. The Canadiens went on to win the game 3–1, and Plante became the first goalie to wear a protective mask regularly. He played goal with superb technical ability and with drama and flair, and he was famous for roving beyond his net. In seventeen NHL seasons, Plante played 837 regular-season and 112 playoff games, and he racked up 82 regular-season and 14 playoff shutouts.

Also on This Day

1847.
Opera singer Emma Albani is born in Chambly, Lower Canada (now Québec). The first Canadian opera singer to attain international fame, Albani toured several continents and attracted such celebrated admirers as composer Charles Gounod and Queen Victoria.

BORN ON THIS DAY

artist Paul-Émile Borduas
1905

1942
politician Ralph Klein

musician and record producer David Foster
1949

NOVEMBER 2

Popular Music Acts from Winnipeg

Randy Bachman
Bachman–Turner Overdrive
Del Barber
Bif Naked (grew up in Winnipeg)
Oscar Brand
Lenny Breau (grew up in Winnipeg)
The Consumer Goods
Crash Test Dummies
Burton Cummings
Joey Gregorash
Harlequin
Terry Jacks
Chantal Kreviazuk
McMaster and James
Holly McNarland
Novillero
Fred Penner
The Perpetrators
Propagandhi
John K. Samson
Remy Shand
The Wailin' Jennys
The Watchmen
The Weakerthans
Neil Young (grew up in Winnipeg)

Courtesy of CBC Still Photo Collection.

The Guess Who performs on a 1968 CBC *Show of the Week* special, hosted by Juliette.

1987. Members of the Winnipeg rock band The Guess Who are inducted into the Canadian Music Hall of Fame. When the band recorded a cover of the British hit "Shakin' All Over" in 1965, producer George Struth released it to radio stations under the name Guess Who?, hoping that radio DJs would play a song by a mysterious British band. The name stuck, and the band—with the pairing of singer-guitarist Randy Bachman and singer-keyboardist Burton Cummings—became one of the most famous Canadian acts. The Guess Who released a series of hit singles in the 1960s and 1970s, including "These Eyes," "No Sugar Tonight," "Laughing," and "American Woman," which was the first song by a Canadian band to hit number one on the Billboard Hot 100 chart. They were Canada's first rock superstars.

BORN ON THIS DAY

1917 — actress Ann Rutherford

1960 — pairs skater Paul Martini

3 NOVEMBER

Library and Archives Canada/Albertype Company/PA-032282.

The Bank of Montreal, in the city for which it is named, ca. 1900.

1817. The Bank of Montreal, the first permanent bank in British North America, opens its doors. It became a source of commercial loans and credit for the growing Canadian economy, and provided backing for many of the key projects spurring national development, including the first canals, the telegraph machine, the Canadian Pacific Railway, major hydroelectric ventures, and early energy and mining enterprises. The Bank of Montreal was the banker for the Canadian government from 1863 until the founding of the Bank of Canada in 1935. It was also the first Canadian bank to establish representation outside the country, with correspondent agencies opening in London and New York in 1818.

Also on This Day

1930.
The Detroit–Windsor tunnel opens to traffic. The 1.6-kilometre tunnel between the Canadian and US border cities—the first underground vehicular tunnel to a foreign country in the world—took twenty-six months to build. The first passenger car it carried was a 1929 Studebaker.

BORN ON THIS DAY

polar explorer, ethnologist, and writer Vilhjalmur Stefansson

1879

1925

author Monica Hughes

Also on This Day

1882.
Hockey Hall of Famer Frank McGee, one of the original nine inductees, is born in Ottawa. Blind in one eye, he was known as One-Eyed McGee and was a legendary player, once scoring fourteen goals in a single Stanley Cup game. His team captured the cup in 1903 and defended it against all challengers until 1906. During the First World War, McGee enlisted in the Canadian Army and died in action in France in 1916.

Who was Canada's first Liberal prime minister? See January 22.

Ryan Remiorz/The Canadian Press.

Prime Minister Jean Chrétien and his wife, Aline, after his election win.

1993. Jean Chrétien is sworn in as Canada's twentieth prime minister. Although the Liberal Party won a strong parliamentary majority that year, two other parties also enjoyed notable victories. Ironically, the secessionist Bloc Québécois, under the leadership of Lucien Bouchard, became Her Majesty's Loyal Opposition. As well, the election saw the rise of the western-based Reform Party under Preston Manning (and the arrival of a young MP named Stephen Harper, who was elected to Parliament for the first time). During his political career, Chrétien helped negotiate the patriation of the Canadian constitution and the Charter of Rights and Freedoms. As prime minister, he led the federal government to its first budget surplus in nearly thirty years; however, his administration also presided over a costly sponsorship program in Québec that sparked one of the worst political scandals of modern times.

BORN ON THIS DAY

child actor and singer Bobby Breen

1927

1930

actress Kate Reid

5 NOVEMBER

© Bev Davies/Library and Archives Canada/e010993751-v8.

Bryan Adams at the CFOX radio station in Vancouver.

1984. Singer-songwriter Bryan Adams releases his internationally successful fourth album, *Reckless*, on his twenty-fifth birthday. With six hit singles, including "Summer of '69," "Run to You," and "It's Only Love" (recorded with Tina Turner), the album went on to sell millions of copies worldwide. Adams's popularity had soared dramatically with the release of earlier singles, such as "Cuts Like a Knife" and "Straight from the Heart." His blue-collar image—including his iconic T-shirt and jeans—mirrored the hard-working values of his music, producing a straightforward style of rock and roll.

Also on This Day

1995.
Prime Minister Jean Chrétien and his wife escape injury when a knife-wielding intruder breaks into their residence at 24 Sussex Drive in Ottawa. Quick-thinking Aline Chrétien shut and locked the bedroom door until security arrived, while the prime minister brandished a stone Inuit carving. Chrétien later said that he initially discounted his wife's claim that she'd heard a noise, telling her, "You're dreaming."

BORN ON THIS DAY

political economist Harold Innis 1894

1931 philosopher Charles Taylor

trap shooter Susan Nattrass 1950

David Suzuki and Internment

Five-year-old David Suzuki and his family were among twenty-two thousand Japanese Canadians forcibly moved from their homes by the government after the bombing of Pearl Harbor in 1942. Many were shipped to internment camps in British Columbia's interior. Properties and businesses were sold without consent, and the damaging economic effects continued to be felt by many families long after the war ended in 1945. Suzuki's family relocated to Ontario after the war—moving east was the only option aside from deportation to Japan. In 1988, the Canadian government formally apologized to those interned and offered compensation, an acknowledgment that these acts were driven more by racism than any real threat.

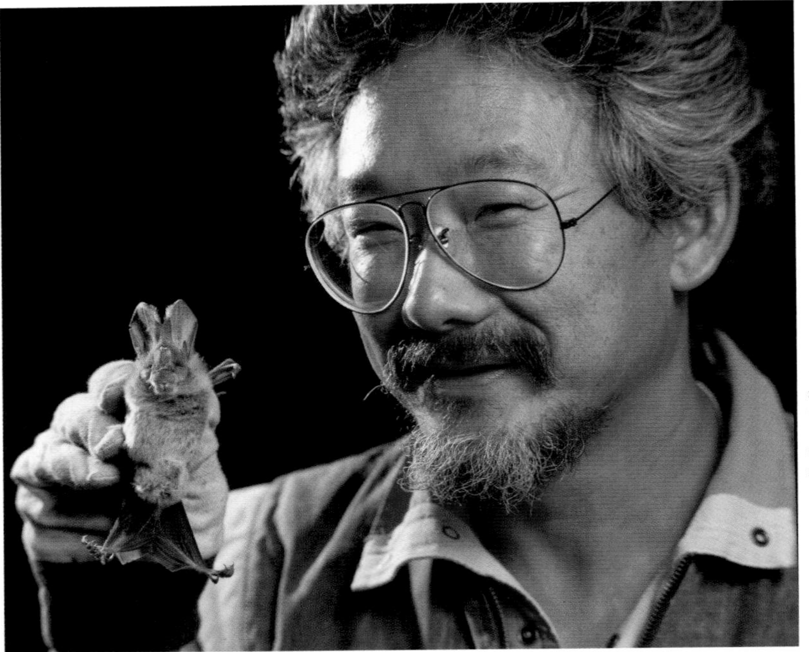

David Suzuki during a *Nature of Things* episode on bats, 1989.

1960. The *Nature of Things* premieres on CBC-TV. It would go on to become the network's longest-running documentary television series. The show was unique in its early days for its focus on the environment. Famed geneticist, environmentalist, and broadcaster David Suzuki took over as host in 1979, and continued to feature scientific discussions on topics such as nuclear power, AIDS, and climate change.

BORN ON THIS DAY

basketball inventor James Naismith

1861

1955

skier Ken Read

7 NOVEMBER

Library and Archives Canada/Alexander Ross/C-003693.

Donald A. Smith driving the last spike to complete the Canadian Pacific Railway.

1885. The symbolic last spike of the Canadian Pacific Railway (CPR) is driven home at Craigellachie, British Columbia, at the western entrance to Eagle Pass. The cash-starved CPR could not afford a fancy party, so this modest ceremony was all that marked the completion of the transcontinental railway. The honour of driving in the last spike was assigned to Donald Smith, the eldest of the four directors of the CPR present. His first blow bent the spike so badly that it had to be replaced. He posed again with hammer uplifted. The camera clicked and clicked again as the blow landed. The driving of the last spike was the great symbolic act of Canada's first century, completing the Confederation promise to link the country from sea to sea.

Also on This Day

1873.
Alexander Mackenzie begins serving as Canada's first Liberal prime minister. Under his government, the Supreme Court of Canada was established and the secret ballot introduced.

BORN ON THIS DAY

1834 folklorist Ernest Gagnon

1860 artist Paul Peel

1936 politician and social worker Audrey McLaughlin

1943 singer-songwriter, guitarist, and painter Joni Mitchell

NOVEMBER 8

Segregation in Canada

Racial segregation permeated many facets of Canadian life well into the mid-twentieth century. Schools were a prime example—the last segregated school did not close until 1983. Like Viola Desmond, many Black Canadians challenged such inequality. Hugh Burnett was a founding member of the National Unity Association (NUA), an organization that advocated racial equality and social justice. Segregation was common in Burnett's home town of Dresden, Ontario, where unequal hiring practices left Black citizens in low-paying jobs, while restaurants and recreational facilities refused them service. The NUA and other activist groups pressured the Ontario government for legal change, leading to the adoption of the province's Fair Employment Practices Act (1951) and Fair Accommodation Practices Act (1954). Full-scale social change was slow to come, but the actions of Hugh Burnett, Viola Desmond, and others like them brought necessary attention to the cause.

Christian Laforce/Halifax Chronicle-Herald/The Canadian Press.

Nova Scotia lieutenant-governor Mayann Francis with a portrait of civil rights leader Viola Desmond at Government House in Halifax, 2010.

1946. Businesswoman Viola Desmond makes a stand against racial segregation in Nova Scotia. Desmond was travelling to a business meeting when her car broke down. While it was being serviced in New Glasgow, she decided to see a film at the local theatre. But when the Roseland Theatre box office would not sell Desmond a ticket for a seat on the main floor, which was reserved for whites only, she decided to sit there anyway. She was confronted by the manager, who called police. Desmond was dragged out of the theatre—injuring her hip and knee in the process—taken to jail, and fined twenty-six dollars. Thanks in part to Desmond's act, which took place almost a decade before Rosa Parks refused to give up her seat to a white person on an Alabama bus, segregation was legally ended in Nova Scotia in 1954. On April 15, 2010, Desmond was posthumously pardoned by Nova Scotia lieutenant-governor Mayann Francis at a ceremony in Halifax.

BORN ON THIS DAY

1881
artist Clarence Gagnon

1932
architect and educator Jack Diamond

1945
Royal Canadian Air Farce member Luba Goy

9 NOVEMBER

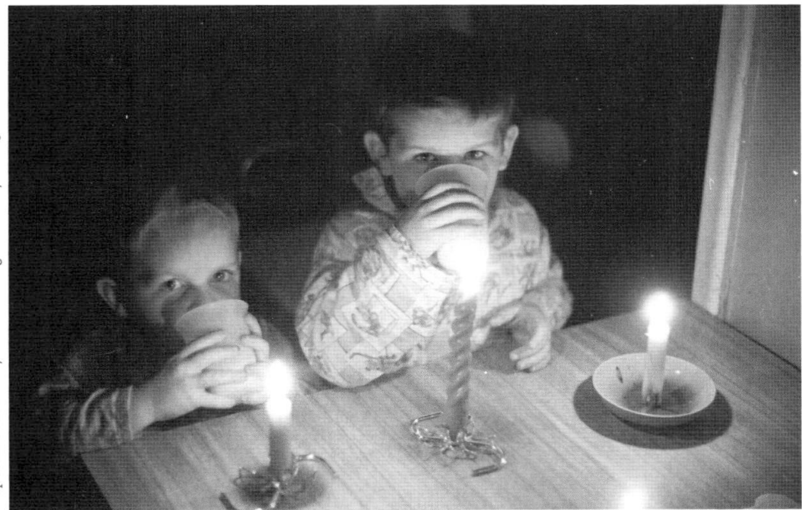

Don Grant./© York University Libraries/Clara Thomas Archives & Special Collections/Toronto Telegram fonds/ASC19000.

Eating dinner by candlelight during the blackout.

1965. The failure of a relay device at a Niagara generating station triggers a massive power failure affecting Ontario, Québec, New York, New Jersey, and much of New England. The Great Northeastern Blackout, which caused traffic chaos, affected about thirty million people and lasted twelve hours. It was the largest power outage in history until the Great Blackout of 2003, which affected more than fifty million people in eastern North America for several days.

Blackouts in Canada

September 20, 1977: 85 percent of the population of Québec affected
March 13, 1989: Six million people left in the dark after a geomagnetic storm causes a power failure
January 4–10, 1998: The Great Ice Storm cuts power to more than four million people in eastern Canada and parts of the United States
August 14, 2003: The Great Blackout affects more than fifty million people in Ontario and the northeastern United States

BORN ON THIS DAY

fur trader and explorer Louis-Joseph Gaultier de La Vérendrye
1717

1869
actress and writer Marie Dressler

politician Clyde Wells
1937

Also on This Day

1975.
The SS *Edmund Fitzgerald* sinks in Lake Superior with her crew of twenty-nine. The ship was used to carry taconite from Minnesota to steel mills located on the Great Lakes. The ship's final voyage began on November 9 from Wisconsin, bound for a steel mill near Detroit, Michigan. As it sailed, the weather continued to worsen and hammered the ship until it was lost near Whitefish Point. There are many theories regarding the cause of the catastrophe, but the 1977 US Coast Guard report cites faulty hatch covers and damage from the impact of heavy seas, among other factors. The bell of the ship was recovered in 1995 and remains on display in the Great Lakes Shipwreck Museum at Whitefish Point.

Gordon Lightfoot, 1966.

1986. Singer-songwriter Gordon Lightfoot is inducted into the Canadian Music Hall of Fame. Born and raised in Orillia, Ontario, where he competed in music festivals as a boy, Lightfoot was drawn into the urban folk music movement by Bob Dylan and others in the 1960s. In that period, some of his songs, including "For Lovin' Me" and "Early Morning Rain," were hits for major acts like Peter, Paul and Mary, gaining Lightfoot a reputation as a songwriter. In the 1970s, he became Canada's most popular male vocalist with his lyrical portraits of everything from relationships to the Canadian landscape to historical events. Among his best known hits are "If You Could Read My Mind," "The Wreck of the *Edmund Fitzgerald*," "Sundown," and "Canadian Railroad Trilogy," the last of which was commissioned by the CBC for Canada's centennial celebrations.

BORN ON THIS DAY

1845 prime minister, judge, and lawyer John Sparrow David Thompson

1921 writer, editor, and activist Doris Anderson

1922 author Constance Beresford-Howe

1954 chess grandmaster Kevin Spraggett

11 NOVEMBER

City of Toronto Archives/Fonds 1244, Item 891D.

Armistice Day at Bay and King Streets in Toronto.

1918. The Armistice ending hostilities in the First World War comes into effect at the eleventh hour of the eleventh day of the eleventh month. More than 600,000 Canadians served in the armed forces between 1914 and 1918, including some 425,000 who went overseas; of those, 60,661 were killed. On November 6, 1919, King George V sent out an appeal to the Empire, urging that the year-old Armistice be marked by the suspension of all activities and the observance of two minutes of silence at precisely 11:00 a.m. on November 11. In May 1921, an Act of Parliament declared that an annual Armistice Day would be held on the Monday of the week in which November 11 fell. However, the roving date was sometimes conflated with Thanksgiving Day, which confused the public and angered veterans. On March 18, 1931, a motion was introduced in the House of Commons to have Armistice Day observed on November 11 and "no other date."

BORN ON THIS DAY

political cartoonist Terry Mosher (Aislin)

1942

1972

actor Adam Beach

Also on This Day

1937.
Statesman and humanitarian Stephen Lewis is born in Ottawa. Lewis was Canada's ambassador to the United Nations, the Special Envoy for HIV/AIDS in Africa, and the deputy executive director of UNICEF. He also established the Stephen Lewis Foundation, which works with organizations that provide care and support to people affected by HIV and AIDS in African countries.

NOVEMBER 12

Also on This Day

1931.
Maple Leaf Gardens, one of the "cathedrals" of ice hockey, officially opens in Toronto. Though the Leafs lost their first game in the arena, they won eleven Stanley Cups during their sixty-eight years playing there. The Gardens also hosted election rallies and concerts by such notables as Elvis Presley and the Beatles. In 1999 the Maple Leafs moved to the Air Canada Centre, and in 2011 much of Maple Leaf Gardens was converted to a massive Loblaws grocery store—complete with large specialty sections dedicated to cheese, tea, and more. In homage to the historic arena, the new store includes some familiar sights: the blue stadium seats were refashioned into the shape of a maple leaf at the store's entrance, a red circle indicates the former location of centre ice, and an original mural was restored and reinstalled by the checkout area.

Neil Young performing at Farm Aid in Kansas City, 2011.

1945. Singer-songwriter Neil Young is born in Toronto. His career in the music business began in the 1960s with rock groups like the Squires and Buffalo Springfield. Young is perhaps best known for his enduring, influential, and often political solo work, including the songs "Southern Man," "Heart of Gold," "Rockin' in the Free World," and "Helpless." He was inducted into the Canadian Music Hall of Fame in 1982. His work has inspired several tribute albums, including in the country and alternative rock genres—a testament to the esteem in which he is held by younger generations of musicians.

BORN ON THIS DAY

artist Agnes Nanogak
1925

1980
actor Ryan Gosling

13 NOVEMBER

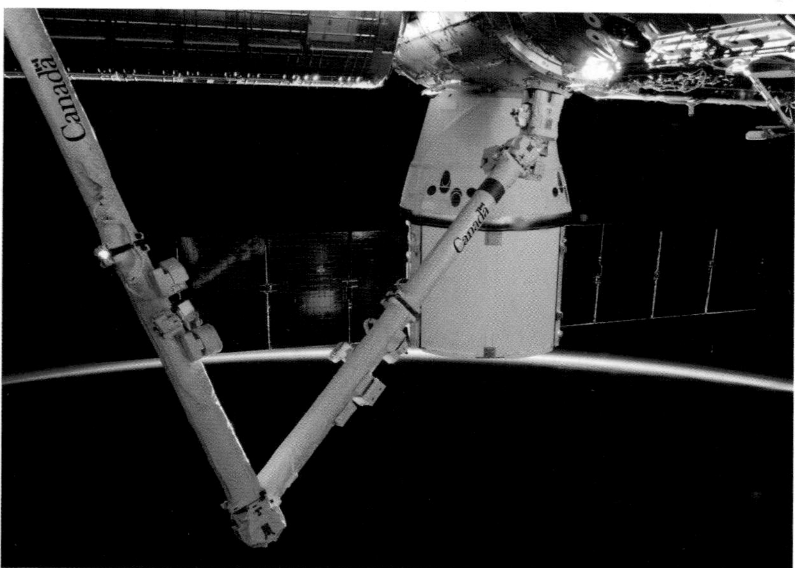

© NASA.

The Canadarm during a shuttle mission.

1981. The Canadian-made Shuttle Remote Manipulator System, more commonly known as the Canadarm, is deployed in space for the first time aboard the space shuttle Columbia. Over the years, it was used like a human arm for deploying, capturing, and repairing satellites; positioning astronauts; and moving equipment and supplies. Canadarm retired in July 2011 (following the final mission of the space shuttle), but its legacy lives on: it cemented Canada's reputation as a leader in technological innovation and inspired a series of Canadian robotics used on the International Space Station, including Canadarm2.

Also on This Day

1903.
Historical novelist Thomas Raddall is born in Hythe, England. He was brought up in Nova Scotia (where a provincial park has been named in his memory), the province he wrote about in works of both fiction and nonfiction. Among his best-known books are *The Governor's Lady* and *The Nymph and the Lamp*, which is about his own experiences as a radio operator on Sable Island after the First World War.

BORN ON THIS DAY

actress Madeleine Sherwood 1922

1932 fashion designer Marilyn Brooks

speed skater François-Louis Tremblay 1980

NOVEMBER 14

Also on This Day

2011. A new Canadian $100 bill begins to circulate, the first in a series of banknotes printed on a polymer material. The new bills, which are stronger and smoother than the old ones, last longer and are designed to be resistant to counterfeiting.

An RCMP officer examines fingerprints inside the identification branch, undated.

1863. Policeman Edward Foster, who would pioneer fingerprinting technology in Canada, is born near Stittsville, Ontario. Foster joined the Dominion Police as a constable in 1890. While at the St. Louis World's Fair in 1904, he was introduced to the controversial science of fingerprint identification. On returning to Canada, Foster advocated the advantages of fingerprinting over the Bertillon system (which used body measurements, such as height and foot size, to identify criminals), and pressed for a central repository of fingerprints. His perseverance resulted in the opening of a national fingerprint bureau in Ottawa in 1911. Foster continued to head the bureau until his retirement in 1932.

BORN ON THIS DAY

1962 — actor and comedian Harland Williams

1964 — rower Silken Laumann

15 NOVEMBER

Library and Archives Canada/The Ottawa Journal/e002505451.

Mackenzie King giving a speech in Ottawa.

1948. William Lyon Mackenzie King, Canada's longest-serving prime minister, resigns. He was succeeded by Louis St. Laurent the same day. As leader of the Liberal Party from 1919 to 1948, and prime minister for almost twenty-two of those years, King was the dominant political figure in an era of major change. He steered Canada through industrialization, much of the Great Depression, and all of the Second World War. By the time he left office, Canada had achieved greater independence from Britain and a stronger international voice, and had overhauled the political landscape in response to industrial development, economic distress, and changing social realities.

Also on This Day

1840.
Author May Agnes Fleming is born in Saint John, New Brunswick. She combined elements of romance and gothic mystery in her novels, and was highly popular in both North America and Britain. With earnings of more than $10,000 annually in the 1870s, she was Canada's first successful professional novelist.

Which prime minister extended the vote to First Nations?
See December 14.

BORN ON THIS DAY

1746 — merchant, poet, playwright, and composer Joseph Quesnel

1936 — TV writer, director, and producer Perry Rosemond

1969 — tennis player Helen Kelesi

NOVEMBER  16

In His Own Words: Louis Riel

"What I have done, and risked, and to which I have exposed myself, rested certainly on the conviction ... [I] was called upon to do something for my country ... I know that through the grace of God I am the founder of Manitoba. I know that though I have no open road for my influence, I have big influence, concentrated as a big amount of vapour in an engine. I believe by what I suffered for fifteen years, by what I have done for Manitoba and the people of the North-West, that my words are worth something."

Where did the North-West Rebellion, led by Louis Riel and Gabriel Dumont, take place?
See May 9.

O.B. Buell/Library and Archives Canada/1966-094, C-001879.

Louis Riel addresses the jury during his trial for treason, 1885.

1885. Louis Riel is hanged for treason in Regina. He had been convicted for his part in the North-West Rebellion after a twelve-day trial in late July. John A. Macdonald's refusal to grant leniency made Riel a symbol of English Canada's oppression of French-speaking people. Since then, Riel's legacy as a leader of the Métis people and founder of Manitoba has made him a central—and at times controversial—figure in Canadian history. (The question of whether Riel had broken either British or Canadian law for his part in the rebellion was never determined in court.) While he was long dismissed as a mad rebel, Riel's legacy has been reconsidered since the 1960s, notably in light of his work negotiating the entry of Manitoba (previously part of Rupert's Land) into the federal union. In 1992, his "unique and historic role" in the creation of Manitoba and the development of Canada was recognized by Parliament and the Legislative Assembly of Manitoba—more than one hundred years after he was hanged for treason.

BORN ON THIS DAY

1836
industrialist
Robert McLaughlin

1839
poet and playwright
Louis-Honoré Fréchette

1942
figure skater
Maria Jelinek

© Hibernia.

The Hibernia platform drills for oil on the Grand Banks, south of St. John's, Newfoundland.

1997. The Hibernia oil field begins producing oil. The oil field was discovered in 1979, in the Jeanne d'Arc Basin off the southeast coast of Newfoundland. On May 19, 1982, the governor-in-council asked the Supreme Court of Canada whether the right to exploit the natural resources of the seabed and subsoil of the continental shelf in the area belonged to the federal or provincial government. Two years later, the court found that those rights were an "extraterritorial manifestation of external sovereignty," and therefore held by the federal government. Following years of development, the $5.8-billion oil platform was positioned on the ocean floor 315 kilometres off Newfoundland. Today the platform, which is taller than the Calgary Tower and half the height of the Empire State Building, is home to approximately 185 people.

Timeline: Offshore Oil Production in Newfoundland and Labrador

1966: The Grand Banks are drilled for the first time.
1976: The first attempt at producing oil at the Come By Chance refinery fails.
1985: The Newfoundland and federal governments sign the Atlantic Accord, giving Ottawa and St. John's joint say over offshore oil and gas reserves and allowing the province to tax the resources as if they were on land.
1997: The Hibernia project results in the province's first offshore oil production.

BORN ON THIS DAY

1861 poet Archibald Lampman

1938 singer-songwriter Gordon Lightfoot

1944 *Saturday Night Live* producer Lorne Michaels

1946 figure skater Petra Burka

1951 actor Brent Carver

1978 actress Rachel McAdams

NOVEMBER  

18

Margaret Atwood's Novels

1969: *The Edible Woman*
1972: *Surfacing*
1976: *Lady Oracle*
1979: *Life Before Man*
1981: *Bodily Harm*
1985: *The Handmaid's Tale*
1988: *Cat's Eye*
1993: *The Robber Bride*
1996: *Alias Grace*
2000: *The Blind Assassin*
2003: *Oryx and Crake*
2005: *The Penelopiad*
2009: *The Year of the Flood*
2013: *MaddAddam*
2015: *The Heart Goes Last*

Bryan Adams/Library and Archives Canada/R11443-60.

Margaret Atwood, 1999.

1939. Poet and novelist Margaret Atwood is born in Ottawa, Ontario. Atwood is known for her craftsmanship and skilful use of language. In her fiction, she has explored the issues of her time, including women's independence, capturing them in the satirical, self-reflexive mode of the contemporary novel. To date, she has written a staggering fourteen novels, eight story collections, seventeen books of poetry, and ten volumes of non-fiction that have collectively garnered two Governor General's Awards, a Giller Prize, a Man Booker Prize, and numerous other accolades. Celebrated for works like *Alias Grace, The Handmaid's Tale,* and *Cat's Eye*, Margaret Atwood is among the most prolific and distinguished writers in Canadian history.

BORN ON THIS DAY

1926
singer Dorothy Collins

1927
newscaster Knowlton Nash

1941
businessman Peter Pocklington

19 NOVEMBER

René Lévesque on stage at the Paul Sauvé Arena, 1973.

1967. René Lévesque forms the Mouvement Souveraineté-Association (MSA) to promote sovereignty in Québec. The following year, he published the organization's manifesto, *An Option for Québec*, which used the term "sovereignty-association" instead of "independence" and promoted the idea of a partnership that would evolve from an agreement under international law and be limited to the economic domain. The MSA was a forerunner to the Parti Québécois, which was formed in 1968 and took up the idea of sovereignty-association, holding a referendum on the subject in 1980.

In what year did the Bloc Québécois first unveil its separatist program in Montréal? See July 25.

Also on This Day

1804.
Canada's first English-language theatre is opened in Montréal, by a Scottish actor named James Ormsby. The plays performed on opening night were *The Busybody*, a comedy by Susanna Centlivre, and *Sultan*, a farce by Isaac Bickerstaffe.

BORN ON THIS DAY

1919 actor Alan Young

1960 guitarist and composer Don Ross

1975 vocalist Matt Dusk

Library and Archives Canada/C-001982.

The birthplace of Wilfrid Laurier.

Also on This Day

1942.
The Alaska Highway, which winds across more than two thousand kilometres of mountain ranges and forest wilderness from Dawson Creek, British Columbia, to Fairbanks, Alaska, opens to military traffic. Five years later, it opened to unrestricted travel.

1841. Sir Wilfrid Laurier is born in Saint-Lin, Canada East (now Québec). In 1896, Laurier became the first French Canadian elected prime minister, a role in which he served until 1911. As leader of the Liberal Party, Laurier was a fervent promoter of national unity during a time of radical change. He also promoted the development and expansion of the country, encouraging immigration to western Canada, supporting the construction of a second transcontinental railway, and overseeing the addition of two provinces, Alberta and Saskatchewan.

BORN ON THIS DAY

insulin co-discoverer James Bertram "Bert" Collip
1892

1906
legal authority J.J. Robinette

21 NOVEMBER

Department of National Defence/Library and Archives Canada/PA-006069.

King George V at the Maple Leaf Club in London, 1919.

1921. The heraldic arms of Canada—which include maple leaves, fleurs-de-lis, a crown, and the words *Desiderantes meliorem patriam* (They desire a better country)—are proclaimed by King George V. At Confederation, in 1867, no arms had been assigned to the new Dominion of Canada. In 1868, the four original provinces—Nova Scotia, New Brunswick, Québec, and Ontario—received arms by a royal warrant that also provided for the Great Seal of Canada. On the Great Seal, the arms of each province appeared separately, two on each side of the figure of Queen Victoria. As additional provinces entered Confederation, armorial bearings were added to the federal shield, creating an unsatisfactory aggregation. A committee was appointed in 1919 and asked to come up with a less crowded design; within a year, this committee had decided on the basic elements of the new coat of arms.

Decoding the Coat of Arms

The design of Canada's coat of arms is traditional, with the shield displaying the arms of England, Scotland, Ireland, and France to symbolize the nation's founders. Underneath the four quarters, on a white field, is a sprig of three maple leaves, representing the new nation of many peoples. Originally green, in 1957 the leaves officially became red, a common autumnal colour, and thus in accord with Canada's national colours, red and white. The motto *A Mari usque ad Mare* (From sea to sea) is from the Bible's Psalm 72:8: "He shall have dominion also from sea to sea, and from the river unto the ends of the earth."

What is the number one ranked Canadian emblem?
See March 24.

BORN ON THIS DAY

1787 merchant, shipowner, and entrepreneur Samuel Cunard

1907 author Christie Harris

1929 broadcaster, author, academic, and senator Laurier LaPierre

1985 singer-songwriter Carly Rae Jepsen

NOVEMBER 22

David Cronenberg Select Filmography

1975: *Shivers*
1977: *Rabid*
1979: *The Brood*
1981: *Scanners*
1983: *Videodrome*
1983: *The Dead Zone*
1986: *The Fly*
1988: *Dead Ringers*
1991: *Naked Lunch*
1996: *Crash*
1999: *eXistenZ*
2005: *A History of Violence*
2007: *Eastern Promises*
2011: *A Dangerous Method*
2014: *Maps to the Stars*

David Cronenberg at the TIFF Bell Lightbox in Toronto.

1992. The film *Naked Lunch*, directed by filmmaker and screenwriter David Cronenberg, dominates the Genie Awards, winning a total of eight, including best picture and best director. The sci-fi thriller, which is an adaptation of William S. Burroughs's 1959 novel, tells the eerie story of an exterminator who slips into paranoid delusions after becoming addicted to insecticide, which he uses as a drug. Although not one of the best-known Cronenberg films, the science-fiction drama proved a hit with critics.

BORN ON THIS DAY

1921 aviator and businessman Maxwell Ward

1923 movie director Arthur Hiller

1943 Hockey Hall of Famer Yvan Cournoyer

1974 figure skater David Pelletier

23 NOVEMBER

Geoff D'Eon. Courtesy of DHX Media Ltd.

Mary Walsh as Marg Delahunty, Princess Warrior, a character from *This Hour Has 22 Minutes.*

1995. The CBC announces that it will drop all American-produced television programs from its prime-time schedule in order to promote more domestic content and protect its identity as a public broadcaster. US hits such as *The Fresh Prince of Bel-Air* would no longer be aired on the network at prime time. Although these programs generated large revenues for the network—which had just announced a $227-million budget cut—CBC president Perrin Beatty said the corporation must remain "resolutely Canadian."

Also on This Day

1916.
Author and artist P.K. Page is born in Swanage, England. She was raised in the Canadian prairies, and her more than thirty published books include poetry, fiction, and children's stories. Also an accomplished artist, Page has works in the permanent collections of the National Gallery of Canada and the Art Gallery of Ontario. To mark the International Year of Dialogue among Civilizations in 2001, Page's poem "Planet Earth" was read simultaneously in New York, Antarctica, and the South Pacific.

BORN ON THIS DAY

United Church moderator Robert Baird McClure
1900

1902
actor, director, and playwright Victor Jory

NOVEMBER  

Also on This Day

1981.
Alpine skier Lauren Woolstencroft is born in Calgary. Despite being born without legs below the knee and no left arm below the elbow, Woolstencroft started skiing when she was four and was racing competitively by fourteen. She skied for Canada at the Paralympic Winter Games in 2002, 2006, and 2010, and became known as the Golden Girl because of her eight gold medals (five from the Vancouver Games alone), one silver, and one bronze.

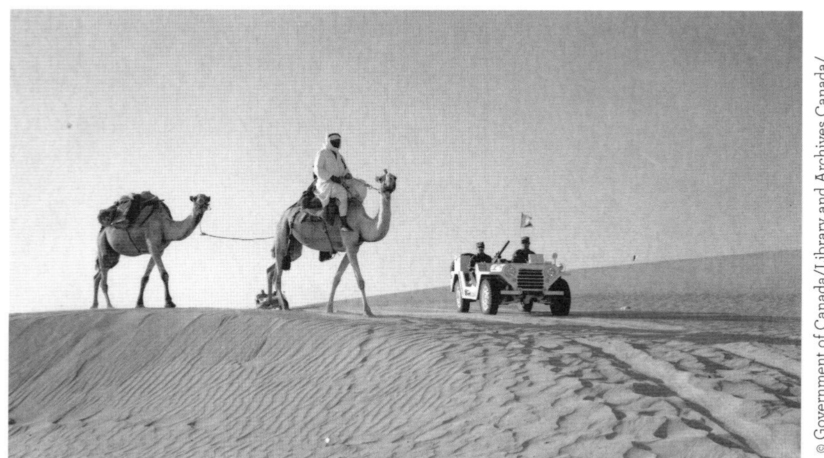

Peacekeepers with a local man travelling through the desert.

1956. The first Canadian peacekeeping troops arrive in Egypt as part of the United Nations Emergency Force (UNEF) tasked with ending hostilities in the Suez Crisis. In July, Egypt had seized the French- and British-owned Suez Canal Company, alarming Western governments, particularly those in Britain and France, who feared their oil supplies would be blocked. But Canada's secretary of state for external affairs, Lester B. Pearson, developed the idea for the UN's first large-scale peacekeeping force. At that time, UN military observers were already being used to monitor cease-fire agreements in Kashmir and Palestine, but a more robust and armoured peacekeeping force had not been tried before. Addressing the UN General Assembly in New York, Pearson made his case for a "peace and police force," saying, "Peace is far more than ceasing to fire." The UN troops that began to arrive in Egypt in November were the first to embody the modern concept of peacekeeping. Pearson won the 1957 Nobel Peace Prize for his initiative. In his acceptance speech, he highlighted Canada's important role in the breakthrough.

BORN ON THIS DAY

1881 sculptor Florence Wyle

1931 financier Andrew Sarlos

1959 skier Todd Brooker

25 NOVEMBER

Library and Archives Canada/1983-28-2634.

Poster for the YWCA by Gil Spear, ca. 1914.

Also on This Day

1851.
Anatomist, surgeon, and pioneer in the field of dermatology, Francis John Shepherd is born in Como, Québec. His diagnostic power, surgical judgment, technical skill, and knowledge of anatomy made him one of the most successful and reliable surgeons of his generation, and his influence revolutionized the teaching of anatomy at McGill University.

1851. Businessmen Francis Grafton and James Clexton establish the first North American chapter of the Young Men's Christian Association (YMCA) in Montréal. Founded in 1844 in London, England, by George Williams, the YMCA spread rapidly to other cities where groups of young men wished to protect themselves against the temptations of modern urban life. The YMCA's original goal was the spiritual improvement of young men through activities that put Christian teachings into practice. For many years, the organization was closely tied to Protestant evangelical churches. Today it serves men and women of all ages, walks of life, races, and religions.

BORN ON THIS DAY

Hockey Hall of Famer Eddie Shore
1902

1963
singer Holly Cole

actress and musician Jill Hennessy
1968

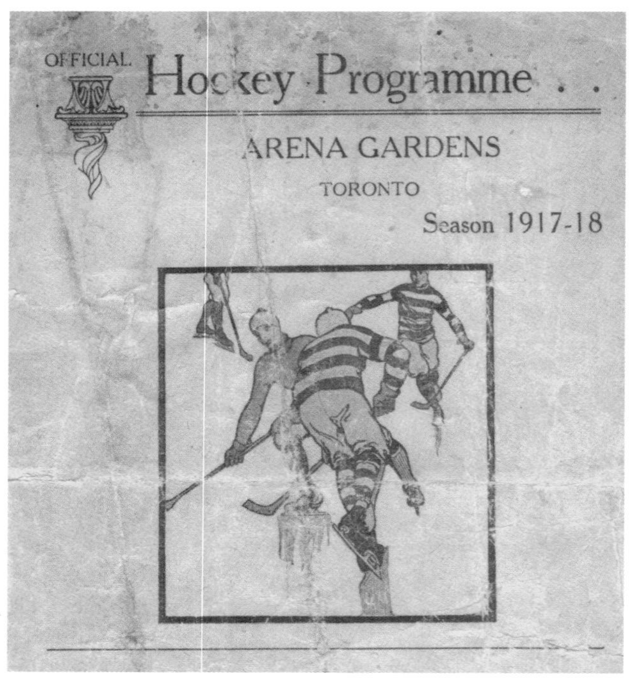

Hockey Hall of Fame.

A Toronto Arenas/Montreal Canadiens program from the 1917–18 NHL season.

1917. The National Hockey League (NHL) is formed. The original teams were the Montreal Canadiens, the Montreal Wanderers, the Ottawa Senators, the Toronto Arenas (predecessors of the Maple Leafs), and the Québec Bulldogs. The first NHL games were played on December 19, 1917, with surprisingly high scores—the Montreal Wanderers beat Toronto 10–9, and the Montreal Canadiens beat Ottawa 7–4. Unfortunately, the league lost two teams early in the season: the Québec franchise folded due to lack of fan support, and the Wanderers dropped out after their stadium burned down. That left only the Montreal Canadiens, the Ottawa Senators, and the Toronto Arenas duking it out to the end of the season. In what would prove to be a poor prediction, the Toronto *Globe* wrote: "Pro hockey is on its last legs."

BORN ON THIS DAY

Old West lawman and journalist William Barclay "Bat" Masterson
1853

1920
director, writer, producer, and actor Daniel Petrie

"Mr. Dressup" Ernie Coombs
1927

1938
impressionist and actor Rich Little

CANADIAN STANLEY CUP WINNERS

Patrick Roy hoists the Stanley Cup.

Calgary Flames: 1989

Edmonton Oilers: 1984, 1985, 1987, 1988, 1990

Kenora Thistles: 1907

Montreal Canadiens: 1916, 1924, 1930, 1931, 1944, 1946, 1953, 1956, 1957, 1958, 1959, 1960, 1965, 1966, 1968, 1969, 1971, 1973, 1976, 1977, 1978, 1979, 1986, 1993

Montreal AAA: 1893, 1894, 1902, 1903

Montreal Maroons: 1926, 1935

Montreal Shamrocks: 1899, 1900

Montreal Victorias: 1895, 1896, 1897, 1898, 1899

Montreal Wanderers: 1906, 1907, 1908, 1910

Ottawa Senators: 1909, 1910, 1911, 1920, 1921, 1923, 1927

Ottawa Silver Seven: 1903, 1904, 1905, 1906

Quebec Bulldogs: 1912, 1913

Toronto Arenas: 1918

Toronto Blueshirts: 1914

Toronto Maple Leafs: 1932, 1942, 1945, 1947, 1948, 1949, 1951, 1962, 1963, 1964, 1967

Toronto St. Pats: 1922

Vancouver Millionaires: 1915

Victoria Cougars: 1925

Winnipeg Victorias: 1896, 1901, 1902

NOVEMBER  

La Presse.

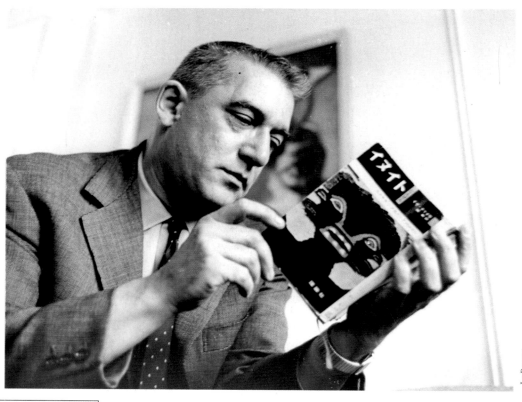

Yves Thériault.

1915. Writer Yves Thériault is born in Québec City. The son of a carpenter, he tried various occupations before earning his living from writing. The 1944 publication of his first book, *Contes pour un homme seul* (Tales for a Man Alone), attracted great public attention, but it was his novel *Agaguk*, published in 1958 and translated into seven languages, that made him famous. Thériault became one of Québec's most popular writers, both in Canada and abroad.

Also on This Day

1829.
The first ships enter the Welland Canal, a waterway built to connect Lakes Ontario and Erie and bypass Niagara Falls. The canal is 43.5 kilometres long and overcomes a height difference of 99.4 metres between the two lakes.

BORN ON THIS DAY

1952 politician Sheila Copps

1965 rower Kathleen Heddle

28 NOVEMBER

Louise Leblanc. Courtesy of Quebec Symphony Orchestra.

The Quebec Symphony Orchestra at the Grand Théâtre de Québec under the direction of Fabien Gabel, 2013.

1902. The Quebec Symphony Orchestra (QSO), with Joseph Vézina as music director, plays its first concert at Tara Hall. Although the First World War and the Spanish flu epidemic disrupted the orchestra's activities—not a single concert was performed between March 1918 and March 1919—it is nevertheless Canada's oldest active orchestra.

Also on This Day

1964.
The BC Lions defeat the Hamilton Tiger-Cats 34–24, winning their first Grey Cup. The Lions played their first game on August 11, 1954, in Vancouver's Empire Stadium. Prior to the team's creation, British Columbia was considered a soccer- and rugby-centered province, and sceptics doubted that a CFL franchise would thrive in the West. The Lions have won the Grey Cup six times since the team was founded (1964, 1985, 1994, 2000, 2006, 2011).

BORN ON THIS DAY

1901 — aviator Carlyle Agar

1949 — bandleader and TV sidekick Paul Shaffer

NOVEMBER  

Also on This Day

1944.
Officers regain control of their troops at the Terrace, BC, army base after five days of mutiny. The soldiers in Terrace were mainly conscripts, many of whom were French Canadian. When news came that they may be shipped overseas for active duty, they began disobeying orders. It was the most serious breach of discipline in the Canadian military during the Second World War.

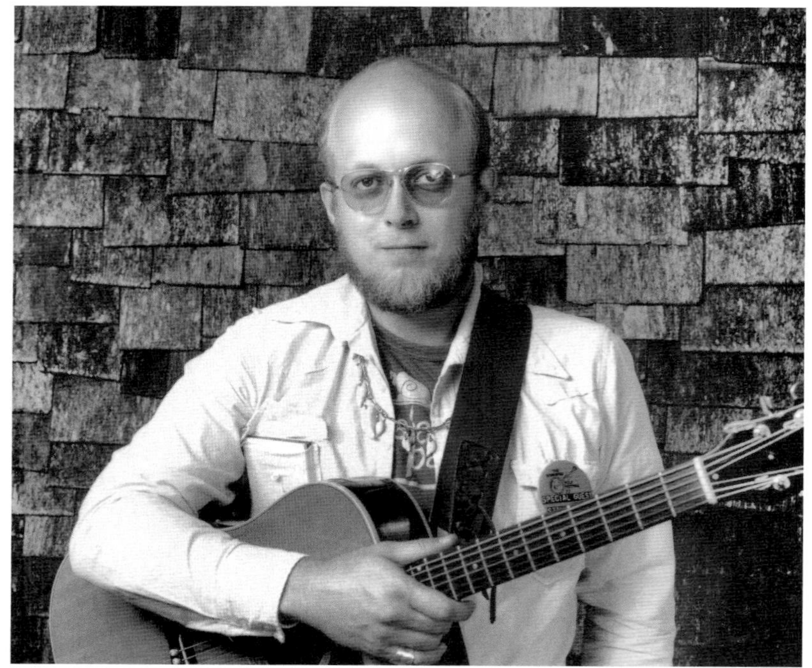

The Estate of Stan Rogers.

Stan Rogers, undated.

1949. Celebrated folk singer Stan Rogers is born in Hamilton, Ontario. Rogers was known for his rich baritone voice and finely crafted folk songs, many of which were written and performed in a traditional Celtic style. With songs such as "Barrett's Privateers" and "Northwest Passage," he drew on historic and poetic aspects of the Canadian experience. His music never received widespread exposure on commercial radio, however, and was largely unknown outside of folk music circles during his lifetime. But his legend grew after his tragic death in an airplane fire in 1983.

BORN ON THIS DAY

1940
singer-songwriter Denny Doherty

1950
author, actress, and director Marie Laberge

1955
comedian, actor, writer, and producer Howie Mandel

© Chantal Gagnon.

The Prince Edward Island birthplace of Lucy Maud Montgomery, author of *Anne of Green Gables.*

1874. Writer Lucy Maud Montgomery is born in Clifton (now New London), Prince Edward Island. Her first novel, *Anne of Green Gables*, published in Boston in 1908, was an instant bestseller. The story of orphan Anne Shirley's bright passage from childhood into adolescence mirrors aspects of Montgomery's own youth in PEI, where she lived with her grandparents after her mother's death. By far the most popular of Montgomery's many novels, *Anne of Green Gables* has remained in print for over a century. It has gone through numerous editions, has been translated into at least fifteen languages, and has several times been adapted for TV and film. It has also been performed annually as a musical in PEI since 1965.

In Her Own Words: L.M. Montgomery

"When I am asked if Anne herself is a 'real person' I always answer 'no' with an odd reluctance and an uncomfortable feeling of not telling the truth. For she is and always has been, from the moment I first thought of her, so real to me that I feel I am doing violence to something when I deny her an existence anywhere save Dreamland. Does she not stand at my elbow even now—if I turned my head quickly should I not see her—with her eager, starry eyes and her long braids of red hair and her little pointed chin? To tell that haunting elf that she is not real, because, forsooth, I never met her in the flesh! No, I cannot do it! She is so real that, although I've never met her, I feel quite sure I shall do so some day—perhaps in a stroll through Lover's Lane in the twilight—or in the moonlit Birch Path—I shall lift my eyes and find her, child or maiden, by my side. And I shall not be in the least surprised because I have always known she was somewhere."

BORN ON THIS DAY

1840 silversmith and jewellery chain founder Henry Birks

1982 actress Elisha Cuthbert

THE TOQUE

In Canada, a toque is a tapered, knitted cap, popular with fishermen, hunters, and other outdoor workers. It's usually made from wool or acrylic fibres.

The word "toque" probably comes from the Arabic *taq*, meaning a veil or shawl. The word came to Canada with Breton settlers, who used it for any kind of hat. A toque is also one name for the tall white hats that chefs wear.

Canadian snowboarders often wear a brimmed toque, nicknamed a *bruque*.

In Phrygia (now part of Turkey), a hat similar to a toque was worn by liberated slaves. During the French Revolution, it was adopted as a symbol of freedom, and in Québec in the 1830s, it became a symbol of rebellion against British rule.

Today, the toque is also part of a yearly homelessness fundraiser run by the Raising the Roof foundation.

Canada's most famous toque-wearers are probably *SCTV*'s Bob and Doug McKenzie. Bob (Rick Moranis) usually wore a green toque with a Canada logo, while Doug (Dave Thomas) sported a blue toque with stripes and a large bobble.

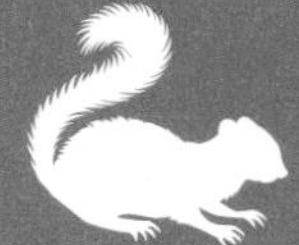

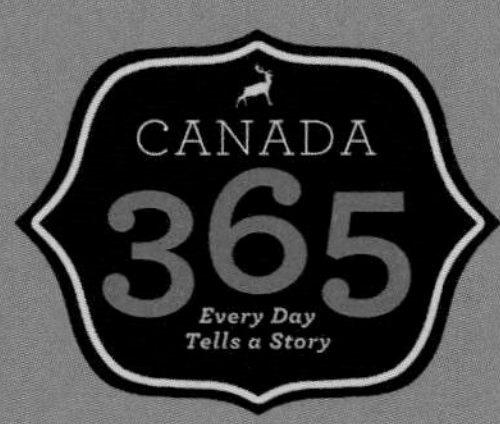
CANADA
365
Every Day
Tells a Story

DECEMBER

DECEMBER  1

What Is Prorogation?

The governor general, on the advice of the prime minister, can (at his or her discretion) suspend a Parliamentary session. This is called proroguing Parliament. A second situation in which the power of the governor general can affect a sitting government is when a prime minister makes a request for the dissolution of Parliament. In 1925, the Liberal government, headed by Prime Minister William Lyon Mackenzie King, advised the governor general, Lord Julian Byng, to dissolve Parliament and call a fresh election after the October 1925 election saw the Conservatives win more seats than the Liberals. King had tried to continue governing after losing the election—as was his right—but he couldn't maintain the confidence of the House of Commons. When King proceeded to ask for a dissolution, Byng refused the request, and instead a new minority government was formed under Conservative leader Arthur Meighen. Eventually Meighen couldn't command the confidence of the House either, so he asked Byng for dissolution, which was granted, and a new election was called. In the ensuing election of September 1926, King campaigned on the constitutional issue, which he described as a British governor general interfering with the right of Canadians to govern themselves, and retook a majority of the seats in parliament. Known as the King-Byng Affair, this would be the last time that a governor general publicly refused the advice of a prime minister.

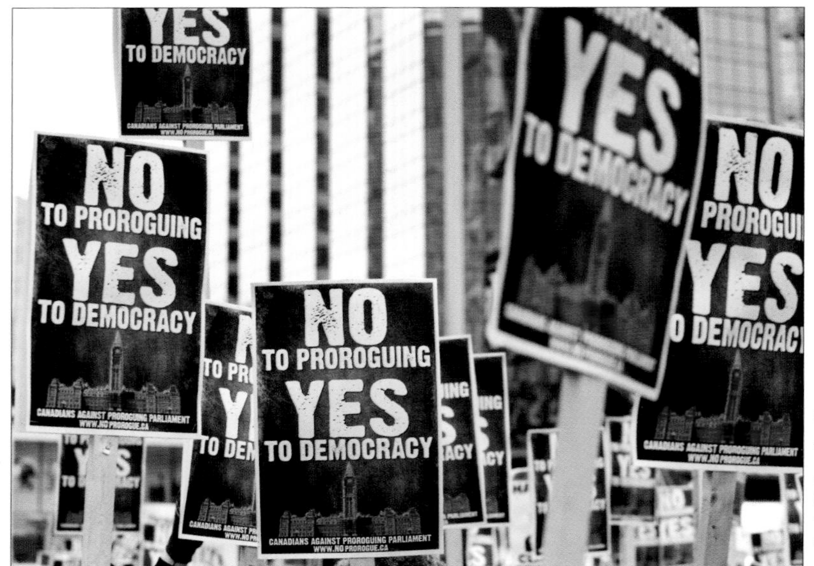

©Tanja-Tiziana Burdi.

A Canadians Against Proroguing Parliament rally in Toronto, 2010.

2008. Following the Conservative government's launch of a series of controversial proposals, the leaders of the opposition Liberal and the New Democratic parties form a coalition to unseat the government with a pledge of support from the Bloc Québécois. Prime Minister Stephen Harper successfully appealed to the governor general to prorogue, or suspend, Parliament until early 2009, which ultimately ended efforts to overturn the government. The government would prorogue Parliament again a year later, in a move critics said was intended to quell controversy surrounding Afghan detainees until after the close of the Vancouver Winter Olympics.

Which more successful coalition helped shape Canada? See March 25.

BORN ON THIS DAY

actress
Allyn Ann McLerie
1926

1962
speed skater
Sylvie Daigle

2 DECEMBER

City of Toronto Archives/Fonds 1231, Item 843.

The Grand Opera House in Toronto, 1921.

1919. In a mystery that would haunt Toronto police for decades, theatre magnate Ambrose Small disappears under suspicious circumstances. In late November, Small had sold his vast theatre holdings for $1.7 million to Trans-Canada Theatres Limited, receiving as a down payment a $1-million dollar cheque, which his wife deposited while he shopped for a new Cadillac and other luxury items. He disappeared after leaving his office on December 2. No kidnappers ever contacted the family, and a large reward was never paid. With his fortune accounted for and no body ever found, many assume he was murdered and the body disposed of. The case remains unsolved.

A Case for Sherlock Holmes?

In 1922, a *Toronto Daily Star* journalist reportedly brought Small's story to the attention of Sir Arthur Conan Doyle, the man who created detective Sherlock Holmes. Though he expressed an interest in the case—the newspaper proclaimed in a headline "Sherlock Holmes to Look into Ambrose Small Mystery"—it seems that Doyle never joined the investigation. But Toronto police are said to have expended every other effort to find the missing magnate, although they refused the services of Maximilian Langsner, a Viennese criminologist who claimed he could solve the case using "thought waves."

BORN ON THIS DAY

Father of Confederation Jean-Charles Chapais
1811

1950
environmental activist Paul Watson

twin hockey players Ron and Rich Sutter
1963

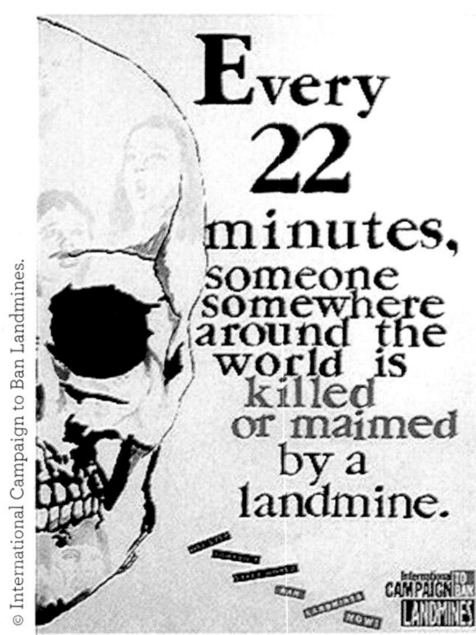

A poster for the International Campaign to Ban Landmines.

1997. Officials from 122 countries gather in Ottawa to sign a treaty aimed at ridding the world of landmines. The Mine Ban Treaty came into force in 1999. It called for member states to destroy stockpiled mines within four years. Delegates were asked to accept the terms of the agreement without further negotiation. It was the first treaty in history to ban a widely used weapon of war. Today there are about 160 parties to the treaty, but roughly thirty-five countries have refused to join, including the United States, China, Russia, North Korea, and South Korea. Many of the signatory countries have voluntarily eliminated their stockpiled landmines. But these weapons remain a problem—every day, about ten people in the world lose life or limb to a landmine or other explosive remnant of war.

Also on This Day

1887.

Saturday Night magazine makes its first appearance as a weekly paper. It would go on sale, for five cents apiece, at 6:00 p.m. every Saturday. It gained critical success beginning in the 1930s, and over the years provided significant political reporting and introduced readers to such authors as Dennis Lee and Margaret Atwood. After undergoing various format changes, it printed its last issue in 2005.

What was the name of the treaty imposed on Germany following the First World War? See June 28.

BORN ON THIS DAY

1927 author Morley Torgov

1968 actor Brendan Fraser

4 DECEMBER

Library and Archives Canada/William Gallaway/PA-067265.

Deanna Durbin, undated.

1921. Actress and singer Deanna Durbin is born in Winnipeg. A popular Hollywood star in the late 1930s, she rivalled Shirley Temple, the biggest box-office draw of the day. After twenty-one feature films and a dozen years in the spotlight, Durbin retired to the south of France. Her last movie, *For the Love of Mary*, was released in 1948, when she was still just twenty-seven years old. Despite numerous attempts to lure her back to the limelight, she refused to come out of retirement. The numerous Deanna Durbin fan clubs worldwide are a tribute to her enduring fame. Durbin passed away in 2013.

Canadians in Classic Films

Ben Blue: *It's a Mad, Mad, Mad, Mad World*; *For Me and My Gal*
Marie Dressler: *Dinner at Eight*; *Tillie's Punctured Romance*
Rockliffe Fellowes: Monkey Business; *Regeneration*
Glenn Ford: *Superman*; *3:10 to Yuma*
May Irwin: *Mrs. Black Is Back*; *The Kiss*
Ruby Keeler: *42nd Street*; *Footlight Parade*
Raymond Massey: *The Scarlet Pimpernel*; *East of Eden*
Mary Pickford: *Coquette*; *Poor Little Rich Girl*
Walter Pidgeon: *Forbidden Planet*; *How Green Was My Valley*; *Funny Girl*
Norma Shearer: *The Women*; *Romeo and Juliet*
Jay Silverheels: *The Lone Ranger* films
Fay Wray: *King Kong*; *Gideon's Trumpet*

BORN ON THIS DAY

1913 — director, editor, writer, and producer Mark Robson
1937 — actor Donnelly Rhodes
1944 — singer-songwriter Anna McGarrigle
1945 — astronaut, physician, educator, and photographer Roberta Bondar
1976 — speed skater Kristina Groves

DECEMBER  5

Also on This Day

1952.
Singer-songwriter Andy Kim is born in Montréal. Kim rose to fame in the late 1960s with such tunes as "How'd We Ever Get This Way?" and "So Good Together." His 1969 surprise hit "Sugar, Sugar," which he co-wrote for The Archies, spent several weeks at number one in Canada, the United States, and elsewhere; the single was inducted into the Canadian Songwriters Hall of Fame in 2006.

City of Toronto Archives/Fonds 1568, Item 311.

Yonge Street, 1909.

1837. William Lyon Mackenzie leads a ragtag contingent of five hundred or so men down Yonge Street from Montgomery's Tavern in an attempt to overthrow the government of Upper Canada. The rebels planned to march to the house of the lieutenant-governor, Sir Francis Bond Head, and perhaps on to city hall. As the force neared Toronto, however, it was dispersed by a few shots from loyalist guards. Mackenzie's Upper Canada Rebellion was inspired by a series of skirmishes in Lower Canada in November. French Canadian nationalist Louis-Joseph Papineau, hoping to upset the political status quo, had sparked those skirmishes between Patriote rebels and trained British soldiers. His rebellion, like Mackenzie's, was handily quashed, but the seeds it sowed, especially the idea of responsible government, would shape the country's modern political system.

BORN ON THIS DAY

Royal Canadian Air Farce member Dave Broadfoot
1925

1962
musician, artist, and actor Kevin Ogilvie

6 DECEMBER

Department of National Defence / Library and Archives Canada / PA-022744.

Soldiers clearing debris after the Halifax Explosion.

1917. At Halifax, the French cargo and munitions ship SS *Mont-Blanc*, which is loaded with explosives bound for First World War battlefields, collides with the Norwegian ship SS *Imo*. The resulting explosion, the largest man-made blast in the world before the advent of the atomic bomb, killed nearly two thousand people, maimed or blinded more than nine thousand others, left twenty-five thousand without proper shelter, and levelled the city's north end in one of Canada's worst disasters.

Railway dispatcher Vince Coleman was among the many who lost their lives in the explosion. As the *Mont-Blanc* burned and drifted toward Pier 6, he remained at his post, tapping out warnings to rail officials to stop all trains headed for the city. His telegraph message, tapped in the last minutes of his life, stated, "Hold up the train. Ammunition ship afire in harbour making for Pier 6 and will explode. Guess this will be my last message. Goodbye boys."

Also on This Day

1989.
The mass murder of fourteen female students and a university employee occurs at Montréal's École Polytechnique. The lone assailant, Marc Lépine, burst into a classroom and separated the women from the men before firing his weapon, shouting, "You are all feminists." In addition to the fourteen young women killed, fourteen other people were wounded. The shooter then turned his gun on himself. Later, investigators found a list of eminent women whom he had identified as "feminists to slaughter." Following the event, debate raged over the significance of the attack, and whether it revealed widespread anti-feminist sentiment and violence against women or was a random outburst of psychological illness. Each year on December 6, vigils are held across the country to remember the victims and to call for an end to violence against women.

BORN ON THIS DAY

author and pioneer
Susanna Moodie
1803

fighter pilot
George Frederick "Buzz" Beurling
1921

author
Tomson Highway
1951

DECEMBER 7

The Canadian Press/Peter Bregg.

Florence Bird, pictured here in November 1982, was the commissioner of the Council on the Status of Women. It was the first Canadian royal commission chaired by a woman.

1970. The Royal Commission on the Status of Women in Canada tables a 488-page report containing 167 recommendations on such matters as equal pay for work of equal value, maternity leave, daycare for children, birth control, and educational and employment opportunities. The commission was struck by Prime Minister Lester B. Pearson in 1967 in response to a campaign organized by a coalition of thirty-two women's groups. It was launched in an era when the influence of the women's movement was increasingly pervading many aspects of Canadian society. By the 1980s, most of the recommendations in the report had been partially or fully implemented.

BORN ON THIS DAY

1910
high jumper
Duncan McNaughton

1911
writer and humorist
Max Braithwaite

1916
dancer, choreographer, and director
Margaret Ruth Carse

1974
singer and actress
Nicole Appleton

WOMEN'S WORK

The report of the Royal Commission on the Status of Women in Canada included a detailed analysis of women's history and some timely statistics on the contemporary conditions for women across the country. Some notable statistics:

National Film Board of Canada/Library and Archives Canada, PA-119766.

- Between 1920 and 1970, only eighteen women were elected to the House of Commons and forty-nine to the provincial legislatures.
- From 1930 (when Cairine Wilson became Canada's first woman senator) to 1970, only eight women were appointed to the Senate, compared to 227 men.
- In 1969, among the 889 judges and magistrates in Canada, only fourteen were women.
- In 1968, female workers accounted for 34.4 percent of the Canadian labour force.
- In 1967, women comprised about one-third of the Canadian graduates in the fields of "arts, pure science and commerce," and more than half the graduates in "education, library science and social work." However, women accounted for less than 5 percent of graduates in law and theology, and less than 12 percent in medicine.

- In 1967, women earned 20.6 percent of wages and salaries in Canada.

Eaton's Santa Claus Parade

Among the lasting legacies of the Eaton's chain is the annual Santa Claus Parade. The first parades set out in 1905 in both Toronto and Winnipeg; Montréal followed in 1925. Eaton's covered all costs for the event and fabricated all costumes, creating an effective promotion strategy for the store. Audiences around the country and even in the United States were able to watch the parade on TV starting in the 1950s. But the boom times were not to last. The Eaton's parade in Montreal was cancelled in 1969 after the FLQ bombings and never returned, and in 1982 the store ended its sponsorship of the parade in Toronto for financial reasons. But the production of the Toronto Santa Claus Parade was taken over by a non-profit organization, ensuring that thousands of Canadians—young and old—would still have their chance to glimpse the man in red.

City of Toronto Archives/Fonds 1266, Item 22538.

Eaton's Santa Claus Parade in Toronto, 1930.

1869. Timothy Eaton opens a tiny dry-goods and haberdashery business with just four employees on Toronto's Yonge Street. His pioneering policies—cash only, no haggling, and "goods satisfactory or money refunded"—helped turn the store into one of the largest retailers in North America. The Eaton's catalogue was introduced in 1884, giving those living in remote farming communities access to a variety of merchandise. By the time of his death in 1907, Timothy Eaton employed over nine thousand people in his stores, factories, and corporate offices. After operating for 130 years, the once-flourishing retailer went bankrupt in 1999.

Mr. Eaton figures as an important character in a popular work by which famous writer? See May 13.

BORN ON THIS DAY

1899

actor John Qualen

1955

actor Kevin McNulty

1959

political commentator Mark Steyn

9 DECEMBER

Library and Archives Canada/Albertype Company/PA-031834.

A post office in Galt, Ontario (now Cambridge), ca. 1900.

1755. The first official post office in Canada is opened in Halifax. Two years earlier, in 1753, Benjamin Franklin had been made deputy postmaster general for the British colonies and was charged with organizing mail delivery in all of British North America. The post office he established in Halifax linked the Atlantic colonies and the existing packet service to England. (A post office limited to local and outgoing mail had been established in Halifax in 1754.) In 1784, courier Pierre Durand was hired to pioneer a route through a thousand kilometres of forest from Halifax to Québec City. The round trip with mail would take only fifteen weeks.

Notable Canadians on Postage Stamps

Pitseolak Ashoona, artist
Frederick Banting, scientist
Norman Bethune, doctor
Billy Bishop, First World War flying ace
Joseph Armand Bombardier, inventor
Ethel Catherwood, athlete
Viola Desmond, activist, businesswoman
Marie Dressler, actress, writer
Gabriel Dumont, Métis leader
Chief Dan George, actor
Germaine Guèvremont, writer
William Hall, naval officer
Pauline Johnson, poet
Paul Kane, artist
Stephen Leacock, writer
Jeanne Mance, religious leader
Marie Travers (La Bolduc), singer
Jennie Kidd Trout, doctor

BORN ON THIS DAY

activist Annie Buller
1895

1969
actor Sebastian Spence

actress Saskia Garel
1977

Other Nobel Prize Winners in the Scientific Realm

1908: Ernest Rutherford (born in New Zealand), Chemistry
1923: Frederick Banting, Physiology or Medicine
1949: William Giauque (born in Canada), Chemistry
1966: Charles B. Huggins (born in Canada), Physiology or Medicine
1971: Gerhard Herzberg (born in Germany), Chemistry
1981: David H. Hubel (born in Canada), Physiology or Medicine
1983: Henry Taube (born in Canada), Chemistry
1989: Sidney Altman, Chemistry
1990: Richard E. Taylor, Physics
1992: Rudolph A. Marcus (born in Canada), Chemistry
1993: Michael Smith (born in the United Kingdom), Chemistry
1994: Bertram N. Brockhouse, Physics
2009: Jack W. Szostak (born in the United Kingdom), Physiology or Medicine
2009: Willard S. Boyle (born in Canada), Physics
2011: Ralph M. Steinman, Physiology or Medicine

John Polanyi, 1984.

1986. University of Toronto professor John C. Polanyi is awarded the Nobel Prize in Chemistry jointly with Dudley R. Herschbach and Yuan T. Lee for developing a new field of research known as reaction dynamics. Specifically, the prize committee cited Polanyi for developing infrared chemiluminescence, "in which the extremely weak infrared emission from a newly formed molecule is measured and analyzed." Born in Germany in 1929, Polanyi was sent to Toronto as a child to escape the dangers of the Second World War. In his later years, he became an active proponent of the peace and disarmament movements. He was the founding chair of the Canadian Pugwash Group—an organization dedicated to providing scholarly insight into the prevention and resolution of armed conflict.

BORN ON THIS DAY

1891
Governor General Harold Alexander

1928
actor John Colicos

1929
musician, composer, and artist Michael Snow

11 DECEMBER

The Canadian Press.

Protestors picket Toronto's Don Jail before the execution of Arthur Lucas and Ronald Turpin.

1962. The last judicial hanging in Canada takes place at Toronto's Don Jail when Ronald Turpin (convicted in the murder of police officer Frederick Nash) and Arthur Lucas (convicted in the murder of Therland Crater, a police informant from Detroit) are executed. In 1976 the country abolished the death penalty for civilian crimes by a majority of just six votes in the House of Commons, but until 1998, under the terms of the National Defence Act, capital punishment could still be used for various military offences, including cowardice, unlawful surrender, and spying for the enemy.

Capital Punishment in Canada

1954: Rape is removed from the list of capital offences.

1962: The last executions in Canada take place.

1966: A motion to abolish the death penalty is defeated in the House of Commons.

1967: Temporary legislation suspends the death sentence for most crimes.

1976: Capital punishment is abolished for all civilian crimes.

1987: A bill to restore the death penalty is defeated in the House of Commons by a vote of 148 to 127.

1998: All references to the death penalty are removed from the National Defence Act.

BORN ON THIS DAY

1838 brewer John Labatt

1922 politician and educator Pauline Jewett

1926 actress Barbara Hamilton

1964 synchronized swimmer Carolyn Waldo

Also on This Day

1985.
The worst air crash in Canadian history occurs in Gander, Newfoundland, when an Arrow Airlines DC-8 crashes seconds after takeoff, killing 248 members of the US 101st Airborne Division and eight crew. The plane was en route to Kentucky from Cairo via Cologne, West Germany, and had stopped to refuel in Gander. Just before the crash, there were reports of freezing drizzle and snow grains.

City of Edmonton Archives/EA-600-3690n.

The Al Rashid Mosque (pictured here in 1950) was relocated to Fort Edmonton Park in the early 1990's to save it from demolition.

1938. Al Rashid, the first mosque in Canada, opens in Edmonton. Canada's Muslim population dates back to the middle of the nineteenth century. The Al Rashid Mosque was built as a place of worship and a centre for community gatherings through the financial contributions of local Albertans, including many of Christian or Jewish faith, and the efforts of a group of Muslim women who first approached Edmonton's mayor about acquiring land upon which a mosque could be built. The Al Rashid Mosque was preserved and relocated to historic Fort Edmonton Park after two new houses of worship were built to accommodate the city's growing Muslim population.

Mosques in central Canada would hit the small screen years later in which popular television show? See January 9.

BORN ON THIS DAY

1921
businessman and Olympic hockey player George Mara

1957
playwright, director, and actor Robert Lepage

1987
actress Kate Todd

13 DECEMBER

© Chantal Gagnon.

The grave of Emily Carr in Victoria's Ross Bay Cemetery.

1871. Painter and writer Emily Carr is born in Victoria, British Columbia. Carr painted a record of the "vanishing" villages, houses, and totem poles in BC, highlighting the Pacific Northwest's distinctive landscape and the culture of its Aboriginal peoples. She was considered one of the preeminent, and perhaps most original, Canadian painters of the first half of the twentieth century, and was one of relatively few major female artists of the period. Much of her work reflected her intimate connection to the natural world. Beside her grave in Victoria is a stone monument celebrating her love of Mother Earth.

In Her Own Words: Emily Carr

"First there must be an idea, a feeling, or whatever you want to call it, the something that interested or inspired you sufficiently to make you desire to express it. Maybe it was an abstract idea that you've got to find a symbol for, or maybe it was a concrete form that you have to simplify or distort to meet your ends, but that starting point must pervade the whole. Then you must discover the pervading direction, the pervading rhythm, the dominant, recurring forms, the dominant colour, but always the thing must be top in your thoughts. Everything must lead up to it, clothe it, feed it, balance it, tenderly fold it, till it reveals itself in all the beauty of its idea."

BORN ON THIS DAY

author
Ross Macdonald
1915

1942
baseball player
Fergie Jenkins

DECEMBER  

The Story of the "Diefenbunker"

During the Cold War, tensions on all sides ran high. To ensure the continued functioning of the Canadian government in the event of a nuclear attack, Prime Minister Diefenbaker commissioned the top-secret construction of an underground safe house in Carp, Ontario, just outside of Ottawa. Known as the Central Emergency Government Headquarters (CEGHQ Carp)—or colloquially, the Diefenbunker—the safe house was completed in 1961 and housed some of Canada's most classified communications. Operation of the Diefenbunker ceased in 1994, the same year the building was designated a National Historic Site.

Prime Minister Diefenbaker visiting Expo 67.

1956. John Diefenbaker is elected leader of the Progressive Conservative Party. Diefenbaker became prime minister in 1957, when he formed a minority government. In 1958 he again led the Progressive Conservatives to power, winning a majority with 208 seats—the highest number held by a single party in Canada to that time. During his time as prime minister, Diefenbaker championed the Canadian Bill of Rights and extended the vote to First Nations. But he was criticized for his indecision regarding nuclear missiles and for his cancellation of the *Avro Arrow* project.

BORN ON THIS DAY

missionary Jean-Baptiste Thibault
1810

1855
artist William Brymner

anthropologist, writer, and ethnobotanist Wade Davis
1953

1954
astronaut Steve MacLean

15 DECEMBER

1890. Sioux chief Sitting Bull is killed, along with thirteen other people, after American authorities order his arrest, provoking a gunfight with reserve police who executed the warrant. Sitting Bull was born around 1831 in present-day Montana or South Dakota. In his youth, he was trained as a warrior, and in the late 1860s, he became leader of the resistance against American expansion into Sioux territory. In response to the encroachment of the settlers, Sitting Bull and his followers sought refuge in what is now Saskatchewan in 1877. The Canadian government, fearing that the Sioux chief's presence would incite intertribal warfare and intent on clearing the Prairies for white settlement, rejected his request for a reserve for his people, forcing them to return to the United States in 1881. Sitting Bull advocated strongly against the American government's attempts to force the surrender of Aboriginal lands, prompting the arrest warrant that ultimately led to his death.

Library and Archives Canada/Duffin and Co./PA-117945.

Sitting Bull, 1885.

Also on This Day

1913.
The opening performance at the Loew's Yonge Street Theatre in Toronto (later renamed the Elgin) is attended by Irving Berlin, who introduced a new song. The Elgin and Winter Garden Theatre Centre is the only double-decker theatre complex still operating in the world.

BORN ON THIS DAY

wheelchair athlete Chantal Petitclerc
1969

1970
actor Michael Shanks

wrestler Eric Young
1979

DECEMBER  

© Jeff Laidlaw.

A view of the Confederation Bridge.

1992. The federal government and the provincial governments of New Brunswick and Prince Edward Island sign an agreement to build a bridge linking PEI to the country's mainland. The bridge cost $1 billion to construct and opened in May 1997. At 12.9 kilometres, it is the world's longest bridge over ice-covered water and takes, on average, ten minutes to cross by car. The bridge is curved to keep drivers alert and reduce accidents. The opening of the bridge significantly increased tourism to the island. Though officially called the Confederation Bridge, the structure has also been dubbed the Span of Green Gables.

The Longest Bridges in Canada

Champlain Bridge
(between Montréal and Brossard, QC), approximately 3.4 km

Sault Ste. Marie International Bridge
(between Sault Ste. Marie, ON, and Sault Ste. Marie, MI), approximately 2.9 km

Garden City Skyway
(between St. Catharines and Niagara-on-the-Lake, ON), approximately 2.2 km

BORN ON THIS DAY

1959 curler Colleen Jones

1967 runner Donovan Bailey

17 DECEMBER

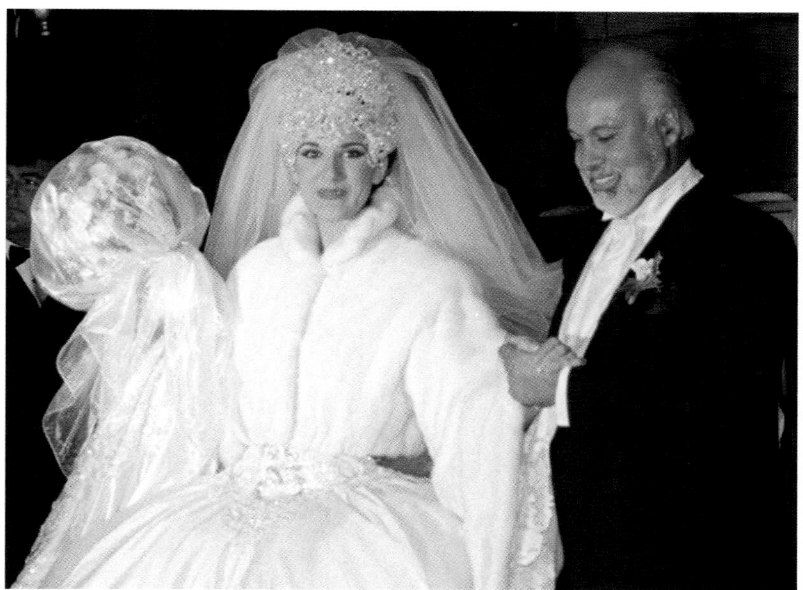

Ryan Remiorz/The Canadian Press.

Céline Dion leaves the church with René Angélil after their wedding ceremony.

1994. Singer Céline Dion marries René Angélil in a lavish ceremony held at the Notre-Dame Basilica in Montréal. The five hundred guests included former prime minister Brian Mulroney. Dion's dress was a show-stopper, with its twenty-three-kilogram train and a headpiece studded with two thousand crystals. Angélil had discovered Dion (the youngest of fourteen children) singing in her family's restaurant in Montréal when she was just twelve years old. He became her first manager, handling what would prove to be a lengthy and successful career, with multiple Grammy Awards, performances at several Academy Awards shows, and a $100-million contract with Caesar's Palace in Las Vegas.

Also on This Day

1946.
Actor, writer, director, and producer Eugene Levy is born in Hamilton, Ontario. An alumnus of the Second City comedy troupe as well as the *SCTV* series, he has appeared in over fifty movies, including all of the *American Pie* films. His role as Mitch alongside Catherine O'Hara's Mickey in *A Mighty Wind* led to the two performing the movie's folk-inspired "A Kiss at the End of the Rainbow" at the 2004 Academy Awards.

SCTV was home to which other talented Canadians? See September 21.

BORN ON THIS DAY

Prime Minister William Lyon Mackenzie King
1874

1968
racing driver Paul Tracy

humanitarian and activist Craig Kielburger
1982

DECEMBER

In His Own Words: James Johnson

James "Vic" Johnson served as an officer in the Royal Canadian Engineers, constructing defences, building structures and clearing minefields during the Korean War.

"A lot of people said it was an engineer's war because we were into a country with no roads. There were very few roads and mountainous—either mountainous or paddy fields. Rice paddies. We had to improve whatever we could there to get roads out so that they could get up to the battalion positions and so forth ... I had to go in and clear mines to arrange for these positions. It was wintertime and there was a fair bit of ice and that, and a lot of the mines were covered with ice, so I would get in there, be laying on my stomach with a bayonet, chipping away very gingerly at the ice around this mine so I could expose the striker on it and put a pin in it to neutralize it."

Frank Smyth/The Memory Project.

Frank Smyth in Korea, handing out clothes and toys donated by his family in Toronto.

1950. Members of the 2nd Battalion, Princess Patricia's Canadian Light Infantry—the first Canadian troops to arrive in Korea—land at Pusan. Initially, Canada had contributed three Royal Canadian Navy destroyers (HMCS *Athabaskan*, HMCS *Cayuga*, and HMCS *Sioux*) and a Royal Canadian Air Force transport squadron (No. 426 "Thunderbird" Squadron). But in response to American, UN, and domestic pressure, Prime Minister Louis St. Laurent announced on August 7, 1950, that the country would expand its UN contributions to Korea with a Canadian Army Special Force (CASF)—later named the 25th Canadian Infantry Brigade. Throughout the Korean War, Canadians battled on unfamiliar and often treacherous terrain, fighting admirably to secure South Korea from the control of North Korea and China.

BORN ON THIS DAY

singer-songwriter Wilf Carter
1904

1927
politician and statesman Roméo LeBlanc

singer and keyboardist Martha Johnson
1950

1961
figure skater Brian Orser

19 DECEMBER

© NASA/iss034e010295.

Chris Hadfield on the International Space Station.

2012. Astronaut Chris Hadfield takes off for the International Space Station (ISS) aboard a Russian Soyuz spacecraft in December. He was the second Canadian to participate in a long-term flight aboard the ISS and the first to command a spaceship when he took over the ISS in March 2013. He returned to earth in May. During his journey in space, Hadfield delighted people around the world through social media with breathtaking photos of the planet from above and lighthearted videos like "Making a Peanut Butter Sandwich in Outer Space" and "Tears in Space (Don't Fall)."

Also on This Day

1995.
Alberta chicken producer Rod Chernos is honoured by the Society for the Prevention of Cruelty to Animals. Unlike other chicken producers, Chernos let his chickens roam free in a barn that was carefully monitored for feed and water levels, temperature, and ventilation. It was common among other chicken farmers to leave poultry in lit barns, which would cause them to eat more and grow faster, but Chernos turned the lights off at night so the chickens would be well-rested and more lively during the day. He believed "a happy chicken is a tasty one."

Which other Canadians journeyed to outer space? See January 30.

BORN ON THIS DAY

1924 hockey Hall of Famer Douglas Harvey

1928 composer Galt MacDermot

1944 guitarist and restaurateur Zal Yanovsky

1965 actress Jessica Steen

DECEMBER 20

In His Own Words: Maurice White

"We went through the town [of Ortona] by blowing holes through from one room to the next. The streets were all filled with rubble almost as high as the houses. So that was our means of getting through, and I believe that a lot of our soldiers with the Loyal Edmonton Regiment were farmers, farm boys. And a farm boy never gets hung up on anything and they always find a way out ... Our way of going about capturing Ortona was to go through from room to room. You'd blow a hole into a room. Generally that would kill or knock out most of the enemy that was in that room, but there would be the next room. There was always the next room."

Lieut. Terry F. Rowe/Canada. Dept. of National Defence/Library and Archives Canada/PA-205255.

Trooper J.W. McConnell, Three Rivers Regiment, examining a knocked-out German PzKpfw III tank, San Leonardo di Ortona, Italy.

1943. Supported by their armoured brigade, Canadian troops attack Ortona, Italy, during the Second World War. Infantry divisions from the Loyal Edmonton Regiment and the Seaforth Highlanders of Canada suffered numerous casualties during the battle, but the Germans were forced to withdraw on the night of December 27. Canadian forces had 1,372 dead at Ortona—almost 25 percent of all Canadians killed in the Mediterranean theatre of the Second World War.

BORN ON THIS DAY

1924

lawyer, politician, broadcaster, and novelist Judy LaMarsh

1959

racing driver Scott Goodyear

1970

actress Nicole de Boer

21 DECEMBER

Robert Bourassa.

1988. Québec's Liberal government under Premier Robert Bourassa adopts Bill 178 (an Act to Amend the Charter of the French Language). The new legislation made it clear that "public signs and posters and commercial advertising, outside or intended for the public outside, shall be solely in French." Public signs, posters, and commercial advertising, however, could be "both in French and in another language, provided they are intended only for the public inside the establishments and that French is markedly predominant." The amendment dissatisfied both Québec nationalists (who opposed any law allowing some use of English) and anglophone and non-French-speaking citizens (who wanted to bring an end to Québec's days as a unilingual province).

Also on This Day

1966.
Actor Kiefer Sutherland—the son of actors Shirley Douglas and Donald Sutherland, and the grandson of Tommy Douglas, father of Canada's medicare system—is born in London, England. His first major role was in the Canadian film *The Bay Boy*, and it was soon followed by the US feature film *Stand by Me*. He is best known for his portrayal of Jack Bauer on the TV series *24*, for which he won numerous awards, including an Emmy and a Golden Globe.

What calling did Tommy Douglas pursue before he entered politics?
See February 24.

BORN ON THIS DAY

- 1885 — Hockey Hall of Famer and league official Frank Patrick
- 1921 — actor and director Jean Gascon
- 1935 — Governor General Edward Schreyer
- 1959 — rower Kay Worthington

Also on This Day

1964.
Angela James, dubbed "the Wayne Gretzky of women's hockey," is born in Toronto. She joined a boys' hockey league at age eight and quickly became the top scorer before league policy was changed in her second year, restricting membership to boys only. In 1990, she played at the inaugural world championship in women's hockey, leading the Canadian team to a gold medal. The winner of numerous awards and accolades, James was inducted into the Hockey Hall of Fame in 2010, one of the first two women and only the second Black athlete to be inducted.

© Ken Dean.

Neil Young, 1988.

1985. The CBC airs a documentary on the creation of "Tears Are Not Enough," a charity single recorded by Northern Lights, a supergroup of more than fifty of Canada's biggest recording artists. Notable participants included Burton Cummings, Oscar Peterson, Anne Murray, Neil Young, Joni Mitchell, Gordon Lightfoot, Bryan Adams, Paul Shaffer, Dan Hill, and Geddy Lee. Inspired by the British charitable single "Do They Know It's Christmas?," "Tears Are Not Enough" was written and recorded to raise funds for famine relief in Ethiopia. The song was also a chart-topping hit in Canada. By 1990, proceeds from the effort had exceeded $3.2 million.

Which member of Northern Lights was inducted into the Canadian Music Hall of Fame in 1986? See November 10.

BORN ON THIS DAY

1938
politician
Lucien Bouchard

1969
biathlete
Myriam Bédard

23 DECEMBER

Jeanne Sauvé, 1987.

1983. Jeanne Sauvé is named Canada's first female governor general. A trailblazer for women in politics, Sauvé was also the first female French Canadian cabinet member and the first female Speaker of the House of Commons. During her political career, she filled the roles of minister of state for science and technology, minister of the environment, and minister of communications. In 1989, Sauvé established the Jeanne Sauvé Foundation, with the goal of empowering a new generation of public leaders.

Also on This Day

1908.
Photographer Yousuf Karsh is born. An Armenian refugee, Karsh immigrated to Canada in 1924. In 1932, he moved to Ottawa, where he opened his own studio with the goal of photographing "people of consequence." Over the course of his career, Karsh would shoot a number of major international figures, including Georgia O'Keeffe, Ernest Hemingway, Charles de Gaulle, Grey Owl, Albert Einstein, and Martin Luther King Jr. One of his most famous portraits, of a formidable-looking Winston Churchill in 1941, graced the cover of *Life* magazine.

BORN ON THIS DAY

poet and author Miriam Waddington — 1917

speed skater Catriona Le May Doan — 1970

actor Corey Haim — 1971

Figures of the War of 1812

Sir Isaac Brock: Major-General Sir Isaac Brock was provisional president of the executive council of Upper Canada and commander of its British forces. He would defend against American attacks into Upper Canada, enlisting the support of First Nations peoples in exchange for the promise of an independent Aboriginal nation. Called the Defender of Upper Canada, Brock was killed on October 13, 1812, at the Battle of Queenston Heights.

Tecumseh: Tecumseh was leader of the First Nations confederacy that was formed to resist American encroachment on Aboriginal land in the late eighteenth and early nineteenth centuries. When the War of 1812 broke out between the United States and Britain, Tecumseh and the confederacy allied with the British. He was killed on October 5, 1813, at the Battle of Moraviantown (also known as the Battle of the Thames).

Laura Secord: Upper Canadian Loyalist Laura Secord overheard American troops stationed at Fort George talk of the impending American advance. Secord trekked over thirty kilometres to warn Lieutenant James FitzGibbon of the attack.

Charles de Salaberry: Charles de Salaberry led the Provincial Corps of Light Infantry (Canadian Voltigeurs), a French-Canadian regiment. On October 26, 1813, his Voltigeurs—along with militia, Aboriginal warriors, and Canadian Fencibles—defeated the Americans at Châteauguay, and Montréal was saved from attack.

Library and Archives Canada/C-005996.

***A Hundred Years Peace. The Signature of the Treaty of Ghent between Great Britain and the United States of America, Dec. 24th 1814,* by Amédée Forestier.**

1814. The Treaty of Ghent is signed in Ghent, Belgium, by Great Britain and the United States, ending the War of 1812. The treaty restored all conquered territories and deferred boundary disputes to joint commissions. At the war's end, the military situation in North America was so well balanced that neither the British nor the Americans had achieved their aspirations. Markedly absent from all treaty negotiations were the First Nations peoples, who today are widely considered to have lost the most during the war. News of the treaty travelled slowly back to North America, and both the Battle of New Orleans and the Battle of Fort Bowyer took place after the agreement was signed.

BORN ON THIS DAY

1879 poet Émile Nelligan

1903 badminton player and shoe designer Jack Purcell

1944 Québec premier Daniel Johnson Jr.

25 DECEMBER

Canadian soldiers mark the Christmas holiday in Ortona, Italy, 1943.

1914. A Christmas Day truce takes place in battle zones on the Western Front, showing the human side of the otherwise devastating conflict. A somewhat spontaneous and unofficial ceasefire between Entente and German soldiers marked the holiday during the first year of the war. Following gestures of goodwill on Christmas Eve, soldiers from both sides entered no man's land, buried their fallen, and exchanged food with the enemy. Impromptu soccer matches were even held before the fighting resumed. No Canadian battalions or regiments were involved in the 1914 truce, but a similar event was reported in a 1916 letter from a Canadian soldier at Vimy Ridge. "We had a truce on Xmas Day and our German friends were quite friendly," wrote Pte. Ronald MacKinnon. "They came over to see us and we traded bully beef for cigars."

Also on This Day

1959.
Jon Kimura Parker, winner of the prestigious Leeds International Piano Competition in 1984, is born in Burnaby, British Columbia. Parker's first public appearance was with the Vancouver Youth Orchestra when he was five years old. Since then, he has performed with orchestras around the world, and on New Year's Eve in 1995 he accompanied an airlift of supplies to Bosnia to play with the Sarajevo Philharmonic. His brother, Jamie Parker, is also an accomplished concert pianist.

BORN ON THIS DAY

1850 — poet and novelist Isabella Valancy Crawford

1889 — *Reader's Digest* co-founder Lila Bell Acheson Wallace

1958 — singer-songwriter Alannah Myles

Also on This Day

1791.
The Constitutional Act of 1791, a statute of the British Parliament, comes into effect. Aimed primarily at reducing expenses by giving colonial assemblies the power of taxation, the act also created Upper Canada and Lower Canada, and therefore was a first step toward Confederation.

Library and Archives Canada/C-57194.

David Milne.

1953. Painter, printmaker, and writer David Milne dies in Bancroft, Ontario. His unique style of painting treated the simplest subjects with significance. Although his rise to fame came more quickly in the United States than Canada, Milne was a fervent nationalist, and he urged Canadians to pay more attention to their art, music, and literature. Celebrated artist Harold Town called Milne "the master of absence" for his ability to reduce a painting and its subject to its essentials.

BORN ON THIS DAY

1927 — dancer and choreographer Arnold Spohr

1933 — poet, artist, and editor Joe Rosenblatt

1935 — Hockey Hall of Famer Norm Ullman

1937 — musician and comedian Ronnie Prophet

27 DECEMBER

© Kris Krug.

Wayne Gretzky, 2006.

1989. Legendary hockey player Wayne Gretzky is named male athlete of the decade by the Associated Press. By his retirement in 1999, after twenty seasons of NHL hockey, Gretzky held or shared sixty-one league records, including those for most regular-season goals in a career, most goals in a single season, and most forty-plus goal seasons. Post-retirement, he has embarked on a number of endeavours, including a restaurant in Toronto. He also, for a time, owned a share of the NHL's Phoenix Coyotes (now the Arizona Coyotes). In the 2002 Olympics, Gretzky was executive director of the Canadian men's hockey team, which earned a gold medal by defeating the United States 5–2.

Selected Wayne Gretzky Records

Most career points: 2,857
Most career goals: 894
Most career assists: 1,963
Most goals in a season: 92
Most goals in the first fifty games of a season: 61
Most points in a season: 215
Most assists in a season: 163
Most playoff points in a career: 382
Most playoff goals in a career: 122
Most playoff assists in a career: 260
Most consecutive MVP awards: 8

BORN ON THIS DAY

1913
writer Elizabeth Smart

1990
tennis player Milos Raonic

LEONARD COHEN

December 27, 1967.

Poet, singer-songwriter, and novelist Leonard Cohen releases his debut album, *Songs of Leonard Cohen*. The influential recording included some of his most well-known works, among them "Suzanne" and "So Long, Marianne." Having already established himself as a poet and novelist with the publication of several books, including *Let Us Compare Mythologies*, *Flowers for Hitler*, and *Beautiful Losers*, Cohen showcased the gravelly voice and captivating lyrics that would make him famous. He would become one of the most acclaimed Canadian artists of the century, a man whose prose and lyrics constantly probe the depths of the human condition with themes of love, loss, and death. His song "Hallelujah" is one of the most covered folk-rock songs, with versions in various languages by over three hundred artists.

Leonard Cohen in Montreal, 1973.

28 DECEMBER

Library and Archives Canada/1977-18-19.

An advertisement for John H.R. Molson & Bros., Ale & Porter Brewers, undated.

1763. Businessman and brewer John Molson is born in Moulton, England. He immigrated to Canada in 1782, and in 1786 began to run a small brewery in Montréal. An astute businessman, Molson used cash payments from his brewery to finance banking activities and build a steamboat line operating between Montréal and Québec City. He also built a hotel and Canada's first distillery, and he financed the country's first railway—the Champlain and Saint Lawrence Railroad. The brewery he established, now Molson Coors, is his most enduring legacy. Known by several names over the years, it became Molson Companies Ltd in 1973, a moniker that reflected its changing nature: from 1967 onward, it diversified to include retail merchandising, marketing of specialty chemicals, and sports and entertainment ventures.

Also on This Day

1945.
A Canadian military court in Aurich, Germany, finds Maj.-Gen. Kurt Meyer guilty of war crimes. He was the only Nazi prisoner imprisoned in Canada after the war. Meyer served five years at the Dorchester Penitentiary in New Brunswick before being transferred to a British military prison in Werl, West Germany, in 1951.

BORN ON THIS DAY

1842 "O Canada" composer Calixa Lavallée

1913 actor Lou Jacobi

1919 humorist, playwright, and journalist Eric Nicol

1928 musician, composer, and arranger Moe Koffman

1929 Hockey Hall of Famer Terry Sawchuk

DECEMBER  29 

Also on This Day

1933.
Fourteen sites in Ontario record their coldest-ever temperatures, including Ottawa at –38.9°C and Algonquin Park at –45.0°C. Record cold temperatures were also set in Manitoba, Québec, and Nova Scotia.

Library and Archives Canada/Peter Winkworth Collection of Canadiana/ e000835920.

***Burning of the* Caroline *on the night of the 29th Decem.* 1837, by J.B. Read, 1838.**

1837. Following the failure of the Upper Canada Rebellion, its leader, William Lyon Mackenzie, retreats with approximately two hundred followers to Navy Island in the Niagara River. Members of the Upper Canada militia, under the leadership of Andrew Drew, pursued Mackenzie and found the *Caroline*, an American ship, moored at Fort Schlosser. The ship was set ablaze and cast adrift, before foundering above the falls and sinking. The incident exacerbated the already strained relations between Britain and America.

BORN ON THIS DAY

Hockey Hall of Famer Nels "Old Poison" Stewart
1902

1926
country and gospel singer Marg Osburne

musician and singer Rick Danko
1942

1942
singer and actress Dinah Christie

30 DECEMBER

Yousuf Karsh/Library and Archives Canada/e010751643.

Winston Churchill, as photographed by Yousuf Karsh.

1941. British prime minister Winston Churchill is photographed on Parliament Hill in Ottawa by internationally famed Canadian photographer Yousuf Karsh. The photo session resulted in the now classic portrait of the leader scowling, an expression brought about when Karsh removed the cigar from Churchill's mouth for the shot. It was considered the definitive representation of Churchill's character. Moments earlier, the prime minister had given a speech to Parliament in which he said that a French general thought England would "have her neck wrung like a chicken" in the war. With his trademark bluster, Churchill exclaimed, "Some chicken! Some neck!"

Also on This Day

1869.
Humorist and economist Stephen Leacock is born in Swanmore, England. He was one of the English-speaking world's best-known humorists in the early part of the twentieth century. Since 1947, an annual award for humour writing has been presented in his honour. Among Leacock's many cherished works are *Sunshine Sketches of a Little Town, Arcadian Adventures with the Idle Rich, My Remarkable Uncle,* and his unfinished autobiography, *The Boy I Left Behind Me.*

BORN ON THIS DAY

Father of Confederation William Henry
1816

1878
radio evangelist and Social Credit Party founder William "Bible Bill" Aberhart

author Matt Cohen
1942

1943
Olympic shooting gold medallist Linda Thom

author Douglas Coupland
1961

DECEMBER  31

1966. Canada's year-long centennial celebration is launched at midnight with a ceremony in Ottawa, during which Prime Minister Lester Pearson lights the Centennial Flame at the entrance to Parliament Hill. Expo 67 and its companion World Festival, both hosted in Montréal, were the most memorable events tied to Canada's hundredth birthday. Festival Canada also promoted a number of countrywide tours for groups like the National Ballet of Canada, the Montreal Symphony Orchestra, and Don Messer and His Islanders, as well as for singers like Gordon Lightfoot and Ian & Sylvia Tyson. Financial assistance was made available to performing arts groups across Canada for productions and commissions.

Canada centennial poster.

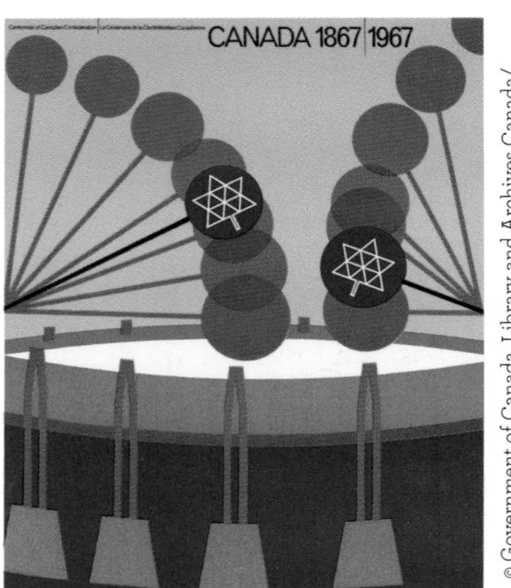

A poster advertising Canada's centennial birthday party.

"What can I do for Centennial?"
Knit a sweater,
Plant a tree.
Travel Canada,

"What Can I Do for Centennial?" poster.

BORN ON THIS DAY

1884 beauty entrepreneur Elizabeth Arden

1935 curler Ron Northcott

1947 singer, musician, and songwriter Burton Cummings

1954 musician, singer, and songwriter Charlie Major

1990 figure skater Patrick Chan

GUY LOMBARDO

1929.

Guy Lombardo and His Royal Canadians play the New Year's Eve celebrations at New York's Roosevelt Grill, beginning an annual tradition that would last thirty-three years. The broadcast of the Royal Canadians' yearly performance at the Roosevelt Grill (and later in the Grand Ballroom of the Waldorf Astoria) became a traditional part of New Year's Eve festivities throughout North America.

At the time of Lombardo's death in 1977, he and his Royal Canadians had released over one hundred records, with recordings of "Winter Wonderland," "Easter Parade," and "Humoresque" selling over a million copies. But no song was more enduring than "Auld Lang Syne." Lombardo's version is the one that still plays in Times Square after the ball drops on New Year's Eve.

Acknowledgements

Historica Canada is the largest independent organization devoted to enhancing awareness of Canadian history and citizenship. This book, directed by Web and Digital Media Manager Chantal Gagnon, is the product of hours of work from many members of our team, including President and CEO Anthony Wilson-Smith, Director of Programs and Development Brigitte d'Auzac de Lamartinie, as well as Davida Aronovitch, Daniel Baird, Laura Bondy, Alexandra Demoe, Alicia Dotiwalla, Calina Ellwand, Richard Foot, Bronwyn Graves, Alexander Herd, Erin James-Abra, Maude Emmanuelle Lambert, Tabitha Marshall, Andrew McIntosh, Nicki Thomas, Zach Parrott, Jill Paterson, and Eli Yarhi.

With files from *The Canadian Encyclopedia* and the Memory Project.